BULB

BULB

by

Anna Pavord

MITCHELL BEAZLEY

Dedicated to Tilly and Argus, Fergus and Captain Jack

BULB
by Anna Pavord

First published in Great Britain in 2009 by Mitchell
Beazley, an imprint of Octopus Publishing Group Ltd,
2–4 Heron Quays, London E14 4JP
An Hachette UK Company
www.hachettelivre.co.uk
www.octopusbooks.co.uk

ISBN: 978 1 84533 415 4

A CIP record for this book is available from the
British Library.

Set in Fairfield

Colour reproduction in Hong Kong by Fine Arts
Printed and bound in China by C&C

Commissioning Editor Helen Griffin
Senior Editor Leanne Bryan
Copy-editor Joanna Chisholm
Proofreader Lynn Bresler
Indexer Helen Snaith
Art Director Tim Foster
Art Editor Nichola Smith
Designer Victoria Easton
Photography Andrew Lawson and Torie Chugg
Picture Researcher Patricia Bridger
Production Manager Peter Hunt

Author's acknowledgements

Andrew Lawson and Torie Chugg, who took the magnificent
pictures for this book, have already made their own list of
acknowledgements but I want to start mine by thanking
them for providing such a sumptuous series of images. Given
the vagaries of the weather and the suicidal tendencies
of some bulbs, they have not had an easy time. But like
magicians, they have produced exactly what I hoped for:
a box of jewels, conjured out of the rain.

David Lamb at Mitchell Beazley has had this book in his
sights for a long time, and I am grateful to him for his constant
support and encouragement. Making a book is a collaborative
effort and Helen Griffin and Leanne Bryan, my editors at
Mitchell Beazley, have been magnificent. The elegant design
is the work of Tim Foster, Victoria Easton and Nichola Smith
with production masterminded by Peter Hunt and
proofreading by Lynn Bresler. Giulia Hetherington oversaw the
picture research. Above all, I need to thank Joanna Chisholm,
the copy editor, for all the painstaking work she has put into
this book. Separated by 650km (400 miles), we met very rarely,
a situation that could have been disastrous if she had not had
the gift of writing the clearest and most helpful notes any
writer could hope to receive. I owe her a great deal.

Anyone who turns to the Bibliography (see p.540) will
already see how indebted I am to Brian Mathew and the
superb books and articles on bulbs that he has produced over
a long period. I first met him more than 20 years ago, and
whenever I have asked him for help he has unstintingly given
it. Now I am in his debt again, for he agreed to check all the
images we wanted to use; he also found time to explain,
among other things, the complications surrounding the names
of various chionodoxa. As always, he taught me a great deal.

Ronald Blom, king of the tulips, kindly found time to
read what I have written here about my favourite flower and
made useful suggestions, which I have been able to include
in the text. Ronald Scamp and Jackie Petherbridge gave
much-needed advice on the best narcissus to grow, and
I was very glad to have it.

I spend more on bulbs than clothes, and although I buy
from many different places by far the greatest proportion of
my purchases over the years has come from Avon Bulbs in
Somerset, where Chris Ireland-Jones and Alan Street grow
the most gorgeous treats that any gardener could wish for.

Closer to home, I'd like to thank Kevin Nunn and
Margaret Dunsford for all their help. I could not have
completed this book without their support. That also applies
to my husband, Trevor Ware, who each season pretends
quite brilliantly that he is as excited as I am by the long-
awaited flowering of a special iris or a hard-to-find tulip.
My final thanks must go to him.

Contents

Foreword

It began, I suppose, with the tulip – of all bulbs, the most desirable. But even in the middle of that love affair, I was growing masses of other bulbs: admiring the fire lit in the white bowl of *Crocus malyi* by its outrageous orange anthers, dazzled by the perfect poise of *Lilium canadense* hanging out over a mound of spurge. Of all types of plant, bulbs (corms, tubers and rhizomes too) intrigue me the most. I like the way they shoot into flower, do their thing, and then thoughtfully put themselves away again. I positively relish the fact that so often I forget I have planted them. Then, at the appropriate season, there they are, not the slightest bit put out that I have not been worrying about them or making them special snacks. As a gardener, I appreciate the way they mark the seasons: aconites giving way to crocus, crocus to daffodils, daffodils to alliums, then lilies, stately galtonias, and a final fantastic flourish of eucomis and nerines. Bulbs are not just a spring thing.

I started keeping notes on all the bulbs I grew. Did *Fritillaria michailovskyi* seem a better plant than *Fritillaria assyriaca*? If so, why? What looked good with an iris such as 'Oriental Beauty' in the garden? I began to add information to these notes about where different things came from, who had first bred them or seen them in the wild. Gradually, over the years, the notes grew as abundantly as the flowers and I felt I had another book coming on, a book that would be filled with enough gorgeous bulbs, corms and tubers to fill a lifetime of gardening. This is it.

OPPOSITE Perfect in every way, a caramel-coloured
bloom of *Tulipa orphanidea* Whittallii Group throws
itself open in the sun.

Introduction

This book is about the most glorious group of plants on earth: bulbs, corms, tubers and rhizomes. They are linked by the fact that they all depend on some kind of storage system to sustain them while they are building up to their next fanfaring performance. A pedant might have insisted the book was called *Monocotyledonous Geophytes*. But could you look a crocus in the face and tell it it was a monocotyledonous geophyte? No. So *Bulb* it is, even though within these pages you will find plenty of plants that grow from corms, tubers and rhizomes too.

For a gardener, the flowers that come from these things are transitory delights. They leap up into growth, do their ravishing thing, then pack themselves away until the following season, when, if you are lucky, you will get a repeat performance. But nothing marks the passage of the seasons in quite the way that bulbs do: the longed-for sight of snowdrops and aconites in late winter, crocus and daffodils in early spring, then tulips, iris and alliums, until high summer explodes with lilies. But that is not the end. As autumn descends on the garden, you can still look forward to cyclamen and colchicum, with fox-coloured leaves lying among the burning yellow goblets of sternbergia. Their very transitoriness is part of their charm.

Bulbs can make carpets in a garden, as snowdrops and cyclamen do, but they can also be displayed like jewels. A single perfect crocus or fritillary, growing in a clay pot, gives as much pleasure as a crowd of daffodils. With a little forethought, you can arrange a non-stop supply of these treasures, bringing them out of a greenhouse or a cold frame to display in season, then, when the petals fall, replacing them with the next delight. Some bulbs are easier to keep in a pot than they are in the open ground, so this treatment suits them too. During the four years I have been working on this book, *Hippeastrum papilio*, *Crocus imperati*, *Fritillaria acmopetala*, *Cyclamen persicum*, *Iris kolpakowskiana*, *Ornithogalum arabicum*, *Sprekelia formosissima*, *Allium flavum* and *Bessera elegans* have all been among the bulbs that have sat next to me, coolly confident of their beauty, coolly disparaging of my attempts to do justice to them.

In these pages you will find about 600 of my favourite bulbs, which is more than enough to sustain a gardener through a lifetime of growing. I am not sure that even a forklift truck could shift a book that tried to describe and illustrate every bulb, corm, tuber and rhizome that exists. For reasons that will be obvious to most gardeners, I have not included begonias, dahlias or cannas. Iris are here, but not the huge race of bearded ones. Iris and crocus could easily have run away with the book, because both groups are so various, so rewarding to grow and cover such a range of seasons. It has not been easy to choose between the extraordinary number of species and varieties. In the most general sense in this book, species predominate. Sometimes that is because the original species remain as beautiful (often

OPPOSITE The 'Spurious Iris' as William Curtis called it, in an eighteenth-century illustration from his famous *Botanical Magazine*. *Iris spuria* gave its name to a whole group of robust, rhizomatous iris.

Publish'd by W. Curtis Botanic Garden Lambeth Marsh.

more beautiful) as any man-made concoctions that have come from them. Sometimes there are no selections or cultivars from which to choose. Growers may not have thought it worthwhile to breed them, or the species itself may not have the capacity to produce the variations on a theme that makes *Tulipa greigii*, for instance, such an astonishing sight on the shale-strewn slopes of the Tien Shan mountains in Kazakhstan. Taxonomists find this natural diversity a nightmare, but for gardeners it is pure joy. It leads though to some overcomplicated tags. The official name for the enchanting, small, spring-flowering cyclamen that gardeners know as 'Maurice Dryden' is *Cyclamen coum* subsp. *coum* f. *coum* Pewter Group 'Maurice Dryden'. But you are scarcely going to wade through all that at your local garden centre are you? So, where there can be no possible ambiguity, I have opted for a simpler process throughout: *Cyclamen coum* 'Maurice Dryden'.

Where bulbs come from

Bulbs (corms, tubers and rhizomes too) have such an efficient way of storing resources that they can flourish in places more permanently present plants would find difficult. So, when you look at a map of the world, it is not surprising to see that so many of the bulbs we grow in our gardens come from areas where winters are cold and summers generally long, hot and dry.

Tickled out of dormancy by changes in day length, temperature, moisture, the bulb grows fast, sending its shoot up towards the light, its roots further down into the crevices between rock and rubble, seeking the water provided by rain or melting snow. It has to work fast, for all its growing and flowering must be done in this tight time frame, before the lack of moisture or a change in temperature makes further development impossible. Then the lavish petals fall, the seed ripens and is scattered, the stem and leaves wither, sending the resources they have gathered to the underground store. To the outward eye, all activity is then suspended until the next mad rush for water and light. But tiny changes continue within the bulb itself: outwardly dormant it may be, but inside the beginnings of the next flower are initiated by the baking summer sun. Inside itself, the bulb is reorganizing priorities. Often, insufficient capital will have been banked by the leaves and stem for the bulb to be able to afford again the extravagance of a flower. It will have to spend a couple of seasons building itself up to strength again. Gardeners have unreal expectations of bulbs, in supposing that each one will flower again and again, year after year. This is not how it is in the wild. If it is sufficiently nourished by its leaves, sufficiently baked by the summer sun, it can produce a flower. If not, not.

So most of the bulbs that gardeners grow without too much difficulty come from the areas round the Mediterranean east into Turkey and central Asia, the Pacific areas of North America, and the southern tip of South Africa. The Himalayas, China and Japan are home to many lilies, but oddly few other kinds of bulb.

Obviously the simplest bulbs to grow are those that are used to your particular climatic conditions. Hardiness may be an issue, but with the notoriously capricious spring seasons that are a feature of gardening life in Britain, gardeners are used to leaping about with sacking and cloches, and providing deep mulches of leaf litter or compost to protect emerging shoots from late frosts. More difficult to provide, for gardeners away from the Mediterranean or the mountains of Kazakhstan, is the summer heat that so many bulbs depend on to initiate their flowers. Yet all gardens have areas that are better than others at trapping heat: the base of a sunny wall, a well-drained slope that faces south, a piece of open, rough, gravelly ground that to you may seem worthless, but to a bulb brought up on a rocky scree in Kazakhstan would be heaven itself.

In many ways, the trickiest bulbs to deal with are those from the opposite side of the equator to your own patch. Lovely bulbs come from South Africa in the southern hemisphere, but for European gardeners their hearts are sometimes set to a different beat. In their own homes, bulbs from the south-west Cape get plenty of rain in winter and flower between August and October. In Britain, though, they want to go on growing through a generally inhospitable winter season, rather different to the conditions they expect at home. So gardeners have to try to trick bulbs by keeping them dormant until about September, then encouraging them to prepare for a flowering between March and June. In other words, they are expected to adjust their inner clocks by six months to catch the best of what they can expect when they jump the equator.

In their own homes, bulbs from the Eastern Cape (such as *Nerine bowdenii*) get summer rain, and this makes them easier propositions for gardeners in the northern hemisphere. They make their growth in our summer and are dormant in our winter. They may not be hardy enough to leave in the ground, but, being dormant, can at least be lifted, dried off and stored in a frost-free shed if necessary.

History

Many central Asian bulbs are tethered by nature to the 40-degree line of latitude north of the equator. From this point, they drifted north until many were stopped by the extreme cold and the lack of a long enough growing period. They drifted south until the heat became too much and a different kind of plant with a different life cycle took over. They moved a little east into China, but mostly they drifted west. As these central Asian bulbs are among the most flamboyant, irresistible superstars of the plant world, merchants found a ready market for them among rich gardeners in Europe.

After the fall of Constantinople in 1453, when European embassies were established in the capital of the new Ottoman empire, the way was clear for these Eastern plants to be introduced into Europe, which they were, in increasingly large numbers. In the hundred years between the

mid-fifteenth and mid-sixteenth centuries, 20 times as many plants entered Europe from the East as had arrived in the previous 2000 years together. Moving along the Silk Road, lilies, fritillaries, hyacinths, anemones, turban ranunculus, crocus, iris and tulips from central Asia travelled with bales of silk through Tashkent, Samarkand, Bukhara, Turkmenistan, then on to Baku and Yerevan before arriving at Constantinople, the springboard for entry into the countries of western Europe.

Imagine the baggage trains, the saddlebags, the hand-made harness, the yurts put up and dismantled, the fires built against bears and wolves, and the practicalities of carrying plants, intact, so far from their natural habitats. They survived, of course, because they were bulbs. Having flowered and gathered their resources back into themselves, they could be carried long distances without any harm, growth suspended. Like the silk that gave its name to this great trade route, they were high-value, low-volume goods, worth a merchant's trouble. These stupendous flowers – crown imperials, tulips, narcotically scented hyacinths – spearheaded the first great wave of strangers that ever came into European gardens. From the mid-sixteenth century onwards, rich gardeners were obsessed with collecting these treasures – and learning how to grow them successfully.

The second great wave of bulbs to hit Europe came from the New World: a completely different tribe of plants – trilliums, erythroniums – woodsy plants used to cooler conditions and often demanding an acid soil, quite unlike the central Asian bulbs, which thrive on limestone. The first British settlement in Virginia was established by 1607. The Pilgrim Fathers landed in 1620. By 1664 Jack-in-the-pulpit (*Arisaema triphyllum*) from the eastern seaboard of America had been introduced into Europe. Erythroniums arrived the following year, trilliums in 1673.

Then, as traders penetrated into the Cape, South African bulbs swept the board – gladiolus, dierama, eucomis – extravagantly illustrated in William Curtis's *Botanical Magazine* set up in 1787 and even more extravagantly displayed in the hothouses of the men growing rich on the back of the trade which exploration of these new areas opened up. Eucomis arrived early in the eighteenth century, beautiful *Amaryllis belladonna* was flowering in Europe by 1712, the arum lily (*Zantedeschia aethiopica*) by 1731, chincherinchee (*Ornithogalum thyrsoides*) by 1757.

The perfect package

All bulbs, corms, tubers and rhizomes are made in a slightly different way. A true bulb (allium, daffodil, tulip) is made up from a number of fleshy scales (they are technically the bottoms of leaves) wrapped around and protecting a growing point in the centre. Fritillaries also grow from bulbs although they may be made up of only one or two very fat scales. The scales of a daffodil are held together by a basal plate, from which the roots grow, and the whole thing is covered by a coat called the tunic. In daffodils, the

OPPOSITE The 'Two-Flower'd Narcissus' from William Curtis's *Botanical Magazine* of 1792. Sweet-scented, he said, and 'found in almost every garden', flowering in late April.

tunic is very robust. In tulips, it is rather thin and papery. Neither lilies nor fritillaries have any kind of tunic and need careful handling so that they do not bruise. Sometimes, as with Juno iris, the bulb has fleshy roots attached. These are an important part of its survival strategy and you have to take great care when planting not to snap them off.

A corm (crocus, gladiolus) is a modified stem covered with a fibrous tunic and grows fresh each year, the new one generally produced on top of the old one, like a stack of doughnuts. The corm of a colchicum, however, develops alongside the old one, characteristically lop-sided. A corm is solid, not made up of overlapping scales, and the main growing point (there may be more than one, as you can see when you plant crocuses) is at the top of the corm. Each of the secondary shoots may be capable of producing a new corm, which is why crocuses can clump up quite fast.

Like corms, tubers (aconites, arums) are also solid, but they do not replace themselves every year. They are thickened stems and just go on getting bigger. Cyclamen tubers can reach the size of dinner plates, the bottom often skin-smooth, with roots being produced from the top or the shoulders of the tuber. New growth comes from the eye at the top.

A rhizome is a modified, swollen stem, which has adapted itself to lie on or under the ground rather than stand upright. Both wood anemones (*Anemone nemorosa*) and lilies-of-the-valley grow from rhizomes, which move about underground sending up flowers and stems at intervals, then wandering on again. They can be problematic to plant, as there is little indication which way up they should be. Sometimes a growing tip will give a clue. Both anemones and lilies-of-the-valley have rather thin rhizomes, while trilliums have very fat ones, with the promising tip of next year's bud jutting out of one end like a finch's beak.

When you are planting bulbs, take time to admire the extraordinary adaptations that each of these plants has made to its circumstances: the pale straw-coloured coat of *Iris reticulata*; the fat white bulb of *Nectaroscordum siculum*, the colour of good bacon fat; *Iris cycloglossa* with long, white fang roots hanging from the tall, etiolated bulb; the pear-shaped, little package of *Leucojum vernum*, eager to get going, probably rooting in its bag even as you unwrap it; the beautiful bright, clean chestnut coats of *Tulipa hageri* and *T. humilis* var. *pulchella*; and the long, thin bits of string which seem to be all that *Paris quadrifolia* needs to support it. Bulbs are miracles of diversity.

A spring-flowering bulb such as a daffodil begins to grow the previous autumn, sending roots down from the basal plate and preparing to send up leaves and (if we are lucky) a flowering stem when the days lengthen and weather conditions improve. The presence or absence of that flower depends not on the conditions the bulb finds when it emerges, but on the circumstances of the previous season, which may or may not have encouraged the incipient flower bud to develop. The leaves go on growing after the flower has finished, and it is important not to get rid of them. They are the means by which the bulb builds up reserves for the following

OPPOSITE The common corn flag (*Gladiolus communis*) in an illustration published in 1789 in William Curtis's *Botanical Magazine*.

season. If it is growing well, a daffodil bulb will also develop offsets, small baby bulbs attached to and growing out from the basal plate. A tulip bulb more often shrivels away after flowering, leaving one or two offsets inside the bulb tunic, which will take a year or two to grow to flowering size.

Spring-flowering bulbs are dormant during summer. Summer-flowering bulbs such as lilies are dormant from late autumn to spring. They are used to dryish winters, which is why it helps (if you can) to keep containers of lilies under cover during winter.

The hardiness of bulbs

All bulbs in this book are listed as either fully hardy, frost hardy, half hardy or tender. A fully hardy bulb should survive a minimum temperature of -15°C (5°F), a frost hardy one a minimum temperature of -5°C (23°F), and a half hardy one a minimum temperature of 0°C (32°F). A tender bulb may be killed if temperatures dip below 5°C (41°F). Hardiness, though, is a complex concept.

Bulbs may well survive a hard frost, if they are growing in perfectly drained ground. Often it is the combination of cold and damp that provides the *coup de grâce*. In Britain and Ireland, many bulbs are perching on the very western edge of their preferred habitats. You sometimes have to work hard to pull the wool over their beautiful eyes. But habitat provides the best clue for gardeners wondering what to expect from their bulbs.

The hardiest of all are those that grow in northern Europe, Siberia, northern China, northern Japan and the eastern states of North America. They include corydalis (many of them at least), *Crocus vernus* and its many varieties, most lilies, narcissus (except the Tazetta types of Division 8), *Scilla bifolia* and *S. siberica*, snowdrops and trilliums. In their natural habitats, these bulbs stay deep underground during the harsh winters and in summer can put up with (sometimes even need) rain. But they are used to a deep covering of snow in winter. The absence of snow combined with sharp, prolonged frost may have an impact on their capacity to survive.

Slightly different in their requirements are the bulbs, corms, tubers and rhizomes that grow in the mountain areas of southern Europe, Turkey, Iran, central Asia and the western states of North America. Here they may also have extremely cold winters but are used to hot, dry summers. In this group, you might include colchicums, most crocus, many fritillaries, bulbous irises and tulips. In the gardens of northern and western Europe, they miss their summer baking though they often do well in places where the roots of neighbouring trees and shrubs dry out the ground around them. Annual flowers, growing in the same ground as the bulbs, perform the same function. Permanent irrigation systems are their worst enemies.

A third group of bulbs favours the Mediterranean areas of Europe, North Africa and Turkey, the coastal fringes of California, Chile and the Cape provinces of South Africa. Winters are mild and damp, with temperatures rarely dropping below -5°C (23°F). Here you might find brodieas, calochortus, *Cyclamen persicum* and *C. repandum*, a few fritillaries and romuleas, all of which will need some protection from cold if grown in northern Europe or the north-eastern states of America. In slightly milder areas, you may find that, well-mulched, they will survive.

Yet another type of bulb has evolved to make the most of the cool dryish winters and warm, wet summers that you find in the Drakensberg mountains of South Africa, southern Chile, Argentina, the Himalayas, and the coastal areas of Oregon and Washington State in North America. They will include arisaemas, eucomis, hardy hippeastrums such as 'Toughie', a few tender lilies, nerines and tigridias, most of which dive underground for winter. That means that gardeners growing them elsewhere can mulch them heavily and keep their fingers crossed. Certainly nerines and eucomis provide few problems in the southern and western parts of Britain. Tigridias are more demanding. Evergreen plants such as dierama and moraea are potentially more tricky, but even if the foliage above ground is cut by frost the underground corms usually survive.

Small blips in general weather patterns may make a big difference to gardeners. North-western Spain and south-western France are broadly considered to be 'Mediterranean' but both can have rain in summer, which means that bulbs from these areas grow very easily in areas further north where summer rain is always built into the weather pattern. That is why gardeners away from the Mediterranean and central Asia find most daffodils (widely distributed in north-west Spain) so much easier to grow than tulips. Easier maybe, but more rewarding? That is a different question. And on the southern shores of the Mediterranean, where the Atlas mountains drift gradually into desert, there are beautiful bulbs that demand even hotter and drier conditions than those on the northern Mediterranean fringe. Gardeners have to fight to grow these bulbs in northern Europe (as will American gardeners on the east coast). In California, though, they will thrive. Altitude matters too. Bulbs that grow high up on a mountain slope may prove hardier than bulbs growing lower down on the same slope.

Snatched from their cradles, as it were, it is scarcely surprising that bulbs sometimes fail to flourish in their new homes. If all the bulbs I have planted had stayed with me, tulips, fritillaries and lilies would be lapping to the boundaries. Sadly, some do not even manage to struggle through the few months from planting to flowering. But I remind myself that the fault is more likely to be mine than theirs. Perhaps I put them in the wrong place. Or perhaps the position I chose for them has changed imperceptibly, sun growing into shade as neighbours spread their arms to cover what was once open space. But the delights of growing bulbs far outstrip any disasters: the first green-white spears of *Galanthus* 'Atkinsii' pushing through a mat of ivy, 'Lady Beatrix Stanley' shaking out its gorgeous blue iris flower over a gravel scree, *Lilium duchartrei* darkly mysterious among fronds of Wallich's wood fern. One of the few infallible rules of gardening is that no garden can have too many bulbs. Splurge. It is the only way.

The Bulbs

FROM LEFT TO RIGHT *Allium* 'Ambassador', *Allium unifolium, Allium stipitatum* 'Mount Everest', *Allium hollandicum* 'Purple Sensation', *Allium schubertii, Allium nigrum*

Acis (Amaryllidaceae)

Acis autumnalis
(*Leucojum autumnale*) ♕

The flowers appear before the leaves, from one to four of them dangling from the stem. The white petals, so pure in their cousins, the spring snowflakes, are flushed and veined with pink. *Acis autumnalis* has been known in gardens since 1629 and does best in a dryish, warm, sunny situation, combined perhaps with powder-blue stokesia. Plant the bulbs 5cm (2in) deep and 8–10cm (3½–4in) apart.

SEASON: September–October
HARDINESS: Fully hardy
HEIGHT: 10–15cm (4–6in)
HABITAT: Southern Europe (Portugal, Spain, Sardinia, Sicily) and north-west Africa where it grows in woodland, scrub and grassland

Acis nicaeensis
(*Leucojum nicaeense*) ♕

Once upon a time this was a leucojum, a miniature one, only 8cm (3½in) high. But the powers that be decided it should be an acis instead. Each stem has just one or two flowers and they look slightly too large for the plant, but the effect is endearing rather than offputting. *Acis nicaeensis* has the quality of a child in grown-up's clothing, very spruce with its dark green leaves setting off the white blooms, each with a pointed orange centre. Unlike their near relatives, the leucojums, the petals do not have green spots. A well-drained alpine bed or trough would be the place for this plant. In the wild it grows on rocky hillsides and it will not thrive in damp, heavy ground. Plant the bulbs 5cm (2in) deep and 8cm (3½in) apart.

SEASON: Late March–May
HARDINESS: Frost hardy
HEIGHT: 8–10cm (3½–4in)
HABITAT: Alpes Maritimes and southern France from Nice to Monaco where it grows on rocky hillsides

Allium (Alliaceae)

Most alliums are built on roughly the same lines: a strong, uncluttered stem with a blob on top. The differences have to do with the proportion of one to the other. *Allium cristophii* is squat, top-heavy, with too much blob for its stem, but has sufficient presence to overcome its inbuilt design problem; *A. caeruleum* has 50cm (20in) of stem, which leads you to expect something rather splendid at the top. In fact the flower is only about 4cm (1½in) across, but the colour is a good, clear sky-blue. If you plant enough of them, the effect is excellent, particularly when they poke through a low sea of something greyish, perhaps a prostrate form of *Artemisia stelleriana*.

The alliums are an enormous group, which includes onions and leeks as well as showpieces such as the enormous purple 'Globemaster'. They are found wild all over the northern hemisphere, in the Alps, the Mediterranean and the Pyrenees, the Middle East, western China and North America. More than 200 sorts have been brought into cultivation, and most are hardy and easy to grow. The flowers are like leeks which you have left to go to seed – large spherical heads made up of hundreds of individual flowers (there are

ABOVE Starry domes of *Allium cristophii*, each made
up of perhaps a hundred narrow-petalled flowers,
explode among brilliant red poppies.

exceptions – beautiful *A. insubricum* has rather few flowers but each is showy). The tallest alliums grow on stems more than 1m (3ft) high, the smallest will fit into a sink garden. Some are sweetly scented. Only when you bruise bulb or leaf do you get a whiff of the kitchen: onions and garlic.

The outline of an allium is strong and well-defined which makes it a useful exclamation mark among mounds of herbaceous plants such as the magenta *Geranium psilostemon* or grasses such as *Stipa tenuissima*. Most are in the pink-mauve-purple part of the paintbox, but *Allium caeruleum* provides a good sky-blue, while *A. moly* 'Jeannine' is as yellow as a daffodil. There is also an increasingly large range of white-flowered varieties such as 'Mount Everest'. Some alliums are as good in death as they are in life. This is especially true of *A. cristophii* and *A. schubertii* which, as they die, become huge greenish or buff domes on stiff but brittle stems. The biggest heads can be more than 40cm (16in) across, perfectly symmetrical, a firework frozen at the moment of explosion.

June is the month for the monster alliums. You can tell them by their names: 'Gladiator', 'Globemaster', 'Mars', 'Mount Everest', all of them more than 1m (3ft) tall. In a garden, this height can be useful. At Hidcote, the National Trust garden in Gloucestershire, UK, tall *A. giganteum* is used down the back of a border of double peonies. The tall alliums also make good companions for the supreme foliage plant *Melianthus major*, perhaps with agapanthus to pick up the baton later. Try them with catmint and the white *Phlox carolina* subsp. *angusta* 'Miss Lingard'. They also look lovely rising from a hazy spread of sky-blue nigella, jostling the rich violet flowers of *Geranium* × *magnificum*, or interplanted with silybum, a

ABOVE Chives (*Allium schoenoprasum*), which grow wild in Europe, Asia and North America, growing with other wildflowers in the Glacier National Park, Montana.

plant like a variegated thistle. Remember though that when these tall alliums' flowers are at their best, their foliage will already be dying back and looking scrappy. You need to arrange them so they float, like extra-terrestrials, over a sea of borrowed foliage, which will disguise their own quietly rotting leaves.

Among the small alliums (and a dozen of the alliums you will find here are no more than 30cm/12in tall) are flowers that spread their performance from March through till August. First into bloom is the pure white *Allium paradoxum*, a quiet beauty, with the added bonus of doing well in shade and on heavy clay soils. The small alliums, such as July-flowering *A. angulosum* and the useful white *A. tuberosum* which flowers in August, are also better behaved in terms of their foliage. It is often reed thin and stays in good condition during flowering time. You get a wider colour range among the

OPPOSITE Tall stems of *Allium* 'Globemaster' push through an underplanting of catmint at Cherkley Court, Surrey. Designer Simon Johnson.

small alliums too: the best pinks, white, brilliant blues (in *A. cyaneum*), and yellows. With the smaller alliums, such as *A. cyaneum* which has flowerheads no bigger than a golf ball, you need correspondingly small companions. Try it on a gravel scree, between low-growing mounds of a variegated thyme, with thrift or among grey-foliaged pinks.

Several of the tall alliums, such as *A. giganteum* and *A. hollandicum* 'Purple Sensation' are excellent planted out in a cutting garden. Here you need alliums with plenty of stem but not too big a head; they are easier to use in arrangements than the vast footballs of varieties such as 'Globemaster'. Mixed perhaps with dark red gladioli, or the bronze-purple foliage of *Cotinus* 'Grace', alliums will last several weeks in a vase. In tubs and pots outside, shorter types such as *Allium cristophii* are more suitable than the giants. Combine them with the grey foliage of helichrysum to cover the alliums' own leaves. Remember though that the flowering stem of an allium rises up alongside the bulb, not from its centre. In too shallow a pot they may tip over at odd angles, especially if they catch the wind. A discreet stake may be necessary.

CULTIVATION

Most alliums are hardy. Some, such as *A. schubertii*, are best treated as frost hardy as they cannot be relied on to survive winter temperatures lower than -5°C (23°F). In chilly areas, stick to the varieties noted below as fully hardy. Most alliums need open ground, doing best in well-drained soil in full sun, but again there are exceptions: the little mouse garlic, *A. angulosum*, grows in shade; so does *A. moly* 'Jeannine'. Planting depth depends on the size of the bulb. The bigger they are, the deeper they should go, but if you intend to grow alliums among herbaceous plants, it is a distinct advantage to plant deeper than the norm, at least 12–15cm (5–6in) down. You will then be less likely to spear the bulbs on your fork during an autumn clean-up, when you may well have forgotten where you put them. Alliums such as *A. senescens* that grow from rhizomes rather than bulbs need to be planted shallowly, just under the surface of the soil. Heavy soil can be improved with coarse sand or grit, mixed in the planting hole. Add a handful of bonemeal as a long-lasting fertilizer. However hideous it looks, do not be tempted to cut back the foliage. Allow it to die down naturally; it feeds goodness back into the bulbs for the next season. Plant bulbs in September or October.

The good news is that neither deer, rabbits nor squirrels seem to fancy alliums. And mice, always demons where bulbs are concerned, will always go for crocus and tulips before they turn to anything else. But being members of the onion tribe, alliums may suffer from common onion problems such as white rot, downy mildew and onion fly. Your best defence against disease is to get the growing conditions right. Remind yourself where alliums grow in the wild (often a mountainous area where the ground drains like a sieve) and try to give them the same conditions in the garden. This usually, but not always, includes a dry rest after flowering. Permanent drip-irrigation systems are anathema to many bulbs.

OPPOSITE Robust heads of *Allium* 'Globemaster' push through mounds of magenta-flowered geranium. The fresh leaves of the geranium are a useful disguise for the allium's own, less attractive foliage.

Allium 'Ambassador'

One of the darkest of the alliums, 'Ambassador' is a rich, eccelesiastical purple, though not quite so bright as 'Purple Sensation'. The flowerheads are not huge, but these medium-sized alliums are in many ways the easiest to use in mixed plantings. The stems are perhaps slightly too thick and clumsy, but they are strong and do not need staking. Let them spear through a sea of tall (not dwarf) forget-me-not, together with a late tulip such as smudgy mauve 'Bleu Aimable'. Plant 12–15cm (5–6in) deep and about 20cm (8in) apart.

SEASON: June–July
HARDINESS: Fully hardy
HEIGHT: 120cm (4ft)

Allium angulosum
MOUSE GARLIC

The leaves are glossy, rich green, and, unlike those of many alliums, still look good when the plant is in flower. The head is a half-sphere of lilac, no more than 5–6cm (2–2¼in) wide, similar to chives, though bigger and paler. This is an easy plant, which will grow perfectly well in damp, heavy soil. It does not mind a little shade. The bulbs are best bought damp-packed as they will still be in leaf in autumn which is when they are offered for sale. They increase rapidly. Plant the little clumps of bulbs 6–8cm (2¼–3½in) deep and about 22cm (9in) apart.

SEASON: Late July–August
HARDINESS: Fully hardy
HEIGHT: 30cm (12in)
HABITAT: Damp grassland, widespread in Europe, through to Siberia

Allium atropurpureum

'Atro...' means dark-coloured and this is an easy, useful, maroon-purple lollipop, with a clutch of basal leaves less than half the height of the flowering stem. The flowerheads, made up of masses of small stars, are half-spheres about 5cm (2in) across – not huge, but pleasing to dot about among bronze fennel or miscanthus. Plant the bulbs in a dry, sunny situation 15cm (6in) deep and about 20cm (8in) apart.

SEASON: June–July
HARDINESS: Fully hardy
HEIGHT: 50–80cm (20–32in)
HABITAT: Dry open places in Bulgaria, Romania and other areas of south-eastern Europe

Allium caeruleum (A. *azureum*) ♟

An unusual colour for an allium, which as a family favours pinks and purples rather than the clear blue of this species. *Allium caeruleum* produces a tight, rounded flowerhead, no more than 4cm (1½in) across, made up of at least 40 individual flowers. Each tiny petal is marked with a dark central vein. Sometimes the flowerhead produces a miniature replica of itself, which grows out from the centre of the ball on a stem 12–15cm (5–6in) long. It creates a charmingly dotty effect, as though the flowers had forgotten that they had already done what they set out to do. Like most alliums, the leaves start to wither before the flower comes out. In the garden, ordinary garden soil is fine, but choose a dryish, sunny spot. If happy, they will clump up quite fast. *Allium caeruleum* was introduced into cultivation in 1830 and is charming among violas, such as lemon-yellow 'Beshlie' or 'Devon Cream'. For a full, rich effect, plant the bulbs 5–8cm (2–3½in) deep and just 3–5cm (1–2in) apart.

SEASON: July
HARDINESS: Frost hardy
HEIGHT: 50cm (20in)
HABITAT: Native of eastern Europe (north of the Caspian Sea) and central Asia south as far as the Tien Shan and the Pamir Alai. There, it favours steppes and brackish, marshy country

Allium carinatum subsp. *pulchellum*
(*A. pulchellum*) ♈

Small, bell-shaped flowers, some drooping, some standing up, grow out of a central point on thread-like stems of different lengths. The effect is charming – like a slightly mad hair cut. This type is magenta-pink, but there is also a fine, white-flowered form, *A. carinatum* subsp. *pulchellum* f. *album*. They seed about, but, because they are so light-limbed, never become a nuisance. The leaves are thin and inconspicuous (good, as they stay around a long time). They are not so tall as the flower stem, which is also thin, but wiry and strong. The bead-like flowers break out of a papery case, deep pink (in the best form – there are muddier colours too) and come out in succession, the outer ones first. *Allium carinatum* subsp. *pulchellum* was introduced into cultivation in 1753 and is a delightful if insubstantial flower, good among tritelia and small pinks such as 'Fair Folly', or between clumps of a smallish agapanthus such as 'Blue Moon' or 'Isis'. It comes into leaf very early, in the autumn before its summer flowering, so bulbs are best bought damp-packed from a supplier who understands their habits. Plant them shallowly in any sunny spot, provided it is not too dry, setting the bulbs 5cm (2in) deep and about 10cm (4in) apart.

SEASON: July
HARDINESS: Fully hardy
HEIGHT: 30–40cm (12–16in)
HABITAT: Widespread in central and southern Europe,
and also found in the Canakkale region of north-west Turkey

Allium cernuum
NODDING ONION

The leaves are flattish, bright green, and still in fine shape at flowering time. The flowering stems too are flattened, taller than the foliage with the flowers enclosed in a papery sheath hooked over at the top of each stem. As the sheath opens the flowers (more than 30 in a head) burst out on stalks of unequal length, the outer ones first. The effect is enchanting – an explosion of pink, each flower showing a long, bell-clapper style in the centre. Try it with the black viola 'Molly Sanderson', blue-grey *Alchemilla erythropoda* or a low spurge such as *Euphorbia* 'Copton Ash'. Once an important food source for the Okanagan-Colville Indians of Washington State, who steamed them in fire pits, it was introduced into cultivation *c*.1800. If you plant *A. cernuum* in a sunny border that does not dry out, you will find the number of flower stems increases very satisfactorily. Unlike many alliums, this one will produce several flowering stems from the same bulb and will give a good display for a month in summer. As it is usually still in leaf in autumn, when suppliers offer it for sale, it is best bought damp-packed, with leaves still attached. Set the bulbs 8–10cm (3½–4in) deep and about 10cm (4in) apart.

SEASON: Early July

HARDINESS: Fully hardy

HEIGHT: 50cm (20in)

HABITAT: North America in an area defined by New York State and British Columbia in the north to Georgia and Arizona in the south. Generally found in mountainous areas, where it grows in gravelly, rocky places

Allium cristophii ♀

Enormous heads, 25cm (10in) across, of a soft greyish mauve, not a striking colour, but the form is good, though the stems are perhaps not quite tall enough for the size of the head. They are strong and do not break, but tend to be pulled forward by the weight of the flowers – small, six-pointed stars, narrow petalled, with a tripartite green button in the centre. There are up to a hundred of them on each head, but you tend not to see them as individuals. The mass is what matters, the whole construction like a geodesic dome. It is extremely showy both in flower and after, as the heads fade well and bleach to a creamy straw colour. It takes a long time to fall apart and is still attractive by the end of summer. The leaves are a disaster, dying noisily just as the flower is coming up to its best. Lovely with lime-green alchemilla, which will disguise the dying foliage. You could also grow them behind a low mound of purple sage, which would provide equally good camouflage. *Allium cristophii* was introduced into cultivation *c.*1903 by the Dutch bulb firm Van Tubergen, and in the garden it likes a hot, dry situation, though even there it will scarcely increase. The bulbs rot away altogether if they are too wet. Plant them 10–15cm (4–6in) deep and about 30cm (12in) apart.

SEASON: June
HARDINESS: Frost hardy
HEIGHT 60cm (24in)
HABITAT: Central Anatolia and north (Khorāsān), east and central Iran, typically growing on rocky slopes at 900–2,250m (3,000–7,400ft)

Allium cyaneum ♀

One of the best of the blue alliums, with deep cobalt flowers holding themselves well above the thin, reedy foliage. There are six or eight flowers hanging on each head, but the whole thing is not more than 2cm (¾in) across. Stamens stick out beyond the ends of each flower, giving a rather feathery effect. It was found by the Russian botanist Nikolai Przewalski on the banks of the Tetung river and introduced to cultivation in 1890. 'I hardly know any plant to compare with it for brilliancy of colour', wrote Col. Charles Grey in *Hardy Bulbs* (1938). 'It should be in every garden.' *Allium cyaneum* needs well-drained soil in full sun, but also requires moisture through its summer growing season. It is practically evergreen. Plant the bulbs 8–10cm (3½–4in) deep and about 10cm (4in) apart.

SEASON: August
HARDINESS: Fully hardy
HEIGHT: 15–25cm (6–10in)
HABITAT: North-west China (Kansu to Sichuan) where it grows in open grassland at 2,400–2,700m (8,000–9,000ft)

Allium 'Early Emperor'

The effect is mottled as each little floret in the big round head has a tuft of pale stamens standing up in the centre, and this makes 'Early Emperor' seem quite grey. The stamens on most other alliums are dark and drift into the background colour of the petals. Tulips in white, deep pink or purple will be spectacular partners. Catmint will carry the patch on through summer. Choose a sunny position and plant the bulbs 12–15cm (5–6in) deep and about 20cm (8in) apart.

SEASON: May
HARDINESS: Fully hardy
HEIGHT: 75cm (30in)

Allium 'Firmament'

A richly coloured, dark variety, which arose from a cross between two fine species – *A. atropurpureum* and *A. cristophii*. The flat-bottomed flowerheads have the starry, netted, slightly metallic look of *A. cristophii* but, though taller, they are not as big. Both these attributes can be an advantage, as these alliums can more easily be set behind other plants, such as *Geranium* 'Brookside' whose foliage will provide good camouflage for the dying leaves of 'Firmament'. The bulbs do best in full sun and well-drained soil. Plant them in small groups, 10–12cm (4–5in) deep and about 20cm (8in) apart.

SEASON: June
HARDINESS: Fully hardy
HEIGHT: 60–75cm (24–30in)

Allium flavum ♀

'Impeccable good manners,' says Dilys Davies, author of *Alliums* (1992). This is a variable species, producing dwarfs suitable for a trough or scree, as well as plants that can take their place in a herbaceous border. Some are scented, some are not. Some have glaucous foliage, some do not. The strange, long, wispy spathe at the top of the wiry stem breaks open to release a crowded umbel of flowers. There may be 30 in a head, clear lemony yellow and held on little stalks unequal in length. The outer flowers open first and hang down, while the buds of the inner ones stand up. Meanwhile the wispy tails of the spathe curve out and down in an elegant parabola. In silhouette, *A. flavum* looks superb. It was introduced into cultivation by 1753 and is easy in a sunny place in the garden. It does not like to dry out completely and so is best bought damp-packed in autumn. Plant bulbs 8–10cm (3½–4in) deep and about 10cm (4in) apart.

SEASON: Late July
HARDINESS: Fully hardy
HEIGHT: 8–30cm (3½–12in)
HABITAT: Southern Europe (France to Greece), western Turkey and outer Anatolia where it grows on dryish hillsides

Allium giganteum ♈

In many ways this is the most useful of the drumstick alliums, as the head, though showy, is not too ridiculously large and the grey-green stems are plenty strong enough for their cargo. It is one of the tallest of all alliums but the foliage is short in relation to the height. Given the leaves' floppiness and their habit of melting noisily at flowering time, this is a great advantage. The deep mauve heads, packed closely with flowers, are about 12cm (5in) across. It is a sturdy allium and does not need staking. Try it with *Digitalis purpurea* 'Sutton's Apricot', rising out of thalictrum foliage or with *Iris* 'Gerald Darby'. For a full purple effect, plant it with *Verbena bonariensis*. It is best at the back of a border, used perhaps as a contrast to *Philadelphus* 'Virginal'. *Allium giganteum* is an easy, adaptable species collected at Merv, Turkmenistan, by the foreign correspondent Edmund O'Donovan ('He could sketch, shoot, lecture, botanize...') and introduced into cultivation in 1883. It needs well-drained soil and full sun. Plant bulbs 12–15cm (5–6in) deep and about 30cm (12in) apart.

SEASON: Early June

HARDINESS: Fully hardy

HEIGHT: 120–150cm (4–5ft)

HABITAT: Iran, Afghanistan, central Asia (Turkistan and the Pamir Alai) where it grows on low, grassy slopes, rarely above 1,200m (4,000ft)

Allium 'Gladiator' ♈

Similar in height to *A. giganteum*, but a paler colour, lilac rather than purple, 'Gladiator' is slightly later than 'Globemaster' and the heads are not as big. Use it with *Geranium palmatum* or the grey-leaved *Hosta* 'Krossa Regal'. It clumps up quite fast, producing three or four offsets every year. Plant the bulbs 12–15cm (5–6in) deep and about 30cm (12in) apart.

SEASON: June

HARDINESS: Fully hardy

HEIGHT: 120–150cm (4–5ft)

NEXT PAGE A firework in disguise, *Allium schubertii*, one of the most eye-catching of all alliums, throws itself into the embrace of dark-flowered iris.

Allium 'Globemaster' ♀

At first, 'Globemaster' produces outrageous footballs, 20cm (8in) across, tightly packed with violet-purple flowers making a perfect globe on a massive, thick, bright green stem. The foliage is equally beefy. In subsequent years the flowers tend to be shorter and smaller and in many ways become easier garden plants, with heads about the size of *A. giganteum*, though only 70cm (28in) tall. At full strength they are almost too dominant. Try them with bronze fennel and the hairy, ginger rosettes of *Meconopsis napaulensis*. 'Globemaster' was bred from *A. giganteum* and was a wonder when first seen at the Royal Botanic Gardens, Kew, UK in the early 1990s. As well as being showy, it has an extraordinarily long flowering season. Plant the bulbs 12–15cm (5–6in) deep and about 45cm (18in) apart.

SEASON: May–June
HARDINESS: Fully hardy
HEIGHT: 130cm (4½ft)

Allium hollandicum 'Purple Sensation'
(*A.* 'Purple Sensation') ♀

Allium hollandicum is a drumstick allium derived from the central Asian species *A. aflatunense*, with masses of starry, purple flowers packed into a round head. It is variable in colour, height and size, but the irregularities add great charm when *A. hollandicum* is planted *en masse*, perhaps with *Cerinthe major* 'Purpurascens' and the lime-green foliage of *Smyrnium perfoliatum*. In the selected form 'Purple Sensation' the flowers are dark, bright purple, one of the darkest and brightest of all the alliums. The well-proportioned sphere balances on a tall, bright green stem. They are about 10cm (4in) across and perfectly globular. The colour is rich and intense, each small flower with a tiny bead at the centre, like a green eye. Use 'Purple Sensation' with pale greeny white astrantias or to precede a show of white galtonias. It needs a well-drained soil in a sunny part of the garden. Set the bulbs 10–12cm (4–5in) deep and about 20cm (8in) apart.

SEASON: May–June
HARDINESS: Fully hardy
HEIGHT: 60–80cm (24–32in)

Allium insubricum ♛

An enchanting small allium, very similar to *A. narcissiflorum*, both in height and in the soft pink colour of its papery flowers. Individually these are quite large – soft, folded skirts, not flat stars – but there are never more than five of them and the hanging head is only about 2cm (¾in) across. At flowering time, the reed-thin leaves are still green and fresh, so there is no need to disguise them. Use *A. insubricum* in a gravel bed, with low-growing thymes and pinks, but do not forget where you have put them. The leaves emerge rather late. Best bought damp-packed as the bulbs do not like drying out completely. Plant them about 5–8cm (2–3½in) deep and 10cm (4in) apart.

SEASON: June–July
HARDINESS: Fully hardy
HEIGHT: 15–25cm (6–10in)
HABITAT: Northern Italy (between Lake Como and Lake Garda) where it grows in limestone hills at about 1,800m (6,000ft)

Allium karataviense ♛

Two very broad, grey-green leaves (rather like those of veratrum, but not so pleated) stay close to the ground and cradle the flower, like the wings sprouting either side of a cherub's head. Though the stem is short, it does not always seem strong enough for its load. The foliage is handsome, not an adjective you often reach for when describing alliums, with the finest of red lines round the edge of each leaf. The flowerhead is pale pinkish grey, 12–15cm (5–6in) across, packed with star-shaped florets. They dry well. *Allium karataviense* was introduced into cultivation in 1878, collected in the Karatau mountains by the Russian plantsman Nikolai Sewerzow. 'Ivory Queen' is a selection, similar in every way, except for the fact that the spiky florets that make up the flowerhead are greenish white, rather than pinkish grey, and the leaves are finely edged with cream rather than red. Use *A. karataviense* in front of the dark emerging foliage of cimicifuga, or with spiky rosettes of *Eryngium bourgatii*. This is an easy plant, if it is planted in well-drained soil in full sun, though the bulbs are slow to increase. Set them 10cm (4in) deep and about 20cm (8in) apart.

SEASON: Late May–June
HARDINESS: Fully hardy
HEIGHT: 25cm (10in)
HABITAT: Central Asia (the Pamir Alai and the western Tien Shan) where it grows in loose limestone scree

Allium 'Lucy Ball'

A hybrid between *A. macleanii* and *A. aflatunense*, named after the American actress Lucille Ball, and bred by the Dutch grower Jan Bijl, the man who gave us 'Globemaster'. The heads are a dark rose-lilac, about 12–15cm (5–6in) wide, and sweetly scented. In season, they give a good show for at least three weeks, but in the long term tend to dwindle away unless you lift them every other year. Separate the clusters of bulbs and replant them in fresh soil to maintain vigour. Plant 'Lucy Ball' in sun or semi-shade, setting the bulbs 10–12cm (4–5in) deep and 12cm (5in) apart.

SEASON: May–June
HARDINESS: Fully hardy
HEIGHT: 100cm (39in)

Allium moly 'Jeannine' ♀

The wild species is found in eastern Spain and south-west France where it grows on mountain screes, often choosing the shady side of a rock. In a garden it can sometimes be invasive, but 'Jeannine' is a selected form, found in June 1978 by the Dutch nurseryman Michael Hoog in the Valle de Roncal in the Spanish Pyrenees. He named it after his wife. It flowers earlier and more reliably than the wild species, usually producing two heads from each bulb. Each head is about the size of a golf ball and is made up of soft, yellow stars. Use it among blue Dutch iris, or between clumps of helenium, which will pick up the yellow theme later in the year. It will also naturalize well under shrubs or trees. Plant the bulbs 8–10cm (3½–4in) deep and 15–20cm (6–8in) apart.

SEASON: May–June
HARDINESS: Fully hardy
HEIGHT: 20cm (8in)

Allium narcissiflorum

A charming miniature allium (the flower stem at 20cm/8in is shorter than the leaves) with grassy foliage which is still fresh and presentable when the flowers come out. These are borne four or five to a head, cup-shaped and pale pink. Although the plant is so small, the individual flowers are rather bigger than the massed florets which make up a typical allium head. They have something of the papery texture of thrift. Inside is a dark purple eye, very neat, with six small, white stamens stuck like tent pegs around it. The leaves emerge in clumps from sheaths, rather like chives, but they are flat, not rounded. It is very similar to *A. insubricum*; the seedheads are the key distinguishing feature. In *A. narcissiflorum* they stand upright. In *A. insubricum*, they hang down. The great alpine gardener Reginald Farrer – not a lover of alliums – made an exception for this species, 'the glory of its race'. Plant the bulbs 8–10cm (3½–4in) deep and the same distance apart.

SEASON: Mid June
HARDINESS: Fully hardy
HEIGHT: 25cm (10in)
HABITAT: Rocky places in southern France and the Alps of north-west Italy

Allium nigrum

The flower is white, not black, as the name suggests. The darkness (actually green) is concentrated in the prominent, button-like ovary that sits in the middle of each flower. The domed head is up to 12cm (5in) across, flattened at the bottom. Known to gardeners since 1762 and good for wilder areas of the garden, where the allium's broad leaves (too broad) can be disguised by mounds of lime-green alchemilla and shaggy astrantia. *Allium nigrum* will do best in a sunny, well-drained soil where it can get a dry summer rest. Plant the bulbs 8–10cm (3½–4in) deep and 25–30cm (10–12in) apart.

SEASON: Early June
HARDINESS: Frost hardy
HEIGHT: 100cm (39in)
HABITAT: Southern Europe east towards Iran, growing usually in fields or among limestone rocks at 100–200m (330–660ft)

Allium oreophilum 'Zwanenburg'
(Allium ostrowskianum 'Zwanenburg') ♉

The wild species is found in the Tien Shan and the Pamir Alai mountains of central Asia. It also grows in eastern Turkey and the Caucasus, favouring stony slopes at 3,000–3,800m (10,000–12,500ft). 'Zwanenburg' is an excellent form introduced by the Dutch firm Van Tubergen, with flowers that are a darker, richer colour than the wild species. Though the heads are small, the individual flowers are quite large and an eye-catching deep pink. Easy in well-drained soil in full sun, used perhaps in a gravel garden with pinks and an airy umbellifer such as *Didiscus* 'Blue Lace'. It makes an excellent cut flower as it is sweetly scented. The bulbs increase well. Plant them 8–10cm (3–4in) deep and 7–8cm (2½–3½in) apart.

SEASON: June
HARDINESS: Fully hardy
HEIGHT: 5–15cm (2–6in)

Allium paradoxum var. *normale*

The wild species, native to Iran and the Caucasus, often produces little more than a head of green bulbils, but this form, introduced from northern Iraq in 1966 by the fine plantsman–artist Paul Furse, is a different thing altogether. It has nodding heads of gleaming white, bell-shaped flowers at the top of a bright green stem, as clean and shining as a spring leucojum. Unusually for an allium, the leaves stay fresh while the flower blooms. *Allium paradoxum* var. *normale* also does well in shade and on heavy soils. Set bulbs 8–10cm (3½–4in) deep and 8–10cm (3½–4in) apart.

SEASON: Early March
HARDINESS: Fully hardy
HEIGHT: 25cm (10in)

Allium 'Pinball Wizard'

'Pinball Wizard', 'Beau Regard', and 'Round and Purple' have similar characteristics, though 'Beau Regard' is smaller and 'Round and Purple' paler in colour than the rich mauve of 'Pinball Wizard'. All of them came from crossing *A. macleanii* with *A. cristophii*. The heads are huge, though the stems are shorter than those of 'Globemaster'. Fortunately they are strong. Plant the bulbs between mounds of catmint or clumps of a large greyish hosta, such as 'Krossa Regal'. Set them 12–15cm (5–6in) deep and about 40cm (16in) apart.

SEASON: June
HARDINESS: Fully hardy
HEIGHT: 60cm (24in)

Allium sativum var. *ophioscorodon*

A very odd form of garlic with narrow stems, madly twisting into loops and corkscrews. The form is the point, not the flower. The stem itself morphs into a long, drawn-out flowerhead, very thin and pointed. The writer Jason Hill likened the whole thing to 'a flamingo at its toilet'. Bizarre, but popular with flower arrangers. In the garden, it needs to be set where its crazy form can be appreciated. It has nothing else to give, being green all over. Try *A. sativum* var. *ophioscorodon* on its own, in a tall, sleek zinc container. Known since 1601, when the French botanist Carolus Clusius included a picture of it in his *Rariorum Plantarum Historia*. Plant 8–10cm (3½–4in) deep and 12–15cm (5–6in) apart.

SEASON: July
HARDINESS: Fully hardy
HEIGHT: 90cm (36in)

Allium schubertii

Introduced into cultivation in 1843 and an outrageously wonderful allium, in its make-up quite different from any other. Half of the green-centred, pink-mauve flowers are clasped quite close to the centre. The rest (the majority) zoom out on long, pinkish green stalks like a firework exploding. It is magnificent, much more interesting than *A. cristophii*. At maturity the heads are almost completely spherical and can measure 40cm (16in) across. Half the height is in the stem, half in the head itself, so it does look slightly top-heavy and may need staking. The foliage is broad, and as usual with this tribe it is at its worst when the flower is at its height. By the time the spectacular seedhead begins to form, the stem is very brittle. If you want to keep it in place, you will have to anchor it discreetly. Silvered, the heads make wonderful decorations for

Christmas. *Allium schubertii* will only settle permanently in good soil in a warm situation where it can get a well-baked rest in summer. The bulbs are large. Beware of planting them too close. To be seen at their best, the umbels need air round them. Set them 8–10cm (3½–4in) deep and about 50cm (20in) apart.

SEASON: Early June
HARDINESS: Frost hardy
HEIGHT: 45–60cm (18–24in)
HABITAT: Widespread in Palestine, Syria, northern Iran and western Turkestan

Allium senescens subsp. *glaucum*

Small, glaucous, scimitar-shaped leaves lie in a flattened whorl, close to the ground, much more handsome than the foliage of most alliums. As the plant pulls itself, very slowly, into flowering mode, the leaves, still twisting slightly, start to lift and point skywards. The flowers are held well above the leaves, soft mauve-pink, clustered in a head that is rarely more than 5cm (2in) across. It takes a phenomenally long time to develop, the flowers opening first round the outside of the head. Bees and butterflies love it. Use *A. senescens* subsp. *glaucum* in a gravel bed, where it can take over from earlier flowering species such as *A. oreophilum* 'Zwanenburg'. It is one of the few alliums that is almost as good in leaf as in flower. Try it between clumps of June-flowering *Iris chrysographes*, with *Thymus vulgaris* 'Silver Posie' or between plantings of spring bulbs such as crocus and species tulips. Plant the rhizomes shallowly, as you might a bearded iris, setting them so their tops are close to the surface of the earth, 3cm (1in) deep and 8–10cm (3½–4in) apart.

SEASON: Late July
HARDINESS: Fully hardy
HEIGHT: 25cm (10in)
HABITAT: Northern Europe and Siberia where it favours dry, rocky places

Allium sphaerocephalon

Tall, thin stems are topped by small, pear-shaped heads, intriguing and wild-looking. At first they appear green with a cap of purple, but gradually the purple floods through the rest of the flower till by the end of July the whole head is glowing. *Allium sphaerocephalon* is an easy, undemanding species tolerant of summer rain. Try it in long grass (as long as it is not cut too early) or perhaps in a rough piece of ground to follow on from opium poppies. It also looks good with grasses such as *Pennisetum alopecuroides* and dries well for winter arrangements. It does best in full sun. Plant 7cm (2½in) deep and 7–8cm (2½–3½in) apart.

SEASON: July
HARDINESS: Fully hardy
HEIGHT: 60cm (24in)
HABITAT: Europe (from England and Belgium right across to the Caucasus), north Africa and Israel where it grows in fields and dry verges

Allium stipitatum 'Mars'

A cross between *A. stipitatum* and *A. hollandicum* 'Purple Sensation' producing fluffy heads of deep mauve (or pale purple), about 15cm (6in) across. Charming and easy to use because, though tall, the flowers are not too big. *Allium stipitatum* 'Mars' clumps up quickly, producing several offsets every year. The bulbs are extraordinary, the colour of pumpkins. Plant them 12–15cm (5–6in) deep and 20cm (8in) apart.

SEASON: Late May–June
HARDINESS: Fully hardy
HEIGHT: 100–120cm (3–4ft)

Allium stipitatum 'Mount Everest'

This has tall, thin, spindly stems, with flowers the size of grapefruit set on top. The general effect is of a large dandelion seedhead. The flower has a flattish bottom unlike the spherical shape of other alliums. Very smart when planted *en masse* against the dark backdrop of a yew hedge, or the blue-grey wall of a wooden shed. Set the bulbs of *A. stipitatum* 'Mount Everest' in a well-drained, sunny spot 10–12cm (4–5in) deep and about 30cm (12in) apart.

SEASON: May–June
HARDINESS: Fully hardy
HEIGHT: 90cm (36in)

Allium tuberosum
CHINESE CHIVES

This allium clumps up quickly in the manner of ordinary chives (*A. schoenoprasum*), though it flowers much later in the season. The flowerheads are small but they come at a good time of year and are held well above the flat leaves, which are half the height of the flower stems. The heads are clusters of starry, white flowers which come out in turn. The outer ones are not always first. In bud they seem tinged with pink because of the thin but very distinct pink line drawn up the midrib of the three tiny outer petals of each star. Use them to make edgings in a potager or plant them among dwarf agapanthus for a Chinese willow-pattern effect. In the tropics, *A. tuberosum* is widely cultivated for cooking, but it seems to be as happy in temperate as in tropical climates though it needs full sun. Best bought damp-packed, as the bulbs are still in leaf when offered for sale in autumn. Plant the little clumps about 5cm (2in) deep and 10cm (4in) apart, or grow it from seed.

SEASON: August–October
HARDINESS: Frost hardy
HEIGHT: 65cm (26in)
HABITAT: East Asia, from India to Japan and China

Allium unifolium ♔

The soft pinkish mauve heads are
made up of relatively large, papery
flowers, up to 30 of them in a single
umbel. It is a charming allium,
introduced into cultivation in 1873,
softer in colour than most, with
flowers that come out in turn (the
outermost ones first) rather than
altogether, as the drumstick types do.
Its strong, sturdy stems allow it to
rise above aquilegia or herbaceous
geraniums such as 'Brookside'. It
needs well-drained soil in full sun,
where it can get a dry, summer rest.
If you think it is unlikely to get this,
cover *A. unifolium* with a cloche
when it has finished flowering or
grow it in a pot in a cold frame.
Plant the bulbs 5cm (2in) deep
and 5–8cm (2–3½in) apart.

SEASON: Mid May

HARDINESS: Frost hardy

HEIGHT: 58cm (23in)

HABITAT: A native of southern Oregon
and northern California where it grows
in moist soil in the pine and mixed
evergreen forests of the coastal region
below 1,200m (4,000ft)

Allium vineale 'Hair'

A curiosity rather than a beauty, with
long, very thin, strong, tough stems.
The heads start off with pointed caps,
like leeks, and remain in this state
for about a month before splitting.
Mad green 'hair' whirls out from the
centre – thread-like and about 5cm
(2in) long. The centre is a congested,
burr-like lump, maroon and pale
green. Useful for cutting, as the
stems take on interesting kinks.
Allium vineale 'Hair' naturalizes
easily and can hold its own in long
grass, which is the best place to
grow it. In borders, it is a thug.
Plant 8–10cm (3½–4in) deep and
12–15cm (5–6in) apart.

SEASON: June

HARDINESS: Fully hardy

HEIGHT: 70cm (28in)

NEXT PAGE *Allium sphaerocephalon* in the cool border at Coughton
Court, Warwickshire. Although the flower heads are relatively small,
this is a charming member of the allium family.

Amaryllis (Amaryllidaceae)

This amaryllis is not the same as the fat, South American flower, expensively packaged in garden centres to bloom indoors after Christmas. Though popularly called amaryllis, those are actually *Hippeastrum*. The true amaryllis, *Amaryllis belladonna*, can be grown outside where winters are not too cold, springing bare-stemmed straight from the ground in late summer and autumn to produce heads of gorgeous trumpet flowers extravagantly at odds with the general *fin de siècle* air of everything else around it. Though a South African, it has settled and naturalized in places such as California where growing conditions are similar to those in its natural habitat. There is only one species, which in the wild produces flowers in various shades from deep pink through to white. Breeders have used it to produce different bi-generic hybrids such as × *Amarine* (amaryllis crossed with nerine), × *Amarcrinum* (amaryllis with crinum, a cross made both in Europe and the US around 1920) and × *Amarygia* (amaryllis with brunsvigia). Are the children more interesting than their parents? Scarcely.

Amaryllis associates naturally with nerines, *Iris unguicularis* and other such plants that need a hot, dry summer rest. The purplish flower stems also look good rising behind low mounds of purple-leaved sage or set in front of a scrambing mass of *Clematis* 'Venosa Violacea'. Avoid over-enthusiastic companions that may shade the bulbs during summer when they need to rest and bake. They make beautiful cut flowers – if you can bear to cut them.

CULTIVATION

Amaryllis belladonna is tougher than its South African home might suggest. Given good drainage (essential) and the shelter of a warm wall, it will settle and slowly increase to make big clumps. In the wild, it is sparked into growth by the onset of autumn rains, coming after a hot, dry summer rest. In the garden, it should be planted in late summer, before growth starts. Set the top of the bulb 10–12cm (4–5in) below the surface of the soil; deep planting gives some protection against frost. Mulch after flowering with a thickish layer of dry leaves, chopped bracken or straw as a further defence against plunging winter temperatures. Remember that foliage will follow the naked flower stems and is likely to swamp smaller subjects growing too close. The bulbs need to stay really dry and as hot as possible during summer. Without this rest and summer baking, they are unlikely to flower well the following season. Give outdoor plants a handful of bonemeal in early spring. This is all the food they will need.

Selections such as 'Bloemfontein', 'Purpurea' and 'Windhoek' make excellent and showy pot plants for a cool conservatory. Set the bulbs firmly in deep pots, using a loam-based compost mixed with grit or sharp sand (two parts compost to one part grit). If the pots are to be kept inside, the bulbs can be set with their necks at soil level. Do not overwater them. When the flower stem starts to show, give rather more water, mixed with a liquid feed, and continue to water and feed until the leaves begin to wither. Allow the flower stems and subsequent leaves to die down naturally, then give the dormant bulbs a dry summer rest. They resent being disturbed. Repot only when overcrowding seems to be having an adverse effect on the production of flowering stems.

Slugs adore amaryllis. That shows good taste on their part but ruins the effect for us onlookers. Take whatever action your conscience allows. If you are growing amaryllis in a greenhouse or conservatory, watch out for common pests such as aphid and red spider mite.

ABOVE The Belladonna Lily (*Amaryllis belladonna*) growing in grassland at the De Hoop Nature Reserve, Western Cape, South Africa. A native of South Africa, the belladonna was introduced into Europe around 1712.

Amaryllis belladonna ♀
BELLADONNA LILY, NAKED LADY

A surprising sight at this time of the year, when the fat, purple-bronze stem erupts naked from the earth to produce a large, loose head of pink, funnel-shaped flowers, six or more on each stem. They are softly scented – a fresh smell, like apples – and astonishingly showy, almost unreal. The stems are thick and juicy, the flowers equally fleshy, flaring out at the tips. This is where the colour is richest; the pink fades away to white at the base of the funnel, both inside and outside the flower. The stamens are creamy, shorter than the style with its dark purplish top hooking upwards from the centre of the protecting funnels. The sheath of strap-shaped leaves comes after the flowers have finished. The foliage does not die down until early summer. *Amaryllis belladonna* was introduced into cultivation in 1712. Outside, plant 10–12cm (4–5in) deep and 30cm (12in) apart.

SEASON: Mid October
HARDINESS: Frost hardy
HEIGHT: 80cm (32in)
HABITAT: Western Cape, South Africa, where it grows on rocky hillsides and along stream banks

Amaryllis belladonna 'Purpurea'

This bears flowers up one side of the stem only, in the manner of a gladiolus. It usually comes into flower earlier than other named varieties. Outside, plant *A. belladonna* 'Purpurea' 10–12cm (4–5in) deep and 30cm (12in) apart.

SEASON: September
HARDINESS: Frost hardy
HEIGHT: 50cm (20in)

Amaryllis belladonna 'Windhoek'

Enormous flowers range round the top of the stem, each with pale pink lips to the petals and pale throats. In a cool conservatory, the scent of *A. belladonna* 'Windhoek' is fabulous. Outside, plant 10–12cm (4–5in) deep and 30cm (12in) apart.

SEASON: September
HARDINESS: Frost hardy
HEIGHT: 60cm (24in)

Ambrosina (Araceae)

Ambrosina bassii

An insignificant aroid is a contradiction in terms, but this one is minute. The oval leaves work heroically to get to 5cm (2in). The comma-shaped inflorescence cannot even reach 2cm (¾in). But, like all aroids, this is a fascinating plant, with the tiny, grey-white spathe intricately patterned in darker streaks and scales. In the wild, ambrosina's seeds are distributed by ants which cart them away to their nests, lick off the sweet outer coating and then abandon them. This suits the seed perfectly since it is then in the best place to germinate and grow. Keep A. *bassii* in a pot. It would get lost in a garden setting. Give it a well-drained, humus-rich compost, and, after it has done its tiny thing, leave it to rest during summer. Plant 3–5cm (1–2in) deep and 5cm (2in) apart.

SEASON: May
HARDINESS: Frost hardy
HEIGHT: 5cm (2in)
HABITAT: Southern Italy, Sardinia and northern Algeria where it
is found in scrubby woodland generally on the north side of a hill

Anemone (Ranunculaceae)

The name, taken from *anemos*, the Greek word for wind, comes from the philosopher Theophrastus, the first man ever to write a book about plants (300 years BC). The anemones listed below grow from twiggy, little rhizomes or small, knobbly tubers and provide flowers through spring and early summer. The popular Japanese anemone (*A. hupehensis*) does not belong here, because it grows as an herbaceous perennial, producing its early autumn flowers each season from a strong, fibrous rootstock. In the wild, anemones are widely spread over Europe and central Asia, but gardeners can think of them as belonging in one or other of two different camps. One group, which includes the wood anemones (*A. nemorosa*), likes the kind of dampish soil, rich in humus, that you find on a woodland floor in spring. The other group (*A. coronaria*, *A. pavonina*) has Mediterranean blood and needs a hot, sunny place in the garden. If they are happy, they will produce a long succession of jewel-coloured blooms. So, cultivation is not a matter of 'one size fits all', but the advantage is that there will certainly be an anemone adapted to fit almost every situation in a garden: hot, dry slopes; gravel; the shaded areas under trees and shrubs. The woodlanders such as *A. nemorosa* can be used like snowdrops to carpet areas which, though shaded once trees and shrubs leaf up, get plenty of light early in the year.

Anemones are 'so full of variety and so dainty', wrote the seventeenth-century gardener John Parkinson, 'so pleasant and so delightsome flowers that the sight of them doth enforce an earnest longing desire in the minde of anyone to be a possessour of some of them at the least, for without all doubt, this one kind of flower... is of it selfe alone almost sufficient to furnish a garden with their flowers for almost halfe the yeare.'

As always, if you set the plants in the kind of place that they want to be, disease will be less prevalent. All species may occasionally be disfigured by leaf spot or powdery mildew. Neither is fatal.

ABOVE Wood anemones (*Anemone nemorosa*) flowering in March in a Hampshire woodland. They are charming, ethereal things, widespread in woods and mountain pastures throughout northern Europe.

Anemone apennina ♀

The flowers are smaller than those of *A. blanda*, but bigger than the wood anemone, *A. nemorosa*. They can be pale mauvish blue or white, with a dozen or more narrow petals spinning round a yellow button centre. *Anemone apennina* var. *albiflora* is a selected, white-flowered form, with a lovely, pale blue wash on the backs of the petals. These are leafy plants and give a pleasingly bulky effect as the foliage is not so deeply divided as the wood anemone's. The flowers are held up above the leaves. *Anemone apennina* does particularly well in soils with plenty of lime, and can cope in grass provided it is not too lush. 'Cope' is not the same as 'thrive', which it will do in soil rich in leaf mould where it can get a dry summer holiday. Hang a large 'Do Not Disturb' notice nearby. The rhizomes are best bought damp-packed, as they hate to dry out. Plant them about 5cm (2in) deep and 15cm (6in) apart.

SEASON: Early March
HARDINESS: Fully hardy
HEIGHT: 15cm (6in)
HABITAT: Southern Europe where it grows in open woodland

Anemone blanda ♀

This is the original wild species from which growers have bred or selected at least a dozen named forms. It is naturally variable, bearing flowers 3–5cm (1–2in) across, that can be blue, pink or white. These are the earliest of the anemones to flower, closely followed by the more fragile-looking blooms of *A. nemorosa*. All this group of anemones are excellent used in large drifts of a single colour, scattered under shrubs or mixed with snowdrops in areas of the garden where ferns might later uncurl. They like sun while they are flowering, and as long as they have sufficient light and moisture in spring they will not mind drying out in summer. You can use *A. blanda* in shallow pots for an early display, but when they have finished flowering they are best planted out in the garden. A free-draining, humus-rich soil is ideal. They also do well on chalk soils.

Give established clumps a top-dressing of leaf mould in autumn. The knobbly tubers look unpromising and by the time they reach your hands may be shrunk and dry. Soak them overnight before planting them out, about 3cm (1in) deep and 7cm (2½in) apart.

SEASON: March
HARDINESS: Fully hardy
HEIGHT: 15cm (6in)
HABITAT: Eastern Mediterranean (Albania, Greece, Turkey, Lebanon) where it grows in scrub, rocky areas and pasture up to 2,000m (6,500ft)

OPPOSITE Given time, *Anemone blanda* will spread to make thick carpets in gardens. Here, both blue and white forms combine to give a fine spring display.

Anemone blanda
blue-flowered

The blooms seem blue, until you compare them with a flower such as *Ipheion* 'Jessie'. Then you see that *A. blanda* blue-flowered is a royal, purplish blue, still wonderful, but quite different. The blue anemones tend to be shorter than the whites, with the many-petalled flowers held only just above the deeply divided foliage. The backs of the leaves are washed over with a deep maroon. They look particularly good scattered around the snub-nosed, magenta flowers of *Cyclamen coum*, or spread in a carpet under an early-flowering cherry. Plant 3cm (1in) deep and 7cm (2½in) apart.

SEASON: Early March
HARDINESS: Fully hardy
HEIGHT: 8cm (3½in)

Anemone blanda
'Radar' ♀

If the flowers are not a searing rich magenta, you have been fobbed off with inferior stock. Towards the centre, each petal fades to white, encircling a creamy yellow boss of stamens, less profuse and fluffy than those of 'White Splendour'. 'Radar' is difficult to propagate so is usually more expensive than other varieties of *A. blanda*. Plant 3cm (1in) deep and 7cm (2½in) apart.

SEASON: Late February–March
HARDINESS: Fully hardy
HEIGHT: 11cm (4½in)

Anemone blanda var. *rosea* ♀

A selected, pink form of the wild species. If you cannot find *A. blanda* var. *rosea*, use 'Charmer' or 'Pink Star' to provide soft sheets of pink under old fruit trees or an early display in a scree or gravel garden. Plant 3cm (1in) deep and 7cm (2½in) apart.

SEASON: March
HARDINESS: Fully hardy
HEIGHT: 13cm (5¼in)

Anemone blanda 'White Splendour' ♀

'White Splendour' is a pure, clean white with just a whisper of pink on the backs of the petals. When the flowers open flat in the sun, though, you see nothing of that. They display themselves well, waving on thin, but strong stems above mats of deeply divided, slightly hairy foliage. In the centre of each flower is a creamy yellow mass of stamens. Wonderful interplanted with *Cyclamen hederifolium* which enjoys the same kind of conditions. Though the cyclamen's flowers are long gone, the marbled foliage still looks fresh in early spring. Plant *A. blanda* 'White Splendour' 3cm (1in) deep and 7cm (2½in) apart.

SEASON: Early March
HARDINESS: Fully hardy
HEIGHT: 13cm (5¼in)

Anemone coronaria

POPPY ANEMONE

The tubers look like dry sheep's dung but from them comes the most astonishing amount of growth. The flowers may be royal blue, intense magenta, brilliant crimson – all stunning, rich, clear colours. Sometimes there are bicolours, with red at the bottom of the petal and white at the top. In wild populations, the most common colour is red. They are enchanting as cut flowers and worth growing in rows for this purpose alone. In its natural habitat (central and eastern Mediterranean), *A. coronaria* flowers in spring, but by planting both in autumn and in spring you can extend the flowering season from April to September. The foliage is strong and finely dissected; it appears before the flowers, as bright and edible looking as parsley. In bud, the flowers are circled by a light ruff of foliage; as they age, they grow slightly away from the ruff. The stems are very fat and juicy. These anemones look good grown in a mixture of colours and are superb bedded out with pink, lily-flowered tulips. But if you grow these anemones in pots, you find there is too much foliage to flower and that, though the flowers are produced in a long succession, not enough of them are out at the same time to make a show. I discovered this the hard way when I planned to use them as table centres for a daughter's wedding.

Introduced into cultivation by 1596, the poppy anemones quickly became favourites with collectors. By 1650, Francesco Caetani, the duke of Sermoneta, had 29,000 of them in his garden at Cisterna, south of Rome. The De Caen Group, raised in Normandy, has single flowers, the Saint Bridgid Group, raised in Ireland, are doubles. They flower about three months after planting so if you start them off in March you will have flowers in June and July; a June planting provides a September show. Plant in September or October for a traditional display in early spring. They will need replacing fairly regularly. Give them a sunny, warm situation in the garden and plant the tubers about 5cm (2in) deep and 15cm (6in) apart.

SEASON: March–September depending on time of planting
HARDINESS: Fully hardy
HEIGHT: 30cm (12in)
HABITAT: Mediterranean areas, from France and Spain in the west to Turkey in the east

Anemone coronaria 'Die Braut' ('The Bride') (De Caen Group)

Though technically a single, the white flowers often have more than six petals. They are arranged round a central, greenish boss and the stamens are buff coloured, so this variety does not have the impact of the dark-centred varieties. But in a mixed planting (and for picking) the white flowers of *A. coronaria* 'Die Braut' leaven the deeply saturated colours of other anemones. Plant the tubers 5cm (2in) deep and 15cm (6in) apart.

SEASON: March–September depending on time of planting
HARDINESS: Fully hardy
HEIGHT: 30cm (12in)

Anemone coronaria 'Hollandia' (De Caen Group)

'Hollandia' is a single variety, but often produces flowers with seven or eight petals. It is a good, clear and uncompromising shade of red, with a neat white circle at the base of each flower. Inside this sits the central, black boss surrounded by a ring of black stamens which add greatly to the charm of the flower. When the flowers go to seed the boss is left behind on the stem. Plant the tubers 5cm (2in) deep and 15cm (6in) apart.

SEASON: March–September depending on time of planting
HARDINESS: Fully hardy
HEIGHT: 30cm (12in)

Anemone coronaria 'Lord Lieutenant'
(Saint Bridgid Group)

The dissected leaves of *A. coronaria* 'Lord Lieutenant' make a thick and meaty basal clump of palish green. From this springs a long succession of many-petalled, blue flowers on tall, fat, strong stems. Unlike those of single varieties the petals of the doubles are narrow and quilled. In the centre is a strong, black knob, covered in dark stubble. Useful among bearded iris. Plant the tubers 5cm (2in) deep and 15cm (6in) apart.

SEASON: March–September depending on time of planting
HARDINESS: Fully hardy
HEIGHT: 40–50cm (16–20in)

Anemone coronaria 'Mister Fokker'
(De Caen Group)

The pleasing foliage of bright parsley green, finely cut, makes excellent ground cover. 'Mister Fokker' is a good, rich blue, the flower pushing up on a chubby stem, with a ruff of greenery clasping the bud. In the centre is a boss of brown stamens. The flowers come out in a long succession, and from a spring planting may still be appearing at the beginning of August. Plant the tubers 5cm (2in) deep and 15cm (6in) apart.

SEASON: March–September depending on time of planting
HARDINESS: Fully hardy
HEIGHT: 30cm (12in)

Anemone coronaria 'Mount Everest'
(Saint Bridgid Group)

Anemone coronaria 'Mount Everest' is the quilled, double equivalent of 'Die Braut', with narrow, white petals surrounding a greenish central boss. Plant the tubers 5cm (2in) deep and 15cm (6in) apart.

SEASON: March–September depending on time of planting
HARDINESS: Fully hardy
HEIGHT: 40–50cm (16–20in)

Anemone coronaria 'Sylphide'
(Mona Lisa Series)

'Sylphide' is a lovely clear shade of amethyst-violet. Use it as an underplanting for the lily-flowered tulip 'William and Mary' or set it among the curving grey foliage of *Euphorbia rigida*. Plant the tubers 5cm (2in) deep and 15cm (6in) apart.

SEASON: March–September depending on time of planting
HARDINESS: Fully hardy
HEIGHT: 30cm (12in)

Anemone coronaria 'The Admiral' (Saint Bridgid Group)

Though the De Caen strain has a composure that the Saint Bridgid anemones lack, the doubles sit well in formal plantings, filling ground that may later be occupied by eucomis or mauve-blue stokesia. *Anemone coronaria* 'The Admiral' is violet-mauve, a double version of 'Sylphide'. Plant the tubers 5cm (2in) deep and 15cm (6in) apart.

SEASON: March–September depending on time of planting
HARDINESS: Fully hardy
HEIGHT: 30cm (12in)

Anemone × lipsiensis 'Pallida' ♀

A hybrid between *A. ranunculoides* and *A. nemorosa* with qualities of both. In growth it is similar to the latter, but *A. ranunculoides* lends its yellow flowers, which is not a colour the wood anemones can produce. 'Pallida' is a wispy, little thing with pale blooms scarcely 2cm (¾in) across, even smaller than the wood anemone. The green knob in the centre of the soft creamy flowers is disguised by a mass of incredibly fine stamens. Try it with the dainty blue flowers of *Scilla bifolia*. It is happiest in light shade, growing in loose, leafy soil, rich in humus, but not too damp in summer. The twiggy rhizomes are best bought damp-packed for autumn planting, as they hate to dry out completely. Lay them flat about 7cm (2½in) below the surface of the soil and 7cm (2½in) apart.

SEASON: Late March
HARDINESS: Fully hardy
HEIGHT: 10–12cm (4–5in)

Anemone nemorosa ♀

WINDFLOWER, WOOD ANEMONE

These anemones flower slightly later than forms of *Anemone blanda* and can usefully follow them as ground cover in wilder places under trees and shrubs, which at this season still allow enough light through for the flowers to open up. In dull, wet weather they remain resolutely closed, protecting the pollen loaded on their fragile stamens. *Anemone nemorosa* is the true, wild windflower, with single, white, usually six-petalled flowers, very much more fragile than the wide, many-petalled flowers of *A. blanda* 'White Splendour'. The two are best kept apart in a garden. It is charming anywhere, but particularly good when used as a link between the edges of a garden and the wider landscape beyond. It can settle under hedges if there is not too much heavyweight competition,

though it does not like excessively dry conditions. If possible, buy these anemones freshly lifted and damp-packed for autumn planting. Dry rhizomes look unpromising – shapeless pieces of fossilized plasticine – but have faith. Though they take time to settle and increase, the transformation from toad to prince is astounding. Soak dry rhizomes in water overnight and plant them flat, not vertically, setting them 5–7cm (2–2½in) deep and 7cm (2½in) apart.

SEASON: Early March
HARDINESS: Fully hardy
HEIGHT: 7cm (2½in)
HABITAT: Woods and mountain pastures throughout northern Europe

Anemone nemorosa 'Allenii' ♚

The impression is of soft lavender-blue, though the petals are washed over on the back with greyish violet. The foliage and stems of 'Allenii' are darker than that of ordinary *A. nemorosa*. Named around 1890 after James Allen of Shepton Mallet, who raised many excellent bulbs, particularly snowdrops. Best bought damp-packed as the rhizomes hate to dry out completely. Plant them 5–7cm (2–2½in) deep and 7cm (2½in) apart.

SEASON: April
HARDINESS: Fully hardy
HEIGHT: 10cm (4in)

Anemone nemorosa 'Blue Beauty'

A low, pale carpet of flowers appears at the same time as the leaves. The flowers may have six, seven or eight petals and are held on thread-like but surprisingly strong stems. They bow outwards to present themselves face-on and are a lovely, soft shade of mauve-blue, darker than 'Robinsoniana', with the usual, elegant, cut foliage. Charming, but easily overwhelmed by neighbours that might be stronger either in constitution or in looks. Use 'Blue Beauty' among the marbled foliage of autumn-flowering *Cyclamen hederifolium*. Plant rhizomes 5–7cm (2–2½in) deep and 7cm (2½in) apart.

SEASON: Mid April
HARDINESS: Fully hardy
HEIGHT: 10cm (4in)

Anemone nemorosa 'Bracteata Pleniflora'

This is not as green (or mad) as
A. *nemorosa* 'Virescens', but is travelling
in the same direction. Each of the
double, white flowers of 'Bracteata
Pleniflora' may have petals striped or
wholly green, and is surrounded by a
wonderful ruff of deeply divided leaves
that are also a mixture of white and
green. These oddities were highly
prized by European gardeners of the
sixteenth and seventeenth century,
who gathered them in with a stamp
collector's ardour. No two flowers are
the same. Plant rhizomes 5–7cm
(2–2½in) deep and 7cm (2½in) apart.

SEASON: April
HARDINESS: Fully hardy
HEIGHT: 10cm (4in)

Anemone nemorosa 'Lychette'

A beautiful form with extra large,
white flowers, made up of seven or
eight petals rather than the normal
six. The green, central button is
surrounded by a froth of creamy
stamens. It naturalizes well and is
showier than the standard species.
Spread 'Lychette' under an early
flowering, pale pink rhododendron, or
let it share quarters with lily-of-the-
valley, which will come into flower
slightly later. It also looks good set
alongside the young, bronze-tinted
foliage of *Corydalis flexuosa* 'China
Blue'. Best bought damp-packed as
the rhizomes hate to dry out totally.
Plant them 5–7cm (2–2½in) deep
and 7cm (2½in) apart.

SEASON: Late March
HARDINESS: Fully hardy
HEIGHT: 15cm (6in)

Anemone nemorosa 'Robinsoniana' ♀

Big flowers in a pale, washed-out lavender-blue, very wistful and appealing against the foliage which is faintly stained on the edges with bronze. The leaves are bigger, less finely cut than those of the wild windflower and the plant stands taller, so calls more attention to itself. This is an old selection, named after himself by the splenetic plantsman William Robinson, owner of Gravetye Manor in Sussex. He discovered it in 1870 growing in the Oxford Botanic Garden, where it had come from Ireland. Though an old performer, 'Robinsoniana' is still one of the most vigorous of the named forms of wood anemone, and is marvellous mixed with primroses. It settles well under deciduous trees and shrubs or anywhere with damp soil, rich in humus. Best bought damp-packed as the rhizomes hate to dry out. Plant them flat, 5–7cm (2–2½in) deep and 7cm (2½in) apart.

SEASON: Late March–April
HARDINESS: Fully hardy
HEIGHT: 14cm (5½in)

Anemone nemorosa 'Vestal' ♀

The centre is a tightly packed powder puff of small, white petals, with a halo of wider petals round the outside. It looks very pure, as there is no darker wash on the reverse of the flower. One of the best of the doubles, introduced by the nurseryman Max Leichtlin and slightly later into flower than others of this group. Plant the rhizomes of 'Vestal' 5–7cm (2–2½in) deep and 7cm (2½in) apart.

SEASON: April
HARDINESS: Fully hardy
HEIGHT: 10cm (4in)

Anemone nemorosa 'Virescens' ♀

A bizarre form in which all the petals (and the centre) have turned themselves into tiny, divided, green leaves, to make a strange, but rather appealing, mossy mop, an excellent cool companion for trilliums. Because there is nothing there to be pollinated, the bloom lasts for a long time in perfect condition. Introduced into cultivation by the fine Irish plantswoman Molly Sanderson, who also gave us a splendid, black-faced viola. 'Virescens' is excellent under deciduous trees and shrubs. The rhizomes are best bought damp-packed in autumn, as they hate to dry out. Lay them flat in cool, moisture-retentive soil, rich in humus, 5–7cm (2–2½in) deep and 7cm (2½in) apart.

SEASON: April
HARDINESS: Fully hardy
HEIGHT: 12cm (5in)

Anemone pavonina
PEACOCK ANEMONE

Flowers of red, pink or a gentle, soft purple rise from a congested mat of leaves, some deeply divided, some not. The flower itself is light-limbed, petals poised round a dark blue centre. *Anemone pavonina* needs a warm, sunny situation if it is to thrive. Grow it with early-flowering tulips such as 'Little Beauty' or slender *Crocus tommasinianus*. It is a good flower for cutting.

SEASON: Mid February–March
HARDINESS: Fully hardy
HEIGHT: 20cm (8in)
HABITAT: Mediterranean areas from France to Turkey where it is found in open, stony places, often on the terraces where olive trees grow

Anemone ranunculoides ♀

The small, yellowish rhizomes produce a mass of bronze-green, fern-like leaves and rich yellow flowers, two or more to a stem, but only five petals to a flower. 'Pleniflora' is a semi- rather than a full double, but the extra set of petals gives the flowers even more panache. In general habit, *A. ranunculoides* is rather like the wood anemones and likes the same kind of humus-rich soil that does not dry out in spring. Leave it alone to creep quietly about under deciduous trees. It naturalizes very readily. Rhizomes are best bought damp-packed as they hate to dry out. Plant them shallowly, laying them flat on the soil no deeper than 5cm (2in) and about 7cm (2½in) apart.

SEASON: April
HARDINESS: Fully hardy
HEIGHT: 10cm (4in)
HABITAT: Widely spread in northern Europe and western Asia from Belgium through to Siberia and generally found in deciduous woodland

NEXT PAGE In a private garden in Oxfordshire, swathes of *Anemone blanda* in white and violet are set against a backdrop of early-flowering narcissus.

Anemonella (Ranunculaceae)

Remember that this plant is a woodlander and give it light shade in well-drained soil with plenty of humus. If it is too wet, the tubers will rot. Soils on the acid side of neutral are ideal, but even in ideal conditions plants are slow to establish and clump up. If they like you, they will seed themselves about. The double form, of course, will not, because it is sterile. The tiny tubers are like those of a dahlia, shrunk in the wash. Buy them damp-packed in autumn and plant them 2–3cm (¾–1in) deep and 30cm (12in) apart.

Anemonella thalictroides
RUE ANEMONE

The flowers are as fragile as wood anemones, and can be white or a very pale, washed-out pink with feathery stamens in the centre. They last in good condition for at least a month. The name reflects the fact that anemonella's foliage is like that of thalictrum, the meadow rue. Leaves and flowers spring out from the same point on the stem. 'Cameo' produces a double flower of soft, icing-sugar pink with the petals stacked up in whorls to make a rounded hummock. *Anemonella thalictroides* is expensive to acquire, but worth it. Plant 2–3cm (¾–1in) deep and 30cm (12in) apart.

SEASON: Late March–April
HARDINESS: Fully hardy
HEIGHT: 10cm (4in)
HABITAT: The eastern states of North America (Maine, Alabama, Arkansas, Oklahoma) where it grows in open woodland

Anthericum (Anthericaceae)

This will naturalize in grass, provided it is not too lush and looks enchanting growing this way, mimicking the plant's natural habitat which is grassy scrub. In Italy, you often see anthericum on roadside verges, with poppies and larkspur, wild roses and orchids. They also last well as cut flowers, though you can never persuade all the flowers on a spike to come out at once. They need full sun.

Anthericum liliago 'Major' ♀
SAINT BERNARD'S LILY

The leaves come first, in clumps, rather like daffodil leaves: long, thin and channelled down the centre. The flower stalks are thin but strong, carrying each spike of white flowers well above the level of the leaves. The flowers make six-petalled stars with orange-tipped stamens in the centre. They open from the bottom up, with 6–8 open at any one time. The advantage is that each spike lasts a long time. *Anthericum liliago* 'Major' is a sweetly scented, airy plant, ethereal and charming but easily overlaid and swamped by noisy neighbours. Its common name commemorates Saint Bernard of Montjoux. Plant the fleshy rhizomes in autumn, setting them 6cm (2¼in) deep and 30cm (12in) apart.

SEASON: Late April
HARDINESS: Fully hardy
HEIGHT: 70cm (28in)

71

A

Arisaema (Araceae)

There has been an explosion in demand for these weird, witchy plants, as gardeners have discovered they are not as tender as their tropical looks might suggest. They have handsome foliage, which stands in splendid fettle after the strange, cobra-headed inflorescences have melted away. These are exaggerated, much more dramatic versions of the cuckoo pint, a hooded spathe protecting a thin column (the spadix) inside. The infinite variations in the structure and markings of spathe and spadix (as well as the handsome foliage, whorled in leaflets on top of tall, bare stems) are what makes these plants so desirable. They are faintly sinister, and fabulously seductive. More than 150 kinds are now in cultivation, but the most useful are the ones that are relatively hardy. Fortunately, beautiful *A. candidissimum* and *A. consanguineum* are among the kinds that can be grown quite easily in areas where winters are not too harsh. Use the taller species with equally imposing ferns, such as *Osmunda regalis*, *Hosta* 'Krossa Regal' and *Thalictrum chelidonii*. The smaller ones can erupt by mounds of *Adiantum pedatum* and the Himalayan maidenhair fern, *A. venustum*. Some arisaemas are sweetly scented.

CULTIVATION
Plant the tubers in spring (this is when they are most usually offered in specialist catalogues), setting them 25cm (10in) deep in moist, well-drained, humus-rich soil in a cool, shady place. They need to be deep because roots come from the top of the tuber, not the bottom. If it is not clear to you which is which, plant the tuber on its side. They are happiest in soils that are the acid side of neutral. Mulch with compost or leaf mould in autumn or winter. If shade is hard to provide in your particular patch, stick to *Arisaema candidissimum*, *A. consanguineum* and *A. jacquemontii*, which can take more sun than the other kinds.

Arisaemas look handsome in containers and grow well in pots, provided they are big and deep enough. Use a loam-based compost mixed with grit (two parts compost to one part grit) adding some well-rotted leaf mould if you have it. Water freely once the leaves start to unfold, and feed with a liquid fertilizer once a month. A dressing of crushed bark on top of the compost helps to retain moisture. Stand the pots outside, once all danger of frost has passed, but remember to bring them in again before temperatures plummet in autumn. Repot each autumn, using fresh compost. Species with potentially large tubers, such as *A. griffithii*, *A speciosum* and *A. tortuosum*, should be in pots at least 25cm (10in) across.

Deer, rabbits and mice leave arisaemas alone, because all parts – tubers, foliage, spathe and spadix – contain an unpalatable oxalic acid. The worst problems come from slugs and snails who are particularly partial to the juicy spears of arisaemas as they come through the ground in summer. A spathe loses its allure once it has been done over by molluscs.

OPPOSITE The cobra-like head of *Arisaema griffithii* rises spookily in the late spring garden. This species has the biggest inflorescence of any of the arisaemas.

Arisaema amurense

The solitary leaf on top of its juicy stem is divided into a hand of five leaflets, each 10–15cm (4–6in) long. The hooded spathe is striped in dark greenish purple and white. Plant *A. amurense* 15–25cm (6–10in) deep and 30cm (12in) apart.

SEASON: June–July
HARDINESS: Frost hardy
HEIGHT: 45cm (18in)
HABITAT: Northern Russia, eastern Siberia, northern China, Korea and Japan

Arisaema candidissimum ♛

The first thing you see is a salmon-pink spear, which encloses both leaf and hooded flower. Then the long, thin, white tip of the hood emerges from this tightly rolled sheath. Gradually, the extraordinary inflorescence develops on top of a juicy stalk, white, very faintly flushed with pink. It makes a cobra head, 8–10cm (3½–4in) tall, striped white and green at the base. The hood folds in at the bottom, making a tube which protects the greeny white spadix. It is a beautifully poised thing, sweetly scented. It bears just one leaf, divided at the top of the stem into three flat leaflets. It does not fully unfurl until the inflorescence has set itself in place. Do not forget where you have planted the tubers as they do not emerge until late in the growing season. This species tolerates more sun than others. It makes an unlikely but very attractive cut flower. Inside, the scent is more noticeable. *Arisaema candidissimum* was first introduced in the 1920s, though new forms were brought in from China in 1993. Plant the tubers 25cm (10in) deep and 30cm (12in) apart.

SEASON: June–July
HARDINESS: Frost hardy
HEIGHT: 40cm (16in)
HABITAT: Western China, especially north-west Yunnan and south-west Sichuan where it grows in pine forests and on steep, shady slopes

Arisaema concinnum

A very pretty arisaema carrying a single leaf, which has 9–10 leaflets radiating out at the top of the stem like a parasol. They are broader than those of *A. consanguineum*, which has similar foliage, and are marked with slanting veins. The spathe, held close against the stem, can be either green or purple, striped vertically in white, like a minty toothpaste. The whole thing emerges from a spear of speckled beige. Plant tubers of *A. concinnum* 25cm (10in) deep and 30cm (12in) apart.

SEASON: May–June

HARDINESS: Frost hardy

HEIGHT: 60cm (24in)

HABITAT: Darjeeling, Nepal, Sikkim, Bhutan into southern Tibet and northern Burma where it grows on the leafy floor of forests at 1,650–3,600m (5,500–12,000ft)

Arisaema consanguineum

The spathe, 10–15cm (4–6in) tall, is palely striped in greenish white and ends in a long, thin tail. The flowers in arisaemas are buried at the bottom of the spadix, so you cannot see them. When pollinated, however, they make brilliant red berries, which stand on the stem long after the spathe and spadix have melted away. The hood is overshadowed by the solitary leaf. This rises on a tall, palely mottled stem and spins out in a Catherine wheel of leaflets, sometimes as many as 20 together. The leaflets are drawn out into long spidery tips which spill water away from the centre of the plant. *Arisaema consanguineum* will tolerate some sun and, in terms of form, is one of the most splendid of all the arisaemas. It was introduced to cultivation in 1893. Plant tubers 25cm (10in) deep and 40cm (16in) apart.

SEASON: May–June

HARDINESS: Frost hardy

HEIGHT: 70cm (28in)

HABITAT: China, Taiwan, Burma, Thailand and the eastern Himalayas where it grows in scrub and light woodland at about 2,000m (6,500ft)

Arisaema griffithii

Arisaema griffithii has the biggest inflorescence of any of the arisaemas. The sinister, wide, dark spathe sits almost on the ground, under the umbrella made by its two leaves. Each is divided into three diamond-shaped leaflets, darkly veined. The spathe is striped at the bottom, veined at the top, and has two flaps either side like elephant's ears. Between them hangs the long, narrow spadix like the tail of a swallowed mouse. Arisaemas are not carnivorous but you feel you do not want to put a finger too close – just in case... In the high mountain areas of the Himalayas, the flattened tubers are used to make a kind of flour, an important winter food in these inhospitable parts. Like cassava (the poisonous tuber used in a similar way by the Macushi and Wapishana of Guyana), the arisaema root needs to be carefully prepared to get rid of toxins. Plant tubers 25cm (10in) deep and 45cm (18in) apart.

SEASON: April–May

HARDINESS: Frost hardy

HEIGHT: 60cm (24in)

HABITAT: Bhutan, Darjeeling, Nepal, Sikkim and the eastern Himalayas where it grows in forest at around 2,500m (8,200ft)

Arisaema jacquemontii

A fat, green stem rises with leaves sheathing off it, the foliage divided into three or five leaflets, in the manner of a horse chestnut leaf. The hood (about 10cm/4in tall) stands up a long way before it folds in on itself. It ends in a long, thin rat's tail, longer by far than the spadix which comes out of the hood, thin and bronzy green. This is not a showy species, as the green hood is narrow and constricted and only faintly striped with white. Nevertheless, *A. jacquemontii* is easy, hardy and will settle in a warmer, more open and slightly drier situation than others of its kind. Plant tubers 25cm (10in) deep and 30cm (12in) apart.

SEASON: Late June–July

HARDINESS: Fully hardy

HEIGHT: 45cm (18in)

HABITAT: Himalayas, covering Afghanistan, Darjeeling, Kashmir, Nepal, Sikkim, Bhutan and south-eastern Tibet where it grows on grassy slopes and in deciduous woodland at 3,000–4,000m (10,000–13,000ft)

Arisaema sikokianum

This produces two leaves: one usually has three oval leaflets, the other five. The hood is wide at the mouth, dark purplish green on the outside, pure white inside, enclosing an unusually broad spadix, shaped like a pestle and glistening white. It is maddeningly slow to clump up, but worth some trouble. The contrast between the porcelain whiteness of the inside and the spooky, dark shades of the hood is particularly dramatic. It was introduced into cultivation in 1938. Plant tubers of *A. sikokianum* 25cm (10in) deep and 35cm (14in) apart.

SEASON: May–June
HARDINESS: Frost hardy
HEIGHT: 25–35cm (10–14in)
HABITAT: The Japanese islands of Honshu, Kyushu and Shikoku

Arisaema saxatile

A charming arisaema, dwarf in habit, and easy. The segmented, mid-green leaves (five leaflets) rise from reddish sheaths alongside the flowering stems. White spathes, hooded in the usual way, shield the central cup from which emerges a long, spidery spadix in a weird shade of green. *Arisaema saxatile* is not as dramatic as *A. candidissimum*, but it is early flowering, clumps up quickly and smells deliciously of lemons. Use it in damp, shady places, perhaps among low-growing deciduous azaleas such as the sweetly scented *Rhododendron viscosum* or *R. vaseyi* 'White Find'. They all enjoy the same growing conditions – leafy, humus-rich soil. Plant tubers 25cm (10in) deep and 30cm (12in) apart.

SEASON: Mid June
HARDINESS: Fully hardy
HEIGHT: 26cm (10½in)
HABITAT: Introduced from the Hubei province of China

Arisaema speciosum

The solitary leaf, divided into three pink-edged leaflets, comes through the ground on a juicy, mottled stem, a snake-like camouflage. The leaf is longer than the hooded spathe, which is purplish brown, striped with white. The spadix leers right out of the mouth of the hood and reaches almost to the ground. In the Chamba valley of Himachal Pradesh, the pounded tubers are used as a dressing for snake bite. *Arisaema speciosum* was introduced into cultivation in 1872. Plant tubers 25cm (10in) deep and 40cm (16in) apart.

SEASON: April–June
HARDINESS: Frost hardy
HEIGHT: 60cm (24in)
HABITAT: The Himalayas, from Nepal to northern Assam and western China where it grows in forests at 2,300–3,500m (7,500–11,500ft)

Arisaema tortuosum

Known in cultivation since 1830, A. *tortuosum* is an unusually tall species with two or three leaf stems that finish in a flat, parasol arrangement of leaflets, sometimes as many as 15 of them in a head. This arisaema is worth growing for its foliage alone. The hooded spathes are not as showy as some, but narrowly elegant, green, with a spadix that may be green or purple. It curls out in the shape of an S, with the point facing skywards. The round tubers have a depression in the centre, like a bun that has collapsed in the oven. Plant them 25cm (10in) deep and 40cm (16in) apart.

SEASON: April–June
HARDINESS: Frost hardy
HEIGHT: 120cm (4ft)
HABITAT: The Himalayan regions of India (Darjeeling, Kashmir, Nepal, the Punjab and Sikkim), Bhutan, Burma and south-western China where it grows in forests at 1,400–2,800m (4,600–9,000ft)

Arisaema triphyllum
JACK-IN-THE-PULPIT

Cool pale green spathes – sometimes striped, sometimes not – stand above the foliage, the tops bending over to protect the equally pale spadix inside. Introduced into cultivation in 1664, *A. triphyllum* is not as weirdly sinister or exciting a plant as the arisaemas from the East, but it is a useful plant for wildish areas, where it can grow with naturalized camassias, Lenten hellebores and primroses. It produces ornamental, red berries similar to those of the wild European arum. Plant tubers 25cm (10in) deep and 30cm (12in) apart.

SEASON: June–July
HARDINESS: Fully hardy
HEIGHT: 30–50cm (12–20in)
HABITAT: Quebec and the eastern states of the USA where it grows in damp woodlands

Arisarum (Araceae)

Arisarum proboscideum
MOUSE PLANT

The flowers, more properly 'inflorescences', cower under the arrow-shaped leaves producing brown-speckled, hooded spathes with ridiculous tails, at least 15cm (6in) long (hence mouse plant). They smell faintly of mushrooms, attracting a fungus gnat which helps to pollinate it. The clever aroid times its flowering to coincide with the first hatch of gnats in spring. They, being rather short of real fungus at this time of the year, are in no position to ask questions of this smellalike. Although you have to hunt to find the 'mice', the glossy, dark green foliage quickly provides good ground cover, a companion for primroses, *Saxifraga stolonifera* and *Cardamine pentaphylla*. Plant the rhizomes of *A. proboscideum* in autumn in moist, humus-rich soil in part shade, setting them about 10cm (4in) deep and 25cm (10in) apart.

SEASON: April–May
HARDINESS: Fully hardy
HEIGHT: 7–8cm (2½–3½in)
HABITAT: Southern Italy and south-west Spain where it grows in woods and other shady places

Arthropodium (Anthericaceae)

Arthropodium candidum

Loose panicles of flowers are carried in airy sprays above thin, grassy leaves. Plant *A. candidum* in fertile, well-drained soil in full sun, adding grit if the ground is heavy. Arthropodiums can also be grown in pots in a cool greenhouse, using a loam-based compost mixed with grit or sharp sand (two parts compost to one part sand). Do not overwater. *Arthropodium candidum purpureum* bears a similar flower, but the foliage has a distinct bronze overlay. Plant tubers 5cm (2in) deep and 10cm (4in) apart.

SEASON: June
HARDINESS: Frost hardy
HEIGHT: 20cm (8in)
HABITAT: New Zealand where it grows in open, sunny areas

Arum (Araceae)

With their menacing spathes, arums are spooky and slightly sinister, an excellent antidote to the sweetness and light ethic promoted by most flowers. The wild European arum, *A. maculatum* (called cuckoo pint or lords and ladies if you are in polite company) has a pale green spathe, like a cowl drawn up to protect the purplish spadix inside. Later in the season, the leaves disappear, leaving a spike of poisonous red berries.

Some gardeners are pre-conditioned to think of them as weeds, for the cuckoo pint is an enthusiastic self-seeder in gardens where it finds the conditions it likes: cool, rich soil and half shade. If it were not so familiar, we would value it more. Forget the faults. Think of the virtues: beautiful, arrow-shaped foliage at a time of the year when most other plants have dived underground, intriguing hooded spathes, elegant in form, often cool in colouring, then spikes of shining, scarlet berries. They are poisonous – yes – but handsome nonetheless, particularly when they are scattered through a froth of Welsh poppy or used to enliven a cool, dark spread of ivy. The handsome foliage is useful for cutting during the winter to bulk up early sprays of catkin and *Lonicera fragrantissima* or provide a dark contrast to a handful of snowdrops. Some spathes are more interesting than others and

ABOVE Having paid rent for a long time in a garden with their handsome leaves, arums such as *A. italicum* provide another treat in late summer with spikes of clear red, though poisonous berries.

these, too, can be cut and brought inside. The more minimal the setting, the better they look.

The fleshy tubers contain a good deal of starch, and the islanders of Portland in Dorset used to boil them up and strain them to produce starch and a kind of arrowroot to thicken sauces. It was big business (though hell on the laundresses' hands), and in 1797 Mrs Jane Gibbs was awarded a gold medal and 30 guineas from the Royal Society of Arts for the perfection of her arum starch.

CULTIVATION

Plant tubers 10–15cm (4–6in) deep in autumn, setting them 15–20cm (6–8in) apart. They like well-drained, humus-rich soil in a site that is partially shaded. They will grow in dry shade, but not so lushly. *Arum creticum* needs full sun. A safer method is to start the tubers off in pots, using a soilless compost. When they are well rooted and spears of foliage are beginning to push through, tip each plant out of its pot and set it in its permanent position outside. Water the plants to settle them in. After that, they will need little attention. *Arum creticum* is susceptible to frost, so in cold areas it may be safer to grow this species in a cool greenhouse or conservatory. Use a big, deep pot and soilless compost mixed with grit (two parts compost to one part grit). Water moderately to bring the arum into growth and water regularly until the leaves start to wither at the end of the growing season. Then keep the tuber dry before starting it into growth the following season.

The 'season' mentioned below is the season when the spathes emerge. The leaves though often have a much longer season, looking good from October right through to April. Remember that if arums produced nothing but leaves they would still be worth growing. Unfortunately badgers seem partial to the arum's underground tubers and, being creatures of great taste and distinction, will always go for expensive named kinds rather than the common native arums. Bamboo cloches anchored over choice plants are usually enough to dissuade them. More troubling is a horrible, rusty looking fungus which sometimes attacks the leaves. They melt into a distressingly ugly heap. There seems to be no cure.

ABOVE The pale spring spathes of wild *Arum maculatum* push through the leaf litter of a woodland floor. Later come columns of bright red, poisonous berries.

Arum 'Chameleon'

The fine foliage spreads into large clumps of big, usually rounded leaves, marbled and swirled in three shades of green. The pale green spathes erupt between April and May, leaving behind stems of berries. By August, these have coloured up to a rich, telling red. Plant tubers of 'Chameleon' in autumn, setting them 10–15cm (4–6in) deep and 15–20cm (6–8in) apart.

SEASON: April–May
HARDINESS: Fully hardy
HEIGHT: 30cm (12in)

Arum creticum

The leaves, appearing in autumn, are plain, dark green, not so arresting as the marvellous foliage of *A. italicum*, but the spathe is wonderful. It is 20–25cm (8–10in) long and a rich, pale yellow, the colour of the best Jersey cream. It scrolls back on itself at the top to show off the stout spadix which is a darker shade of yellow. It is very sweetly scented, which is a surprise: freesia and lemons. *Arum creticum* was introduced into cultivation in 1853. Plant tubers in autumn, setting them 10–15cm (4–6in) deep and 15–20cm (6–8in) apart.

SEASON: April–May
HARDINESS: Frost hardy
HEIGHT: 40cm (16in)
HABITAT: Stony hillsides on the Greek islands of Crete, Kárpathos, Rhodes and Sámos

Arum italicum

Arum italicum was already in cultivation by 1693, which is not surprising as the foliage is superb, in shape, texture and patterning. The glossiness of the leaves is astonishing and the solid arrow shape makes a fine foil for other less well-endowed neighbours: pale early narcissus perhaps. The marbling is laid on in a very particular though not exactly symmetrical way, so that each leaf (they can be up to 30cm/12in long) has a plain green border. The spathes are cool, pale green, but are not readily produced unless the plants are in a warmish situation. Sometimes the orange berries that follow the spathe last right through until the new crop of leaves begins to emerge the following October. *Arum italicum* subsp. *italicum* 'Marmoratum' (an AGM plant sometimes called 'Pictum') is a selected form with marbling that is creamy rather than silver. Plant tubers in autumn, 10–15cm (4–6in) deep and 15–20cm (6–8in) apart.

SEASON: April–May

HARDINESS: Fully hardy

HEIGHT: 30cm (12in)

HABITAT: Europe, northern and western Turkey, Algeria, Morocco and Tunisia where it grows in scrubby woodland

Arum nigrum

The plain green leaves of A. *nigrum* make good ground cover early in the year, arrow-shaped and slightly bigger than the common cuckoo pint, A. *maculatum*. The plant clumps up quickly in leafy soil and part shade. In spring wonderfully sinister, furled, black spikes emerge under the clump of leaves. These develop into glossy, purplish black cowls which tend to bend over the dark, central spadix. It feels like rubber. The whole thing is very weird and splendid. At the base, where it curls round the spadix, the spathe is pale green, drifting gradually into dark shades above. Plant tubers in autumn, setting them 10–15cm (4–6in) deep and 15–20cm (6–8in) apart.

SEASON: Mid April

HARDINESS: Fully hardy

HEIGHT: 35cm (14in)

HABITAT: South-eastern Europe

Babiana (Iridaceae)

This sweetly scented member of the iris family will be too tender for gardens where winter temperatures drop below 5°C (41°F). Grow it in a pot in a cool greenhouse or conservatory, where the smell can fill the air in spring. Plant the corms in autumn, setting them shallowly in soil-based potting compost. Water sparingly until the plant has come into growth. Keep the pot in full light. As the foliage begins to die down, stop watering and keep the pot dry until the cycle of growth begins again. If you feel like chancing it outside, plant in gritty, well-drained soil in full sun.

Babiana stricta ♀

The name comes from *babianer*, the Dutch word for the African baboon that feasts on the corms of this genus. The flowering stem is twice as tall as the spiky iris leaves and may produce sheaves of blue, purple or yellow flowers, sweetly scented. *Babiana stricta* has been known in gardens since the second half of the eighteenth century. Plant corms 20cm (8in) deep and 8cm (3½in) apart.

SEASON: May–June
HARDINESS: Tender
HEIGHT: 10–30cm (4–12in)
HABITAT: South Africa where it grows on open, grassy hillsides

Bellevalia (Hyacinthaceae)

In general form these are very similar to grape hyacinths and flower at the same time. They like full sun but will put up with half shade; spread them under deciduous trees which, at the season when these bulbs flower, allow plenty of light through to the ground beneath. Plant them with cyclamen, both autumn- and spring-flowering kinds, or scatter them between hose-in-hose primulas, purple-leaved *Viola labradorica* and erythroniums. Where happy, they will self-seed.

ABOVE *Bellevalia paradoxa* has struggled to establish its own identity. For a long time, it was lumped in with the grape hyacinth (*Muscari*), which it closely resembles.

Bellevalia paradoxa
(*B. pycnantha, Muscari paradoxum*)

The flower is rather like that of a grape hyacinth (it is sometimes listed as one), but the leaves grow as big and fleshy as bluebells, while the flower spike is still short and undeveloped. It stretches into a dense pyramid, the colour strange and intriguing, dark blackish turquoise at first, then blackish blue, with the green settling on the inside of the small bell-flowers. They are pinched at the mouth and the pale creamy stamens only just show through the crack. The bottom bells have finished before the top ones have started, but they do not die noisily and the staggered performance means that you get a long show in the garden. Plant the bulbs of *B. paradoxa* about 10cm (4in) deep and 10cm (4in) apart.

SEASON: Mid April
HARDINESS: Fully hardy
HEIGHT: 18cm (7in)
HABITAT: The Caucasus, eastern Turkey, Iran and Iraq

Bellevalia romana

This gives a more recessive effect than its cousin, as the flowers, loosely arranged in a spike, are white tinged with green. Close up, they are enchanting – the anthers being chic dots of navy-blue. The leaves are more than twice as long as the flowers, straggling on to 45cm (18in). But they are narrow and will be well disguised if you spread *B. romana* under Solomon's seal or between clumps of pale blue scillas or wild primroses. If it is warm enough, it releases a gentle smell of almonds. Plant the bulbs about 10cm (4in) deep and 10cm (4in) apart.

SEASON: Early April
HARDINESS: Fully hardy
HEIGHT: 15cm (6in)
HABITAT: Mediterranean areas of southern France and Greece

B

Bessera (Alliaceae)

Bessera elegans

The leaves are few, thin and grassy, appearing during the summer before the flowers startle late summer with their brilliant exhibition. They hang out like little lanterns from the top of the stem, seven or eight of them, individually small, but beautifully made. The colour, brilliant orange-red, is surprising. Even greater is the surprise when you look inside one of the lanterns (they come out one at a time) and see how beautifully marked the six petals are: a bright red stripe over a cream overlay; the stamens, tipped with lime-green, cluster round a central cream cone. This is a dear plant, fighting well above its apparent weight. You wait half a lifetime for the buds to open into flowers, but it is worth it. *Bessera elegans* was introduced into cultivation by the German plant hunter Count Wilhelm Karwinsky who found it at Sultepec on his first expedition to Mexico, 1826–31. The corms are small; in cold areas, it may be safer to keep them in pots, planting them in a loam-based potting compost. Five will fit comfortably in a deep 15cm (6in) pot. Water them moderately and bring them into full sun once growth is established. When the leaves begin to die down, keep them dry. If they are damp during their resting time, they rot. Repot in fresh compost the following April. Outside, plant no sooner than mid to late April, setting the corms in well-drained soil in full sun 6cm (2¼in) deep and 10cm (4in) apart.

SEASON: September–October
HARDINESS: Frost hardy
HEIGHT: 30cm (12in)
HABITAT: South-west and south-central Mexico where it grows in scrub and grassy slopes

Bongardia (Berberidaceae)

Bongardia chrysogonum

Taxonomists have decided that this is a berberis, even though it grows from a tuber and dies down completely in summer. Why don't all plants? It saves so much effort. At first, *B. chrysogonum* seems rather a weedy thing with a spray of bright yellow, star flowers held on a reddish bronze stem. Give it time. You may still feel the flowers are not adding much to the gaiety of nations (though they smell faintly of honey), but when the foliage clumps up you begin to appreciate the attraction of this plant. Each leaflet of the pinnate, pewter-coloured leaves is marked at the base with a horseshoe of maroon. The foliage dies down in summer, and then the tubers need a warm, dry rest. If they are too wet, they rot. Buy the corky tubers damp-packed in autumn, and plant them in light, well-drained soil in full sun. Set them 10–15cm (4–6in) deep and 20cm (8in) apart.

SEASON: April–May
HARDINESS: Frost hardy
HEIGHT: 20cm (8in)
HABITAT: Greece, Turkey, central Asia, Afghanistan and Pakistan where it grows in dry uplands

Bowiea (Hyacinthaceae)

Bowiea volubilis

A strange, succulent plant, curious rather than beautiful. It does not appear to have any leaves, but produces a tangle of green stems peppered with insignificant, starry flowers of greenish white. *Bowiea volubilis* is unlikely to thrive outside unless you can give it a minimum winter temperature of 13°C (55°F). Grow it as you might a cactus, resting the bottom half of the fleshy, green bulb in a pot of gritty compost (two parts of a loamy compost to one part grit). Top off the pot with a layer of pure grit. Stick canes or bamboos round the pot to provide a climbing frame for the stems. It should be at least 1m (3ft) tall. Water sparingly throughout and stop watering entirely in May when the stems start to die back. Once they have withered completely, cut them away and store the bulb carefully until the following October when you can start it into growth again. Encourage dormancy by putting another pot upside down over the bulb in its own pot. Coming from the southern hemisphere, the bowiea's clock is set to a different rhythm from plants that grow north of the equator.

SEASON: December–April
HARDINESS: Tender
HEIGHT: 4m (13ft)
HABITAT: South Africa

Brimeura (Hyacinthaceae)

Brimeura amethystina ♀

Think bluebell, seen down the wrong end of a telescope. Then take away the thuggish element of bluebells and plan on using brimeura in a gravel bed or planted in a trough with saxifrages and cotton-topped sempervivums. *Brimeura amethystina* is a light-limbed plant, with bells that may be pale or dark blue scattered alternately up strong, wiry stems. There may be as many as 16 of them, and insects seem to love them. The leaves are thin and grassy and do not overwhelm the picture. 'Alba' is a selected form of the species, bearing pure white flowers. Use it with erythroniums and after snowdrops in partial shade, or spread it around under shrub roses such as 'Felicia' or 'Buff Beauty' that will come into flower later in the season. Plant the bulbs in well-drained soil, either in sun or in partial shade, setting them 5cm (2in) deep and 5–7cm (2–2½in) apart.

SEASON: Mid May
HARDINESS: Fully hardy
HEIGHT: 30cm (12in)
HABITAT: The Pyrenees where it grows in maquis and high meadows

B

Brodiaea (Alliaceae)

Brodiaea californica

This bears big, loose umbels of flowers, which can be pink or a soft lavender-mauve. The tall, thin buds open into wide stars, each petal striped down the middle with green. There can be more than 20 on each wiry stem. Give *B. californica* a home on a sunny bank in light, well-drained soil, planting the corms in full sun or part shade about 8cm (3½in) deep and 20cm (8in) apart. See also *Triteleia*.

SEASON: June–August
HARDINESS: Frost hardy
HEIGHT: 45–50cm (18–20in)
HABITAT: USA (northern California) where it grows
on gravelly slopes in the foothills of the Sierra Nevada

Bulbocodium (Colchicaceae)

Bulbocodium vernum

If this flowered in autumn, you would think it was a colchicum, but it does not and it is not. 'It is at present a rare plant in our gardens', wrote William Curtis in *The Botanical Magazine* of April 1791, 'which we attribute to its bulbs not admitting of much increase, as well as its... requiring more care than it might be thought entitled to from its appearance.' The flowers are bright magenta-pink and sit on the ground, with no stem or throat, the petals jagged and uneven. The leaves come later and are neither as meaty nor as demanding of space as the colchicum's. Give *B. vernum* a sunny, well-drained slope and it should settle and increase. It is also worth trying to naturalize *B. vernum* in grass, provided the grass is not too lush. Plant in autumn, setting the corms in rich, well-drained soil in full sun 8cm (3½in) deep and about 12cm (5in) apart.

SEASON: March–April
HARDINESS: Fully hardy
HEIGHT: 4–5cm (1½–2in)
HABITAT: Pyrenees and western Alps where it grows in alpine meadows

Calochortus (Liliaceae)

'Calochortus? No!' wrote Reginald Farrer wildly in *The English Rock Garden* (1919). 'The utmost they will do in England is to arise just once from their elaborate beds, wave at the world their painted waxen heads and delicate fringes and then go on to join the Onocyclus Irids in a better land.' So if you get them to flower you will feel ridiculously pleased and proud. The six petals are arranged three and three, with the inner set much bigger and showier than the outer one. The foliage is negligible, the stems thin and wiry. Calochortus hate cool summers and soggy winters, so for practical reasons it is probably best to grow them in deep pots, even though the plants have rather a lanky habit and actually look best scrambling through some other companion that can lend them bulk and support. Plant about 6cm (2¼in) deep in a free-draining mix (two parts loamy compost, one part sand and one part grit) and bring the pots under cover for winter. Even better is to grow calochortus in a bulb frame, where the roots can run around more freely. After they have finished flowering, put the frame lights back on the frame and keep them there until autumn, so that the bulbs can bake and ripen. When growing, they need as much light as possible. They are unwilling to put up with conditions less congenial than those of their native California so gardeners in other places do not find them easy to please.

ABOVE The intricate flowers of *Calochortus superbus* lolling happily in bright sunlight. Without this, they refuse to open.

Calochortus superbus

Calochortus superbus was introduced in 1893, and the flowers, facing up towards the sky, can be white, cream, yellow or a lovely, soft lavender-blue. To get one particular shade you need to buy plants already in flower, rather than dry bulbs. Plant in a pot, setting the bulb about 6cm (2¼in) deep.

SEASON: May–June
HARDINESS: Frost hardy
HEIGHT: 40–60cm (16–24in)
HABITAT: USA (California)

Calochortus venustus
MARIPOSA TULIP

The big, showy flowers (up to 7cm/2½in across) can be white, deep red or a multitude of shades in between; cream is the commonest. The plain coloured petals are flimsy, folded round each other rather like the California poppy. At the centre, they become much more complicated, with strong, dark blotches joined by a circle of freckles; the blotches mark the nectaries – a signpost for pollinating insects. The leaves are thin and grassy. *Calochortus venustus* makes a good cut flower, but you need plenty of plants if you are to have enough to pick. It was introduced to cultivation in 1836. Best in a pot, with the bulb planted 6cm (2¼in) deep.

SEASON: June–July
HARDINESS: Frost hardy
HEIGHT: 20–40cm (8–16in)
HABITAT: Central and southern California from Mendocino County to Los Angeles and also the Sierra Nevada where it grows in grassland or open wooded sites, favouring light, sandy soil over a wide range of altitudes, 300–2,600m (1,000–8,500ft)

Caloscordum (Alliaceae)

Caloscordum neriniflorum

This Asian native is a bit like an allium on a diet: pink flowers on long, thin, green stalks sparsely spaced on the head. The foliage, scant at best, has often withered away entirely by the time the flowers are produced. Give *C. neriniflorum* a well-drained home in a sunny spot. Set the bulbs 7cm (2½in) deep and about 15cm (6in) apart.

SEASON: July–August
HARDINESS: Fully hardy
HEIGHT: 20cm (8in)
HABITAT: Mongolia, north and west China and east Siberia where it grows on dry slopes

Camassia (Hyacinthaceae)

In the wild, camassias are found in damp, fertile ground, so naturalize comfortably in grass and in the kind of heavy, damp clay soils that many other kinds of bulb find difficult. Mix them with pheasant's eye narcissus (*N. poeticus* var. *recurvus*) which enjoy the same kind of conditions. Beautiful clumps of them flourish in the long grass alongside the path leading to the front door of Great Dixter, the late Christopher Lloyd's home in Sussex, UK. If you grow them in grass, do not mow until July, by which time all trace of the camassias will have disappeared. They will grow on the margins of pools, but also settle comfortably in light woodland though you will probably get better flower spikes if you plant them in the rich, well-fed soil of a border. Combine them with *Geranium psilostemon* or *G. wallichianum* 'Buxton's Variety' which later in the season will fling its long arms over the empty spaces where the camassias once ruled. They make good cut flowers, though you need to pinch off the bottom-most flowers on the spike as they fade. Plant the bulbs in autumn, in moist, fertile soil in sun or partial shade. They increase slowly by offsets or seeding and seem mercifully free of pests and diseases.

ABOVE Wild camassias blooming in the Beacon Hill Park, Victoria on Vancouver Island, British Columbia. The camassias, or quamash, thrive in damp, heavy ground.

Camassia leichtlinii 'Alba Plena'

This is a double form of the wild species with flowers of creamy white. Use 'Alba Plena' between unfolding ferns, such as *Dryopteris wallichiana* or *Polystichum setiferum* 'Pulcherrimum Bevis'. You could also use it to follow on from the greeny white flowers of *Helleborus argutifolius*. Set the bulbs 20cm (8in) deep and 30cm (12in) apart.

SEASON: May
HARDINESS: Fully hardy
HEIGHT: 60–120cm (2–4ft)

Camassia leichtlinii subsp. *leichtlinii* ♔

The flowering stem towers over the lax, bright green leaves with the spidery, star flowers quite widely spaced up it. They are white with tawny yellow anthers. As with all camassias, they open from the bottom upwards, so although the spike lasts a long time it never delivers the knock-out blow you are waiting for. *Camassia leichtlinii* subsp. *leichtlinii* was found in the Umpqua valley, Oregon by the Scottish plant hunter John Jeffrey and was first described in Andrew Murray's *A Botanical Expedition to Oregon* (1853). Introduced into cultivation by W C Cusick in 1914, it is named after Max Leichtlin, the nineteenth-century director of the botanic garden at Baden-Baden and one of the great plantsmen of his day. Grow it through a mat of the enchanting *Viola* 'Belmont Blue'. Plant bulbs 20cm (8in) deep and 30cm (12in) apart.

SEASON: May
HARDINESS: Fully hardy
HEIGHT: 60–130cm (2–4½ft)
HABITAT: USA (Oregon)

Camassia leichtlinii 'Semiplena'

This has half double flowers of a soft creamy, greenish white, which make much more of a splash than the single types of camassia. But *C. leichtlinii* 'Semiplena' is also a good plant for naturalizing in grass, in an orchard perhaps, set in large drifts under apple trees. It will not mind late summer dryness, providing the soil stays damp in its growing season. Plant in sun or half shade setting the bulbs about 20cm (8in) deep and 30cm (12in) apart.

SEASON: June
HARDINESS: Fully hardy
HEIGHT: 90cm (36in)

Camassia leichtlinii subsp. *suksdorfii*

The leaves, bright green, are about 30cm (12in) long, the flowering stem usually twice that height, covered with large, blue, widely expanded flowers. Although camassias were introduced to gardens relatively recently, there has been a great muddle about their names. Only now is the blue form separated from the white in the cumbersomely named *C. leichtlinii* subsp. *suksdorfii* Caerulea Group. The colour varies but is generally a soft blue, not so intense as *C. quamash*. Inside the six petals are set six prominent stamens, not so gold as those of *C. quamash*. The leaves are scarcely a third of the height of the flowering stem. They are strong, deep green, and firmly channelled up the centre. The stem is extremely strong and upright, bearing about 50 of the blue, star-like flowers; they start at the bottom of the spike and are still emerging three weeks later. These camassias are more likely to cope in long grass if you start them into growth in a pot, and plant them out when the shoots first show through. By then, they will have developed a good root system which can sustain them against the competition. They will slowly settle and naturalize in areas where the grass is not too lush and bossy. This subspecies, *suksdorfii* was first collected in 1880 by W N Suksdorf in wettish meadows in the Falcon valley, Washington State, USA. Plant bulbs 20cm (8in) deep and 30cm (12in) apart.

SEASON: May
HARDINESS: Fully hardy
HEIGHT: 115cm (3¾ft)
HABITAT: West coast of Canada and USA
(British Columbia to California)

Camassia quamash
(Camassia esculenta)
QUAMASH

Smaller and neater in growth than *C. leichtlinii* subsp. *suksdorfii* with grassy leaves of a greyish green and thin, wiry stems, perfectly capable of standing up to competition. There are about eight flowers on a stem, bright blue rather than grey-blue, and with more prominent centres than *C. leichtlinii* subsp. *suksdorfii*. This is because the anthers are so bright. The flowers arrange themselves with five petals standing upright, the other hanging down and out almost like the lip of an orchid. *Camassia quamash* is a charming thing and in many situations is a better plant to naturalize in grass than *C. leichtlinii*. Sometimes that can look too gardenesque. This was an important food plant for the native Americans of the north-west, who dried the bulbs over their fires and stored them to eat in winter. Meriwether Lewis and William Clark, then on the homeward leg of their great expedition through the north-western territories of America, found it in 1806 growing on the Weippe prairie in Clearwater County, Idaho. It was introduced into cultivation in 1827 by the Scottish plant hunter David Douglas. In *C. quamash* 'Blue Melody', the flowerheads are somewhat sparse but the leaves have broad, cream edges, a natural choice for those who like variegated plants. Plant the bulbs about 10cm (4in) deep and 10cm (4in) apart.

SEASON: May
HARDINESS: Fully hardy
HEIGHT: 40cm (16in)
HABITAT: Southern Canada and northern USA from British Columbia to California where it grows in marshy grassland

Cardiocrinum (Liliaceae)

These are vast plants and need correspondingly vast amounts of food if they are to produce the spectacular heads of flowers that took Major Edward Madden's breath away when he first saw *C. giganteum* flowering in India in 1841. He was an officer in the Bengal Artillery, one of the many soldiers and civil servants in India who introduced the beautiful plants of that vast sub-continent to gardeners in Europe and America. Cardiocrinums are monocarpic, which means that after the monumental effort they have put into flowering they die. They leave offsets behind them, but these will take four or five years to grow on to flowering size. For a display you can rely on each year, you need bulbs at every stage of growth, which is not easy to arrange. You also need very particular growing conditions: damp, acid soil in a setting which mimics the semi-shaded woodland of the cardiocrinum's native habitat. They are most comfortable in the kind of slightly wild garden where large species rhododendrons and magnolias grow.

At every stage of growth they are handsome: the leaves are huge, glossy and heart-shaped (the name *Cardiocrinum* comes from *kardia*, the Greek word for heart), but vulnerable to frost as they come through in spring; protect them if necessary with straw, bracken or a permeable membrane. Even the seedheads are wonderful. Gardeners use them as a subtle way of showing off, cutting the vast stem of seedheads and using it in a winter arrangement of dried stems and leaves. I have never met anybody who has actually cut a stem of flowers. It would seem almost sacrilegious to fell it in its prime, but actually you get more offsets that way. All the energy that might have been directed towards producing seed is instead spent on fattening up daughter bulbs.

CULTIVATION

Plant the huge bulbs in autumn, setting them so the tops are only just beneath the surface of the soil. They need a cool, partly shaded, sheltered site and really deep, moist but well-drained soil with plenty of humus (leaf mould is ideal). It should be on the acid side of neutral. When they are growing, they need plenty of water, but they must never be so drenched that they are waterlogged. To encourage offsets to grow, add a liquid fertilizer to the water. Treat cardiocrinums to a thick blanket of leaf mould in the autumn and top this up in winter to provide extra protection against frost. They are used to cold, but in the wild they are covered so thickly in snow that the ground underneath never freezes. If you can afford more than one bulb, set them at least 90cm (36in) apart to allow space for the leaves to develop. Seed is slow (it needs two successive periods of winter chilling before it shows a leaf) but those who have done it say the best flower spikes come from plants grown this way. They would, wouldn't they,

given that the seed takes seven to ten years to develop into a flowering-size bulb. There has to be some tangible reward for gardeners of such staggering tenacity and devotion that they can wait ten years for a result. The easier way is to dig up the offsets, and replant them in freshly prepared ground. There will still be a wait, but not such a long one, before the offsets deign to flower.

Cardiocrinums are prone to the kind of virus diseases from which lilies sometimes suffer and for which there is no cure. Slugs adore them. Take precautions. They will surely notice the emergence of the juicy, new spears of foliage before you do.

Cardiocrinum giganteum

The biggest leaves are at the base, where they can be up to 45cm (18in) long. As they rise up the stem towards the flowers, they get progressively smaller. This stem (when it is finally produced) is like a tree trunk, very thick at the bottom and tapering at the head; the hill people of Nepal use them to make musical pipes. At the top of the stem are the flowers, up to 20 huge, hanging trumpets, 15cm (6in) long, the petals slightly reflexed. They are white, striped inside with maroon, and swoonily scented. In flower, the cardiocrinum is the most spectacular of all bulbs, but it is also choosy. Do not kill more than three before allowing some other more fortunate gardener to take the honour of getting it to flower. The subspecies *C. giganteum* var. *yunnanense* is found in central and western China and, though not so imposingly tall, has leaves and stems of a super-sophisticated bronze-purple. The flowers at the top of the spike open first and the white trumpets are often tinged with green. They are held out in a more face-on fashion than those of *C. giganteum*. Plant each massive bulb with its nose level with the surface of the soil. Set them at least 90cm (36in) apart.

SEASON: July–August

HARDINESS: Fully hardy

HEIGHT: 1.8–4m (6–13ft)

HABITAT: Himalayas (Nepal and north-east India), north-west Burma and south-west China where it grows in damp woodland and scrub at 1,600–3,300m (5,250–11,000ft)

OPPOSITE The handsome seed pods of *Cardiocrinum giganteum* will stand all winter outside. Seed may take up to ten years to grow to a bulb of flowering size.

C

Cautleya (Zingiberaceae)

SEASON: Late August

HARDINESS: Fully hardy

HEIGHT: 85cm (34in)

HABITAT: Himalayas, from north-east India to Sikkim, where they grow among shrubs in shady ravines up to 2,000m (6,500ft)

Cautleya spicata

Cautleyas look a bit like gingers (*Hedychium*), with stiffish, oblong leaves and lippy flowers which grow out from a central spike. They are keener on shade than the gingers though and are most likely to flourish in a border where they are not in sun all day. The leaves (about 30cm/ 12in long) are strongly veined and handsome, and rise alternately up the reddish stems. The stiff flowering spike (at first about 20cm/8in tall) rises up from the top of the stem, sheathed in maroon-coloured bracts. From these, orange-yellow flowers open up, two-lipped, like mouths waiting to be fed. The contrast between the two colours is startling. The seedhead is also handsome: black seeds in white jackets. 'Robusta' is the form to look for, bigger and sturdier in all its parts, as its name suggests. It spreads slowly to make handsome clumps, which can look surprisingly effective in a woodland garden, provided the soil does not dry out. They like good, rich earth around them, plenty to drink and a thick mulch in autumn. Plant the rhizomes in spring, setting them about 15cm (6in) deep and 45cm (18in) apart.

Chasmanthe (Iridaceae)

Chasmanthe aethiopica

The flower spike rises from a sheath of sword-like leaves and produces tubular flowers, narrow and hooded, arranged either side of the stem. The top part of the curving tube is reddish, drifting to an orange-green at the bottom, with the stamens poking out under the hood. The flowers open from the bottom of the spike upwards, and at first the upper buds are crammed closely together. The whole spike lengthens as the flowers develop. Plant C. *aethiopica* in a big pot and plunge it in fertile, well-drained soil in full sun. That way, you can lift pot and plant together with the minimum of fuss and bring them under cover for winter. Or treat them like gladiolus, and plant them in a row in the cutting garden. They were introduced in 1759 and make interesting cut flowers. They will last a long time in water, if you remember to tidy up the dying flowers from the bottom of the spike. After flowering, they die down completely. That is when you can lift them and store the corms ready for the following season. If you keep them, repot them in fresh compost each autumn. You can also treat them as if they were annuals and plant fresh corms each spring. Left to their own devices they will try and revert to their South African clocks and produce flowers in the impossible (for them) conditions of mid-winter. Plant the corms in spring, setting them in a pot or in the ground about 9cm (3¾in) deep and 10cm (4in) apart.

SEASON: July–August
HARDINESS: Tender
HEIGHT: 70cm (28in)
HABITAT: South Africa

Chionodoxa (Hyacinthaceae)

GLORY OF THE SNOW

*C*hionodoxa, together with grape hyacinths, *Scilla* and × *Chionoscilla* provide the chorus in the opera of spring's arrival. From a distance, they all seem to be singing the same tune, providing a gentle background to the arias of bigger, pushier stars – magnolias, daphnes, camellias. Whichever of these little blue bulbs you choose, you need lots of them, spreading in great pools under shrubs, where they can seed about to their (and your) heart's content. If you grow them in a pot or a trough, they will be closer to view and you can admire the delicacy of each blue star and the fresh, almost edible greenness of the strap-shaped foliage. And the proportion of leaf to flower is good: just two leaves for every stem of stars. The common name is a literal translation of the proper name – *chion* is the ancient Greek word for snow and *doxa* means glory.

ABOVE Most chionodoxas are blue. 'Pink Giant' is a selected form with mauve-pink flowers, which grows rather taller than other kinds.

CULTIVATION

Plant the bulbs in autumn. They will flower best in a position where they get full sun in spring and early summer. They will not mind if a tree or shrub canopy closes over them later in the growing season. Use each kind separately and spread them in large masses. If you are planting chionodoxa in pots use a loam-based compost, mixing two measures of compost with one measure of grit. In a container, the bulbs can be set closely together. Top off the pots with a layer of grit which keeps the flowers clean as they come through in spring. It also stops blackbirds tossing the compost about. Water the pots well after planting, then keep the compost moist but not soggy through winter. When they are in active growth, add a liquid fertilizer to the water (tomato fertilizer, high in potash, is ideal). Stop watering when the foliage dies down and allow the bulbs a summer rest. Plant the bulbs 4–8cm (1½–3½in) deep and 4cm (1½in) apart.

OPPOSITE When chionodoxa are happy, they seed about with abandon as they have done here at the Royal Botanic Gardens, Kew, where they grow in thinnish grass.

Chionodoxa forbesii

The stem bears only a few, upward-facing, starry flowers of a rich sky-blue. Each has an indistinct, white eye. It is an enchanting species, because the flowers look up at you as you look down on them. This makes a carpet of them seem bluer than a spread of the kinds whose flowers look out or down. It was introduced to cultivation in 1871 and named after the Manx naturalist Edward Forbes, who travelled through western Anatolia in 1842. The true *C. forbesii* is a rare plant. Shown here is the much more commonly cultivated '*C. forbesii* of gardens', probably a form of *C. siehei*. Plant the bulbs 4–8cm (1½–3½in) deep and 4cm (1½in) apart.

SEASON: Late March

HARDINESS: Fully hardy

HEIGHT: 12–15cm (5–6in)

HABITAT: South-west Turkey in the mountains where it grows on the snowline above 2,500m (8,250ft)

SEASON: March
HARDINESS: Fully hardy
HEIGHT: 10cm (4in)
HABITAT: Western Turkey

Chionodoxa luciliae ♀

The first reports of this scilla-like beauty drifted back to gardeners in Europe in 1842, when the Swiss botanist Pierre Edmond Boissier found it growing on the snowline of the Boz Dag, in the Tmolus mountains of western Turkey. More than 30 years later, George Maw, the tile manufacturer turned plantsman, thought he had collected it on Nymph Dag, near the Turkish village of Taktalie. Even his Greek and Turkish servants, he said, became 'botanically excited' at the sight of this flower, growing in huge drifts along their path, 'forming one of the most sumptuous displays of floral beauty I ever beheld.' This plant, though, turned out to be *C. siehei*. *Chionodoxa luciliae* has flowers that are usually a paler, softer blue than those of *C. forbesii* but individually they are the biggest of all the chionodoxas, with 1–3 on each stem. They face upwards and last a long time, the blue softening almost to white at the centre of each flower. Use *C. luciliae* in generous spreads with small, early crocus. It is good in borders too, where it fills in the early gaps between perennial plants. By the time these are swelling into their space, the chionodoxa will have ducked underground. If you want to try naturalizing chionodoxa in shortish grass, this is the species that is most likely to succeed. It thrives in almost any soil, but prefers light ones. Set the bulbs 4–5cm (1½–2in) deep and 4–5cm (1½–2in) apart.

Chionodoxa 'Pink Giant'

This selected form has very pale mauve-pink flowers, up to six on a stem, each with its own long stalk, the colour is slightly deeper at the tips of the petals. In bud the flowers are like little ridged balloons, the petals hanging on to each other at the top, while the bud swells underneath. Two relatively broad leaves clasp each bronze-stained stem. They are roughly the same height as the flowers. 'Pink Giant' is not a showy thing, but looks charming mixed with blue grape hyacinths, or spread in a mat under an early flowering cherry with equally pale blooms. Scatter them between the silver-variegated leaves of *Cyclamen hederifolium* or round plum-coloured *Helleborus orientalis*. This pink form usually grows slightly taller than the various blue forms of chionodoxa, but you can plant close. Set the bulbs 4–8cm (1½–3½in) deep and 4cm (1½in) apart.

SEASON: Late March
HARDINESS: Fully hardy
HEIGHT: 15cm (6in)

Chionodoxa sardensis ♀

This species is named after the ancient city of Sardis in Turkey and differs from the others in that the smallish flowers do not have such distinct white eyes and the stems rather than being green are stained a deep bronze. The colour is the same intense shade of blue as *C. forbesii* and there are plenty of flowers on a stem (as many as 20 are promised, but I have never had more than a dozen). *Chionodoxa sardensis* was first found growing in the mountains near Smyrna and had been cultivated for years before it was officially christened in the German plant magazine *Gartenflora* in 1887. It is often the first of the chionodoxas to flower, lovely in bud when the colour is an intense sapphire, purplish at the tip. Try it with a small daffodil such as *Narcissus* 'Canaliculatus'. Set the bulbs 4–8cm (1½–3½in) deep and 4cm (1½in) apart.

SEASON: March
HARDINESS: Fully hardy
HEIGHT: 14cm (5½in)
HABITAT: Western Turkey, especially on the hills east of Izmir where it grows in shady woods

Chionodoxa siehei ♀

This has larger flowers than *C. forbesii* and there are up to 12 of them on the stem. The general effect is paler though, as the petals are a soft violet rather than bright blue and the central, pale eye is bigger. They face out rather than up. *Chionodoxa siehei* seeds about very freely and if it is left in peace will in time make huge colonies. Set the bulbs 4–8cm (1½–3½in) deep and 4cm (1½in) apart.

SEASON: March
HARDINESS: Fully hardy
HEIGHT: 12cm (5in)
HABITAT: Western Turkey

× Chionoscilla (Hyacinthaceae)

SEASON: Late March
HARDINESS: Fully hardy
HEIGHT: 10cm (4in)

× *Chionoscilla allenii*

A marriage (brought about by nature rather than man) between *Chionodoxa siehei* and *Scilla bifolia*. It was described in 1889 and named after the brilliant James Allen of Shepton Mallet who first noticed this newcomer in his Somerset garden. It is a very sweet thing with sky-blue flowers (up to six) borne on stems slightly longer than the leaves. The individual flowers are larger than those of either parent. Three flowering stems may come from a single bulb, with four flowers on each stem (three come out at once, leaving a bud for later). Each little star has a dark blue knob in the centre, surrounded by short, slightly creamy, slightly bluish stamens. The stamens of chionodoxa are plain creamy white. The leaves are bright green, glossy and narrow. 'Fra Angelico' is the form to look for, as it has flowers of a deeper, richer blue than the natural hybrid. × *Chionoscilla allenii* does not produce seed, but clumps up by producing offsets. It looks good combined with pulmonaria. Plant the bulbs in autumn, in sun or partial shade, setting them 8cm (3½in) deep and 5–8cm (2–3½in) apart.

Colchicum (Colchicaceae)

AUTUMN CROCUS, NAKED LADIES

The name comes from Colchis (an ancient kingdom – and home of all sorcery – set between the Caucasus to the north and Armenia to the south) where the first plants are said to have sprung from drops of the potion brewed by the enchantress Medea, daughter of the king of Colchis, to restore youth to the ageing Aeson. They are certainly powerful plants, since all parts yield the drug colchicine, a cure for gout, as the medieval physicians of Islam discovered.

Many of the best garden kinds erupt into bloom without any leaves. These follow later when the flowers are long gone and persist until early summer. Remember this when you are planting them. The foliage takes up more room than the flowers and has nothing to recommend it. The sturdier kinds – C. autumnale and C. speciosum – look excellent in grass, which is how they grow in the wild. Damp meadows in the west of England were once full of them. If you grow them in grass, you cannot mow after late August nor start again until late June the following year, by which time the foliage of the colchicums will have died down completely.

ABOVE The enchantress Medea rejuvenates her husband's father, Aeson, giving him a young man's body, but an old man's mind.

CULTIVATION

Colchicum corms are generally available in late summer but they are not convenient things for bulb merchants to deal with; as flowers and leaves emerge separately, they are in active growth over a long period. All the species listed here like deep, fertile soil that is well-drained but does not dry out completely. Though they will put up with some shade, they flower most freely (and do not fall over so quickly) in an open site in full sun. Deer, rabbits and mice seem to leave them alone but you need to guard against slugs. After three or four years, you may need to lift and split overcrowded clumps. This is a job best done in late summer, before flowering begins. Replant the corms in soil refreshed with a few handfuls of bonemeal.

Colchicums are sometimes recommended for growing indoors; just set on a saucer with no soil or water. They will flower, because in the wild they are used to hot dry summers and only produce roots after flowering, when the autumn rains begin. But unless you plant them outside as soon as they have finished their display, this method of growing them will weaken the corm. It may then take a season to build itself up again.

Colchicum agrippinum ♛

The pink-and-white flowers are funnel-shaped, opening almost flat in the sun. They are chequered all over in a smudgy, tessellated pattern, which makes them instantly recognizable. *Colchicum agrippinum* is a generous plant, producing masses of flowers with thin, pointed petals about 5cm (2in) long. In the centre are three thread-like styles, like the wavering legs of an insect that has burrowed too far to investigate the soft, orange spots at their base. No one seems to have found this species in the wild so it may be a hybrid between C. *autumnale* and C. *variegatum*, known in gardens since at least 1874. The leaves are relatively narrow, which makes it a good choice where space is restricted. Try it in association with caryopteris or with banks of lavender, which benefits from a pick-me-up towards the end of summer. Plant the corms 10cm (4in) deep and about 15cm (6in) apart.

SEASON: August–September
HARDINESS: Fully hardy
HEIGHT: 8–10cm (3½–4in)

OPPOSITE An autumn treat, with both pink and white forms of *Colchicum speciosum* growing among the pale flowers of *Cyclamen hederifolium*.

Colchicum autumnale
MEADOW SAFFRON

Gerard in his famous *Herball* (1633 edition) wrote that meadow saffron grew in England 'in great abundance, in fat and fertile medowes, as about Vilford and Bathe, as also in the medowes neere to a small village in the West part of England, called Shepton Mallet, in the medowes about Bristoll, in Kingstroppe medow neere unto a Water-mill as you go from Northampton to Holmeby House, upon the right hand of the way, and likewise in great plenty in Nobottle wood two miles from the said towne of Northampton, and many other places.' Alas, no longer, though they still grow plentifully in Wychwood Forest. 'It is good to knowe this herbe that a man maye isschewe it,' wrote William Turner, the first Englishman ever to write a book about plants (*The Names of Herbes* 1548). 'It will strangell a man and kyll him in the space of one daye, even as some kinde of Todestolles do.' So a poisonous plant then, but a beautiful one and vigorous, springing through the ground in autumn with stubby goblet flowers of pale, almost translucent lavender-pink, eight or more from each corm. The long, purplish styles are tickling through the top of each bud before the petals have even begun to open up. Unfortunately the shock of arrival seems almost too much for the flowers to bear and then they keel over. Try *C. autumnale* in grass, which disguises this untoward habit, or plant it among the trailing stems of *Euphorbia myrsinites*, which will also offer support. It is even strong enough to push through spreads of dark, evergreen *Vinca minor*. The leaves start developing in spring and have withered away by the end of June. The stem-like throats are very white, compared with the pale greenish tinge on the throats of the later-flowering *Crocus speciosus*. Plant the corms 10cm (4in) deep and about 15cm (6in) apart.

SEASON: September
HARDINESS: Fully hardy
HEIGHT: 15cm (6in)
HABITAT: Mainland Europe and Britain

Colchicum autumnale 'Album'

Enchanting, pure white flowers (about the size of a crocus) open above long, thin, white throats. There may be as many as 11 in a clump, pushing up vigorously with pale centres and stamens the colour of clotted cream arranged round a white, tripartite stigma. They make a good contrast to the dark foliage of *Helleborus foetidus* or you can use them to fill in between leaves of biennial *Eryngium giganteum*. 'Album' is a great beauty, a fragile treat at this time of the year (though not quite as good as *C. speciosum* 'Album'). The leaves follow in March – big sheaves of bright mid-green. Plant the corms 10cm (4in) deep and about 15cm (6in) apart.

SEASON: Mid September
HARDINESS: Fully hardy
HEIGHT: 18cm (7in)

Colchicum autumnale 'Nancy Lindsay' ♀

Nancy Lindsay, who died in 1973, was the daughter of the more famous Norah, garden designer and great friend of Lawrence Johnston of Hidcote in Gloucestershire, UK. Her colchicum produces big, strong pink flowers with deeper pink throats. The leaves are relatively small. Set 'Nancy Lindsay' alongside the searingly blue-flowered shrub *Ceratostigma willmottianum* or between clumps of early spring-flowering *Helleborus orientalis*. Plant the corms 10cm (4in) deep and about 15cm (6in) apart.

SEASON: Mid September
HARDINESS: Fully hardy
HEIGHT: 18cm (7in)

Colchicum byzantinum ♀

This is another colchicum that has never been found in the wild, but has been long cultivated in Europe. Carolus Clusius, one of the greatest plantsmen of the sixteenth century, knew it, named it and wrote about it in his *Rariorum plantarum historia* of 1601. His plants came from Viennese friends, who had received them from Constantinople in 1588. It may be a hybrid derived from *C. cilicicum* and certainly has a hybrid's vigour, producing up to 20 smallish flowers from a single, huge corm. The lilac-pink petals are as long as those of *C. agrippinum* but narrower, with a pale stripe running up the centre of each one. The anthers are bright crimson. Set *C. byzantinum* between clumps of ferns such as *Polypodium interjectum* 'Cornubiense' whose own fresh fronds produced late in summer are beautifully timed to complement the colchicum's flowers. The colchicum's spring foliage is big and strongly ribbed or pleated. Give it plenty of room. Plant the corms 10cm (4in) deep and about 20cm (8in) apart.

SEASON: September–October
HARDINESS: Fully hardy
HEIGHT: 12cm (5in)

Colchicum cilicicum

The purplish pink flowers have narrow, blunt, rounded petals, deeper in colour round the edges than they are at the centre and with a distinct, white rib down the centre of each petal. It is similar to *C. byzantinum*, but flowers a little later, with a delicious scent. It is a very free-flowering species and the stem-like tube or throat of the flower is stout and relatively short, so it is not so prone to collapse as others of this tribe. Use with narrow-leaved *Hosta lancifolia* or to spread under a bush of grey-leaved sage. *Colchicum cilicicum* was introduced to cultivation in 1896 by the German plant collector Walter Siehe, who lived in Turkey for 25 years and made a superb garden in Mersin province, destroyed by French troops in the First World War. Plant the corms 10cm (4in) deep and about 15cm (6in) apart.

SEASON: September–October
HARDINESS: Fully hardy
HEIGHT: 10cm (4in)
HABITAT: Turkey, Syria and Lebanon where it grows on rocky slopes, often in light woodland

Colchicum 'Pink Goblet' ♔

This selection came from Dick Trotter's garden near Inverness, UK and is, as its name suggests, distinctly goblet-shaped, with pink, unchequered flowers swelling from long, bronze-pink throats. Plant the corms of 'Pink Goblet' 10cm (4in) deep and about 15cm (6in) apart.

SEASON: September
HARDINESS: Fully hardy
HEIGHT: 15cm (6in)

Colchicum 'Rosy Dawn' ♔

This variety was raised by the famous bulb firm Barr & Sons, founded in 1862 (as Barr & Sugden) in King St, Covent Garden, London, and it is a fine, vigorous seedling that produces up to six flowers from each corm. At first they are rounded goblets, but in the sun the petals splay open and then they become more like trumpets, exposing the brilliant gold anthers inside. Outside, the petals seem to be rich pinkish violet, striated, though very faintly. Inside the colour drifts into white which covers almost half the petal. The stem-like throats are long but strong and the scent, though fleeting, is delicious. Use 'Rosy Dawn' between the silver-spotted leaves of pulmonaria or to make a splash in thin grass under birch trees. Plant the corms 10cm (4in) deep and about 15cm (6in) apart.

SEASON: September
HARDINESS: Fully hardy
HEIGHT: 15cm (6in)

SEASON: Late September

HARDINESS: Fully hardy

HEIGHT: 20cm (8in)

HABITAT: Caucasus, north-eastern Turkey and Iran where it grows in light woodland or sub-alpine meadows up to 3,000m (10,000ft)

Colchicum speciosum ♔

This species was first found in the Caucasus in 1828, but was not introduced into cultivation until *c.*1850. The flowers, in the best forms, are taller and a much richer pink than those of *C. autumnale*, though they are not produced in such quantity. Usually no more than four elegantly globe-shaped blooms emerge from each corm, with orange-yellow anthers held upright in the deep greeny white throats. If you have room for only one type of colchicum, this is the one to choose (especially the white form, *below*) as the flowers are bigger and stronger than those of *C. autumnale*. *Colchicum speciosum* looks good spread under the stems of Pemberton musk roses, which produce their second flush of flowers during August and September. In flowering time, it follows on after *C. autumnale*, a useful trait where you want to extend autumn interest in the garden. The three-branched style is white, unlike the purple topped antlers of *C. autumnale*. Plant the corms 10cm (4in) deep and about 15cm (6in) apart.

Colchicum speciosum 'Album' ♔

A very pure, delicate flower, spearing through the ground naked of leaf. Most of the height (10cm/4in) is in the long, pale celadon-green throat which flares out into the flower. It is rather loath to open up and when it does scarcely opens enough for you to see into the centre of the flower. Everything inside is pale. The filaments carry faintly grey sacks of pollen, the stigma is divided into three thin, white threads. 'Album' is an immensely elegant thing and despite its ethereal quality surprisingly resistant to wild autumn weather. 'Cannot be equalled for beauty in the late autumn,' said the Edwardian gardener E A Bowles, one of the many who rate this the best of all colchicums. It was raised in the Yorkshire nursery of Messrs Backhouse and sold at the end of the nineteenth century for five guineas a bulb. Spread it in quantity round the base of shrubs such as *Cotinus coggygria*, or close to the low, sweeping branches of *Hydrangea aspera* Villosa Group. Plant the corms 10cm (4in) deep and about 15cm (6in) apart.

SEASON: Early October

HARDINESS: Fully hardy

HEIGHT: 15cm (6in)

Colchicum tenorei ♀

This is one of the first of the colchicums to appear, producing a rather upright, rich pink flower with petals that are very faintly tessellated. In size and colour, *C. tenorei* is similar to *C. autumnale*. Each petal has a narrow, white stripe leading down the centre and disappearing into the throat. On the outside, the white lines make more conspicuous, white ridges. The distinguishing features of the species are the three styles, which crook over at the top to make tiny, purple knobs. Because it is relatively short, it stands up well in the garden. It was introduced in 1858 and looks splendid between clumps of the handsome, marbled arum. Plant the corms 10cm (4in) deep and about 15cm (6in) apart.

SEASON: Mid September
HARDINESS: Fully hardy
HEIGHT: 10cm (4in)
HABITAT: Southern Italy, especially around Naples

Colchicum 'Waterlily' ♀

This is undeniably a showy colchicum, introduced *c*.1905, one of the many crosses made by J J Kerbert of Zocher & Co.'s nursery at Haarlem. Unfortunately, in the open, the double flowers (20 petals or more) have a tendency to flop under their own weight and lie on the ground. When the buds first push through, they seem almost white with a pale pink tip. They open into messy, full blooms of purplish pink, very much the same kind of shade as autumn cyclamen. There can be eight flowers from a single bulb with the stamens hidden inside the outer ring of narrow, strap-shaped petals. The fat, white, juicy throat of the flower acts almost as a stem. Plant the corms of 'Waterlily' 10cm (4in) deep and about 15cm (6in) apart.

SEASON: Late September
HARDINESS: Fully hardy
HEIGHT: 13cm (5in)

NEXT PAGE The outrageous powderpuff flowers of *Colchicum* 'Waterlily' push naked through the ground; a surprising sight in an autumnal garden. Leaves follow later in spring.

Convallaria (Convallariaceae)

LILY-OF-THE-VALLEY

'The lily-of-the-valley is the worst of all delicious weeds when it thrives,' wrote the king of rock gardens, Reginald Farrer. But you need to remember that it may not thrive and will have its own ideas about where it wants to be, which is not always where you put it. The smell is gorgeous of course, which is why old privies often had huge spreads of lily-of-the-valley round them. These outdoor lavatories were usually set in shady, dark corners and the plants liked that too. They much prefer cool, moist growing conditions to hot, sunny ones. It is not a plant that you ever see in a key position in a garden because for each flower stem there will be far too many leaves. You need a huge spread of the stuff if you are ever to have enough to pick. It spreads quietly by means of underground stolons and is best in a forgotten corner where it can be left to its own devices. It can do without the privy, but must have a fairly rich, moist soil.

Lily-of-the-valley grows wild all over Europe, especially in the cooler, northern regions. Gardeners started cultivating it not only because it was beautiful but also because it became an important ingredient in the home-grown medicine chest. Lily-of-the-valley liquid, made by infusing flowers for a month in water, strengthened weak memories, cheered the heart, was an important ingredient in love potions and more prosaically cured gout. If you could find an anthill in which to bury the bottled liquid, it became even more powerful. Sadly, no one seems to believe in love potions any more, but in France *muguet* are still an essential part of the May Day holiday. As we bring holly inside at Christmas, so the French celebrate May's arrival with a posy of lily-of-the-valley, set on the table, the waxy, white bells neatly sheathed by an oval, green leaf.

'I shall never forget it in May 1918', wrote Colonel Charles Grey in *Hardy Bulbs*, 'in the woods between the Chemin des Dames and the Aisne, presenting a dense carpet of green and white, and so scenting the air as to dominate the smells of the shell-devastated area less than half a mile away. It was a most astonishing experience, rendered even more astonishing by the fact that through the wire, which we had been at such pains to put up, burst two wild boars, apparently as unconcerned by war and tumult as the lilies of the valley themselves.'

CULTIVATION

Lily-of-the-valley is best bought damp-packed as it hates to dry out. It has long, thong-like rhizomes which you lay horizontally just under the surface of the soil. Water them in and give them a mulch of leaf mould or good compost. Then leave them alone. They hate to be chivvied. If you already have a colony and want to start another one, just dig out a square with a spade, as though you were lifting a turf of grass. Set the lifted clump firmly

OPPOSITE A peaceful spot in cool, moist ground is all that lily-of-the-valley (*Convallaria majalis*) needs to produce its waxy, deliciously scented white flowers.

in its new home, sift compost over it, making sure there are no gaps at the edges, and water it in. It likes shade and grows best in leafy, fertile soil, rich in humus. If you want to give lily-of-the-valley a treat, top-dress it with leaf mould each autumn.

Gardeners in the country houses of Queen Victoria's Britain were expected to produce vast quantities of lily-of-the-valley over a long season, for buttonholes, posies and scented pots for cool corridors. At Scone Palace in Scotland, 0.4ha (1 acre) was taken up with this one single flower; the gardeners dug up the plants in rotation and forced them gently under glass to provide decorations for the dining table or bouquets for the boudoir. 'Pips' (the growing bud and roots of lily-of-the-valley), specially treated for forcing, are sometimes available in November. If you cannot find any, do as the Scone gardeners did and dig up some from your garden. A dozen plump 'pips' will fill a container roughly 15cm (6in) across. Plant them in a fast-draining compost (Victorian gardeners mixed their own using equal quantities of loam, leaf mould and sand). Stand the container in a cool greenhouse or frame until January, then bring it into the warm (18–21°C/65–70°F is ideal) to persuade the plants to flower. Remember that you cannot push them on as fast as you can hyacinths. Keep them well watered all the time and stand the pots on trays of damp pebbles so that they are always surrounded by moist air. They will last much longer in a cool room than an overheated one.

Convallaria majalis ♀

The best flowering spikes of C. majalis may have a dozen small, white bells climbing the stem, each bell flipping out at the end to make an enchanting, scalloped edge. The leaves are long and pointed, and wrap themselves round the flowering stems to make a natural buttonhole. 'The sweetest and most agreeable perfume', wrote John Lawrence in The Flower Garden (1726), 'not offensive nor overbearing, even to those who are made uneasy with the perfumes of other sweet scented flowers.' In 'Géant de Fortin' the bells are bigger, tubbier, the leaves broader and the scent unimpaired. This variety generally flowers a week or ten days later than the ordinary kind of lily-of-the-valley. Plant both, for the longest possible season. Convallaria majalis var. rosea has bells flushed over with pale pink, which is fine for gardeners who think pink. But the white is better. Plant the rhizomes 5–7cm (2–2½in) deep and 20cm (8in) apart.

SEASON: April–May

HARDINESS: Fully hardy

HEIGHT: 23cm (9in)

HABITAT: Britain, northern Europe and the Allegheny mountains of the USA

Corydalis (Papaveraceae)

Bulbs, corms, rhizomes and tubers rarely have foliage that is good enough to grow on its own, even if no flowers ever appeared. Corydalis is an exception and has beautiful, soft greyish green leaves, as finely cut as a fern's. The flowers are distinctive, flared, long-necked trumpets, with a horn on the upper side. The small selection listed here grow from tubers. The well-known *C. flexuosa* is a fibrous-rooted perennial, so does not belong in this company.

CULTIVATION

Most of the corydalis below will tolerate partial shade, which does not mean the kind of dustbowl among tree roots that some cyclamen will put up with. Peaty soil suits most of them, light and full of humus. The simplest method is to buy plants already in growth in spring. Water them in well. If you are growing from tubers supplied in autumn, grow these on in 7cm (2½in) pots and set the plants out in spring when you can see where they are. Then you will remember to protect them against slugs and snails. The tubers hate to dry out. Good suppliers move them on as fast as possible, packed in damp moss or compost.

ABOVE *Corydalis solida* in its typical form, with soft, dull purplish flowers. The leaves are almost as pretty, making good ground cover in light, humus-rich ground.

Corydalis caucasica

The leaves near the base of the plant are carried on longish stems and are divided into rounded lobes. The horned flowers are usually lilac, more rarely white, borne down one side of the flowering stem. This is an easy plant, provided it has shade and a light, peaty soil. Spread *C. caucasica* in carpets under small species rhododendrons or under shrubs such as philadelphus or lilac. It smells of honey. Set the tubers (or plants) 5–8cm (2–3½in) deep and 15–20cm (6–8in) apart.

SEASON: February–April
HARDINESS: Fully hardy
HEIGHT: 15cm (6in)
HABITAT: South-west Georgia where it grows on mountain slopes among shrubs and trees

Corydalis schanginii subsp. *ainii* ♀

'One of the noblest and most large flowering species in the section,' writes the Latvian plantsman Janis Ruksans, who discovered this sub-species growing in Berkara Gorge in the Karatau mountains of Kazakhstan. The colour of the flowers is extraordinary, a white or pale pink tube and horn, which switches to bright greenish yellow towards the lip. The inner petal is finished off with a chocolate tip. The foliage, much divided, is an attractive, glaucous grey-green. Use *C. schanginii* subsp. *ainii* under shrubs where it can spread into mats, or mix it with white-flowered erythroniums. It eventually makes huge tubers and increases steadily. Set the tubers (or plants) 5–8cm (2–3½in) deep and 15–20cm (6–8in) apart.

SEASON: May–June
HARDINESS: Fully hardy
HEIGHT: 20cm (8in)
HABITAT: Karatau mountains of Kazakhstan

Corydalis solida FUMITORY

This is a very variable species with more than
20 named forms now available. The prettiest one
I have grown is pale pink, but in the wild the most
common colour is a soft, dull purple, the flowers
held above attractive, much divided, grey-green
foliage. Wisps of leaf alternate with the flowers
on each spike, the flowers themselves poised like
small birds with upturned tails. This corydalis does
not mind some shade, so you can spread it about
under shrubs such as *Magnolia stellata* or mix it
with white, spring-flowering hellebores. If your
stock is increasing well and you have plants to
spare (lift and split them in late spring after
they have flowered), you could try planting this
corydalis in grass. Although early, and seemingly
fragile, *C. solida* is surprisingly resistant to rough
weather. Best bought damp-packed and planted
in well-drained soil 5–7cm (2–2½in) deep and
10cm (4in) apart.

SEASON: Early March–April
HARDINESS: Fully hardy
HEIGHT: 20cm (8in)
HABITAT: Widespread in Europe, east to Russia and
Turkey where it grows in meadows and woodland

Corydalis solida subsp. *solida* 'George Baker' ♛

Pretty leaves, divided into lobes, and
topped in spring by spurred flowers in
a soft, rich red, the colour of ancient
bricks. It is slow to increase, a jewel
to be displayed in a pot, rather than
liberated into the hurly-burly of the
wider garden. Once it has done its
thing, 'George Baker' disappears
to lie dormant through the summer.
Best bought damp-packed and
planted 5–8cm (2–3½in) deep and
10cm (4in) apart.

SEASON: Early March
HARDINESS: Fully hardy
HEIGHT: 10cm (4in)

Corydalis solida 'White Swallow'

A miniature plant with a prettily divided leaf, though the foliage is not so much of a feature as it is, for instance, in C. *flexuosa* 'China Blue'. The basal clump of leaves lying flat against the ground provides a platform for the flowering stems, which have much smaller leaflets directly under the white, lippy flowers. They have long, curved horns at the back, like aquilegias. A charming plant but easily lost in a crowd. Use 'White Swallow' with small species crocus or iris and keep it away from bullies. Best bought damp-packed and planted 5–8cm (2–3½in) deep and 10cm (4in) apart.

SEASON: March
HARDINESS: Fully hardy
HEIGHT: 7cm (2½in)

Crinum (Amaryllidaceae)

Crinums bring a wonderfully dangerous whiff of the tropics to gardens set in more sober, temperate parts of the world. The huge scale of the plant and the poise of the trumpet flowers, drooping slightly on top of the massive stem that supports them, carry tremendous drama at the end of summer when gardens often need a boost. Only the leaves disappoint. They need to be big to feed the appetite of the monster bulb below but not even the most enthusiastic fans of the crinum could say they embellish the scene. Never mind. Plant them anyway.

CULTIVATION

In the wild, crinums choose damp places to grow: the banks of streams or along lake shores. Sometimes they even put themselves in shallow water and grow as lushly as zantedeschias do in Irish ditches. So although they need full sun, they also require moist soil, deep fertile stuff with plenty of porridge in it to feed the vast, strappy leaves and huge, fat stems that, in late summer, produce the heads of trumpet flowers. The bulbs are huge and are best planted in spring, if you can get hold of them then. Set them so the end of the bulb's extraordinarily long neck is just above the surface of the soil. Water it well, especially in its first growing season when the roots will be working hard to get together enough food and drink to support the vast storage organ of the bulb. In cold areas, mulch during winter to provide extra protection. Fidgety gardeners are unlikely to succeed with crinums for, once established, they hate to be disturbed.

ABOVE The vast trumpet flowers of *Crinum × powellii*, one of the hardiest of this tribe, bring drama to the late summer garden.

Crinum moorei

The huge bulbs have very long necks and require some thought as to where they might safely grow, as they are not as hardy as *C. × powellii*. In cold, frost-prone areas, *C. moorei* might be best planted in a greenhouse border or in a big pot that can be dragged under cover for winter. The huge, strappy leaves, bright green, can be 90cm (36in) long and this needs thinking about too, because the bulbs do not like to share their living space too closely with other plants. At the top of the tall, purple-flushed stem, there may be up to ten soft pink flowers flaring out in wide trumpets and the effect is spectacular. They are scented too – an added bonus. The species was introduced from South Africa in 1874. Plant with the neck of the bulb just above the surface of the soil, 45–50cm (18–20in) apart.

SEASON: August
HARDINESS: Half hardy
HEIGHT: 90cm (36in)
HABITAT: South Africa, especially southern Kwazulu-Natal and Eastern Cape

Crinum × powellii ♀

This hybrid form was raised (it may have been the work of the keen, early nineteenth-century plantsman Dean Herbert) by crossing *C. moorei* with another slightly hardier crinum, *C. bulbispermum*. Because *C. × powellii* is relatively hardy, it is the best type to grow in gardens that are more temperate than tropical. The strappy foliage is not easy to accommodate in a mixed border, which may be why, in old gardens, you often find this crinum growing on its own in a narrow, south-facing border. The foot of a greenhouse wall is an ideal location. The pink, trumpet flowers are elegantly held on their long, swan-like necks, but you sometimes wish that, like their cousins the belladonnas, they would flower without their leaves. Plant so that the nose of the bulb is level with the surface of the soil, and set them 50–60cm (20–24in) apart.

SEASON: Early August
HARDINESS: Fully hardy
HEIGHT: 90cm (36in)

Crinum × *powellii* 'Album' ♟

Alongside sheaves of untidy leaves rises the fat stem of 'Album' with its trumpet flowers at the head. This white form is spectacularly lovely, with wide, flaring, trumpet flowers, up to a dozen on each head. They come out in turn, four or five at a time. Each has a long, greenish neck (actually a tube) with white stamens and style. Lovely with cleome, selinum and agapanthus, or set against the sea-green foliage of *Euphorbia mellifera* or melianthus. The leaves are channelled and more than 60cm (24in) long. This bulb is a beauty and it comes at a good time of year. Plant so that the nose of each one is level with the surface of the soil, and set them 50–60cm (20–24in) apart.

SEASON: Early August
HARDINESS: Fully hardy
HEIGHT: 90cm (36in)

Crocus (Iridaceae)

Splurging is the only way with crocus, whether the spring-flowering ones (pp.138–55) or the autumn-flowering ones (dealt with separately on pp.155–66). It is no good planting five of a kind together. You have got to have at least 20. Like snowdrops, they are flowers best seen *en masse*. An exception can be made for some of the difficult-to-get-hold-of, autumn-flowering kinds. Grow these one to a pot and show them off, like the crown jewels, in season. 'They are all of them very beautiful', wrote the Reverend William Hanbury in his *Complete Body of Planting and Gardening* (1770), 'and their having a Spring-like appearance puts you in mind of that reviving season, when Nature, in other respects, seems to be in total decay.'

ABOVE Crocus lover, E A Bowles (1865–1954) who spent a lifetime selecting new forms of his favourite flower.

Species crocus are generally lighter-limbed, more finely textured, and earlier into flower than the big, fat *C. vernus*, the type generally known as Dutch. E A Bowles, the Edwardian gardener and author of a famous monograph on the crocus, said that in bud the species crocus reminded him 'of a smart new umbrella compared with the thicker, clumsier buds of *C. vernus* which are more of the "gamp" style.' Both sorts have their uses, but it is better to plant them separately. A bantam weight such as *C. chrysanthus* will be knocked sideways by a heavyweight Dutch such as *C. vernus* 'Pickwick'. Use species with alpine plants in a scree or gravel bed: they like the same open, well-drained situation as dwarf pinks and saxifrages, sempervivums and thrift and are built on a similar Lilliputian scale. They are not ideal subjects for herbaceous borders. The time of maximum activity in borders is exactly the time when the crocus's small corms are lurking out of sight and usually out of mind as well. Even if you do not actually spike them, you will worry and upset them by disturbing the ground round about.

Choosing crocus is not difficult: in the end you are painting in just three different colours – yellow, white and various shades of purplish mauve. The biggest selection is among the purples and mauves. Though catalogues often describe crocuses such as *C. vernus* 'Remembrance' as blue and use names such as *C.* 'Blue Bird' or *C.* 'Blue Pearl', no crocus really is blue. The small species offer more complex combinations than the big Dutch crocus. *Crocus chrysanthus* 'Ladykiller' is a very chic combination of deep purple and white, and *C. sieberi* subsp. *sublimis* 'Tricolor' really is sublime. In some of the autumn-flowering species, the central sculpture of stamens and stigma becomes the most mesmerizing part of the whole flower, the many-branched, bright orange stigma as complex as a piece of coral.

OPPOSITE *Crocus sieberi* subsp. *sublimis* 'Tricolor', the insides of its flowers neatly ringed round with circles of yellow, white and purple.

CULTIVATION

Though the heartland of the crocus lies in Turkey and south-eastern Europe, they have flung themselves out over vast areas of central and southern Europe, the Middle East, central Asia and western China, so it is not surprising that, in a garden, some require different treatment to others. The majority do best in well-drained soil in full sun, where they can find enough warmth to open their flowers in spring and keep their underground corms reasonably dry in summer. In the list below, crocuses that need this kind of treatment are marked Cultivation Group 1. Other, slightly fussier crocus are probably best grown in a bulb frame or cold frame. Though they are perfectly hardy, the frame keeps the plants bone dry after flowering, which some species need. And in the shelter of a frame, some of the fragile autumn crocus can display their flowers to perfection, which can be difficult in an autumn garden, raked over by squalls and equinoctial gales. Species marked Cultivation Group 2 are safest grown this way, though in favoured, sheltered gardens ambitious gardeners can try growing them outside, like Group 1 crocuses. A third group is of particular interest to those of us who garden in places where the summer is rarely quite hot or dry enough or the winters cold enough to satisfy crocuses from central Asia. European species, such as spring-flowering *C. etruscus* and autumn-flowering *C. banaticus*, are well adapted to grow on fertile, dampish soil, provided it still drains adequately. These good-natured crocus are marked Cultivation Group 3. Unlike most crocuses, they do not demand sun. Even generous crocuses such as *C. tommasinianus* remain sulkily shut up on overcast days and unfortunately there are plenty of those in late winter and early spring. Do not necessarily be ruled by the suggested cultivation groups. They are fluid divisions. Microclimates exist in all gardens; if you think you can get away with growing spring-flowering *C. malyi* outside, do it. Conversely, species such as *C. tomassinianus* will happily colonize quite damp areas of grass.

To naturalize crocuses in grass, you can use a long-handled bulb planter to take out a plug of soil but this allows you to plant only one corm at a time. If you want to cover an area faster, slide a spade under the turf and peel it up. Roughly break up the ground underneath, add some bonemeal to provide long-term sustenance, and plant the corms in groups. You can put them quite close together. Then roll the turf back over the ground. When the crocuses start seeding themselves about, you will know they are happy in the home you have given them. But if you want that seeding, which is the only way to get really natural-looking spreads in grass, do not mow for at least two weeks after the crocus foliage has died down. The seed capsule sits almost on the ground and takes a little time to ripen and shed its seed.

Good drainage is vital. Even easy-going *C. nudiflorus* will not survive if it sits in a puddle. Grit – either 6mm (¼in) or 10mm (⅜in) – is wonderful stuff and plenty of it, incorporated into heavy clay soils, can transform your chances of success. On any soil, a top-dressing of grit is also effective.

OPPOSITE Crocus growing wild in a spring meadow
below the snow-capped Karwendel mountains of
Bavaria, Germany.

It stops earth splashing the flowers, which by their nature grow very close to the surface of the soil. It acts as a slight deterrent to slugs and snails and also, to some extent, stops mice burrowing down to gobble your crocus. A top-dressing of grit also reminds you where you have put bulbs and corms, so that you do not immediately spear a handfork through their hearts while planting something else. The grit gradually works its way down into the soil and that is good too. You can scarcely ever use too much grit, where crocus are concerned. Top it up regularly.

Do not ever be tempted to chop back the leaves, which develop at a tremendous rate once the flowers have finished. The foliage is important for the crocus's survival strategy. They grow from corms, which look like flattened bulbs and each season a new corm develops, sitting on top of the old one. The new corm depends on the foliage for sustenance, so it can grow to the size it needs to be to flower the following season. Without the leaves, it will not do so.

ABOVE Crocus have distinctive corms, the inner heart wrapped round with a stringy protective covering almost like coconut coir. Each corm may produce more than one growing point.

Spring-flowering crocus need to be planted in autumn, autumn-flowering ones (not seen around half as much as they deserve) as soon as you can get hold of them in late summer. With some of the more expensive types, such as autumn-flowering *C. banaticus* and *C. longiflorus*, you can indulge in jewel-box gardening. Buy just one corm and set it in a clay pot in a free-draining mix of two parts John Innes No 3 to one part 6mm (¼in) grit. Top-dress the pot with more gravel. Within six weeks or so of planting, your crocuses will start to emerge and you can range them in a row on a plant stand by your front door, or have them inside with you on a sunny windowsill – a wonderful place to catch the rich sweet scent of a species such as autumn-flowering *C. hadriaticus*. Remember to pick off the dead flowers before the melting petals attract botrytis, which may affect the corms.

Corms in pots are also a bit safer from mice, one of the worst scourges of the crocus. It seems always to have been so. An engraving in the first nurseryman's catalogue ever compiled, the *Hortus Floridus* published in Utrecht in 1614, shows a mouse nibbling a crocus corm. E A Bowles was a psychopath where mice were concerned: 'Mice need fighting in all months and by any means,' he wrote. 'Break back traps baited with Brazil nuts are very useful weapons. Nor should one neglect the aid of cats, poison, virus, sunken jars, or any other method of destroying the field vole, which nibbles off leaves and buds, and the long-tailed wood mouse, which digs up and devours the corms.' He had some no-nonsense ways with birds and caterpillars as well. But this was a man who was prepared to wait patiently for 30 years before his programme of cross-fertilization produced a pure white seedling of the Greek species *C. sieberi*. Such dedication excuses a certain paranoia. He gave us some wonderful plants.

Crocus can be forced in pots to bring inside, but they need to be treated gently. Plant them up in a shallow, terracotta pot, water them and store them somewhere dark and cool for 11 or 12 weeks. Keep them safe from mice. As soon as you see the green spears coming through bring them into the light. Keep them as cool as possible indoors and do not let them dry out. They should flower about three weeks after they come out of hiding. Types of *C. chrysanthus* such as 'Snow Bunting' and 'Gipsy Girl' will flower first, followed by the big Dutch crocuses such as *C. vernus* 'Remembrance' and *C.v.* 'Pickwick'.

Bowles was right. Mice are the crocus's worst enemy. Corms are most vulnerable when they are first planted in autumn, which is when mice are anxious to build themselves up for the winter ahead. They do not seem so intent on attack once the corms are in growth in spring. You can outwit them by planting corms in plastic pots (five or seven corms will easily fit into a 12cm/5in pot). Keep the pots in a cold frame – with traps set around them if you are really paranoid – and then plant out the crocus, whole potfuls at a time, when the green shoots first start to spear through the compost in late winter.

Birds are more difficult to deal with, as they attack crocuses, more particularly the yellow ones, when they are in flower. Check out William Curtis's solution (see *C. flavus* subsp. *flavus*, p.144).

ABOVE Autumn-flowering *Crocus sativus* illustrated by Crispin de Passe in the first nursery catalogue ever produced, the *Hortus Floridus* of 1614. Then as now, mice were a major problem.

Spring-flowering Crocus

Crocus angustifolius ♀

A fiery, bright golden-yellow crocus, brushed over on the three outer petals with deep bronze-purple markings. Sometimes this darker colour is arranged in stripes, sometimes it is a more general overlay. In the best forms, such as 'Oreanda' (named after the place in the Crimea where it was first found), the markings are beautifully placed: two dark parallel lines up the centre of the petal with feathering reaching out from each line towards the rim. When tickled into action by early spring sunshine, the narrow petals roll back on themselves in an extravagant way and show off the yellow filaments and style. The foliage overtops the flowers but is so thin and grassy, it is in no danger of swamping them. Where it is happy, *C. angustifolius* increases well both by seed and offsets. Cultivation Group 1 or 2. Plant 5–8cm (2–3½in) deep and 5–8cm (2–3½in) apart.

SEASON: Late February
HARDINESS: Fully hardy
HEIGHT: 9cm (3¾in)
HABITAT: South-west Russia (Armenia, the Crimea, southern Ukraine) where it grows on hillsides or in scrub at 300–1,500m (1,000–5,000ft)

Crocus biflorus 'Miss Vain'

Crocus biflorus is a taxonomist's nightmare since it grows over a huge area – the Peloponnese, Italy, south-eastern Europe, Rhodes, the Crimea, the Caucasus, Turkey, northern Iraq and north-west Iran – and produces different-looking flowers in each place. 'Miss Vain' is a selected form with ivory-white flowers, flushed outside at the bases with a soft dove-grey. Inside the flower is pure white with the rich gold stigma rising above the stamens of a less intense yellow. Use it to push through the snaking, blue-grey arms of *Euphorbia myrsinites* or act as a prelude to later-flowering *Anemone coronaria* De Caen Group. It sometimes seems reluctant to open, more reluctant than usual that is, for none of these light-limbed crocus will open up without some warmth and sun. Cultivation Group 1. Plant 5–8cm (2–3½in) deep and 5–8cm (2–3½in) apart.

SEASON: February–March
HARDINESS: Fully hardy
HEIGHT: 6cm (2¼in)

Crocus 'Blue Bird'

'Blue Bird' is charming and prolific, producing up to five flowers from a corm. In bud, the flowers appear purple, as the outer three petals have only a thin edge of white. The three inner petals are all white, as is the inner surface of the outer petals. At the base is a brownish yellow blotch, with the startlingly orange stigma glowing out from it. These stigmas are extraordinarily large, the three parts curling round each other. All types of *C. chrysanthus* do best planted in full sun and well-drained soil. Cultivation Group 1. Set the corms 5–6cm (2–2¼in) deep and 5cm (2in) apart.

SEASON: Late February
HARDINESS: Fully hardy
HEIGHT: 8cm (3½in)

Crocus 'Blue Pearl' ♀

A paler flower than *C. sieberi* 'Violet Queen' and bluer in tone. The outsides of the petals are washed over with a dark greyish purple, which continues all the way down the stem-like throat of the flower. In bud, *C.* 'Blue Pearl' looks mysterious, though recessive. Inside, there is a soft yellow base, the orange stamens nowhere near as showy and important as those of *C. sieberi* 'Violet Queen'. Cultivation Group 1. Set the corms 5–6cm (2–2¼in) deep and 5cm (2in) apart.

SEASON: Early February
HARDINESS: Fully hardy
HEIGHT: 8cm (3½in)

Crocus chrysanthus 'Cream Beauty' ♀

Flowers and leaves break from very fat, robust sheaths, the foliage at flowering time about the same height as the flowers. These are the colour of proper Jersey cream, with a slight smudge of charcoal at the base of all the petals. The blotch drifts up the three outside petals, fading halfway up into indeterminate feathers. Inside, the base of the flower is slightly darker, but the contrast on 'Cream Beauty' is nowhere near as marked as it is on 'Snow Bunting'. Cultivation Group 1. Set the corms 5–6cm (2–2¼in) deep and 5cm (2in) apart.

SEASON: Mid February
HARDINESS: Fully hardy
HEIGHT: 9cm (3¾in)

Crocus chrysanthus 'E A Bowles'

Golden-yellow flowers, feathered on the outside with a bronze-purple, just a little darker (and smaller) than the similar 'Gypsy Girl'. The three inner petals do not have the feathering, just a greyish blotch at the base on the outside. This seedling, handsome even when the flower is not open, was raised by the famous Dutch grower J M C Hoog of Haarlem in The Netherlands. Cultivation Group 1. Set the corms of 'E A Bowles' 5–6cm (2–2¼in) deep and 5cm (2in) apart.

SEASON: Early February
HARDINESS: Fully hardy
HEIGHT: 10cm (4in)

Crocus chrysanthus 'Gypsy Girl'

This has bigger flowers than other crocuses of the *chrysanthus* tribe. They are taller too, butter-yellow, feathered on the outside with deep brownish purple. It is similar to 'E A Bowles' but just a whisper paler, as well as bigger in all its parts. If you were being really picky you might say that the feathering on the outside is not as finely done as it is on 'E A Bowles'. But 'Gypsy Girl' is a showy crocus, and opens flat in warmth and sun. Cultivation Group 1. Set the corms 5–6cm (2–2¼in) deep and 5cm (2in) apart.

SEASON: Early February
HARDINESS: Fully hardy
HEIGHT: 13cm (5¼in)

Crocus chrysanthus 'Ladykiller' ♀

A designer's delight, providing almost the sharpest contrast that a crocus can produce. The inside of the flower is shining white, but the outsides of the three outer petals are plated over with deep purple. The three inner petals only have a blotch at the base and it is bluish rather than purple. Inside, as always, shines the little, orange light of the style. The *chrysanthus* tribe have more throat and less cup than a Dutch crocus such as *C. vernus* 'Grand Maître' and so are inclined to loll. Prop them up between primroses or spread them around tussocks of an old-fashioned pink, whose grey foliage will provide an excellent backdrop. Cultivation Group 1. Set the corms of 'Ladykiller' 5–6cm (2–2¼in) deep and 5cm (2in) apart.

SEASON: Late February
HARDINESS: Fully hardy
HEIGHT: 13cm (5in)

Crocus chrysanthus 'Romance'

The foliage, at flowering time, is just a little taller than the flowers themselves. They are robust, vigorous, though not quite so large as 'Gypsy Girl'. The colour is a clean shade of pale yellow, unmarked except for a smudge of grey at the base of each outer petal. 'Romance' is neat, good for naturalizing and, if the sun shines on it, richly scented. Cultivation Group 1. Set the corms 5–6cm (2–2¼in) deep and 5cm (2in) apart.

SEASON: Early February
HARDINESS: Fully hardy
HEIGHT: 12cm (5in)

Crocus chrysanthus 'Zwanenburg Bronze' ♡

A very vivid, egg-yolk orange-yellow, with no contrasting colour at the base. The three outer petals are striped on the outside with a dark brownish purple while the three inner petals have the same deep colour at the base on the outside, but no stripes. 'Zwanenburg Bronze' is a vigorous variety, but prone to attack by birds. Cultivation Group 1. Set the corms 5–6cm (2–2¼in) deep and 5cm (2in) apart.

SEASON: Early February
HARDINESS: Fully hardy
HEIGHT: 5cm (2in)

Crocus corsicus ♡

In bud *C. corsicus* looks like a smartly striped, tightly furled umbrella, but the stripes, deep purple on a buff ground, show only on the outside. Inside, the flower is the colour of lilac, clean and bright, with the orange style branching like a little tree in the centre. Unfortunately, it is slow to increase. Cultivation Group 1 or 2. Plant 5–8cm (2–3½in) deep and 5–8cm (2–3½in) apart.

SEASON: March–May
HARDINESS: Fully hardy
HEIGHT: 8–10cm (3½–4in)
HABITAT: Central and northern Corsica where it grows on rocky hillsides at 500–2,300m (1,650–7,500ft)

Crocus etruscus

Like so many of the species crocuses, this is a different beast when it opens up to show its lilac-grey flowers. In bud, *C. etruscus* is a pale silvery grey or buff, feathered and veined in fine threads of violet. It is a charming, light-limbed crocus, the orange of the stigma shining out with great brilliance in the centre of the pale flower. In the wild, it is often found in the semi-shade of deciduous woods and does not cry out for the hot, dry baking that so many other crocuses demand during their summer rest period. Cultivation Group 3. Plant 5–8cm (2–3½in) deep and 5–8cm (2–3½in) apart.

SEASON: Mid February
HARDINESS: Fully hardy
HEIGHT: 8cm (3½in)
HABITAT: Tuscany region of north-western Italy where it grows in meadows and light woodland at 300–600m (1,000–2,000ft)

Crocus flavus subsp. *flavus* ♀

A delicious scent comes from the flowers when they open in the sun, glowing all over, inside and out in pure, brilliant gold. Crocuses derived from *C. flavus* were the first yellow crocuses that European gardeners ever knew, and they have been grown (and pulled apart by birds) for more than four hundred years. William Curtis had the right idea. Writing in the *Botanical Magazine* in 1787 he said, 'The most mischievous of all our common birds, the sparrow is very apt to commit great depredations amongst them when in flower. We have succeeded in keeping these birds off, by placing near the object to be preserved the skin of a cat properly stuffed.' Cultivation Group 1. Plant corms 5–8cm (2–3½in) deep and 5–8cm (2–3½in) apart.

SEASON: March–April
HARDINESS: Fully hardy
HEIGHT: 8cm (3½in)
HABITAT: Bulgaria, central and northern Greece, Romania, north-western Turkey and Kosovo where it grows in dry grassland or scrub from sea level to 1,000m (3,300ft)

Crocus imperati

In bud, this seems a subdued crocus, buff coloured or, at its most adventurous, veined on the outside with purple. When *C. imperati* flings itself open to the sun, it shows its other side: a purple stunner with a central obelisk of golden stamens, longer than the style inside. The leaves are longer and slightly wider than most crocus and loop down to the ground, away from the flower. The name commemorates a sixteenth-century Neapolitan botanist and pharmacist, Ferrante Imperato. Cultivation Group 1. Plant corms 5–8cm (2–3½in) deep and 5–8cm (2–3½in) apart.

SEASON: January–March
HARDINESS: Fully hardy
HEIGHT: 10cm (4in)
HABITAT: Western Italy where it grows in grassland and light woodland up to *c.*1,200m (4,000ft)

Crocus × *luteus* 'Golden Yellow' ♛

A very vigorous. egg-yolk yellow crocus, good for naturalizing (though birds always seem to attack yellow crocus more madly than they do the purples and whites). As many as five flowers may be produced from each corm of 'Golden Yellow'. Cultivation Group 1. Plant 5–8cm (2–3½in) deep and 5–8cm (2–3½in) apart.

SEASON: March
HARDINESS: Fully hardy
HEIGHT: 8–10cm (3½–4in)

Crocus malyi ♀

A thick, white sheath pushes through the ground, covered in a fine, tissue-paper coat. The leaves (four or five) are at first narrow and short. About 3cm (1in) above ground they break from their sheath and fan out in a star round the base of the flower. *Crocus malyi* makes a chubby bud, creamy white with purplish markings that turn brown as the flower develops and the petals become long (4cm/1½in) and thin. Inside, the base is suffused with a rich bronze-yellow. The style is very long, the tip showing as an orange spot at the top of the flower even when it is in tight bud. It is like the tip of a tongue poking out from a lippy mouth. The flower has a sturdy, strong base, like the trunk of a tree, and does well in gardens provided the ground is well drained. It needs an open situation with plenty of sun. Cultivation Group 2. Plant the corms 5–8cm (2–3½in) deep and 5–8cm (2–3½in) apart.

SEASON: February–March
HARDINESS: Fully hardy
HEIGHT: 12cm (5in)
HABITAT: Velebit mountains of Croatia where it grows in short grass at 300–1,000m (1,000–3,300ft)

Crocus sieberi ♀

In this crocus, the brilliant orange, usually confined to the stamens and style, washes out over the bottom third of the petal, making a stunning contrast with the purple of the upper part. It is a capricious species: the petals may be pale or dark lavender, even white, sometimes there is a white band between the orange and the purple segments of the petal, sometimes not. Plant *C. sieberi* in soil rich in humus and in full sun. Cultivation Group 1. Set the corms 5–8cm (2–3½in) deep and 5–8cm (2–3½in) apart.

SEASON: February–March
HARDINESS: Fully hardy
HEIGHT: 5–8cm (2–3½in)
HABITAT: Widespread in Greece

Crocus sieberi subsp. *sublimis* 'Tricolor' ♔

As its name suggests, this is one of the best of the *sieberi* selections, a tricolor triumph originally found on Mount Chelmos in Greece. It is a sturdily upright crocus, emerging strongly from a thick sheath and not inclined to loll, as *C. chrysanthus* is. The leaves are packed tight in the sheath at flowering time, only the tips showing. The flower is outstanding, purple, with a white band separating it from the yellow at the bottom (better than it sounds). Dark bronze runs down the throat into the sheath. The flower is neat, compact and slightly reluctant to open wide, but remarkable for the depth and intensity of its colour. The outside banding is replicated inside with a neat, orange blotch of anthers. The same markings appear on all six petals, which is perhaps what makes this crocus so striking. Often, the markings show only on the three outer petals. 'Tricolor' will thrive in sun or part shade, but must have fertile, well-drained soil where it can bake during summer. Cultivation Group 1. Plant the corms 5–8cm (2–3½in) deep, 5–8cm (2–3½in) apart.

SEASON: February–March
HARDINESS: Fully hardy
HEIGHT: 5–8cm (2–3½in)

Crocus sieberi 'Violet Queen'

A rich violet colour, with petals the same colour on the outside as they are on the inside. There is a contrasting yellow base, and the anthers erupt in a brilliant orange spray, much larger and more prominent than those, say, in *C. tommasinianus*. The flower is rather bulbous, bowl shaped in form. An exceptionally early crocus, which flowers before the tommys come into bloom. Cultivation Group 1. Set the corms of 'Violet Queen' 5–8cm (2–3½in) deep and 5–8cm (2–3½in) apart.

SEASON: Mid January
HARDINESS: Fully hardy
HEIGHT: 5–8cm (2–3½in)

NEXT PAGE Big, fat Dutch crocus, including white 'Jeanne d'Arc' naturalize well in grass, provided it is not too coarse. Birds are less tempted to attack the white and mauve kinds than they are the yellow.

Crocus tommasinianus ♔

The petals, a clear bluish mauve, fade to white towards the centre, each one striped with three darker lines, top to toe. In the centre rises the golden pillar of stamens and style. It is this contrast between the gold and the blue that makes species crocus so enchanting, but without sun they resolutely refuse to open up and let you see into their secrets. *Crocus tommasinianus*, named by the great plantsman Dean Herbert after Muzio de Tommasini, a nineteenth-century botanist from Trieste, is narrow-petalled and light-limbed, and when warm enough it opens right out into a flat star. Where it is happy, it seeds about in the kind of thin grass you might find under a beech tree on a lawn, or strays into gravel paths. Once I tried to make a river of it beside a path on a sunny bank. It was not happy there, but seeded with relief into the lawn below. Fortunately, it flowers before grass needs to be cut, though there is a danger that if you cut too early you mow off the seed capsules before they have ripened. *Crocus tommasinianus* prefers light soil but will grow well in grass, provided it is not too lush. Cultivation Group 1. Plant 5–8cm (2–3½in) deep, setting the corms in small groups, 5–8cm (2–3½in) apart.

SEASON: February–March

HARDINESS: Fully hardy

HEIGHT: 8–10cm (3½–4in)

HABITAT: North-west Bulgaria, Montenegro, Bosnia and southern Hungary where it grows in deciduous woods or on rocky hillsides at 100–1,500m (330–5,000ft)

Crocus tommasinianus 'Barr's Purple'

A selected form, named after the great Victorian nurseryman Peter Barr, whose Covent Garden firm for a time rivalled the Dutch growers in breadth and expertise. 'Barr's Purple' produces purple flowers (not such a red tone as 'Whitewell Purple') washed on the outside with silver. Cultivation Group 1. Set the corms 5–8cm (2–3½in) deep and 5–8cm (2–3½in) apart.

SEASON: February–March

HARDINESS: Fully hardy

HEIGHT: 8–10cm (3½–4in)

Crocus tommasinianus 'Roseus'

A lovely, little crocus, wild looking and seemingly fragile (though not). The petals are narrow, the interior colour a tranquil pinkish mauve, the three outer petals washed over on the outside with dove-grey. It is one of the pinkest crocus you can grow. The style and stamens are much the same colour, but longer than in C. 'Blue Bird', where the centre is more compact and arresting. *Crocus tommasinianus* 'Roseus' is enchanting and holds its own well in gravel, under a standard bay tree perhaps, or anywhere that is sunny and well drained. Cultivation Group 1. Set the corms 5–8cm (2–3½in) deep and 5–8cm (2–3½in) apart.

SEASON: Mid February
HARDINESS: Fully hardy
HEIGHT: 8cm (3½in)

Crocus tommasinianus 'Ruby Giant'

With its strong, deep colour and wider petals, 'Ruby Giant' is a pumped-up version of the original species, and equally obliging in settling and spreading, though it is sterile, so does not seed about. Though neither ruby, nor a giant, it is a beautiful crocus, the three outer petals faintly stippled with paler streaks. The purple colour drifts down the throat and is as intense inside the flower as out. Use it to follow on from pink *Cyclamen coum*, or to spread in sheets under wintersweet and daphne. Cultivation Group 1. Set the corms 5–8cm (2–3½in) deep and 5–8cm (2–3½in) apart.

SEASON: Late February
HARDINESS: Fully hardy
HEIGHT: 7cm (2½in)

151

Crocus tommasinianus 'Whitewell Purple'

The foliage is very thin and tends to lie flat against the ground once the flowers appear. The leaves are rather smart, each with a thin, silvery stripe down the centre. The flower, an attractive deep rich purple, is about the same height as the foliage, the colour as dark on the outside as on the inside of the petals. The stigma is brilliant orange, the stamens paler, though you need sun to see the beauty of the inside, when the flower opens flat like a spreadeagled sunbather. Cultivation Group 1. Set the corms of 'Whitewell Purple' 5–8cm (2–3½in) deep and 5–8cm (2–3½in) apart.

SEASON: Mid February
HARDINESS: Fully hardy
HEIGHT: 9cm (3¾in)

Crocus 'Vanguard' ♛

This is bigger than the race of crocus bred from *C. chrysanthus* or *C. tommasinianus*, but not quite so bossy as most of the large Dutch crocus that usually flower early in March. It seldom produces more than two flowers from each bulb, so it is not especially prolific but each bloom is beautifully put together. The three outer petals are dove-grey on the outside, mauve on the inner, so the flower looks much paler in bud than it does when it opens to show off the startling stigma of burning hot orange. This is a flower with style, selected by J C M Hoog from a batch of bulbs sent to him from Russia, and the variations in the markings give an intriguing effect when 'Vanguard' is planted *en masse*. Spread it under *Daphne odora* or *D. mezereum*. Cultivation Group 1. Set the corms 5–8cm (2–3½in) deep and 8cm (3½in) apart.

SEASON: Late February
HARDINESS: Fully hardy
HEIGHT: 10–12cm (4–5in)

Crocus vernus 'Grand Maître'

A very vigorous crocus, with three flowers zooming out of each small corm. The colour is a good, clear bluish purple, darker at the throat, but otherwise fairly uniform in colour. The flower is strong and stands up well (better for instance than *C. chrysanthus* 'Ladykiller' which has a much longer, thinner throat and lolls about like a tired teenager). As with all crocuses, the centre is considerably enlivened by the wonderful central column of the style and stigma, frilly and bright orange. Use 'Grand Maître' in sheets in grass or under *Rhododendron luteum*, not yet in flower. If you are planting in grass, do not mow until the foliage has died down completely. Cultivation Group 1. Set the corms 8cm (3½in) deep and 8cm (3½in) apart.

SEASON: Late February–March
HARDINESS: Fully hardy
HEIGHT: 12cm (5in)

Crocus vernus 'Jeanne d'Arc'

A showy, prolific, white flower (well, with a name like this, she could scarcely be yellow, the colour of cowardice). The blooms make huge goblets, a lovely shape when closed, but even better when they open – never extravagantly – to show the brilliant orange stigma glowing inside like an ember. Dark purple stains the bottom of the flower where it meets the throat, though this colouring is not constant. Some flowers are white all the way through. All though carry three fine lines like cats' whiskers which rise inside the flower and mark the three inner petals. The purple seems longing to escape; occasionally small random blotches of it appear on the white petals. Anarchic flowers are always to be encouraged. Why stick to the rules when your own ideas are so much more interesting than those in the script that the breeder has written for you? A superb crocus. Cultivation Group 1. Set the corms of 'Jeanne d'Arc' 8cm (3½in) deep and 8cm (3½in) apart.

SEASON: Late February–March
HARDINESS: Fully hardy
HEIGHT: 12cm (5in)

Crocus vernus
'King of the Striped'

A very strong, vigorous crocus, producing up to three flowers from each bulb. 'King of the Striped' is very similar to 'Pickwick', though perhaps a shade lighter (and later). The background colour is white, heavily striped in purple, the purple strongest on the inner surface of the outer petals. The inner petals are striped equally on both sides. The darkest colour is at the throat, deep purple, almost black, the colour drifting halfway down the stem-like throat. No discernible scent. Cultivation Group 1. Set the corms 8cm (3½in) deep and 8cm (3½in) apart.

SEASON: Late February–March
HARDINESS: Fully hardy
HEIGHT: 15cm (6in)

Crocus vernus
'Pickwick'

This is an enormous crocus, the vast goblet flowers easily overtopping the narrow leaves, which are neatly striped with a silver line down the centre. The striped blooms play with various combinations of purple and white in patterns as complex as the delta of the Nile. The markings show as strongly on the inside of the flower as they do on the outside. Mostly there is more white than purple, but where the goblet narrows to meet the stem or throat of the flower deep purple suffuses the base of the petals and runs halfway down the throat too. Inside of course is the amazing orange beacon of the stigma, intricately carved. 'Pickwick' is a very vigorous, showy crocus which should not be planted too near the lighter-limbed species. It will overpower them. Cultivation Group 1. Set the corms 8cm (3½in) deep and 8cm (3½in) apart.

SEASON: Late February
HARDINESS: Fully hardy
HEIGHT: 15cm (6in)

Crocus vernus 'Queen of the Blues'

'Queen of the Blues' is very similar to 'Grand Maître', producing a rich, clear bluish purple flower, darkening slightly towards the base, a wonderful contrast to the bunch of orange stamens and the style at the centre. Cultivation Group 1. Set the corms 8cm (3½in) deep, 8cm (3½in) apart.

SEASON: March
HARDINESS: Fully hardy
HEIGHT: 10–12cm (4–5in)

Autumn-flowering Crocus

Crocus banaticus ♈

In form, this is unlike any other crocus. The three inner petals are smaller than the outer ones and throughout the flower's life stay determinedly upright. The three outer petals, which are wider as well as taller than the inner ones, gradually splay outwards, first becoming horizontal and then, as the flower is going over, drooping downwards like a spaniel's ears. The style is different too. In most crocus it is a searing orange. Here, it is lilac, the same colour as the petals, and it divides delicately and elegantly into many branches. *Crocus banaticus* is at home in leafy soil and dampish ground, another unusual trait, and in the garden does not mind light shade. Cultivation Group 3. Plant corms 5–8cm (2–3½in) deep and 5–8cm (2–3½in) apart.

SEASON: September–October
HARDINESS: Fully hardy
HEIGHT: 10cm (4in)
HABITAT: Central, western and north-western Romania where it grows in meadows and deciduous woodland at 150–700m (500–2,300ft)

Crocus cartwrightianus ♀

In colour, very variable, veering from quite a rich purple through lilac to an albino version, which may or may not be stained or streaked with purple. Leaves and flowers break through the fat, white sheath at the same time in late autumn. For a gardener, this crocus has the useful habit (which it shares with C. *tournefortii*) of keeping its flowers open, whatever the weather or time of day. This gives the lucky passer-by the best possible chance of admiring the extraordinary orange style; the three branches so long that they do not stand up but flop out sideways between the petals. *Crocus cartwrightianus* is perhaps the original saffron crocus, from which C. *sativus* was selected. It is very generous with its flowers (up to eight from a single corm) and sweetly scented. The name is from a British consul who served at Constantinople in the first half of the nineteenth century. Cultivation Group 2. Plant corms 5–8cm (2–3½in) deep and 5–8cm (2–3½in) apart.

SEASON: Late October–November
HARDINESS: Fully hardy
HEIGHT: 7cm (2½in)
HABITAT: Greece, including Crete and the Cyclades, where it grows on rocky hillsides in grass or scrub from sea level to about 100m (330ft)

Crocus goulimyi ♈

A smooth, soft lavender flower, the three outer petals slightly larger and very slightly darker than the three inner ones. The stigma is the same soft yellow as the stamens, not as dramatic in colour or form as those of some other autumn-flowering crocus. The overall form of the flower is enchanting, the thin, tightly scrolled bud opening into a wide, shallow bowl on top of a long, creamy throat. The leaves, at flowering time, form no more than a tiny, bright green frill round the base of the flower. This is a lovely, delicate thing, worth persevering with. It is much keener to open up its flowers than *C. niveus*, which, though beautiful, is a little sullen in this respect. Outside its native habitat, *C. goulimyi* needs a really warm, sunny spot in soil that drains like a sieve. If you cannot provide that, grow it in a pot and bake it during summer under the lights of a cold frame. The flowers have a soft, delicious scent. *Crocus goulimyi* subsp. *goulimyi* 'Mani White' is a pure white selection, which arose in cultivated stocks and was named after the Máni peninsula where *C. goulimyi* is at its happiest. It is a very beautiful thing, though not the easiest crocus to please in the cooler, damper gardens of northern Europe. Cultivation Group 1 or 2. Plant corms 5–8cm (2–3½in) deep and 5–8cm (2–3½in) apart.

SEASON: Early November
HARDINESS: Fully hardy
HEIGHT: 12cm (5in)
HABITAT: Southern Greece, particularly on the Peloponnese, where
it grows under figs and olives or close to stone retaining walls

Crocus hadriaticus ♀

Though this crocus is relatively short and stubby in growth, the white flowers are big, stained at the throat with yellow (inside) and dark purplish green (outside). When the bud first breaks out of its white sheath, the leaves are just thin wisps of green round the base of the flower; eventually they grow to the same height. *Crocus hadriaticus* is a long-lasting marvel, producing up to five flowers from a single bulb, rather more generous than *C. banaticus*, which can only squeeze out one. The scent is magnificent, rich, slightly spicy, like wallflowers. Cultivation Group 1 or 2. Plant corms 5–8cm (2–3½in) deep and 5–8cm (2–3½in) apart.

SEASON: Mid October

HARDINESS: Fully hardy

HEIGHT: 9cm (3¾in)

HABITAT: Western and southern Greece where it grows in grass or scrub on rocky hillsides at 250–1,500m (800–5,000ft)

SEASON: Early October

HARDINESS: Fully hardy

HEIGHT: 8cm (3½in)

HABITAT: Central and southern Turkey and south to the Lebanon where it grows in mountain meadows and thin scrub

Crocus kotschyanus ♀

A crocus-sized crocus, unlike *C. speciosus*, which seems enormous by comparison. This is usually the earliest of the autumn crocuses to come into flower. It is a prolific species, with rounded flowers of a very pale, washed-out mauve. Darker veining on the petals leads down to a neat series of orange dots which join to make a circle round the style and creamy stamens. These are not as extravagantly formed or coloured as on some crocus, but the neat bull's-eye effect of the dotted circle around them is very appealing. *Crocus kotschyanus* was first described in 1853 and named after the nineteenth-century Austrian explorer and botanist Theodor Kotschy, who travelled widely in Turkey. It is an easy species to grow because it does not demand the hot, sunbaked summer rest that many other eastern bulbs need. And it is generous, increasing rapidly by means of offsets. Cultivation Group 1 or 2. Plant corms 5–8cm (2–3½in) deep and 5–8cm (2–3½in) apart.

Crocus longiflorus ♀

A sheaf of narrow, green leaves appears with the flowers, so their appearance is not as dramatic as those that produce their foliage after they have finished flowering. An enchanting flower of soft mauve, it is much readier to open out in the sun than C. *nudiflorus*. In the centre are three heavily laden, golden anthers ranged round a deeper orange stigma. Keep C. *longiflorus* in a bulb frame, well forward, as it is a miniature, but also because you will want to poke your nose into it whenever you pass. It is very sweetly scented. It is also a generous plant, flowering and increasing well wherever it can catch enough sun. It was introduced into cultivation in 1843. Cultivation Group 2. Plant corms 5–8cm (2–3½in) deep and 5–8cm (2–3½in) apart.

SEASON: Early October

HARDINESS: Fully hardy

HEIGHT: 7cm (2½in)

HABITAT: South-west Italy, Sicily and Malta where it grows in rocky and grassy places, usually on limestone

Crocus medius ♀

The flowers appear before the leaves, a good bright purple in the best forms, though they can be paler. An amazing style rises in the centre, much branched like a piece of fantastical, orange coral. It is a safe garden plant but it also grows well in a pot, especially if you give it a hot summer baking and remember to feed it in early spring when the leaves are gathering resources to send back down to the bulb to fuel the next autumn flowering. *Crocus medius* looks wonderful spread about under nerines and tall clumps of purple *Verbena bonariensis*. Introduced into cultivation in 1843. Cultivation Group 1. Plant corms 5–8cm (2–3½in) deep and 5–8cm (2–3½in) apart.

SEASON: October–November

HARDINESS: Fully hardy

HEIGHT: 8cm (3½in)

HABITAT: North-west Italy (especially the hills behind the Ligurian coast) and south-east France where it grows in mountain pastures and woodland at 200–1,400m (660–4,600ft)

Crocus niveus

A big flower, later than *C. hadriaticus*. Both are white, but *C. niveus*'s petals are less pointed and the staining at the throat is deep yellow both inside and out. At flowering time, the narrow, rush-like foliage is almost as tall as the flower, unlike *C. hadriaticus* where the leaves do not fully develop until the flower is over. It needs a really sheltered, sunny position to increase in the garden. If you cannot give it this, grow *C. niveus* in a pot in a bulb frame – jewel-box gardening. It was first described in 1900 by the Edwardian gardener and crocus fanatic E A Bowles, who thought it 'far and away the most beautiful of all white-flowered autumnal species'. Cultivation Group 1 or 2. Plant the corms 8–10cm (3½–4in) deep and 8cm (3½in) apart.

SEASON: Early November
HARDINESS: Fully hardy
HEIGHT: 12cm (5in)
HABITAT: Southern Greece where it grows in olive groves and among limestone rocks at 50–750m (165–2,500ft)

Crocus nudiflorus

This is smaller and perhaps just a whisper darker than *C. kotschyanus*, but flowers at the same time. Unlike *C. kotschyanus* which produces four flowers from a bulb, *C. nudiflorus* produces one, so, though charming, it is reticent. The inner three petals are the same soft mauve or purple colour as the outer ones with the colour drifting down the throat to meet the greenish sheath below. It increases by means of underground stolons and will grow on a grassy bank, provided the grass is not too coarse and the ground does not get too hot and dry in summer. It will naturalize in areas where it can be left undisturbed. It has been cultivated

in gardens for a long time: the seventeenth-century botanist John Parkinson knew it, though it was not properly described until 1798. In England, it was used as a source of saffron because it was easier to grow than *C. sativus*, the true saffron crocus. The leaves come long after the flowers. E A Bowles noted that it had become naturalized in several English counties and 'was at one time plentiful in meadows near Nottingham. Unfortunately for the crocus this has now become a built-up area. I have been told', he continued, 'that a few flowers of this brave little die-hard push up annually between the paving stones.' Cultivation Group 3. Plant corms 5–8cm (2–3½in) deep and 5–8cm (2–3½in) apart.

SEASON: Early October
HARDINESS: Fully hardy
HEIGHT: 15–20cm (6–8in)
HABITAT: South-west France and eastern Spain where it grows in rich, moist meadows

Crocus ochroleucus ♀

Fragile in appearance, and one of the latest of the autumn crocuses to flower. The small, creamy white blooms are not equipped to weather wild autumn rain and gales. Grow *C. ochroleucus* in the shelter of a bulb frame. If you want to try it outside, find a sheltered spot that is not too hot or dry in summer. Introduced into cultivation by Joseph Dalton Hooker, the future director of Kew, after his plant-hunting trip to the Lebanon in 1860. The leaves come at the same time as the flowers. Cultivation Group 1 or 2. Plant corms 5–8cm (2–3½in) deep and 5–8cm (2–3½in) apart.

SEASON: November
HARDINESS: Fully hardy
HEIGHT: 5cm (2in)
HABITAT: Southern Syria, Lebanon and Israel where it grows on rocky hillsides up to 1,000m (3,300ft)

Crocus pulchellus ♀

A paler colour and slightly later into flower than its close ally *C. speciosus*, the delicately veined petals finish in a flourish of yellow at the throat. *Crocus pulchellus* was first described in 1841 by the Rev. William Herbert, one of those fortunate, mid-nineteenth-century parsons who seemed to have plenty of time to indulge in their own interests. Writing to the British consul in Constantinople, he asked him 'to have the kindness to send some person into the forest of Belgrad' where he thought this crocus, which he had first seen in the herbarium at Kew, was most likely to be found. He was right. It increases freely in the garden and is happy in sun or light shade, even in grass, provided it is not too coarse. It occasionally hybridizes with *C. speciosus*, if the two species are grown close together. Try it among clumps of *Saxifraga fortunei* or *S. stolonifera*. Cultivation Group 1. Plant corms 5–8cm (2–3½in) deep and 5–8cm (2–3½in) apart.

SEASON: October
HARDINESS: Fully hardy
HEIGHT: 10–12cm (4–5in)
HABITAT: Macedonia and Bulgaria, northern Greece and north-western Turkey where it grows in damp meadows

NEXT PAGE Huge spreads of *Crocus tommasinianus* are naturalized in the grass at the Royal Botanic Gardens, Kew. These are earlier flowering than the big Dutch crocus, but the two are best kept apart in a garden.

Crocus sativus

The flower, just 6cm (2¼in) tall, is less than half the height of the narrow, rush-like leaves and pushes up between them, so that they range themselves all round the flower with its extraordinary, three-branched stigma. The arms are so long that they cannot stand upright but loll down between the petals, leaving the creamy stamens standing stiffly alone in the middle of the flower. The mauve petals are long (4cm/1½in) and narrow, beautifully veined with darker purple. This is a strange and lovely crocus, though not so bombastically eye-catching as the earlier flowering C. *speciosus*. Once open, the flowers stay open, which is wonderful if the weather is kind, not so good if it rains continuously when the petals melt and the wonderful style is bedraggled. The scent is exceptionally sweet. This is the famous saffron crocus, the expensive wisps of orange used for centuries to flavour rice and sauces. It was also used extensively in medicine, though in his *Herbal* (published between 1719 and 1730) the French botanist Joseph Pitton de Tournefort warned that it needed to be used with care. He had seen, he said, 'a lady of Trent almost shaken to pieces with laughing immoderately for a space of three hours, which was occasioned by her taking too much Saffron.' It likes the sun and when it does not get it refuses to flower. Plant it in warm, well-drained ground that dries out in summer. Give the corms a feed of potash in autumn and spring. *Crocus sativus* is sterile and can only increase by producing offsets. Cultivation Group 1 or 2. Set the corms 8–10cm (3½–4in) deep and 8–10cm (3½–4in) apart.

SEASON: Mid October
HARDINESS: Fully hardy
HEIGHT: 14cm (5½in)
HABITAT: Not known in the wild and probably a selected form of *C. cartwrightianus*

Crocus speciosus ♉

A breathtaking crocus, especially when it opens out and shows the gorgeous, delicate veining on its six blue-mauve petals. The blueness is extraordinary, though the three inner petals are paler and more heavily veined than the outer ones. They are shorter too, framing a frilly stigma of brilliant orange. The flowers come through the ground on long throat-stems, which are tougher than they appear. The lack of leaves at this stage makes the appearance of the flowers all the more dramatic. Use *C. speciosus* to take over from spreads of *Nigella hispanica*, which by this stage will be shedding seed from its extravagantly horned seedpods. It is happy in sun or light shade and will even grow in grass, provided it is not too coarse. Cultivation Group 1. Set the corms 8–10cm (3½–4in) deep and 8–10cm (3½–4in) apart.

SEASON: Early October

HARDINESS: Fully hardy

HEIGHT: 15–18cm (6–7in)

HABITAT: The Crimea, Caucasus, Turkey and Iran where it grows in woods and meadows at 800–2,350m (2,600–7,700ft)

Crocus speciosus 'Conqueror'

This selection produces an absolutely gorgeous flower which gives a long-lasting display, especially in the second and subsequent seasons after planting. The buds come through without leaves, a dramatic arrival, supported on thin but strong throats. At 12–13cm (5–5¼in), these flare out into six-petalled flowers of a beautiful blue-mauve. On the outside, the petals are feathered with pale lines; on the inside, they are veined. Remarkable stamens are brilliant orange, with the style branched like the antlers of a deer. 'Conqueror' is an *extremely* showy crocus, especially when the flower opens in the sun. Elegant, delicate, altogether delicious. Cultivation Group 1. Set the corms 8–10cm (3½–4in) deep and 8–10cm (3½–4in) apart.

SEASON: Mid September–late October

HARDINESS: Fully hardy

HEIGHT: 19cm (7½in)

Crocus tournefortii ♧

Leaves and flowers emerge together. The soft lilac-coloured flowers open into flat, round-petalled stars and once open stay open all the time. At first, the frilly, orange stigma (a great feature of *C. tournefortii*) stands up in the middle, extraordinarily exposed, then it lolls down between the petals. It needs a really warm, sunny spot to do well in the garden and is probably best grown in a bulb frame, where it can bake during summer. The species was introduced in 1831 and named after Joseph Pitton de Tournefort (1656–1707), explorer and professor of botany at the Jardin du Roi in Paris. Cultivation Group 1 or 2. Plant 5–8cm (2–3½in) deep and 5–8cm (2–3½in) apart.

SEASON: Late October–November
HARDINESS: Fully hardy
HEIGHT: 10cm (4in)
HABITAT: The Cyclades and Crete where it grows in scrub and open, stony ground

Cyclamen (Primulaceae)

Cyclamen are Old World flowers and though they drift towards the Black Sea and down to Lebanon, the land bordering the Mediterranean and the Adriatic is their cradle. In Croatia, for instance, they are strewn over the verges as thickly as dandelions. But you never see cyclamen in gardens there; too common to bother with, perhaps.

In this area, they grow in scrub of myrtle and holm oak, under battered fig and pomegranate trees or in abandoned olive groves. In the wild, autumn cyclamen such as *C. hederifolium* flower after the first rains of late summer, pushing snub-nosed, pink flowers through ivy and thistles, demanding passage. Limestone country is what this species likes best and they seem to grow particularly well where they are shaded by a top storey of trees and shrubs. This position suits them in gardens too. They do not mind dry soil provided they are not at the same time frizzling in full sun and will grow happily between the roots of beech trees and other potentially difficult places. It is one of the reasons why gardeners, outside that favoured Mediterranean basin, rate them so highly. They are essential delights in either a spring or an autumn garden.

ABOVE John Gerard (1545–1612) author of a rather unreliable *Herball* published in 1597. His position as superintendent of Lord Burghley's London garden brought him many foreign plants.

Although *C. hederifolium* grows wild over a great swathe of Europe from France to Turkey, it seems never to have been native to Britain. The pushy apothecary John Gerard had it in his garden by 1597 and considered it a great rarity. It is of course a beautiful plant, the marbled leaves just as important as the flowers, but for Gerard it was a potential gold mine too. European apothecaries used ground cyclamen tubers in a vast number of ways: as a hair restorer, as 'amorous medicine', to ease childbirth. It was considered so effective in bringing on labour that Gerard fenced his cyclamen round with sticks in case a pregnant woman stepped over the plants and consequently dropped her baby on top of them. The fate of the plants was his concern – not the baby.

In old gardens, you sometimes see great sheets of cyclamen growing perhaps under an old beech tree on a lawn, looking as natural as they do in the wild. Ants do the work of spreading seed about and it germinates quite easily. First-year seedlings have a corm the size of a peppercorn with a single, little, ivy-shaped leaf attached, but established corms can grow as big as dinner plates, each producing hundreds of flowers, followed later by silvery marbled leaves.

Cyclamen hederifolium, flowering in late summer and autumn, is one of the easiest species for gardeners to use in quantity. The other is *C. coum*, which flowers in winter and early spring. Both have excellent foliage, which lasts even longer than the flowers and both will succeed in shade. Of the two, *C. hederifolium* is the most accommodating and will grow almost anywhere. It looks particularly ravishing under beeches, when the tree's nut-brown autumn leaves begin to fall around the cyclamen's own brightly marbled foliage. Though you might carefully plan one all-white patch of cyclamen here, an all-pink patch there, the flowers themselves may have different ideas. So may the ants.

Both these species are hardy. *Cyclamen purpurascens* is too, but is not so easy to please away from its native habitat. The most tender species are *C. africanum*, *C. cyprium*, *C. rohlfsianum* and *C. persicum*. Only the last appears in the list below, because it is the one that breeders have used to produce the huge and popular potted plants that appear in shops and garden centres in the month before Christmas. It has very specific requirements, which you will find under *C. persicum*.

CULTIVATION

Most outdoor cyclamen will grow in sun or light shade and prefer a light, permeable soil, high in humus. The species listed below are divided into two cultivation groups. Plant the hardiest types (Cultivation Group 1) in a situation that is partly shaded and drains well. The tubers should have about 3cm (1in) of leafy soil on top of them. Top-dress them every autumn with more leaf mould or humus-rich soil sifted and laced with a handful of bonemeal. Cyclamen in Cultivation Group 2 are not quite so hardy. In mild areas, they will be happy outside. Otherwise, grow them in pots in a cool greenhouse or cold frame, using a compost mixed from equal parts of loam, leaf mould and sharp sand. Water moderately when they are in growth, mixing liquid fertilizer (tomato food is ideal) with the water. Reduce food and drink once the leaves start to die back. They like to be really dry while they are dormant.

The tubers do not split, divide or grow offsets. They just get bigger and bigger, and produce more and more flowers. So the only way to propagate cyclamen is by seed. In the garden, ants do the necessary work, because they like the sticky stuff that coats the seeds inside the capsule. You can dig up the tiny seedlings, a single leaf on a thread-like stem, and grow them on in trays. Or you can leave them to their own devices to spread about as they please. No cyclamen is ever in the way. And no garden can ever have too many of them.

When possible, buy plants rather than dry corms. Cyclamen hate to dry out and you are unlikely to get good results from corms that have been hanging around too long out of the ground. There is another advantage in buying plants in full leaf and flower: you can choose exactly the colour and foliage forms you want. In such a variable group as the cyclamen, this matters. All are lovely, but some are more lovely than others.

OPPOSITE Rich pink *Cyclamen coum*, spreading in thick mats, make a cheerful picture in February. The leaves, marbled here in silver, can be as various as the flowers.

Spring-flowering Cyclamen

Cyclamen coum ♀

The foliage, rounded, glossy and often marbled in interesting ways, is around longer than the flowers. The buds sprawl on the ground, tantalizingly showing a streak of colour, for a long time through November before the stems lift themselves up to flower. Then the blooms appear sporadically all the way through from Christmas until March. The colour range is similar to that of *C. hederifolium*: various pinks from deep magenta (in the wild generally found round the Black Sea coast) to baby's breath pink and a lovely white (*right*). But outside the flowering season, you can generally tell the two apart by their leaves (*C. hederifolium* has much more pointed foliage). The flowers of *C. coum* are stubby, wider than they are high, and blunt-nosed, as though they have run into a brick wall at speed. It gives them great appeal. *Cyclamen coum* grows more slowly and in a more straggly fashion than *C. hederifolium* so you do not get the huge, dense mats of foliage that the other produces. But the fabulous intensity of the tiny flowers on a grim February morning is one of the most cheering sights of late winter. All types of *C. coum* look terrific grouped in plain terracotta pots. If you have got plenty, you can make carpets of it between species rhododendrons or let it wander about at the foot of a yew hedge. Along the Black Sea coast of Turkey, *C. coum* grows with the Lenten hellebore (*H. orientalis*) and this is a good companion in the garden too. Further inland in Turkey it is found with the pinkish purple flowers of *Primula vulgaris* subsp. *sibthorpii*, another excellent partner. It is better not to mix *C. coum* with *C. hederifolium*. Though in principle this may seem like a good idea – the spring species followed by the autumn-flowering one – in practice it is like setting a heavyweight boxer against a bantam weight. *Cyclamen hederifolium*, which grows more vigorously, is likely to crowd cautious *C. coum* right out of the bed. The roots of this species come from the base of the tuber. Cultivation Group 1. Plant 3cm (1in) deep and 10–15cm (4–6in) apart.

SEASON: December–March

HARDINESS: Fully hardy

HEIGHT: 5–8cm (2–3½in)

HABITAT: Bulgaria, Crimea, Caucasus, Turkey, north-west Syria and Lebanon where it grows in dampish ground in beech or pine woods and scrub up to 2,000m (6,500ft)

Cyclamen coum 'Maurice Dryden'

This selected form is an amalgam of the best qualities of
'Album' and the Pewter Group: red-mouthed, white flowers
and foliage plated over with dull pewter. A plain green margin
runs round the edge of each leaf. This form was selected by
the fine gardener Kath Dryden and named after her husband.
It is not vigorous but you could try and spread 'Maurice
Dryden' around under early flowering daphnes, such as
D. mezereum. Cultivation Group 1. Plant 3cm (1in) deep
and 10–15cm (4–6in) apart.

SEASON: December–March

HARDINESS: Fully hardy

HEIGHT: 5–8cm (2–3½in)

Cyclamen coum f. *pallidum* 'Album'

The flowers are palest pink in bud, opening almost white with
deep pinkish red at the mouth. The rounded leaves are glossy
but more often plain than marbled. Use 'Album' among
pale-coloured primulas, which will like the same dampish
conditions. Cultivation Group 1. Plant 3cm (1in) deep and
10–15cm (4–6in) apart.

SEASON: December–March

HARDINESS: Fully hardy

HEIGHT: 5–8cm (2–3½in)

Cyclamen coum Pewter Group ♛

Cyclamen coum is extraordinarily variable – a delight for
gardeners, but a nightmare for the botanists whose job it is to
name and sort and order. It has pink flowers, but the defining
feature of this particular clique is its foliage, plated all over
with a rich, dull pewtery sheen. It is less vigorous than the
plain green-leaved form of *C. coum* so is probably best grown
in a separate place. Use Pewter Group plants under *Garrya
elliptica* or with the lemon-yellow tassels of *Corylopsis
pauciflora*. Cultivation Group 1. Plant 3cm (1in) deep and
10–15cm (4–6in) apart.

SEASON: December–March

HARDINESS: Fully hardy

HEIGHT: 5–8cm (2–3½in)

Cyclamen coum
Silver Group

An enchanting, variable group with
foliage plated over with silver, muted,
but shinier than the leaves of the
Pewter Group. Each leaf has a plain
green margin. Without this contrast,
the silvering on Silver Group would
be much less telling. The texture of
the leaves is thick and leathery while
the leaves themselves are held quite
stiffly on their dark bronze stems.
The flowers are pink whorls, five
petals held vertically and scrunching
together in a pale ring at the mouth.
Expect at least 20 from each small
corm, though only a few will be fully
out at any one time. Cultivation
Group 1. Plant 3cm (1in) deep and
10–15cm (4–6in) apart.

SEASON: December–March
HARDINESS: Fully hardy
HEIGHT: 5–8cm (2–3½in)

Cyclamen libanoticum

When the leaves first appear, around
Christmas, they are folded flat together,
the undersides showing their bright
beetroot livery. Flower buds may be
showing at the same time, but take a
couple of months to work up sufficient
enthusiasm to develop. The tease has to
be endured. They are worth waiting for
– flowers of a clear, almost translucent
pink with wide, untwisted petals. The
smell unfortunately is vile. Tubers are
small and increase in size much more
slowly than those of other cyclamen.
Grow several together in a clay pot,
which you can keep in a frost-free place
through winter. *Cyclamen libanoticum*,
introduced to cultivation by E Hartman
in 1895, is not reliably hardy. It also
needs a really dry, warm rest during
summer and is much more likely to get
that under cover than in the garden.
Cultivation Group 2. Plant tubers 2–3cm
(¾–1in) deep and 5–8cm (2–3½in) apart.

SEASON: February–March
HARDINESS: Half hardy
HEIGHT: 10cm (4in)
HABITAT: Lebanon where it grows in the
mountains east of Beirut in shady, rocky
places at 750–1,400m (2,500–5,000ft)

Cyclamen persicum

The wild species is a gorgeous and very variable creature, producing blooms in white and many different shades of pink, usually with a rim of darker magenta round the mouth of the flower. They hover like a cloud of butterflies over the marbled foliage, which is equally diverse in its markings. This variability has been exploited by breeders of florists' cyclamen (the big potted ones sold as houseplants) to extend even further the colour range of the wild forms and select flowers with particular characteristics such as frilly petals or foliage with exceptional variegation. The Victorians were mad on cyclamen that looked like orchids, with wide, spreading, unreflexed petals. They also developed a flower with bearded petals, the beards running up the centre of the petals, as they do on iris.

These cyclamen, bred from *C. persicum*, arrive in shops and garden centres just as the autumn-flowering types are finishing outside in the garden. Treated properly, they will continue to flower well into the new year. But leaving the greenhouses where they have been cosseted since March is a great shock to their systems. Under the care of a commercial grower, all their whims have been gratified. The plants have been well fed, doctored against botrytis, kept cool and well aired. Then suddenly the lulling routine comes to an end. There is no more capillary matting, no more temperature control, none of those little attentions to which a potted plant can so easily get accustomed. Cyclamen mind that and are not afraid of showing it.

If you are buying, avoid plants standing for sale outside in the cold. They do not like this any more than we do, although they are slower (and quieter) to show their displeasure. Look for plants that are compact with healthy dark foliage and choose those that have plenty of buds and not too many fully open flowers.

At home, remember that cyclamen hate central heating. The room in which you have them should be a steady 15–16°C (59–61°F), or even cooler. The pots should stand in a bright, airy place, as far away as possible from radiators or fires. But though cyclamen like it cool, they do not like draughts, nor sudden fluctuations in temperature.

Plants should be watered sparingly with tepid water and the compost allowed to dry out a little between one drink and the next. The usual advice is to water from the bottom rather than from the top. That is fine, as long as you do not leave the pot standing too long in water. If you do, the compost at the bottom of the pot will get saturated and the cyclamen's tuber will rot. Wilting of leaves and flowers is just as likely to be caused by overwatering as underwatering.

When leaves or flowers die, pull them sharply and cleanly away from the tuber. Check that there are no broken bits of stem still lingering there for they will be magnets for grey mould (botrytis). Before you buy

them, the plants will have been fed regularly with a fertilizer rich in potassium. Continue to feed with a balanced liquid fertilizer. Although cyclamen grow in containers that seem impossibly small for the amount of growth they produce, do not be tempted to put them in bigger ones. Root disturbance is the last thing a cyclamen needs when it has more than 50 leaves, nine fully opened flowers and 27 waiting buds to support. If the plastic pot offends you, use a cache-pot.

The flowers of the wild *C. persicum* are in the usual shades of pink and white. Breeders of the big potted cyclamen have developed salmon and scarlet shades as well. In breeding for size, growers have lost the sweet delicate scent that is a feature of the wild *C. persicum*, but fortunately the scent has been reintroduced in a smaller, more delicate group of florist's cyclamen that come into garden centres in November. The scent is likely to be more pronounced in white flowers than pink or red. They are compact and, like the wild species, have more flowers out at the same time than the big cyclamen. That means, of course, that they do not flower over such a long period.

The petal of a good wild plant would be about 3cm (1in) long. The petals of a typical florist's cyclamen are twice as big. A hundred years of breeding has produced the doubling but some elegance has been lost along the way. The wild flower has the swept-back petals, the general look of a small animal caught in the teeth of a gale, that gives all wild cyclamen enormous charm. This neatness of form has to a large extent disappeared in the flowers of the biggest florist's cyclamen, though not in the daintier strains now available. Plant the tuber with its nose at the surface of the potting compost.

SEASON: March–April

HARDINESS: Tender

HEIGHT: 20cm (8in)

HABITAT: Scrubby, rocky places in southern Greece and Turkey, Cyprus, Jordan and Lebanon

Cyclamen pseudibericum ♀

The leaves are very dark, sometimes hooked at the edges like a holly leaf, while the flowers rise on top of dark stems, the broad magenta petals marked at the base with chocolate-coloured blotches. They smell of violets. *Cyclamen pseudibericum* is not fully hardy, so is probably best grown in a pot, though in mild areas it would be worth risking it outside under the canopy of trees where frost may not penetrate. In the wild, it grows with *Anemone blanda* and corydalis, primroses and *Cyclamen coum*, combinations worth trying in the garden too. The tubers root from the base. Cultivation Group 2. Plant 3cm (1in) deep, 10–15cm (4–6in) apart.

SEASON: Early March

HARDINESS: Frost hardy

HEIGHT: 9cm (3¾in)

HABITAT: Southern Turkey (Amanus mountains)

Cyclamen repandum

In the wild, *C. repandum* is a woodlander and its distinctive, toothed leaves are easily damaged by direct sunlight. They start to grow in late summer and may be well established by Christmas. In some forms, the leaves are spotted and dashed with silver, instead of the more usual marbled pattern. The pinkish purple flowers are long but not so elegantly restrained in form as *C. mirabile*. The twisted petals sometimes zoom off in unexpected directions. They smell faintly of violets. This species is trickier to establish in gardens than *C. coum*. It does not like to be too exposed and is only borderline hardy, so, although it does well in areas with relatively mild winters, elsewhere it may be best to grow it in a pot and give it shelter during periods of exceptionally cold weather. If you are going to risk it outside, try it with gentle *Anemone nemorosa* or dark-leaved *Viola riviniana* Purpurea Group. Cultivation Group 1 or 2. Plant 3cm (1in) deep and 10–15cm (4–6in) apart.

SEASON: April–May

HARDINESS: Borderline hardy

HEIGHT: 10–15cm (4–6in)

HABITAT: Widely distributed round the Mediterranean basin: southern France, Corsica, Sardinia, Italy, Sicily and south-eastern Europe where it grows in rocky places, woods and scrub up to 500m (1,650ft)

Autumn-flowering Cyclamen

Cyclamen cilicium ♀

Leaves and flowers appear together, the foliage spoon-shaped, unlike that of any of its cousins. The flowers are produced in a wide range of dark and pale pinks, the petals long and sharply pointed, unlike the blunt little flowers of *C. coum*. They smell deliciously of honey. *Cyclamen cilicium* was introduced to cultivation in 1872 and is not as hardy as some species, but in the right situation it is not a difficult garden plant. It also grows well in a pot, which means you can whisk it into a cold frame if you think it needs protecting from a particularly bitter bout of winter weather. Cultivation Group 1 or 2. Plant 3cm (1in) deep and 10–15cm (4–6in) apart.

SEASON: Late September

HARDINESS: Frost hardy

HEIGHT: 5cm (2in)

HABITAT: Southern Turkey (Antalya to Adana) where it grows in pine woods (and occasionally olive groves) at 700–2,000m (2,300–6,500ft)

Cyclamen hederifolium ♀
SOWBREAD

An enchanting and variable cyclamen which can produce flowers from white through palest pink to a rich, deep magenta. They are darkest at the mouth, scrunched into five pleats, from which the five petals flare back. It is a lovely way to show themselves off. The petals are fairly flat, and do not have the propeller form of *C. purpurascens*. Some flowers have longer petals than others. The leaves are even more various in size, shape and markings. Some showy types have leaves that are covered all over in a lichen-coloured silvery green (in shade, they glow). Others are marbled to a greater or lesser extent and look wonderful with ferns such as *Adiantum venustum* or *A. aleuticum* 'Miss Sharples'. All are superb garden plants.

The flowers of *Cyclamen hederifolium* start to appear in mid July and go on until the end of November; a mature corm may produce a hundred of them. The gorgeous leaves have an even longer season. They begin to push through three to five weeks after the first flowers and last until the following May. The corms which, when you buy them, may be no bigger than a 50p coin, eventually get enormous and, where happy, may last for a hundred years or more. When they get big, they sometimes heave themselves out of the ground. That does not seem to stop them flowering, though they would think it a treat if you sifted some leaf mould over them in their brief summer resting time.

Buy ready potted plants in flower in late summer or early autumn so you can choose the widest possible range of flower colour and leaf form. They will establish better as growing plants than they do from dried tubers. These are too often sent out in autumn, at a time when the cyclamen is longing to be fat and in full leaf, not sitting wizened and starved on a warehouse shelf. Once established, you could not wish for a more accommodating plant, nor a longer-lasting one. Show them off under the wine-coloured foliage of *Cotinus* 'Grace' or mix them with autumn-flowering *Crocus speciosus* for a stunning show-stopper in the garden. The early snowdrop *Galanthus reginae-olgae* is another good companion, for a cooler, more restrained effect. If you are planting bare tubers, remember that the roots of this species come from the shoulders and the sides, not the bottom. The upper surface is often slightly concave, the base smooth and rounded, a help when you are wondering which way up to put the tuber. Cultivation group 1. Plant 3cm (1in) deep and 10–15cm (4–6in) apart.

SEASON: July–November
HARDINESS: Fully hardy
HEIGHT: 10cm (4in)
HABITAT: Mediterranean from southern France to Greece and Turkey where it grows in woods and rocky places, often taking itself into olive groves and orchards

Cyclamen hederifolium f. *albiflorum*

This delectable, little flower shoots straight from the ground on a strong, darkish stem. The scrolled buds, very tightly rolled, open into the well-known, five-petalled flower; the petals sometimes have a distinct twist. An amazing number of flowers comes from a single tuber and they face in all directions, making a charming clump. Although this is a white-flowered form of the species, the mouth is flushed with pink. The first tentative leaves start appearing three to five weeks after the flowers. They are gorgeous: ivy-shaped and marked with silver in patterns as various as fingerprints. Set *C. hederifolium* f. *albiflorum* where it can glow from the base of a yew hedge. But feed it. Cultivation Group 1. Plant 3cm (1in) deep and 10–15cm (4–6in) apart.

SEASON: August–November
HARDINESS: Fully hardy
HEIGHT: 10cm (4in)

Cyclamen mirabile ♛

In many ways *C. mirabile* is similar to *C. cilicium*, with flowers beautifully poised on their stems. Each pale pink petal has a neat, upward twist, so the profile of the flower is rather narrow and elegant. Sometimes the marbling on the rounded leaves is pinkish rather than silver. This species was introduced in 1906. Cultivation Group 2. Plant 2–3cm (¾–1in) deep and 15–20cm (6–8in) apart.

SEASON: Late September–October
HARDINESS: Frost hardy
HEIGHT: 8cm (3½in)
HABITAT: South-western Turkey around Mugla and Isparta where it grows between limestone rocks at 500–1,000m (1,650–3,300ft)

NEXT PAGE The shuttlecock blooms of *Cyclamen hederifolium* can be any shade from white to a deep, rich pink. The first flowers push through before the leaves and are produced over a very long period.

Cyclamen purpurascens ♀

The tuber is knobbly and round, rather than flattish, and the roots shoot out from all over it. The foliage is more or less evergreen, unlike *C. hederifolium*, but *C. purpurascens* is a variable species. The cultivar I have grown is 'Lake Garda', with kidney-shaped evergreen leaves, quite small and silvered all over. The flowers are small, too, with narrow, twisted petals that give the effect of whirling propellers. Though they look white in bud, the flowers open in an intense magenta. For scent, this is one of the best cyclamen, the smell rather like lily-of-the-valley. It was a great favourite with Reginald Farrer, the famous plant collector: 'In all the garden there are no plants that more completely take my heart, they are so invariably, so indefatigably beautiful. Their whole personality so winning and sweet.' The seedpods are borne on the usual coiled spring of a stalk. This species cannot stand being dried out. Buy it as a living, growing plant. Even though it is perfectly hardy, it does not settle as easily as *C. hederifolium* and needs excellent drainage. Try it in a leaf-littered place under the canopy of tall trees. Cultivation Group 1 or 2. Plant 2–3cm (¾–1in) deep and 10–15cm (4–6in) apart.

SEASON: Early June
HARDINESS: Fully hardy
HEIGHT: 9cm (3¾in)
HABITAT: Central and eastern Europe where it grows in woods, often of beech or hornbeam, at 250–1,300m (800–4,250ft)

Cyrtanthus (Amaryllidaceae)

Cyrtanthus elatus (Vallota speciosa) ♀
SCARBOROUGH LILY

What has this South African plant got to do with the Yorkshire seaside town of Scarborough you might ask? It would be more at home in the tropics. The explanation you choose to believe depends on the amount of romance in your soul. Some say it was brought back from South Africa by a sailor for his sweetheart. Others believe that it was washed ashore from a Dutch ship wrecked with its cargo of bulbs off the Yorkshire coast in about 1800. The truth is that it was introduced to Britain from South Africa in 1773 when Francis Masson brought it back to the Royal Botanic Gardens at Kew.

Cyrtanthus elatus has bright scarlet, trumpet-shaped flowers (they can be 10cm/4in across) rising from a mass of sword-shaped foliage. There may be up to nine on a stem, each with six crisp, yellow anthers in the centre. Most of us will have to grow these elegant plants in a greenhouse or on a sunny windowsill. They need a winter temperature that does not drop below 5–10°C (41–50°F). Plant the bulb in a 13cm (5in) pot of loam-based compost such as John Innes No 2 mixed with sharp sand or grit (two parts compost to one part grit) and set it with its neck level with the top of the compost. Keep the pot in a warm, sunny place where the temperature is 16–18°C (61–65°F). When the plant is growing strongly, give it plenty of water, and feed with a liquid fertilizer high in potash. Reduce watering as growth begins to die down. It is by nature evergreen, so should never be allowed to dry out completely, though in winter, while it is resting, it needs hardly any water at all. Do not be in a hurry to repot it. It flowers better when it is slightly cramped. If you want to try it outside, give it the same growing conditions as you would a nerine: the sunniest, most sheltered border you have. Heap leaves over it in winter to provide extra protection against frost. Plant 10–15cm (4–6in) deep and 15–20cm (6–8in) apart.

SEASON: August–September
HARDINESS: Half hardy
HEIGHT: 30–60cm (12–24in)
HABITAT: South Africa (Western Cape)

Cyrtanthus falcatus ♀

The flowers of C. falcatus hang down from dark stems: thin tubes, pale pink flushed with a yellowish green. They are gathered tightly into a head and the effect is of a very full pleated skirt, quite different to the wide-mouthed flowers of the Scarborough lily. Cultivation as for C. elatus. Plant 10–15cm (4–6in) deep and 15–20cm (6–8in) apart.

SEASON: August–September
HARDINESS: Half hardy
HEIGHT: 30cm (12in)
HABITAT: South Africa (KwaZulu-Natal)

Dichelostemma (Alliaceae)

Dichelostemma congestum

At the top of each wiry stem is a head of flowers gathered together like chives but each flower is bluer, bigger, and there are less of them in the cluster. The foliage is thin and wiry. Plant *D. congestum* on very well-drained soil in a sunny, sheltered site 7–10cm (2½–4in) deep and 5–7cm (2–2½in) apart.

SEASON: June
HARDINESS: Frost hardy
HEIGHT: 50cm (20in)
HABITAT: USA (California, Oregon, Washington) where it grows in grassland and open woods

Dichelostemma ida-maia
CALIFORNIAN FIRECRACKER

In 1867, Alphonso Wood described how the plant had been 'first noticed by Mr Burke, the stage driver, in his daily route. He had given it the name Ida May in affection for his little daughter – a name quite appropriate, moreover, as on the Ides (that is, the 15th) of May the plant begins to flower'. It is a charming thing, with long, tube-like flowers (up to 12 of them) gathered together at the top of the stem. In bud, they are red with lime-green tips, and when the flower opens the green scrolls back to reveal a creamy frill round the stamens. Choose a sunny, sheltered site with well-drained soil and plant 7–10cm (2½–4in) deep and 5–7cm (2–2½in) apart.

SEASON: May–June
HARDINESS: Frost hardy
HEIGHT: 25–30cm (10–12in)
HABITAT: USA (northern California, southern Oregon) where it grows in grassland and deciduous woodland at 300–1,500m (1,000–5,000ft)

Dierama (Iridaceae)

ANGEL'S FISHING ROD, WANDFLOWER

These are uncommonly graceful South African plants with flowers that hang out along the arched branches like baubles on a Christmas tree. Each is held on its own thread-like stem, so that it moves independently from its neighbours and talks only to its own papery bract. The flowers open in succession from the bottom upwards, so each stem lasts a long time. Although they may look fragile, they are not and the clumps do not need staking. Indeed, the way they move is one of their great gifts to a garden. Do not muddle dierama up with other herbaceous plants. Set them so that the flowering stems can hang out over paving, or even better over water. They may be slow to establish, but where they are happy they will increase into satisfyingly large clumps. They hate to be disturbed, so if you are a fidgety sort of gardener, leave them alone and fidget somewhere else. By nature, dieramas (the name comes from the Greek word for funnel) do not have a dormant period, so you will be offered them as plants rather than dry corms. Bulb merchants send them out in spring, the roots packed in damp compost, the tough foliage cut down to size. Spring, not autumn, is the right time to plant in rich, well-drained soil in full sun. The dieramas' natural habitat is damp grassland; plants must never dry out.

ABOVE The dangling flowers of *Dierama pulcherrimum* displayed in the best possible way, hanging out over water and the flat pads of water lilies.

Dierama dracomontanum

Dense, vigorous clumps of evergreen grassy foliage
are overtopped by arching stems of wide, bell flowers,
which may be pale or deep pink, sometimes veering
towards purple. *Dierama dracomontanum* is the earliest
dierama to flower and, as it is slightly more upright in
growth than *D. pulcherrimum*, is a good choice for
small gardens. It also seems to clump up faster than
other dieramas. In time, *D. dracomontanum* builds
up a chain of underground corms, the new ones sitting
on top of the old like montbretias. Plant 8–10cm
(3½–4in) deep and 40–50cm (16–20in) apart.

SEASON: June
HARDINESS: Frost hardy
HEIGHT: 60cm (24in)
HABITAT: South Africa (Drakensberg mountains from Free
State to Eastern Cape) and Lesotho where it grows on grassy
mountain slopes at 1,500–2,800m (5,000–9,000ft)

Dierama 'Guinevere'

A pure white selection, which looks more than
usually angelic. Give *D*. 'Guinevere' full sun and
well-behaved companions – melianthus perhaps or
a low mat of a grey-leaved hosta such as 'Halcyon'
or 'Fragrant Blue'. Plant 8–10cm (3½–4in) deep
and 60–80cm (24–32in) apart.

SEASON: July–August
HARDINESS: Frost hardy
HEIGHT: 1m (3ft)

Dierama 'Lancelot'

A vigorous clone, and tall, with pink flowers, produced in
abundance. This is perhaps one of the best of the dieramas to
start with, as it clumps up well. Hang *D*. 'Lancelot' over a low
mat of the excellent dark red *Dianthus* 'Hidcote', which will
now have shot its bolt as far as flowering is concerned and
let the dierama reinvigorate the dianthus's grey foliage.
Plant 8–10cm (3½–4in) deep and 60–80cm (24–32in) apart.

SEASON: July–August
HARDINESS: Frost hardy
HEIGHT: 1.3m (4½ft)

Dierama pendulum

An imposing plant, with arching stems of purplish pink flowers, each one 4–5cm (1½–2in) long, rising from tussocks of grassy foliage. They spread out to make wider trumpets than those of *D. pulcherrimum*. Though in a garden you may not think there is much to choose between them, these species keep themselves quite separate in the wild, *D. pendulum* to the west of Eastern Cape, *D. pulcherrimum* to the east. Plant *D. pendulum* 8–10cm (3½–4in) deep and 60–80cm (24–32in) apart.

SEASON: July–August

HARDINESS: Frost hardy

HEIGHT: 60–100cm (2–4ft)

HABITAT: South Africa (Eastern Cape) though it has now become naturalized in South Australia and New South Wales and has also jumped over garden walls in New Zealand

SEASON: August

HARDINESS: Frost hardy

HEIGHT: 1.5–1.8m (5–6ft)

HABITAT: South Africa (Eastern Cape, KwaZulu-Natal, Mpumalanga, Limpopo) and Lesotho where it grows in damp grassland at 900–1,700m (3,000–5,750ft)

Dierama pulcherrimum

This species (as beautiful as its name suggests) was introduced to gardeners in 1866 by the famous Yorkshire nurseryman James Backhouse and over the next 50 years became well established in gardens such as Inverewe on the west coast of Scotland. It is still the dierama you are most likely to see in cool-temperate gardens and will probably have drooping flowers of silvery pink, though a white form flowered at the Royal Botanic Gardens, Kew, UK in 1898 and purple forms have been seen in the wild. The flowers develop into attractive seedheads which hang like beads from the stem. In the wild, *D. pulcherrimum* comes from dampish habitats and, though it likes sun, should never be allowed to become too dry. Some fine selections of this species were made in the 1950s by Leslie Slinger at the Slieve Donard nurseries in Northern Ireland, most of them named after birds. Try it with *Thalictrum dipterocarpum* or let it hang out over mauve-blue-flowered stokesia. Plant 8–10cm (3½–4in) deep and 80–100cm (32–39in) apart.

D

Dietes (Iridaceae)

These are the iris of the tropics, with sword-shaped leaves and flat-faced flowers rather like those of *Iris ensata*. Though the flowers only last a day (*D. grandiflora* will do three), there are lots of them. They are mostly found in the tropical regions of Africa with a strange outpost on Lord Howe Island in the Pacific. They are too tender to grow outside where winters are very cold, but they thrive in borders in mild areas. Elsewhere, grow them in pots in a greenhouse or conservatory. Use a loam-based compost such as John Innes No 2. Give plenty of water while the plants are growing, less when they have finished flowering; when dormant, they will need practically none. In the growing season, feed every two weeks with a fertilizer rich in potash (tomato feed is ideal).

ABOVE *Dietes iridioides* opens its elegant, flat-faced flowers. Each one only lasts a day but there are plenty of them on each spike.

Dietes grandiflora

The flowering stems tower over the leaves, which in *D. grandiflora* can be up to 10cm (4in) wide. The flowers are very lovely: the wide petals blotched with yellow and the styles, standing up in the centre, a soft mauve-purple. Plant rhizomes with their noses level with the ground and 40cm (16in) apart.

SEASON: April–June
HARDINESS: Tender
HEIGHT: 1.2m (4ft)
HABITAT: East Africa, South Africa (Western Cape to KwaZulu-Natal)

Dietes iridioides

As its name suggests, this is the most iris-like of the dietes, with the leaves held in a basal fan, like the bearded iris. The three larger petals of the white flowers are blotched with yellow, and the styles, which look like petals themselves, stand purplish in the centre. Do not be tempted to cut back the flowering stems of *D. iridioides* when the flowers have died. Unlike the iris of more temperate zones, these stems are perennial. Plant rhizomes with their noses level with the ground and 40cm (16in) apart.

SEASON: April–June
HARDINESS: Tender
HEIGHT: 30–60cm (12–24in)
HABITAT: South Africa (Western Cape) and Kenya where it grows along the banks of streams

D

Dracunculus (Araceae)

Dracunculus vulgaris
(Arum dracunculus)
DRAGON ARUM

A great deal of fuss is made about the smell of the dragon arum. Think rotting meat. But you are hardly going to camp out alongside it while it is in flower. Instead of complaining, marvel that this arum has sufficient *savoir-faire* to abandon sweet, which is overdone in the plant world, and do obnoxious instead. It is an extremely effective ploy, designed to attract flies which do the job of pollination. The leaves come through in early spring, packed into a tight, sharp, spearing point. The stalk, as it develops, becomes like a tree trunk, strangely mottled with greenish purple on a cream background. At the base, the stem can measure 8cm (3½in) across, but it needs to be strong to support the enormous amount of growth above. The leaflets are held on bizarre, semi-circular ribs, a characteristic (the arc) that was caught in the earliest pictures of the plant, made in the sixth century. There may be up to 14 leaflets on each stem, all of them feathered with white. At the base of the spathe is a pale green balloon, from which the whole massive edifice gradually unfurls. In mid May, the purple spadix, 60cm (24in) long, is already lolling out of the top when the spathe begins to unfurl. It is huge (70cm/28in tall), strange, and very showy. Frightening even. It takes a long time to unfurl completely, but can be as much as 25cm (10in) across. Each has a different texture, the spathe matt, dull purple, the spadix slightly darker and shiny. Try D. *vulgaris* among *Helleborus argutifolius* or beside *Euphorbia mellifera*. Plant in rich soil that does not dry out and give the tubers a thick mulch of some nutritious stuff every spring. Set them 15cm (6in) deep and 45–60cm (18–24in) apart.

SEASON: Mid May

HARDINESS: Frost hardy

HEIGHT: 1.5m (5ft)

HABITAT: Central and eastern Mediterranean from Sardinia and Sicily eastwards to southern Bulgaria, Greece and southern Turkey where it grows on the margins of fields and in other disturbed habitats

Eranthis (Ranunculaceae)

WINTER ACONITE

The winter aconite has made itself so at home in Britain that it seems like a native. It is not but it was introduced a very long time ago. Already by 1578, the writer Henry Lyte was talking about these 'venomous and naughtie hearbs' planted 'in the gardens of certain Herborists'. John Gerard knew them too and described in his famous *Herball* (1597) how they 'came foorth of the grounde in the dead time of

winter, many times bearing the snowe upon the heades of his leaves and flowers; yea, the colder the weather is and the deeper that the snowe is, the fairer and larger is the flower; and the warmer that the weather is, the lesser is the flower, and worse coloured.' Winter aconites seem to grow particularly well on light soils, and they do well under trees too. You often see huge colonies of them spread out under a horse chestnut or a weeping ash. The grass under trees is usually too thin to hinder the aconites, which seed outwards under the canopy like the ripples of a pond. They are often planted with the common snowdrop (*Galanthus nivalis*), a natural companion since their flowering times overlap, but do not be afraid to let aconites out on their own. Try spreading them under wintersweet or witch hazel or some other deciduous shrub, which will allow them plenty of light during their growing season. The tubers

ABOVE John Gerard's *Herball* was the most widely read plant book of its age, and gives a useful insight into the flowers that were available to gardeners of the late sixteenth century.

look unpromising – hard, misshapen, little things like dried sheep's dung – and are best planted quite shallowly. But like snowdrops, aconites hate to dry out, and often the best way to establish them is to buy them 'in the green', lifted just after they have finished flowering and sent out in little clumps with leaves and stems still attached. They need to be replanted as quickly as possible. Do not try to pull the clumps apart. You can do this with snowdrops, but aconites are better left alone. If dry tubers are all you have got, soak them overnight before planting them.

Eranthis hyemalis ♀

Nobody goes crazy about aconites, the way they do about snowdrops, but this dear flower often beats the first snowdrops into bloom. It is a familiar and very welcome sign of a new season starting. The stems sit under the centre of enchanting, bright green ruffs of leaves so each opens in a flat parasol on top. The flowers are surrounded by similar green ruffs, though there are not so many 'fingers' of green as there are with the leaves. The blooms are bright yellow throughout, the same colour on both the inner and outer surfaces of the petals. The bright boss of stamens in the centre is the same shade of yellow. The texture of the petals is thin, though, and the veining shows. Plant tubers of *E. hyemalis* 3cm (1in) deep and 7–8cm (2½–3½in) apart.

SEASON: Mid–late January
HARDINESS: Fully hardy
HEIGHT: 10cm (4in)
HABITAT: France, Italy and south-eastern Europe, but widely naturalized in Europe. In the wild, it favours woods and stony places

---

Eranthis hyemalis Cilicica Group

The blooms of the Cilicica Group are very similar to those of the ordinary winter aconite, but they are a bit bigger and the leaves more finely cut. In most seasons, they flower slightly later than *E. hyemalis*; by using both, you can extend the display. Give them sun. Plant tubers 3cm (1in) deep and 7–8cm (2½–3½in) apart.

SEASON: February
HARDINESS: Fully hardy
HEIGHT: 5–8cm (2–3½in)

Eranthis hyemalis 'Guinea Gold' ♀

The new foliage has a distinct, bronze cast, subtle but noticeable if you plant this selection close to the ordinary winter aconite. The flowers are a slightly deeper shade of yellow. 'Guinea Gold', introduced to cultivation in 1923 by the Dutch bulb growers Van Tubergen, is a bigger plant too, though size is relative when, even drawn up to your full height, you are only a few centimetres off the ground. It is sterile (and relatively expensive) so is not the one to choose for naturalizing. Plant tubers 3cm (1in) deep and 7–8cm (2½–3½in) apart.

SEASON: February
HARDINESS: Fully hardy
HEIGHT: 8–10cm (3½–4in)

Erythronium (Liliaceae)

Only one kind – dog's tooth violet (*Erythronium dens-canis*) – grows in Europe and seventeenth-century gardeners such as John Parkinson, author of a beautiful plant book, *Paradisus* (1629), were tremendously excited by new sorts coming in for the first time from America, where so many different species grow. 'Wee have had from Virginia a roote sent unto us', he wrote 'which the naturall people holde not onely to be singular to procure lust, but hold it as a secret, loth to reveale it.' At that time, the obsession with aphrodisiacs was matched only by a corresponding quest for plants that might provide a cure for syphilis. The Tartars of Russia had a more prosaic view of erythroniums. They made soup from the roots, 'nourishing and excellent', said Johann Gmelin, an eighteenth-century professor of botany at St Petersburg.

CULTIVATION
Ideally, erythroniums need humus-rich ground in shade, a home that is damp in spring but dries out a little in summer. They prefer soils that are on the acid side of neutral. Because erythroniums hate to dry out, they are best bought damp-packed in autumn. Get them in the ground as soon as you can and use them on their own under trees and shrubs. They are not robust enough to fight pulmonarias or other over-excited perennials. Plant the bulbs with the pointed end uppermost, 10cm (4in) deep and about the same distance apart.

ABOVE Yellow-flowered erythroniums grow happily with cream-edged hostas in the woodland garden at Stone Crop, New York.

Erythronium californicum 'White Beauty' ♀

The leaves are subtly but beautifully marked in white, like feathers on a bird's back. Enchanting, small, creamy white flowers (up to three on a stem) have a strange necklace of brownish maroon round the stamens. These are the same creamish white as the flowers and very prominent. This is in every way an enchanting plant and increases quite quickly by offsets. If you are longing to give 'White Beauty' a companion, try it with the compact form of blue-flowered *Omphalodes cappadocica*, 'Cherry Ingram'. Plant the bulbs 10cm (4in) deep and about the same distance apart.

SEASON: Early April
HARDINESS: Fully hardy
HEIGHT: 13cm (5in)

Erythronium dens-canis ♀
DOG'S TOOTH VIOLET

The leaves are beautifully mottled and blotched – indeed the foliage plays almost as important a part as the flowers in paying rent in a garden. The flowers themselves may be white or various shades of a rather purplish pink, the petals very abruptly swept back from the mouth of the flower away from the purplish stamens. There is just one flower on each stem, so it is not as showy as some of its cousins, but it is usually one of the first to flower. If your soil is on the limy side, *E. dens-canis* is the one to grow. In this respect, the American erythroniums are fussier. If you are lucky, you may be able to naturalize dog's tooth violet in grass, but only where the turf is fine rather than coarse. Light, sandy soils are likely to provide the right conditions, provided there is also enough humus. The great plantsman Christopher Lloyd grew *E. dens-canis* with the little, yellow daffodil *Narcissus minor*. Plant the bulbs 10cm (4in) deep and about the same distance apart.

SEASON: Early April
HARDINESS: Fully hardy
HEIGHT: 15cm (6in)
HABITAT: Europe (Spain, Portugal, Austria, Romania, Bulgaria) where it grows in woods, scrub and meadows up to 1,700m (5,750ft)

Erythronium dens-canis 'Old Aberdeen'

The foliage is wide and ground hugging, but nowhere near as meaty as *E.* 'Sundisc'. It is pale grey-green, mottled in large blotches with ox blood. The flower is very delicate, swept back in the way of all erythroniums, and a good pink, the same kind of colour as *Cyclamen hederifolium*. At the centre of the flower is a gingery brown ring, with the stamens – very prominent – sticking out in the opposite direction to the petals. It is a charming variety, but miniature. Although of course 'Old Aberdeen' does not flower at the same time as *C. hederifolium*, the two make good companions; plant them alongside each other, rather than intermingled. 'Old Aberdeen' is not as vigorous as the cyclamen. Plant the bulbs 10cm (4in) deep and about the same distance apart.

SEASON: Late March
HARDINESS: Fully hardy
HEIGHT: 8cm (3½in)

SEASON: Early April
HARDINESS: Fully hardy
HEIGHT: 27cm (11in)

Erythronium 'Joanna'

The broad, green, arum-like leaves are only lightly marked with darker colour, so in this respect 'Joanna' is not as showy as 'Sundisc'. There can be from four to eight flowers on a stem, all borne quite close together at the top. The petals are washed on the back with a pale purplish pink. Inside, the centre is bright yellow, drifting out to purplish pink at the edges. It is a strange colour, more complex than either 'Sundisc' or *E. californicum* 'White Beauty'. The yellow colour comes from *E. tuolumnense*, a parent of 'Joanna'. Plant bulbs 10cm (4in) deep and about the same distance apart.

Erythronium 'Pagoda' ♧

The yellow flowers, paler than those of *E. tuolumnense*, are supremely elegant, hanging in swept-back Turk's caps over huge, green leaves. These are only slightly mottled, but stained beetroot colour at the base where they first shoot from the ground. 'Pagoda' is one of the tallest of the erythroniums, and some growers have reported finding ten flowers on a single stem. Usually the plant is less ambitious, producing four or five. That is not disappointing. Try it with the little, blue-flowered navelwort *Omphalodes cappadocica*. Plant the bulbs in the dappled shade under deciduous trees and shrubs, setting them 10cm (4in) deep and 12–15cm (5–6in) apart.

SEASON: April
HARDINESS: Fully hardy
HEIGHT: 30cm (12in)

Erythronium revolutum ♧

The leaves are deep green, heavily mottled with brown, and in the best forms are worth growing for the foliage alone; it provides a handsome underpinning for the purplish pink flowers. There may be up to four flowers on a stem, each 4–7cm (1½–2½in) across. *Erythronium revolutum* may take time to settle in, but if it decides it likes you it will start seeding itself about. Seedlings take three or four years to grow into flowering-size bulbs. It looks wonderful among the emerging fronds of shuttlecock fern (*Matteuccia struthiopteris*). Plant the bulbs 10cm (4in) deep and about the same distance apart.

SEASON: April
HARDINESS: Fully hardy
HEIGHT: 22cm (9in)
HABITAT: Canada (Vancouver Island, British Columbia) and USA (Washington, Oregon, northern California) in coniferous forests and along the banks of streams up to 1,000m (3,300ft)

Erythronium 'Sundisc'

The leaves are very large and wonderfully marked in featherings of dark maroon-brown. The flowers (three on a stem) are clear bright yellow, slightly paler on the reverse. A necklace of brownish red marks circles the stamens, though they are not such a prominent feature as they are on *E. californicum* 'White Beauty'. 'Sundisc' is a good plant, though the flowers are in danger of being overwhelmed by the size of the leaves. Plant the bulbs 10cm (4in) deep and about the same distance apart.

SEASON: Early April
HARDINESS: Fully hardy
HEIGHT: 26cm (10½in)

SEASON: Early April
HARDINESS: Fully hardy
HEIGHT: 30cm (12in)
HABITAT: USA (central California in the foothills of the Sierra Nevada) where it grows in woods of pine and evergreen oak around 500m (1,650ft)

Erythronium tuolumnense ♀

The broad, shiny leaves are plain bright green and slightly crinkled at the edges. On each of the dark-stained stems are yellow flowers, up to four of them, the petals swept back in the enchanting way of all this tribe. There is no contrasting colour at the centre, nor are the stamens as long as they are on *E. dens-canis* 'Old Aberdeen', but this is an easy erythronium which fits comfortably into a wild setting. It gets its name from the place where it was first found – Tuolumne County in California. When *E. tuolumnense* is happy it clumps up fast by means of offsets. Give it an open situation where it can dry out a little during summer and plant the bulbs 10cm (4in) deep and about the same distance apart.

E

Eucharis (Amaryllidaceae)

Eucharis amazonica ♀

This is sometimes called the Peruvian daffodil, which is idiotic, since it is nothing like a daffodil. It is far more dangerous, the white flowers (there may be up to eight of them) arching out in a head from long tubes which flare into six wide petals. In the centre is a greenish white cup, ringed round with six strange, little horns. The cup is made from the stamens which have fused all together, and the horns are the anthers on top of the stamens. The scent is rich and heady. In tropical countries, *E. amazonica* is a popular cut flower, but I cannot imagine ever being brave enough to cut one. I have seen eucharis glowing from the understorey of the Guyanese rainforest and looking impossibly glamorous in gardens of the Caribbean. It is happy in those places, where winter temperatures never dip down below 10°C (50°F). The rest of us will have to be content with growing it in a pot. Use a loam-based compost such as John Innes No 2, mixed with grit (two parts compost to one part grit or sharp sand). When the plant is growing strongly, give it plenty of water and feed once every two weeks with a fertilizer rich in potash (tomato feed is ideal). Never allow the bulbs to dry out. Set them with their noses level with the surface of the compost.

SEASON: September–October

HARDINESS: Tender

HEIGHT: 70cm (28in)

HABITAT: Colombia and north-eastern Peru

Eucomis (Hyacinthaceae)

PINEAPPLE FLOWER

These are fleshy, strange creatures with a pineapple tuft of leaves set on top of a cylinder of flowers. They are stronger on form than colour, though purple-leaved 'Sparkling Burgundy' provides both. You can plant them on their own in pots (three bulbs will fit into a tub about 30cm/12in across), though in this situation you may feel the foliage is too dominant; or else use them in borders to give a late summer boost to earlier flowering companions such as eryngium. Eucomis last a long time and develop interesting seedheads as autumn advances. In rich soil, they grow almost too well: the foliage becomes floppy and coarse and the flowering spike too tall for its own good. They tend to flop, and because of the way they are made are not easy to stake. Try propping them up with mounds of *Geranium* 'Brookside' or let them lean against the stout, leathery foliage of beautiful *Helleborus argutifolius*.

CULTIVATION
Eucomis need warm, fertile soil, plenty of sun and lots to drink during summer. Remember that they are only borderline hardy, so in cold areas mulch to protect the bulbs from frost and do not expect to see new shoots until May. The chief difficulty is keeping them upright. They are not easy to stake; the flowers cover so much of the stem that you can only tie them in at the bottom, which is usually too low to be useful.

ABOVE The strange topknot of leaves on top of the stem gives the eucomis its common name, the pineapple flower. It is a welcome addition to the garden in late summer.

Eucomis autumnalis ♀

The leaves are narrower than those of the similar *E. bicolor* 'Alba'; the flowers are whiter and are held facing outwards rather than as drooping, greenish bells. The stem is plain pale green, and the foliage has no spots on the underside. Introduced to cultivation in 1760, *E. autumnalis* is a handsome thing, as all eucomis are but, in its first year at least, does not seem as vigorous or as showy as *E. bicolor* 'Alba'. It comes into flower slightly later though, which is a useful attribute. Plant 15cm (6in) deep and 30–40cm (12–16in) apart.

SEASON: August
HARDINESS: Borderline hardy
HEIGHT: 30cm (12in)
HABITAT: South Africa (Eastern Cape, North West Province, Mpumalanga, KwaZulu-Natal), Botswana, Malawi, Swaziland and Zimbabwe where it grows on grassy mountain slopes

Eucomis bicolor ♀

Strange, rather arresting, this is a classy, long-lasting eucomis, with six fleshy, shiny leaves that droop at the tips and fold away from the midrib. They are bright dark green, spotted underneath, the spots thick at the base, then running out halfway up the stem. The flower stalk is very thick and fleshy, darkly spotted, and streaked like the leaves of *Tulipa greigii*. The actual flowering spike (15cm/6in long) opens from the bottom up, finishing in a small topknot of greenery which cannot decide whether it is petal or leaf. The flowers are tiny, pale celadon-green, the petals edged with maroon. At the centre of each is a small green bead which swells as the flowers age. *Eucomis bicolor* has been cultivated since 1878. Plant the bulbs 15cm (6in) deep and 30–40cm (12–16in) apart.

SEASON: Late July
HARDINESS: Borderline hardy
HEIGHT: 45cm (18in)
HABITAT: South Africa (KwaZulu-Natal) where it grows on rich, damp grassland and by streams up to 2,500m (8,250ft)

OPPOSITE Each separate flower in this stem of *Eucomis comosa* is a miracle of complexity, each petal edged finely with purple, each creamy flower with a bead-like purple centre.

Eucomis bicolor 'Alba'

Gorgeous 'Alba' is even better than *E. bicolor*. The foliage is much the same, broad and fleshy, though the dark spots on the undersides of the leaves of *E. bicolor* are reduced here to faint shadows. The thick stem is plain pale green (unlike *E. bicolor*'s mottled snakeskin), and pale greenish white flowers cluster round under the topknot, which is larger and showier than that of *E. bicolor*. The bells are plain white, each with a small, green button in the centre. 'Alba' is obviously attractive to flies, though the scent (unpleasant) is faint. Try it with a full-hearted lily such as *Lilium speciosum*. Plant the bulbs 15cm (6in) deep and 30–40cm (12–16in) apart.

SEASON: Early August

HARDINESS: Borderline hardy

HEIGHT: 60cm (24in)

Eucomis comosa

The stem is rather too tall for its own good (the flowering spike alone is 50cm/20in long) and, although stout and juicy, cannot hold upright the huge cargo above. So it lolls. Staking is not the answer because you can only tie the stem in beneath the flowers, which is too low to be helpful. Prop *E. comosa* up with *Geranium wallichianum* 'Buxton's Variety' or give it mounds of *Helleborus argutifolius* to lean against. The foliage is bright green, up to 60cm (24in) long, the leaves arching out from a central growing point and dark-purple spotted on the undersides like a snake's skin. Tiny, purple-edged leaflets climb up the stem between the white, star flowers, each minute petal also edged with purple. The bead-like centres of the flowers are purple, surrounded by lemon-yellow stamens. The tuft of leaves that crowns the flowering spike is not as showy as it is in other types. Plant the bulbs 15cm (6in) deep and 30–40cm (12–16in) apart.

SEASON: August–September

HARDINESS: Borderline hardy

HEIGHT: 90cm (36in)

HABITAT: South Africa (Eastern Cape, KwaZulu-Natal)

Eucomis comosa 'Sparkling Burgundy'

When the leaves first come through in spring, they are deep, rich purple and hold themselves upright. As the season progresses, the colour changes to a duller bronze and the foliage (11cm/4½in wide and very heavy) starts turning over on itself, often sprawling on the ground. The flower stems are rich maroon-purple, fat, though not strong enough to hold the spike upright (a problem with most eucomis except dwarf *E. vandermerwei*). The flowers open from the bottom of the spike up, a strange pinkish cream, stiff and fleshy, with prominent, cream stamens. As they go over, the central knob develops into a solid, little button. Try 'Sparkling Burgundy' among the tawny brown flowers of *Helenium* 'Moerheim Beauty'. Plant the bulbs 15cm (6in) deep and 30–40cm (12–16in) apart.

SEASON: Late August
HARDINESS: Borderline hardy
HEIGHT: 90cm (36in)

Eucomis pallidiflora ♀

An elegant plant, pale as its name suggests, with greenish white flowers on a long spike that takes up more than half of the flowering stem. The leaves are also pale, with markedly crinkled edges. Be prepared for them to flop over neighbours. They can be up to 70cm (28in) long. Plant the bulbs of *E. pallidiflora* 15cm (6in) deep and 30–40cm (12–16in) apart.

SEASON: September–October
HARDINESS: Frost hardy
HEIGHT: 45–75cm (18–30in)
HABITAT: South Africa (Free State)

Eucomis pole-evansii

The species was collected by the director of the Botanical Survey of South Africa, the magnificently named Iltyd Buller Pole-Evans, along the edges of streams in the Transvaal. In cultivation it seems often to be muddled with *E. pallidiflora*. 'If I owned a sheltered garden in Devonshire or Wigtownshire I would without delay ask the Department of Agriculture at Pretoria to supply me with seed,' wrote Colonel Charles Grey, author of *Hardy Bulbs*. And, being an army man, he would of course expect to get it. *Eucomis pole-evansii* makes a huge bulb. You could stun a burglar with it, and it produces an equally huge plant with stems up to 2m (6½ft) topped by a creamy yellow flower spike. It is probably best in the hands of gardeners who are not easily intimidated by their plants and confined in gardens where the winters are relatively mild. Plant the bulbs 15cm (6in) deep and 50–60cm (20–24in) apart.

SEASON: August–September
HARDINESS: Borderline hardy
HEIGHT: 1.5–1.8m (5–6ft)
HABITAT: South Africa (North West Province, Mpumalanga) and Swaziland

Eucomis vandermerwei

When tiny *E. vandermerwei* first comes through it looks more animal than plant, the leaves pressed flat to the ground like a star fish, darkly speckled with purple. The edges of the leaves are faintly crinkled and scarcely more than 15cm (6in) long, six or seven of them evenly arranged in a star. The miniature flowerhead with its topknot of leaves (green, finely edged with purple) has deep maroon flowers, hanging down, with tufts of stamens protruding from the mouth. It is good in gravel (it likes sun) to follow on from dwarf spring bulbs – species tulips or crocus. Plant the bulbs 15cm (6in) deep and 30–40cm (12–16in) apart.

SEASON: Mid August
HARDINESS: Borderline hardy
HEIGHT: 13cm (5in)
HABITAT: South Africa (North West Province) where it grows in grassland

OPPOSITE Eucomis are only borderline hardy and need plenty of sun if they are to thrive. In this species, *E. comosa*, the topknot of leaves is not such a feature as it is with other types.

F

Freesia (Iridaceae)

These are popular cut flowers and not too expensive so you may feel that you can let commercial growers lie awake at night worrying about their needs and treat yourself occasionally to a couple of bunches from the florist instead. But, but, but… There is a driving force in all gardeners to get to the heart of anything that grows, to try and understand what plants are trying to tell them, and if they succeed they feel – well – just a little bit wiser than they did before. I have only once been able to grow a couple of decent pots of freesias to bring into the house, but I felt ridiculously proud every time I passed them in the sitting room, glowing out from a windowsill.

The colours are jewel bright and the scent glorious – stronger from the yellow kinds than from any other. In the wild, freesias are mostly creamy or yellow, and from this restricted paintbox breeders in England, France, Italy and The Netherlands have coaxed flowers of red, white, mauve and pink, both singles and doubles, with much of the breeding centring on a plant brought into Europe from Port Elizabeth in 1898.

Gardeners are rarely offered any of the 15 species that grow wild in South Africa: white-flowered *F. alba*, which grows in rocky, sandy soil on the Cape's

ABOVE Yellow freesias bloom with *Hyacinthoides italica* and provide a blend of scents that no perfumier could ever quite match.

southern shores, *F. caryophyllacea* with white flowers dramatically blotched with orange (and the most heavenly scent of any freesia), *F. corymbosa* in pinkish purple, a flower of the Eastern Cape, and yellow *F. speciosa*, which has the biggest flowers of any of the wild freesias. Sometimes, if you are lucky, you may be able to get hold of *F. fucata*, which in the wild grows on clay soils near Worcester, just east of Cape Town. The delicious scent is not there for our benefit but to pull in pollinating insects. Green-flowered *F. viridis* turns on its perfume at night, to attract moths. *F. grandiflora* and *F. laxa* depend on butterflies. If you can get freesias flowering for you, the smell will fill a greenhouse or conservatory in a most glorious way.

The strong, branched flowering stems (up to 40cm/16in) tower over the fans of leaves, and the flowers are all held on one side of the stem. If you intend to grow freesias in a greenhouse, you can plant corms in late summer or early autumn and keep them frost-free through winter (a temperature around 10°C/50°F is about right). Six will fit comfortably into a 13cm (5in) pot; push in some twiggy sticks to support the stems as they begin to grow. Sometimes you can get hold of specially treated corms which you plant in late spring to flower in late summer. If you are planting outside, choose a well-drained soil in full sun. When the plants are established, feed them with a fertilizer rich in potash (tomato feed is ideal). Only in the mildest areas will freesias survive outside through the following winter. So then you have to buy fresh corms, at which point you may ask yourself whether it would not be better to spend the money on cut flowers instead. Few named varieties are available to gardeners. Freesias are mostly sold as mixtures.

Freesia cultivars

The freesia is named after Friedrich Freese, a physician from Kiel, Germany, and the corms, usually in mixtures of singles and doubles, are available in spring to flower outside in late summer. Cultivated forms of freesia have been bred from the white-flowered species *F. alba*, native to Western Cape, South Africa, which has been crossed with scented, yellow *F. leichtlinii*. Do not be tempted to plant corms before the end of April. Set them 5cm (2in) deep and 7–8cm (2½–3½in) apart.

SEASON: January–April (indoors); July–August (outdoors)
HARDINESS: Half hardy
HEIGHT: 40cm (16in)

F

Fritillaria (Liliaceae)

'An enormous number of Fritillaries have stinking bells of dingy chocolate and greenish tones,' complained the pleasingly opinionated gardener Reginald Farrer. But that did not stop him growing them. Fritillaries are like that. They creep up on you quietly, for noise is alien to them. Their colours are muted, and apart from the famous crown imperial they are mostly spindly, frail plants. But some of us like khaki and welcome this restrained palette of colours at a time when we are being assaulted by hyacinths that are too pink, daffodils that are too yellow. Even in the wild, few fritillaries make massive spreads – the exceptions are *F. meleagris* and *F. pyrenaica*. Mostly they are solitary creatures, which makes them perfect for jewel-box gardening. Plant a single bulb in a clay pot and as each comes into flower bring it to a place – the front door perhaps – where you will see it often. Stand different pots together on a plant stand outside a window, where you can admire the perfection of each individual bloom. Because their colours are so muted, fritillaries can get lost in the general hurly-burly of a garden. Displayed like the crown jewels, each flower in its own pot, their sophistication is more apparent. There is another advantage too: you can manipulate the growing conditions more easily. Some fritillaries are fussy and need to be really dry when they are dormant. A plant in a pot can be whisked under cover at the appropriate time, which is much simpler than trying to balance panes of glass over the things in the open garden. At the Royal Botanic Gardens, Kew, UK, choice fritillaries are kept in clay pots plunged up to their rims in frames of damp sand.

ABOVE Reginald Farrer (1880–1920), the plant collector, traveller, writer and famous builder of rock gardens.

Sadly for gardeners, many fritillaries seem determined to die. You will get a flower the first year (most suppliers are kind enough to ensure at least that brief satisfaction). After that, you may cosset them all you like, but the death wish seems embedded in their souls. 'Why?' I asked the ghost of my *Fritillaria pallidiflora*. 'Why can't I make you happy? What is it in the sloping meadows of the Zhungar Alatau in Kazakhstan that you are pining for? What am I doing wrong?' *F. pallidiflora* is actually one of the easier fritillaries to grow, but I lost several batches in the garden before I started to keep them in pots, which in my situation and soil seems to delay (I dare not say cure) their suicidal tendencies.

Part of the charm of fritillaries lies in the way they are made – the hanging bell suggesting a kind of bashfulness which is very appealing. There

OPPOSITE Snake's head fritillaries (*Fritillaria meleagris*) in white and chequered purple grow with scillas in a classic spring planting.

are people like that. You need to give them time. And space. The diversity of the flowers is mirrored in the bulbs themselves, some rather large (*F. pallidiflora*, *F. raddeana*), but composed of few scales, others like the North American species *F. camschatcensis* made up of many tiny rounded scales often called rice grains. In the wild, the grains fall away from the mother plant and grow into separate plants, exactly the same as the parent.

CULTIVATION

When you are growing fritillaries, you need to know where they come from – their requirements in cultivation correspond fairly closely to their natural habitats. The fritillaries listed below are divided into four different groups. Cultivation Group 3 is the odd man out. The others need, in varying degrees, a damp spring followed by a dry summer and winter. The fritillaries in Cultivation Group 1 are the most tolerant types, happy and easy in a garden setting as long as they have fertile, well-drained soil and full sun. Cultivation Group 2 are fussier about getting wet. They are reasonably tolerant but need to be in really well-drained ground and full sun. They will not be happy if, as predicted, winters get even wetter. The fritillaries in Cultivation Group 3 are those that, in the wild, choose damp places to grow (like *F. meleagris*). They like soil rich in humus where they never dry out completely. They positively enjoy cool, damp summers and will grow in sun or light shade. Cultivation Group 4 fritillaries are for advanced gardeners, who have worked their way through the easier ones. These hate wet and are best grown under cover in a cold frame or greenhouse. When they are dormant, they need to be really dry. If you grow fritillaries in pots, use a loam-based compost such as John Innes No 2 mixed with grit (two parts compost to one part grit) and repot every summer in fresh compost, while the bulbs are dormant. For a real splash, you can fit ten of the cheaper, smaller kinds into a 20cm (8in) pot. At all times handle the bulbs with care. They are rather naked, not protected by tunics as daffodil bulbs are, and they bruise easily. Get hold of them as soon as you can in autumn. They start rooting rather earlier than many spring bulbs. Watch out for bright red lily beetles which unfortunately are as partial to fritillaries as they are to lilies. If you have never grown fritillaries before, start with some of these easy ones: *F. acmopetala*, *F. camschatcensis*, *F. imperialis*, *F. meleagris*, *F. michailovskyi*, *F. pallidiflora*, *F. pontica*, *F. pyrenaica*, or *F. uva-vulpis*.

OPPOSITE Once a common native of damp grassland, snake's head fritillaries are now rare in Britain. This meadow, close to Magdalen College in Oxford, is a miraculous survival.

Fritillaria acmopetala ♀

This has a larger flower than
F. uva-vulpis on a stem less than half
the height. The three outer petals
are green with some dark marks, the
three inner ones darkly smudged
where they emerge from the stem,
matched by a similar smudge at the
tip of the petal. The inner petals are
far wider than the outer ones. The
bell flips outwards at the bottom, so
you get a clear view of the inside of
the flower: jade green, very finely
veined in darker green and quite
staggeringly shiny. Six thin leaves
clasp the stem. This is an intriguing
flower, introduced to cultivation in
1874, but you need to be close to
see it properly. Give *F. acmopetala*
well-drained soil, perhaps under an
early-flowering daphne such as
D. mezereum. Cultivation Group 1.
Easy. Plant 10cm (4in) deep and the
same distance apart.

SEASON: Early April
HARDINESS: Fully hardy
HEIGHT: 30cm (12in)
HABITAT: Cyprus, south-western Turkey, Syria and
Lebanon where it grows on stony limestone in pine
woods, scrub and cornfields up to 1,200m (4,000ft)

Fritillaria assyriaca

In outline, *F. assyriaca* is a slender
plant with grey-green leaves climbing
alternately up the stem. The bells are
also narrow, the muted purple-brown
petals flipping out very slightly at the
bottom. Imagine the bloom on a
bunch of grapes, add it to this flower,
and you perhaps have an idea of its
strange allure and texture. It was
introduced to cultivation in 1874, but
is often confused with *F. uva-vulpis*.
Cultivation Group 2 or 4. Easy. Plant
10cm (4in) deep and the same
distance apart.

SEASON: Late March
HARDINESS: Fully hardy
HEIGHT: 20cm (8in)
HABITAT: Eastern Turkey, western
Iran and northern Iraq where it
grows on limestone pastures up to
2,500m (8,250ft)

Fritillaria camschatcensis

When *F. camschatcensis* is established, each flowering stem produces up to eight black bell flowers, among the darkest of all fritillaries. This needs a place that is damp in spring, when it is in active growth, and shady and cool in summer. It flowers later than most fritillaries so is a useful ally if you are trying to arrange a succession of these enigmatic beauties. This species does not like to dry out completely, so is best bought damp-packed for autumn planting. It likes the kind of slightly acid soil that rhododendrons favour and is a natural companion for them. Unusually, the bulbs are made up from scales, like lilies. Cultivation Group 3. Easy. Set them 10cm (4in) deep and the same apart.

SEASON: Mid May–early June
HARDINESS: Fully hardy
HEIGHT: 40cm (16in)
HABITAT: Eastern Siberia, Japan, Canada and USA (Alaska down to Washington State) where it grows in damp meadows

Fritillaria davisii

A charming, dwarfish fritillary with one or two flowers hanging down from the stem. The two basal leaves are much wider than the others, which cluster close to the top of the stem. The bells are dull purplish green on the outside, slightly chequered in the manner of *F. meleagris*. Inside, the petals are much shinier, a bright khaki, slightly yellower at the edges. On each petal is a neat, dark, basal blotch. *Fritillaria davisii* was introduced in 1940, and advanced gardeners make it look enchanting in stone troughs with other spring treasures. In the right conditions it can increase quite quickly, the offsets getting to flowering size in two to three years. If you plant deeply though, at 10cm (4in), you will get fewer offsets but more flowers. It is best under cover. Cultivation Group 4. Difficult. Plant 10cm (4in) deep and the same distance apart.

SEASON: Late April
HARDINESS: Fully hardy
HEIGHT: 15cm (6in)
HABITAT: Southern Greece (Máni peninsula) where it grows in scrub, olive groves and cornfields up to 150m (500ft)

Fritillaria elwesii

This is a light-limbed, minimal plant, intensely vertical, with narrow leaves (up to five) held alternately up the wiry, mottled stem. At the top, a leaf arches out over the flowers like a narrow horn. The bells (one to three) hang down, long and narrow, so that it is difficult to see inside. Outside the petals are striped in yellowish green and murky purple. If you peer inside the bell, you see the same colours, but the yellow becomes a more pronounced stripe. Introduced in 1884 and named after Henry John Elwes of Colesbourne, Gloucestershire, UK, *F. elwesii* is similar to *F. assyriaca* and is an engaging thing, but easy to miss in a garden setting. Cultivation group 2 or 4. Easy. Plant 10cm (4in) deep and the same distance apart.

SEASON: Early March
HARDINESS: Fully hardy
HEIGHT: 30cm (12in)
HABITAT: South-western Turkey where it grows in pine scrub at 500–900m (1,650–3,000ft)

OPPOSITE *Fritillaria uva-vulpis* is a native of south-eastern Turkey and northern Iraq. Knowledge of its original habitat is the key to understanding what it needs in a garden: long, hot, dry summers.

Fritillaria imperialis
CROWN IMPERIAL

The fritillaries are a big gang, but this is by far the most dramatic of them – a sensation when it first appeared in Western gardens. Like the tulip, it came into Europe in the sixteenth century, in the first great influx of strange plants, many of them bulbs, ever to find their way over the water from Constantinople. *Fritillaria imperialis* was in Vienna by 1576, introduced by the been-everywhere, seen-everything plantsman Carolus Clusius. John Gerard had it in England soon after and in his *Herball* noted a characteristic of the crown imperial that struck all who saw it in flower for the first time – the terracotta bells (up to six of them) hanging down from the stem under their strange topknot of green leaves. 'In the bottom of each of these bels', wrote Gerard, 'there is placed six drops of most cleare shining sweet water, in taste like sugar, resembling in shew faire orient pearles: the which drops if you take away, there do immediately appeare the like, notwithstanding if they may be suffered to stand still in the floure according to his owne nature, they will never fall away, no not if you strike the plant until it be broken.'

Some people object to the foxy smell of crown imperials, most apparent when the plant first pushes through the ground in spring, but that is a spurious reason to exile it from a garden. Indeed, John Parkinson, author of *Paradisus* (1629), wondered if 'the strong scent… might be applied to good purpose'. What could he have had in mind? The crown imperial's heroic moment actually came in the Second World War when vast numbers of bulbs were gathered from the Fens and sent to Addenbrooke's Hospital in Cambridge. Here surgeons used a paste made from the bulbs in their earliest attempts to graft new skin on the wounds of badly burned pilots.

The bulbs are huge (up to 13cm/5in across). Plant them as soon as you can in late summer or early autumn, setting them in rich, well-manured soil that is alkaline rather than acid. If you set each bulb on its side, there is less chance of damp seeping down through the open centre and rotting the heart. Use grit, too, if your soil is heavy. The bulb can rest on a bed of grit with more added as a counterpane over the top before topping off with soil. Shallow planting is the most common reason for crown imperials refusing to flower. Mulch them every year with mushroom compost or some other treat rich in humus. They will lap up liquid feeds too. They do not like being disturbed and take a while to settle into a garden. But if they do, they will in time fatten into imposing clumps. Then you may have to split them, a great token of success, but not something to undertake lightly. If you must split, do it as soon as the plants have finished flowering. Replant in fresh soil in a new position. Cultivation Group 1. Easy. Plant 30cm (12in) deep and the same distance apart.

SEASON: April

HARDINESS: Fully hardy

HEIGHT: 60–90cm (24–36in)

HABITAT: Eastern and south-eastern Turkey, northern and western Iran, north-west Iraq, Afghanistan, Pakistan and Kashmir where it grows in scrub and among rocks at 700–2,200m (2,300–7,225ft)

Fritillaria imperialis 'William Rex'

The fat stems are stained bronze at the base and also under the head of flowers. These are a rich, intense reddish orange, darker at the top where they join their stalks. The bells hang down, each petal veined inside with a darker colour, which, close up, adds a great deal to their allure. In the centre are powdery cream stamens, the style hanging lower and paler. 'William Rex' is a strong plant, dramatic in flower with its shiny green foliage and topknot, both of which catch and reflect the light. It has been known in gardens since 1746 and looks wonderful with *Euphorbia characias* subsp. *wulfenii* or standing behind a strong tulip such as 'Prinses Irene'. Set the bulbs in rich, loamy soil and give them an annual feed of a fertilizer rich in potash (tomato food is ideal). They appreciate a dry rest in summer. Cultivation Group 1. Easy. Plant 30cm (12in) deep and the same distance apart.

SEASON: Early April
HARDINESS: Fully hardy
HEIGHT: 60–90cm (24–36in)

Fritillaria imperialis 'Maxima Lutea' ♚

Yellow forms of crown imperial have been known in gardens since 1665, but they do not seem to be as common in the wild. Vast snouts push through the ground in spring and unfurl in fat, fleshy stems with whorls of shiny, pale green leaves. This is a fine selection with big, yellow bells up to 6cm (2¼in) long and 5cm (2in) wide. Unfortunately the colour fades as the bells age. Let 'Maxima Lutea' rise from a carpet of mahogany-coloured wallflowers or, for a stronger contrast, interplant them with the dark double tulip 'Black Hero'. Cultivation Group 1. Easy. Plant 30cm (12in) deep and the same distance apart.

SEASON: Early April
HARDINESS: Fully hardy
HEIGHT: 75–90cm (30–36in)

NEXT PAGE Less than half the height of *Fritillaria uva-vulpis*, *F. acmopetala* has gorgeous bell flowers of the smudgy greenish-brown so typical of this tribe.

Fritillaria meleagris
SNAKE'S HEAD FRITILLARY

An enchanting plant with wide, chunky, square-shouldered bells, just one on each stem, as broad as they are long. The petals, a subdued purple (occasionally white) are chequered over with darker and lighter colour to make tiny squares all over the surface. John Gerard called *F. meleagris* the Ginnie Hen flower, because of its appearance 'checquered most strangely: wherein Nature, or rather the Creator of all things, hath kept a very wonderfull order, surpassing (as in all other things) the curiosest painting that Art can set downe'. He thought it had been brought into England from Orleans by a French apothecary, Noel Caperon, killed in the Massacre of St Bartholomew in 1572, but it is now considered an English native, a rare one, well established in a few sites such as the meadows of Magdalen College, Oxford and also near Cricklade, Gloucestershire. *Fritillaria meleagris* var. *unicolor* subvar. *alba* (what a ridiculously overcomplicated name) is a fine white selection of the snake's head fritillary, particularly effective in grass as the pale colour shows up more clearly than the purple. *Fritillaria meleagris* likes damp, heavyish soil and is used to growing in grass, but if you want to establish it in a meadow-like situation it may be better to start the bulbs off in pots, say five to a 10cm (4in) pot. Plant the potfuls, disturbing the roots as little as possible, when the leaves show above the compost in early spring. Do not be tempted to mow before early autumn as the plants must be allowed to die down naturally. After that, cut the grass a few more times so the turf is low and tight when the bulbs come through in spring. Cultivation Group 1 or 3. Easy. Plant 10cm (4in) deep and the same distance apart.

SEASON: April

HARDINESS: Fully hardy

HEIGHT: 30cm (12in)

HABITAT: Europe (southern England to the northern Balkans and western Russia). Naturalized in Scandinavia

Fritillaria michailovskyi ♀

A showier plant than *F. assyriaca* but similar in height and foliage with bigger, brighter and more telling flowers. The narrow stem leaves, greyish green, get smaller and thinner as they rise. Of the four bell flowers, the bottom two are held together on a stem, the others as singles, but all gather in a graduated clump at the top of the stem. They are bright purplish brown, 2cm (¾in) long, with a broad mustard-yellow band round the bottom of the petals. The inside is a handsome, shiny mustard-yellow, but given the way the bells hang you have to lift them up to admire it. *Fritillaria michailovskyi* was first collected near Kars by S J Michailovsky in 1904, but was lost in cultivation until it was reintroduced in 1965 by the brilliant Brian Mathew, whose wife Margaret found it growing in the Sarikamis Pass in north-eastern Turkey. Cultivation Group 2 or 4. Easy. If you are growing these bulbs in open ground plant them 10–15cm (4–6in) deep and 15cm (6in) apart.

SEASON: Late March
HARDINESS: Fully hardy
HEIGHT: 25cm (10in)
HABITAT: North-eastern Turkey from Erzurum to Kars where it grows on scree and sub-alpine meadows up to 1,800m (6,000ft)

Fritillaria pallidiflora ♀

The leaves are relatively wide, glaucous grey-green, exactly the right colour to set off the chunky, wide bells which are palest lemon-yellow, almost green, quietly luminous. Typically there are four squareish bells on a stem (though there can be more), each about 4cm (1½in) long and 3cm (1in) wide, generally with a small topknot of greenery arching over them. At the very centre of each flower is an intriguing, small, dark blotch. Stamens and stigma are equally pale and ethereal. *Fritillaria pallidiflora* was introduced into cultivation by Eduard von Regel, president of the Russian Horticultural Society, and needs a rich but well-drained soil, a little shade and shelter from wind. Cultivation Group 1 or 3. Easy. Plant 10cm (4in) deep and the same distance apart.

SEASON: April
HARDINESS: Fully hardy
HEIGHT: 40cm (16in)
HABITAT: Central Asia, especially in mountainous areas such as the Tien Shan, the Ala Tau and the Russian-Chinese border where it flowers on damp, sub-alpine slopes up to 3,000m (10,000ft)

Fritillaria persica 'Adiyaman' ♀

Fritillaria persica is a tall fritillary, widespread in southern Turkey, Syria, Lebanon, Israel, Jordan, Iraq and western Iran where it grows among rocks in scrub and on the edges of cornfields up to 2,500m (8,250ft). 'Adiyaman' is a selected form named after the Turkish town where it was first found, and as a garden plant it is better in every way than the ordinary species. The handsome, twisted leaves whirl ghostly grey round the fat stems, the purple bells are bigger, darker, and more closely gathered on the flowering spike at the top of the stem. There may be up to 30 flowers on a 25cm (10in) spike, each individual flower a neat, little cone of purple so dark it is almost black, bloomed like a grape. The cones, narrow at first, open out to reveal creamy stamens inside. This is a wonderful plant, known to John Gerard (the species, rather than 'Adiyaman') as the Persian lily. In his *Herball* of 1597 he described its 'little bels, of an overworn purple colour, hanging down their heads, every one having his own foot-stalke of two inches long, as also his pestell or clapper from the middle part of the floure'. Thanks to the 'industrie of Travellers', he said the flower was well known in London gardens. *Fritillaria persica* comes into growth sooner than you expect. By early February there are huge, fat fists of glaucous foliage pushing into the foul weather this month so often produces. Although hardy, plants may need protecting from frost; they will probably do best in a sunny border with some shelter at their backs. Be prepared to stake them if necessary. The bulbs are big, egg-shaped things, up to 12cm (5in) long. Cultivation Group 1. Easy. Plant 25–30cm (10–12in) deep and 15cm (6in) apart.

SEASON: March

HARDINESS: Fully hardy

HEIGHT: 65cm (26in)

Fritillaria pontica ♀

This is a much chunkier plant than
F. elwesii with fat stems, stained purple
at the base and broad, glaucous leaves,
quite thickly textured. Typically, each
stem carries three bells (3cm/1in across)
in a green that is slightly yellower than
that of the leaves, but of the same matt
texture. Outside, the bells are lightly
flushed with reddish brown. The inside,
as so often with fritillaries, is much more
highly polished. At the base of the petals
are six dark brown spots, very neat and
correct. The flowers droop, with the last
leaves clustered over them like little
umbrellas. Introduced in 1826, you could
never call *F. pontica* showy, but it is
deeply intriguing and will cope with the
hurly-burly of a border. Cultivation
Group 1 or 2. Easy. Plant 10cm (4in)
deep and the same distance apart.

SEASON: Late April
HARDINESS: Fully hardy
HEIGHT: 25–30cm (10–12in)
HABITAT: Albania, Bulgaria, Kosovo,
Macedonia, northern Greece and
north-western Turkey where it grows
in scrub and on wooded hillsides up
to 2,100m (7,000ft)

Fritillaria pyrenaica ♀

The bells are chequered, in the manner
of the snake's head fritillary, but the base
colour is yellow, overlaid with purple.
The bell (usually one, very occasionally
three to a stem) flips out at the base
showing off the highly polished, yellow
interior. *Fritillaria pyrenaica* is easy going
enough to risk in a border. In the wild,
it grows in alpine meadows, so you
could also try it in grass, but it must be
fine turf, not coarse. If you can grow
F. meleagris then you will most likely
succeed with this close relative.
Cultivation Group 1. Easy. Plant 10cm
(4in) deep and the same distance apart.

SEASON: April
HARDINESS: Fully hardy
HEIGHT: 30–45cm (12–18in)
HABITAT: Pyrenees of southern France
and north-western Spain in sub-alpine
meadows up to 2,000m (6,500ft)

Fritillaria raddeana

In form, this is rather like crown imperial, with the bell flowers (up to ten of them) gathered together at the top of the stem surmounted by a topknot of narrow, green leaves. But this plant is smaller and the bells are the palest lemon-yellow. Inside each one, the stamens, unequal in length, clasp the stigma which divides into three elegant curls. The foliage whirling around the stem under the beautiful bell flowers is bright glossy green. *Fritillaria raddeana* was first found by Dr Radde in 1886 and bears his name, but most of the bulbs that are now available come from the few collected in the 1960s by Rear Admiral Paul Furse and his wife, Polly, in the Golestān forest, Iran. Give *F. raddeana* a favoured, free-draining site in good soil and full sun. It comes into growth early, the flowers opening when the fat spike is scarcely 25cm (10in) high. Guard it against slugs. Bulbs are best bought damp-packed as they hate to dry out. Cultivation Group 1 or 3. Easy. Plant 10cm (4in) deep and the same distance apart.

SEASON: Late February–March
HARDINESS: Fully hardy
HEIGHT: 60cm (24in)
HABITAT: North-eastern Iran and Turkmenistan especially the Elburz mountains and the Kopet Dag where it grows in scrub and rocky places up to 600m (2,000ft) often in the shade cast by trees

SEASON: Early April
HARDINESS: Fully hardy
HEIGHT: 30–45cm (12–18in)
HABITAT: South-eastern Turkey, northern Iraq and western Iran where it grows in moist cornfields and hay meadows at 900–1,800m (3,000–6,000ft)

Fritillaria uva-vulpis

This fine species was introduced into cultivation from Iran in the 1960s by Rear Admiral Paul Furse and his wife, Polly, and, though not as showy as *F. michailovskyi*, is not difficult to establish. The two are similar in height. *Fritillaria uva-vulpis* has a single flowering stem that emerges from a clump of short, shiny, bright green leaves, spear-shaped and only 6cm (2¼in) tall. There are six or eight of them round each flowering stem. The drooping flowers are usually held singly, narrower in outline than *F. michailovskyi* though the same length and pinched at the mouth. The colour is a dark purplish brown, with a bloom that is almost pewter; around the edge of each flower is a narrow rim of mustard-yellow. In a garden setting, the flowers are recessive. They do not need bossily bright neighbours. Or any neighbours at all, except more of their own kind. In cultivation, *F. uva-vulpis* (which was first described by Martyn Rix in 1974) is often muddled with *F. assyriaca*. Like so many fritillaries, it is intriguing, rather than showy, but will only be happy outside in areas where the summers are hot and dry. It does well when potted up and kept in a cold frame, but it needs good compost and frequent repotting. If bulbs do not get enough to eat, they do not get fat enough to flower. They produce plenty of offsets though, which need to be grown on for a few years before they reach flowering size. Cultivation Group 2 or 4. Easy. Plant 10cm (4in) deep and the same distance apart.

Gagea (Liliaceae)

Gagea lutea

A bulb for gardeners who have got everything else and, like stamp collectors, feel they want to complete the spring set. One broad leaf accompanies each stem of small, starry, greenish yellow flowers, up to seven of them in a little umbel. They are scarcely show-stoppers. So was Sir Thomas Gage, an eighteenth-century botanizing baronet of Hengrave Hall in Suffolk, UK, pleased when the gagea was named after him or did he secretly wish he could have been a snowdrop instead? *Gagea lutea* is suitable for a woodland garden, where it can grow under trees as it does in the wild. Plant the bulbs 5cm (2in) deep and the same distance apart.

SEASON: March–April
HARDINESS: Fully hardy
HEIGHT: 8–10cm (3½– 4in)
HABITAT: Widespread in Europe where it grows in woods and meadows

Galanthus (Amaryllidaceae)

Snowdrops attract a particularly fanatical band of admirers, but you need special qualities to be a snowdrop buff: a circulation system of cast iron and brilliant eyesight. To most of the world, a snowdrop is a snowdrop, single or double. But since the 1990s, new varieties have been appearing faster than rabbits out of a magician's hat. Though there are only 18 species, you can now get hold of at least 150 different kinds, including one called 'Nothing Special'. Quite. When all is said and done, snowdrops have a limited repertoire of tricks.

ABOVE Henry John Elwes (1846–1922) sportsman, naturalist and plantsman, who made a huge collection of snowdrops at his home, Colesbourne in Gloucestershire.

Though aconites regularly beat snowdrops for the title of first flower of the year, they have never acquired the same charisma as snowdrops, the Garboesque, I want to be alone quality that brings acolytes flocking in droves around them during late January and February. Invitations to select snowdrop parties are 'to die for' as my American friend says, but you are not likely to be asked unless you can recognize 'John Gray' at 30 paces.

Actually, 'John Gray' would be kid's stuff to real galanthophiles. They could pick it out at 60, let alone 30 paces AND tell you the difference between this and 'Mighty Atom', another snowdrop that came originally from John Gray's Benhall garden in the UK. You have to get used to the pitying looks that come your way from true snowdrop fanatics. 'But surely you grow *rizehensis*?' they will say, and if you don't, you get The Look (Bluffer's Guide: *G. rizehensis* is an insignificant, little snowdrop like *G. nivalis* shrunk in the wash, with leaves of dull, dark green).

To the uninitiated, the differences between the various kinds are often minimal. You soon learn, however, that the presence or absence of green markings is a critical indicator. 'Pusey Green Tip' got its name because the three outer petals are tipped with green; usually they are white. The inner segments of single snowdrops join together to make a frilly little cup and markings on these are much more difficult to distinguish. And surely there are better times of the year to be on your hands and knees counting green spots? Other differences are more obvious. Some flowers have a distinctly yellow look about them. Your first thought might be that these are rather sad, sick creatures, suffering perhaps from a chlorotic overdose of lime. Not at all. The yellowish ones, such as 'Lady Elphinstone' and *G. nivalis* Sandersonii Group turn out to be the most highly prized of all.

OPPOSITE Snowdrops (*Galanthus nivalis*) growing in woodland at Burford Priory, Oxfordshire.

One of the best things about snowdrops – the name comes from the greek *gala* (milk) combined with *anthos* (flower) – is that they come when they are most needed. There is nothing more cheering, when a searing north-easterly wind is cutting you in half, than seeing a snowdrop such as 'Anglesey Abbey', named after the fine Cambridgeshire garden where it was first found, bravely hanging on to its hat in the teeth of the gale. Collectors love to collect, but for me snowdrops are flowers best seen *en masse* not loitering palely on their own with labels like tombstones stuck beside their solitary stems. Plant the easy ones first and plant lots of the same kind together. Try them with the dark, leathery foliage of *Euphorbia amygdaloides* var. *robbiae* or let them share a bed with the autumn-flowering cyclamen, *C. hederifolium*. The marbled leaves of the cyclamen provide a cool foil for the piercingly white flowers of the snowdrop. All of them are scented, some more strongly than others. The best way to pick up the smell is to bring them inside. The taller types such as 'Atkinsii' are lovely bunched in posies, with a few dark ivy leaves added round the outside of the bunch. Outside, individual flowers will last for at least a month, inside of course, rather less.

ABOVE *Galanthus* 'Magnet', bred by James Allen of Shepton Mallet, Somerset, has a particularly elegant habit, the flower on its long, thin stem bending over in a graceful curve.

They are tougher than they look. In the shoots that push out from the underground bulb the outer leaf hoods over the inner one to make an astonishingly hard tip, almost like a drill bit, which is pushed up above the soil as the cells under them fill with water pumped up by the roots. While looking down at 'Magnet' – already recognized as a star at the time of the first Snowdrop Conference held in 1891 – it is bizarre to think of it as a piece of hydraulic engineering. But that is what it is.

CULTIVATION

Snowdrops, at least the ordinary kinds, are adaptable creatures. They will grow in shade as well as sun. They will push their way through thick ground-covering mats of ivy and grow in soil under trees, though they will do better there if you give them a top-dressing of leaf mould or compost every autumn. They increase quite rapidly by producing bulb offsets underground and by seed which is spread about by ants. Remember though that seedlings will not necessarily be the same as their parents, particularly if you are growing different named varieties close together. The ideal regime is a cool, moist growing period in spring, followed by a dryer summer dormancy, though bulbs should never be allowed to dry out completely. An alkaline soil is better than an acid one, and a cool root run is better than one that is baked dry. Though they may hang on in poor soils, snowdrops will naturally do much better in deep, rich ones, and they positively thrive where soil is on the heavy side.

The traditional advice is to establish snowdrops 'in the green'. This means getting hold of them and planting them just after they have finished flowering, while there are still green leaves growing from the bulb. Some suppliers now send bulbs out in late summer, fresh dug and damp-packed, but before they have started to root; connoisseurs think that this is an even better time to move them. Unfortunately there are not many nurserymen who want to go to this trouble as snowdrops are so much more difficult to locate and dig up then. The worst thing to do is to buy dry bulbs, which have been hanging around for too long in a shop or garden centre. Snowdrops hate drying out, and very few of these poor, shrivelled lumps are ever likely to grow. But where they are happy, they clump up fast and you will need to divide them, probably every three years.

For naturalizing in grass or under trees, it is perhaps best to stick to the ordinary single and double kinds of *G. nivalis*. Set small clumps of bulbs together, with a pinch of bonemeal under them for encouragement. With a trowel or a bulb planter, take out a plug of turf, put the bulbs in (in leaf) and then fill the hole with soil sifted from the compost heap. This is easier than trying to press the turf plug back into the hole without breaking the leaves of the snowdrop in the process. If you've got spare labour to call on, you can plant bulbs as singletons. Do not let the roots dry out. Keep some damp sacking folded over the bulbs while they are out of the ground. And for yourself, get some warm underwear, so that when your snowdrops flower you can enjoy them in comfort.

Galanthus 'Atkinsii' ♛

A very vigorous, early snowdrop, the foliage glaucous like that of *G. nivalis*, but bigger and broader. This was the Edwardian gardener E A Bowles's favourite snowdrop and it is mine too: it comes very early and builds up into lavish displays with very little effort. The flowers are enormous, at least 5cm (2in) across, with outer petals held almost horizontal. Inside, the bell is white, with a broad ^ shape marked in green. Odd petals fly away occasionally to break the symmetry, and in some seasons flowers carry four outer petals instead of three. Use 'Atkinsii' with dark hellebores or among the glorious marbled leaves of *Arum italicum* 'Pictum' which is at its best at this time of the year. 'Atkinsii' is thought to be a cross between *G. nivalis* and *G. plicatus* and was named by the great snowdrop grower James Allen of Shepton Mallet, Somerset, UK, after another snowdrop maniac, James Atkins of Painswick in Gloucestershire, UK, who had got it from a friend in the 1860s. The flower hangs from an unusually short stalk. Plant 7–10cm (2½–4in) deep and the same distance apart.

SEASON: Early January–February
HARDINESS: Fully hardy
HEIGHT: 26cm (10½in)

Galanthus elwesii ♀

Named after Henry John Elwes – big game hunter, naturalist, arboriculturist, lily-fancier, soldier, ornithologist, traveller, botanist – who was born at Colesbourne, Gloucestershire, UK, in 1846. Was there anything he could not do, you may ask? Probably not. Except stay at home. In the years between his leaving school and his death in 1922 Henry Elwes scarcely spent a year at a time in Gloucestershire. Yet he managed to plant an extraordinary arboretum there and build up one of the greatest collections of bulbs in the world. His snowdrop, like the man himself, is bigger and bolder than the rest. In 1874, Henry Elwes had been in Anatolia, collecting plants in Smyrna, Sámos and Kos – places then of more interest to archaeologists than plantsmen. On the way home, all his bulbs were stolen, but a Greek friend he had made in Smyrna later sent him a replacement parcel of bulbs, which included the famous snowdrop. You are most likely to recognize G. *elwesii* by its leaves which are very broad and very grey. It is also tall, twice the height of G. *nivalis*. It has two green blotches on the white inner petals, one above the other but sometimes they join together so that the entire inner petal appears green. Use it to leaven the beefy foliage of colchicums, clumps of which begin to emerge towards the end of the snowdrop season. Plant 10cm (4in) deep and the same distance apart.

SEASON: February–March
HARDINESS: Fully hardy
HEIGHT: 12–22cm (5–9in)
HABITAT: Macedonia, Bulgaria, north-eastern Greece, southern Ukraine and Turkey where it grows in woods and scrub at 800–1,000m (2,600–3,300ft)

Galanthus 'Galatea'

An astoundingly lovely snowdrop, better (in my form at least) than the very similar 'Magnet' and just as big. Like 'Magnet', 'Galatea' was raised by the snowdrop grower James Allen of Shepton Mallet some time before 1890. The foliage is soft grey-green and the flowers dangle on unusually long, thread-like stalks, crooked at a right angle. The livery is the usual one: plain white outer petals and a small, three-petal cup inside with the standard ^ markings in green, not quite such a yellowish green as 'Atkinsii'. 'Galatea' is at its best as 'Atkinsii' is beginning to go over. It is a showy snowdrop and increases well. Try spreading it under the bare, arched stems of *Rubus* 'Benenden'. Plant 10cm (4in) deep and the same distance apart.

SEASON: Late January
HARDINESS: Fully hardy
HEIGHT: 25cm (10in)

Galanthus 'Hill Poë'

The outer petals stretch over the mass of inner ones like an overstuffed cushion. The flower is a cheerful blob-double, with a translucent ring at the point where the petals join the ovary. It is neater than many doubles, with perhaps a couple of dozen inner petals crammed between the longer outer ones, so the inside is a muddle of green and white, with a bunch of white petals at the centre slightly longer than the rest. There are usually five outer petals, though occasional flowers have six of reasonably equal size and shape. When the flowers come out, the leaves, narrow and grey, are still short. First found early in the twentieth century by James Hill Poë at Riverston, Ireland where it was growing under a walnut tree by the dining room window. Mine came from a kind Dorset neighbour, the late John Poë. Use 'Hill Poë' in the bare spaces among deciduous ferns such as *Dryopteris affinis* 'Cristata' or *Polystichum setiferum* 'Divisilobum Densum'. You will, of course, have remembered to cut down the old, dead fronds so the snowdrops are not smothered as they emerge. Plant 10cm (4in) deep and the same distance apart.

SEASON: Mid February
HARDINESS: Fully hardy
HEIGHT: 20cm (8in)

Galanthus 'Magnet' ♀

'Magnet' has a very elegant habit: the flower is so big it pulls over the top of the stem into a graceful curve, even before it has freed the long, thread-like flower stalk – its trademark – that emerges from the greenish white sheath at the top of the stem. This is a beautifully balanced snowdrop, the three outer petals more than 3cm (1in) long, and the cup white (green inside) with a very strong ^ mark in green at the bottom of the inner petals. The foliage is not particularly broad, a soft greenish grey, but nowhere near as glaucous as *G. elwesii*. Like so many good snowdrops, 'Magnet' was raised before 1894 by James Allen of Shepton Mallet, Somerset, UK. Spread it under the beautiful, purple-flowered *Daphne mezereum*. Plant 10cm (4in) deep and the same distance apart.

SEASON: Late January
HARDINESS: Fully hardy
HEIGHT: 20cm (8in)

Galanthus nivalis ♀

The bashful, drooping head is part of the charm of a snowdrop. The purity appeals too, a clear, clean combination of green and white. In *G. nivalis*, the three outer petals are pure white and twice as long as the three inner ones which overlap each other to make a little cup. At the bottom of each of these inner petals is a ^ shape in green, and the same green is striped over the inside of the cup, leaving a narrow, white margin round the edges. *Galanthus nivalis* made itself so at home in western Europe that we tend to think of it as a native, but the Dutch artist Crispin de Passe, who in 1614 drew the pictures for the first ever nursery catalogue, *Hortus Floridus*, said that: 'This plant abounds in Italy, but is not to be found here, except in the

gardens of the curious.' It is best seen in large spreads. Get into the habit of digging up at least one clump every year after flowering and spreading the bulbs about: under dogwoods, under hydrangeas, under hedges, among hostas and rodgersias, whose shoots are not showing at all at this bare time of year. Snowdrops can give this spare ground a new lease of life. But be lavish. Plant 10cm (4in) deep and the same distance apart.

SEASON: January–February
HARDINESS: Fully hardy
HEIGHT: 10cm (4in)
HABITAT: Europe (Pyrenees to the Ukraine); naturalized in Britain, The Netherlands, Belgium, Scandinavia and USA where it grows in woods and scrub at 300–600m (1,000–2,000ft)

Galanthus nivalis 'Anglesey Abbey'

Unlike the majority of snowdrops, which have leaves of a bluish grey, 'Anglesey Abbey' flowers among clumps of bright green foliage, which has the effect of making the flowers seem even more than usually pure. They are about the same length and width as those of *G. nivalis*, a perfect foil for the flowers, which are long, compact and exceptionally pure with plain white exterior petals. The interior bell is often all white too, with just the faintest hair lines of green on the inner surface. Some flowers have a misshapen ^ notch of green on the outside of the bell. 'Anglesey Abbey' is named after the Cambridgeshire garden where it was first discovered. Spread it under the fine *Mahonia × media* 'Lionel Fortescue'. Plant 10cm (4in) deep and the same distance apart.

SEASON: Early February
HARDINESS: Fully hardy
HEIGHT: 15cm (6in)

Galanthus nivalis 'Flore Pleno' ♔

The flowers are fat and full, so do not hang as gracefully as the single form. But if you are wanting to make a big splash fast, these are the snowdrops to use. The flowers vary a good deal with anything from three to six outer petals bulging over the muddled inside. This is usually greenish whitish, flecked with the orange-yellow dots of the stamens. Use 'Flore Pleno' among hart's tongue ferns, the old foliage cleared away, the new fronds crouching in furry humps, ready to uncurl. Plant 10cm (4in) deep and the same distance apart.

SEASON: Early February
HARDINESS: Fully hardy
HEIGHT: 10cm (4in)

Galanthus nivalis 'Viridapice'

Introduced into cultivation by the Dutch nurserymen Van Tubergen of Haarlem, where it was found as a chance seedling in the nursery. Both outer and inner white petals are tipped with green. Though not elegant, 'Viridapice' is vigorous and clumps up quickly. Plant 10cm (4in) deep and the same distance apart.

SEASON: Early February
HARDINESS: Fully hardy
HEIGHT: 10cm (4in)

Galanthus plicatus ♀

A splendidly robust snowdrop with leaves that droop down slightly at the edges (a good, quick recognition tag for a bluffer). The inside petals of the elegant, white bells are marked on the tips with green. It increases well from offsets and is also later than most other snowdrops – a useful attribute if you want to extend the snowdrop season. Though *G. plicatus* has been known in gardens since the sixteenth century, the best form, called 'Warham', was brought back from the Crimea in 1855 by a Captain Adlington who was fighting in the war there. Lovely among ferns such as *Dryopteris affinis* 'Crispa Gracilis' or *D. cycadina*. Plant bulbs 10cm (4in) deep and the same distance apart.

SEASON: March

HARDINESS: Fully hardy

HEIGHT: 20cm (8in)

HABITAT: Crimea, Romania and north-western Turkey in woods at 1,000–1,300m (3,300–4,250ft)

Galanthus reginae-olgae

A surprising autumn arrival, given the snowdrop's image as the harbinger of spring. The bright green stem (paler towards the base) comes through the ground naked of leaf, like so many autumn-flowering bulbs (crocus, colchicum etc.). The flower – which in size and general appearance is very like the common spring snowdrop (*G. nivalis*) – hangs on a short stalk, with three outer petals of pure white and green ^ shapes on the inner petals. The leaves, when they come through, have a distinctive, silvery stripe down the centre, like a crocus leaf. The flower scent of *G. reginae-olgae* is strong and musky, powerful for so small a flower, but with too much of old sock about it to be entirely pleasing. This species was first collected on Mount Taygetus in the Greek Peloponnese and in 1876 was named after Queen Olga of Greece, the Duke of Edinburgh's grandmother. Give it a warmish, sunny site. Plant bulbs 10cm (4in) deep and the same distance apart.

SEASON: Late October

HARDINESS: Frost hardy

HEIGHT: 8cm (3½in)

HABITAT: South and north-west Greece, Corfu and Sicily where it grows in dryish woodland at 600–1,000m (2,000–3,300ft)

Galanthus 'S Arnott' ♀

In style 'S Arnott' is like *G. nivalis* but it is twice the size with a showy, dangling, single flower. It is a deliciously juicy thing, named after a Scottish snowdrop fancier, Sam Arnott, who was born in Dumfries in 1852. He worked in the family's bakery business until ill health forced a move to Carsethorn, a seaside town on the Solway Firth. Here he not only made a notable garden but also founded a library, a Sunday school and started a local regatta. Snowdrops (and colchicums) were Sam Arnott's specialities. He grew both in his Scottish garden and in 1904 published a pamphlet on snowdrops, 'The Fair Maids of February'. 'S Arnott' came from his own garden, and he distributed it to several snowdrop fanciers, including Henry Elwes at Colesbourne. 'S Arnott' recently came top of a poll to choose the best-ever snowdrop, and fortunately it is not the slightest bit difficult to grow. It has a wonderful scent, most pronounced when you pick a posy of flowers and bring them into the warm. Plant 10cm (4in) deep and the same distance apart.

SEASON: February
HARDINESS: Fully hardy
HEIGHT: 20cm (8in)

Galanthus woronowii ♀

The foliage is the first clue to identifying *G. woronowii*: the leaves are broad (2cm/¾in) and glossy green. The flower is nowhere near the size of 'Atkinsii' or 'Galatea', and it bears petals that are quite narrow and finely textured, thin enough for you to see the orange stigmas glowing through the opaque white at the top of the flower. The cup inside is rather short, less than half the length of the three outer petals. The ^ marks on the cup are a paler, more yellowish green than those on 'Galatea'. *Galanthus woronowii* is naturalized in our Dorset valley where it grows on greensand in quite deep shade. Plant 10cm (4in) deep and 10cm (4in) apart.

SEASON: Early February
HARDINESS: Fully hardy
HEIGHT: 23cm (9in)
HABITAT: Southern Russia, Georgia, Armenia, Azerbaijan and north-eastern Turkey where it grows in woods and scree at 70–1,400m (200–4,600ft)

Galtonia (Hyacinthaceae)

This genus gets its name from Francis Galton, one of the many colonizing Brits who in the nineteenth century wandered around South Africa enjoying the extraordinary plants of this well-endowed land. In gardens, galtonias must have fertile, well-drained soil that does not dry out. In really cold areas, *G. viridiflora* may need some protection in winter. If, each autumn, you mulch thickly with mushroom compost, you provide food, blotting paper and protection all at the same time. Galtonias need plenty to drink when they are in growth. Although they are quite imposing plants, you need at least five in a group to make an impact in a mixed border. In cold areas, you can start the bulbs into growth in pots and plant them out in late spring when the weather warms up. Watch out for slugs which seem able to consume prodigious amounts of new growth.

ABOVE *Galtonia candicans* is an unexpected treat in late July, when it erupts into the scene like a star expected in spring but mysteriously held up along the way.

Galtonia candicans ♔

Tall, strong, juicy, green stems rear up in late summer with 30 or more white, waxy bells packed into a head. Each bell emerges from a papery sheath and as they come out, from the bottom up, the spike gets longer. Just seven or eight flowers are out at the same time, so the spike lasts a long time. The top buds stand upright, but as they prepare to flower they hang down on arched, green stems. The only colour comes from the anthers: lime-green at first, dark blackish green later. Introduced in the 1860s, *G. candicans* is elegant among eryngium, eucomis and white bleeding heart (*Dicentra spectabilis* 'Alba') which will disguise the fact that the galtonia's foliage gets ravaged by slugs and is beginning to turn yellow by the time the flowers come out. Plant the bulbs 15cm (6in) deep and 10cm (4in) apart.

SEASON: Late July
HARDINESS: Fully hardy
HEIGHT: 1.15m (3¾ft)
HABITAT: South Africa (Limpopo, Mpumalanga, Free State, KwaZulu-Natal, Eastern Cape) and Lesotho where it grows in sandy soils at 1,500–2,000m (5,000–6,500ft)

Galtonia viridiflora

In terms of form, this is very similar to the more common *G. candicans* but the bells are very pale, icy green. The flowers of *G. viridiflora* are extraordinarily elegant, but the leaves are unfortunately twice as wide as those of *G. candicans*, the slug holes consequently twice as obvious. Disguise them with mounds of blue-flowered *Geranium* Rozanne. Plant the bulbs 15cm (6in) deep and 10cm (4in) apart.

SEASON: Late July
HARDINESS: Frost hardy
HEIGHT: 1m (3ft)
HABITAT: South Africa (Free State, Eastern Cape) and Lesotho where it grows in the Drakensberg mountains at around 2,500m (8,250ft)

Gladiolus (Iridaceae)

M odern gladioli belong with the diamanté specs and knockout handbag of Dame Edna Everage, Barry Humphries's *alter ego*. With their vast flowers and unyielding stems, they are more at home on the show bench or in a vase than in a garden. In the right setting, though, gladioli make dramatic cut flowers, suitably unreal for the make-believe world of the flower arrangers: 'Journey into Space', 'Nimbus Revisited'. For the longest display in a vase, cut the spikes as soon as the first buds are colouring up.

The gladioli listed below are all good garden plants: they will get on well with neighbours in a border or you can grow them in pots either outside or in a cool conservatory. Most are wild species, and all but one comes from South or eastern Africa. The others, in style, are close to the species, with flowers that can stand up to rain and which do not need to be lashed to a stake, as the show varieties do. If you want lots to cut (they do make very good, if stiff, cut flowers), line out corms in a kitchen plot or cutting garden. For the best results, you will have to buy fresh corms each year, but you can also lift the corms in late autumn, clean them off and store them in a frost-free place before planting the following spring.

In catalogues, you will find gladioli sorted into three main groups: in the Grandiflorus group are the show types; in the Nanus group are smaller hybrids that flower in early summer; and in the Primulinus group are hybrids mostly derived from *G. primulinus* (now known as *G. dalenii*), first found growing on a ledge doused by the spray of the great Victoria Falls.

CULTIVATION

Gladiolus communis subsp. *byzantinus* is hardy, so can be planted in autumn and left where it has been put. The South African species, together with the hybrids derived from them, are not and there are two ways you can deal with them. In mild areas, you can risk them outside – *G. cardinalis* for instance has flourished outside in my garden for many seasons. Plant in late April or early May in fertile, well-drained soil in full sun, setting the corms 10–15cm (4–6in) deep and 10cm (4in) apart. If the soil is heavy, add grit to improve drainage. When the spikes are about 15cm (6in) high, feed them with a fertilizer high in potash (tomato feed is ideal). In cold areas it may be safer to plant the corms in pots (five corms will fit comfortably in a 15cm/6in pot) and start them into growth in a greenhouse or cold frame, protected from the frost. Plant them out in May when they will already be well-established plants. Either way, gladioli should be in bloom three months after you have planted them. If you want to keep the corms, lift them when the foliage has died back in autumn. A new corm will have grown on top of the old one. Clear away the old leaves and snap the new corm away from the old one (which you can throw away). Store the new corms somewhere that is dry and free from frost until it is time to plant in the following spring.

Gladiolus cardinalis

Astonishing cardinal-red flowers, four
or five of them, come out in turn
(the lowest first) on a thin, wiry stem,
strong enough not to need staking.
The flowers (5cm/2in across) have
six (occasionally eight) petals, the
two uppermost all red, the lower
ones arranged in a fan of red, boldly
centred with white. On the outside,
white drifts up from the base to
splash over the backs of the petals.
If there are eight petals, there are
four stamens, just three if there are
six. At the beginning they are pale,
but gradually they acquire a mauve
flush. The style is airy, splitting into
three (or four) curled flourishes, like
the swoop of an italic script. The
foliage is sword-shaped, grey-green.
Gladiolus cardinalis contrasts well
with the lime-green flowers of
Euphorbia 'Copton Ash' and is equally
good in front of a dark-leaved
cimicifuga. Wherever you put it, it is
a thrilling plant, known in cultivation
since 1789. Set the corms 10–15cm
(4–6in) deep and 10cm (4in) apart.

SEASON: Mid July
HARDINESS: Half hardy
HEIGHT: 60cm (24in)
HABITAT: South Africa (Western Cape) where it lives
on damp ledges at the edge of waterfalls

Gladiolus 'Charm'

An enchanting gladiolus in the
Nanus group with slightly frilly, bright
pink flowers (4cm/1½in across) on
spikes 30cm (12in) long. Typically
four or five of the eight buds will be
open together. Use 'Charm' with the
smoky seedlings of a bronze fennel or
to fill up spaces where April tulips
have come and gone. Set the corms
10–15cm (4–6in) deep and 10cm
(4in) apart.

SEASON: Mid May
HARDINESS: Half hardy
HEIGHT: 70cm (28in)

OPPOSITE In the wild, *Gladiolus communis* subsp. *byzantinus* grows in
Spain, Sicily and north-west Africa, but it is surprisingly tolerant of cooler
climates. It grows here with *Allium cristophii*.

239

Gladiolus × colvillii 'The Bride' ♀

The × *colvillii* hybrids were raised from a cross between *G. cardinalis* and *G. tristis* and named after the plantsman James Colville, who in the 1820s had a nursery in Chelsea, UK, when Chelsea was a place for plants not expensive boutiques. 'The Bride' has small spikes of white flowers, from four to seven on a stem. Each is about 8cm (3½in) across, and the three lower petals have an indistinct, cool lemon stripe down the middle. Corms planted in October will flower in early June. However, 'The Bride' is not hardy, and in cold areas you may have to lift the corms and overwinter them before planting again the following spring; they will then flower in late July. This cultivar looks lovely in a pot, though you need to tidy up the leaves which at flowering time are beginning to wither. Unfortunately the flowers do not have such a swoony scent as their *G. tristis* parent. Set the corms 10–15cm (4–6in) deep and 10cm (4in) apart.

SEASON: Early June or late July
HARDINESS: Half hardy
HEIGHT: 65cm (26in)

Gladiolus communis subsp. *byzantinus* ♀

This, in essence, is like any other gladiolus, but it grows like an herbaceous plant, self-supporting and strongly upright in growth. It is surprisingly good in grass, where it can easily hold its own if it is planted out when in growth, rather than as a dry bulb. *Gladiolus communis* subsp. *byzantinus* is particularly pleasing in bud, when the flowerhead turns over in an elegant curve. On most gladioli, the flowers are produced on one side of the spike and all face the same way. This gladiolus, however, has flowers that are less blinkered, facing sideways as well as to the front. There may be up to 20 of them on a spike, each about 5cm (2in) wide. Use it as a prelude to phlox or set it beside the brilliant lime-green flowers of *Euphorbia palustris*. It also sits well with Mediterranean companions such as rosemary and grey-leaved cistus. Beware the pale imitation, *G. italicus*, in which the colour is a wishy washy pink, nowhere near as telling as the real, bright magenta thing. Set the corms 10–15cm (4–6in) deep and 10cm (4in) apart.

SEASON: Early June
HARDINESS: Fully hardy
HEIGHT: 60cm (24in)
HABITAT: Spain, north-west Africa and Sicily

Gladiolus murielae ♀
(*Acidanthera bicolor*)

Foliage and flower stems are roughly the same height, the stems thin and wiry, the leaves pleated longitudinally in the manner of *Crocosmia* 'Lucifer'. The flowers (up to eight on a stem) droop down slightly when open, which they do in succession, so G. *murielae* lasts a long time, but you never get one monumental blast of bloom. Each flower has a tube at least 7cm (2½in) long which emerges from a green sheath and flares into a white, six-petalled bloom with a deep maroon

blotch at the centre. It is gorgeously scented and excellent in pots to grow either outside or in the house. The purpose of the scent is to attract the hummingbird hawk moth which pollinates the flowers, but it does a good job in drawing in people too. In a border you might grow G. *murielae* among clumps of *Paeonia lactiflora* or use it between stands of grey-leaved *Rosa glauca*. It is not hardy, but in certain well-mulched places in my garden it survives the winter, though the flowers come into bloom a couple of weeks later than those from fresh corms planted the same season. It is a useful backup for a gardener. Plant up spare pots of G. *murielae* in late March or early April and use them to fill late-summer disaster areas (there always are some). If by any chance they are not needed, you can bring them inside. Unfortunately they are too tall for all but the grandest windowsills but can look wonderful on a low table. Set the corms 10–15cm (4–6in) deep and 10cm (4in) apart.

SEASON: Late August

HARDINESS: Half hardy

HEIGHT: 1m (3ft)

HABITAT: Eastern Africa from Ethiopia and Somalia to Tanzania and Malawi where it grows in grass and on damp cliffs at 1,200–2,500m (4,000–8,250ft)

Gladiolus 'Nymph'

This is one of the Nanus group, and it produces spikes of white flowers 8cm (3½in) across. The three lower petals look as though they have been kissed by Marilyn Monroe, a bright pink lipstick impression left neatly in the centre of each one. The spikes are about 25cm (10in) long and, typically, each will bear six flowers, of which four or five are likely to be out together. 'Nymph' is a wonderful gladiolus for cutting. If you hate raiding your borders, plant out some corms in a spare sunny place and raid that instead. Set the corms 10–15cm (4–6in) deep and 10cm (4in) apart.

SEASON: Early June

HARDINESS: Half hardy

HEIGHT: 45–50cm (18–20in)

Gladiolus papilio

A spindly, strange, waif-like gladiolus, first collected by a Mr Arnott near Colesberg in Natal and introduced to cultivation in 1866. The flowering stems are twice the height of the sword-like foliage, which is pale green and not markedly pleated as the leaves of *G. murielae* are. There are up to eight hooded flowers on a stem, all facing the same way, cream overlaid with dirty purple. The stamens are a surprisingly bright blue. It is not a showy species, as the cup-shaped flowers are narrow and do not open out much, but it is deeply intriguing. Inside, the flowers are a smoky pale mauve, with spoon-shaped blotches of pale acid-yellow on the two lower petals, frilled round with more mauve (mauve is the gift *G. papilio* passed on, via a complicated programme of cross-breeding, to the big show-bench gladioli). The stems squirm about like dancing snakes, and need staking. Although it has a wistful, not-long-for-this-world air about it, *G. papilio* is actually quite tough, spreading by underground runners to make a large clump. Most gladioli need sun but this one likes to be cool, and it must never be short of water. Set the corms 10–15cm (4–6in) deep and 10cm (4in) apart.

SEASON: Early August
HARDINESS: Frost hardy
HEIGHT: 90cm (36in)
HABITAT: South Africa (Limpopo, Mpumalanga) and Lesotho where it grows in damp, grassy places up to 1,600m (5,250ft)

Gladiolus tristis

This species was already being grown in the Chelsea Physic Garden, London by 1745 where it was much admired for its ivory, funnel-shaped flowers. There may be eight of them on a spike, each 5cm (2in) wide, streaked with yellow, and sometimes flushed or spotted with mauve. The leaves are very narrow, often twisting at the top. Choose a warm, sunny place to plant *G. tristis* where it can remain undisturbed. In cold areas, protect the plants if necessary with straw or bracken. It has the most wonderful scent, particularly in the evening and so is an ideal choice for a cool conservatory where you can grow the corms in pots and keep them inside. Flowers on cut spikes do not hold their scent half so long. Set the corms 10–15cm (4–6in) deep and 10cm (4in) apart.

SEASON: May
HARDINESS: Half hardy
HEIGHT: 50–100cm (20–39in)
HABITAT: South Africa (Western Cape) where it grows in damp, sandy places up to 1,800m (6,000ft)

Gloriosa (Colchicaceae)

Gloriosa superba ♈
GLORY LILY

Glossy leaves narrow into tendrils, which is how this plant hauls itself through a support, for its own stems are spindly and weak. The flowers are sensational with long, narrow, twisting petals sweeping back like a Turk's cap lily, equally long stamens dangling below. In the wild, the flowers may be red, purplish or yellow. 'Rothschildiana' (*above*) is a selected form introduced from Africa in 1904, with bright red flowers up to 10cm (4in) across, edged in an equally bright yellow. Commercially, glory lilies are much in demand as cut flowers, but so far my plant has produced only one bloom. To cut that would have been sacrilege. For most of us, this will be a plant for the greenhouse or conservatory. The tubers are generally available in spring rather than autumn. Plant in a loam-based compost mixed with grit (two parts compost to one part grit) setting the tuber 7–10cm (2½–4in) deep in a pot at least 20cm (8in) across. Water the tuber in and keep the pot in a place where the temperature does not drop below 10°C (50°F) – keep it slightly higher if you can afford the heating bill. Begin watering again when the plant comes into growth and make sure it has some kind of support. It has a lot to achieve in a relatively short time and is more likely to succeed if it gets a liquid feed every two weeks. Praise *G. superba* extravagantly while it is in bloom and then allow it to die back naturally so that it can have a dry rest period in winter.

SEASON: July–August

HARDINESS: Tender

HEIGHT: 2m (6½ft)

HABITAT: Africa and India where it grows in tropical forests, scrambling through other trees and shrubs

Habranthus (Amaryllidaceae)

Habranthus robustus ♔

RAIN LILY

The rain lilies were introduced to cultivation in the 1820s, and as their family name suggests look rather like amaryllis, or belladonna lilies, pushing through the ground on leafless stems to produce wide-mouthed, pale pink, trumpet flowers (6cm/2¼in across), just one to a stem. Of course, the colour is much more subtle than 'pale pink' suggests: the throat is greenish, then whitish, the pink gets darker towards the edges of the petals, which are also veined in a darker colour, the anthers are softly golden… It is even less hardy than the belladonna so is only worth risking outside in very mild areas, where it will need the sunniest spot you can find and extra protection in winter with a loose blanket of bracken or straw. Otherwise plant 10cm (4in) deep in a pot in a mixture of loam-based compost and gravel (two parts compost to one part 6mm/¼in gravel). You can fit five bulbs into a 15cm (6in) pot. Water freely while they are growing. Afterwards, allow the foliage to die back naturally and keep watering to a minimum during the bulbs' spring dormancy. They flower best in pots when they are a little cramped, so do not hurry to pot them on. In the wild, habranthus is programmed to respond to late summer rain. The same is often true in a sheltered garden border when it will spear through the ground a couple of weeks after a good soaking. Plant the bulbs 10cm (4in) deep and 20cm (8in) apart.

SEASON: September

HARDINESS: Half hardy

HEIGHT: 15–20cm (6–8in)

HABITAT: Brazil where it grows on dry uplands

Haemanthus (Amaryllidaceae)

Haemanthus albiflos ♀
SHAVING BRUSH PLANT

Introduced to cultivation in 1791, this is best treated as a rather bizarre houseplant as it is too tender for most gardens, needing a minimum winter temperature of 10°C (50°F). The leathery, razor-strop leaves are evergreen, and in autumn and early winter a fat stem pushes up between them, crowned with tiny white flowers, which are more stamen than petal (left), in a bunch 7–8cm (2½–3½in) across. Its common name, the shaving brush plant, is very apt. Grow it in a 25cm (10in) pot of loam-based compost mixed with grit (two parts compost to one part grit) setting the big bulb so its neck is level with the surface of the soil. Keep the plant on a sunny windowsill – it needs good light – where the temperature is 13–16°C (55–61°F). Feed it every two weeks with a fertilizer high in potash (tomato food is ideal). Like many plants from this region, it needs to be rather dry during the rest it takes after performing, but when grown inside haemanthus is evergreen so do not hold back completely on the watering. It flowers best when slightly pot bound. Do not be in too much of a hurry to give it a bigger root run.

SEASON: September
HARDINESS: Tender
HEIGHT: 15–25cm (6–10in)
HABITAT: South Africa (Eastern Cape, Western Cape) where it grows along river banks

Hermodactylus (Iridaceae)

Hermodactylus tuberosus
(*Iris tuberosus*)
WIDOW IRIS

Though it is easy to walk past widow iris in a garden, even in late February when there is little else to look at, this is an astonishing flower, made like an iris, with three 'mouths' of weird olive-green. The lip is bronze-purple, drifting into lime-green at the throat. These three dark mouths (if it was an iris you would call them falls) lie horizontal with the edges of the petals curving in slightly. The green 'ears' (or standards) stick up vertically. The tube of the flower is as long as its stem; the two make a sharp angle where they join, so the stem looks as though it has been snapped over. The sheath that has enclosed the flower stands up at twelve o'clock between the two petals at two and ten o'clock. The texture of the flower is like the best, most expensive satin, though no designer could ever come up with such subtle, bizarre colours. But they are silent colours and you need to plant this carefully, between primroses perhaps, or under a Judas tree, not yet in bloom. Do not put it next to anything noisy. Hermodactylus may naturalize in grass, if the turf is not too coarse, but unless the summer sun can bore through to its tubers it will produce foliage but few flowers. The leaves are thin and grassy like those of a Spanish iris and come through the ground very early. By flowering time they are much longer (up to 50cm/20in) than the stems of flower. As they lengthen, they collapse and lie on the ground in a straggly way. By May, they have disappeared entirely. Plant the tubers in autumn in sharply drained soil in full sun. They will do especially well on chalk, and on soils they like they will creep about underground to form quite large colonies, though they may need protecting from slugs. Like so many flowers from the Mediterranean and central Asia, they flower best after a hot summer the previous season. They are lovely to pick. Though they do not last long in a vase, the flowers are scented and it is much easier to appreciate that in a warm kitchen than it is outside in a February gale. Plant 10cm (4in) deep and the same distance apart.

SEASON: February–mid March
HARDINESS: Fully hardy
HEIGHT: 27cm (11in)
HABITAT: Southern France east to south-eastern Europe, Israel and Turkey where it grows on dry, grassy hillsides and between rocks

Hippeastrum (Amaryllidaceae)

AMARYLLIS

*H*ippeastrum bear the big, fat, trumpet-shaped flowers that most of us (wrongly) still call amaryllis. Do not be snooty about them. They are fabulous things and the whole point of them is their ludicrous size and their ability to knock you out from the far side of a room. From enormous, beefy bulbs, they grow indoors at a phenomenal rate producing stems thicker than broom handles with at least four blooms on each one. From a single bulb, my best ever hippeastrum 'Fairytale' conjured four stems, each bearing six huge flowers. So you have got to hope you like them when they emerge. Fortunately, an explosion has recently taken place in the amount, style and scale of hippeastrums on offer. Not long ago they were sold, like potatoes, as 'red' or 'white'. Red was usually 'Red Lion', white was usually 'Apple Blossom' (actually quite pink). Now even the dustiest, most parochial garden centre will have its autumn and winter shelves stacked with amaryllis that look like orchids, striped in strange ways and with fancy colours. Nearly 80 different kinds are listed in *RHS Plant Finder*, and each year new arrivals are introduced.

ABOVE Though an old variety, introduced in 1954, *Hippeastrum* 'Apple Blossom' is still popular and deservedly so, the pale blooms streaked in a darker pink.

The bulbs make excellent Christmas presents for small children, because they grow very fast and have flowers fit for a Walt Disney cartoon. Plant them and get them into growth first. Waiting for a shoot to appear is, for them, the boring bit, but after that there is plenty of action. Hippeastrums have also become popular cut flowers as they last such a long time in water. If you do cut them, run a thin cane up inside each hollow stem before you put them in a vase. This will prevent them collapsing under the weight of the flowers on top. The cane should jam in at the top of the stem just under the flowers; if it does not, plug it in place by stuffing cotton wool inside the bottom of the fat stem. If you quickly wrap a wide rubber band round the bottom too, this will stop the stem splitting and curling. But if you are growing plenty of hippeastrums in pots, there is scarcely any need to cut. Experiment instead by planting the bulbs themselves in tall, thick glass vases. You need to be careful about watering, as there will be no drainage holes at the bottom, but the final effect is wonderful, very spare and spacey. Add slender twigs of beech, twisty willow or branches of catkin if you want a fuller effect. You can stick the stems straight in the compost.

Last season, in early November, I planted seven amaryllis, all new to me. Some were quicker into flower than others, but it is difficult to know whether earliness is an inherent trait (as it is with hyacinths) or whether some small difference in aspect, feeding, watering or temperature advanced some and retarded others. I thought I was treating them all exactly the same, but perhaps they felt differently. Of the seven I grew then, 'Aphrodite' was the earliest, 'Pink Floyd' the latest.

CULTIVATION

Invest in top-size bulbs and check that they are firm and have plenty of fleshy roots. Kits containing pot, compost and bulb are not such good value as buying bulbs on their own. Check that the nose of the bulb is not damaged. Soak the roots for 12–24 hours, by balancing the bulb on top of a jar of tepid tap water. Do not get the base itself wet, or it may rot. Choose 15cm (6in) pots for smallish bulbs (though small is a relative term here, 28–30cm/11–12in around the waist of the bulb), 18cm (7in) pots for medium-sized bulbs (30–34cm/12–14in) and 20cm (8in) pots for big ones (34–38cm/14–15in). You do not need to leave much space between the edge of the bulb and the edge of the pot, but the deeper the pot the better. Plastic is easier to manage than terracotta (though does not look so good). The pots must, of course, have drainage holes. The compost you use must be nutritious and free draining. The Royal Botanic Gardens, Kew, in the UK, which puts on spectacular winter shows of hippeastrums in its glasshouses, makes up its own special mix: 45 per cent coir, 45 per cent composted twigs and bark mix and 10 per cent loam, with added slow-release fertilizer. I have had decent results simply by mixing multipurpose compost with gravel or grit (two parts compost to one part grit). Add a slow-release fertilizer to the mix. Put a layer of your compost mix in the bottom of a pot. Hold the bulb in one hand with its roots hanging down and firm more compost mix round the roots. The nose of the bulb should poke up above the rim of the pot, and its shoulders should be above the surface of the compost. Water with tepid water and put the pot in a warm, light, well-ventilated place, free from draughts. A temperature around 21°C (70°F) is said to be ideal but I grow them in much cooler conditions.

Let the compost dry out on top before watering. Always water from the top, never from the bottom. Do not wet the nose of the bulb or allow the pot to stand in water for a long period. When the first shoot appears, start feeding by adding a liquid fertilizer when you water. Give the pot a quarter turn each day to keep the stems growing straight. You may need to stake them as they grow. When the buds start to open, move the pot to a cooler place so the flowers last as long as possible. Suppliers suggest that hippeastrums will come into flower six to eight weeks after planting. They have never been that fast for me. Ten weeks is perhaps more realistic.

After the plants have flowered, cut off the dead heads and continue to feed and water the plants throughout summer until about the middle of October. Never cut off the leaves. Pots can stand outside for the summer.

OPPOSITE Hippeastrum are not hardy, so it is only in frost-free gardens such as this one in Brisbane, Australia, that they can grow outside. Here their partners are tropical codiaeums.

Give them as much light as possible. A temperature of 21–29°C (70–84°F) is ideal. Check regularly for pests such as thrips, aphids and mealy bugs and deal with them before they build up to epidemic proportions. In mid October bring the plants inside, where the temperature is no more than 9–13°C (48–55°F). Keep the compost in the pots just moist. Stop feeding them and let the bulbs tick over quietly for ten weeks, then wake them up by cutting off any remaining foliage 10cm (4in) above the neck. If an old bulb has made less than four leaves, it is unlikely to produce a flower. Rather than repotting (the roots hate being disturbed), just remove the top 6cm (2¼in) of compost and replace it with a fresh mix. Move the pots back into the warm and start to grow them on in the same way as before.

All those words may give the impression that hippeastrums are difficult to grow. They are not. They are among the easiest and most rewarding of all houseplants. Occasionally a bulb will refuse to start into growth. This may be because it has rotted (too much water), but if you can feel it with a finger stuck in the compost, and it is still plump, do not throw it away. It may surprise you by coming into growth while it is outside, in which case it will flower in October. Bulbs that you save after flowering may take more than a season to build up again to flowering size, and when they do flower will come on later than newly bought bulbs.

ABOVE The vigorous new *Hippeastrum* 'Fairytale' produces elegant trumpets, with petals more pointed than 'Apple Blossom'.

Hippeastrum 'Aphrodite'

'Aphrodite' is a creature of the boudoir, a powder puff of a flower, one of many variations on the pink and white theme, but double. Each flower looks like three single flowers, one fitted inside another with the petals of the innermost slightly narrower than the outer ones. The background colour is creamy greeny white, each petal finely edged and flushed with pink. It is the absolute antithesis of a hippeastrum such as 'La Paz'. You miss the elegant stamens, here transformed to petals. I had two stems from one bulb, with four flowers on the first stem, two on the second. As they age, they grow out on their stalks and hang heavily down. The broad, fleshy leaves, at flowering time, are half the height of the flowering stem. 'Aphrodite' was bred by the Miyake Nursery in Japan and introduced in 1994. It gets into growth quite quickly; after eight weeks you can expect to see flowers.

SEASON: Late January
HARDINESS: Tender
HEIGHT: 60cm (24in)

Hippeastrum 'Apple Blossom'

From a November planting, flower spikes begin to appear in the new year. I had two stems from a single bulb, each bearing six flowers. Though large, it is an elegant variety, deservedly popular ever since its introduction in 1954. The foliage, strap-shaped and bright, clean green, is only just poking through at flowering time. The stems are fat and hollow and in this variety a rather pale celadon-green. When the great package on top of the stem breaks open, the buds are standing upright, but they drop to the horizontal just before they unfurl. At this stage, they are very green. The flowers, when fully open, are at least 15cm (6in) across, widest in the lower half where two big petals at five o'clock and seven o'clock stand either side of a narrower one at six o'clock. The colour, a pale, streaked pink, is most pronounced in the top half of the flower and deeper on the inner surface of the petal than the outer. Long, white stamens and style hang down against the bottom petal. 'Apple Blossom' is a showy variety and long-lasting too, a splendidly outrageous response to the cold and wet outside.

SEASON: January–February
HARDINESS: Tender
HEIGHT: 60cm (24in)

Hippeastrum 'Black Pearl'

'Black Pearl' produces a strong deep red flower, though nowhere near the black promised in the name. My bulb had three stems with four flowers on each. Is height and flower power in hippeastrums dependent on the size of the bulb, or are some varieties really taller and more prolific than others? This is a solid-coloured beast, with none of the fine markings of 'Picotee' or 'Fairytale'. The flowers are wide (13cm/5in across), the three outer petals wider, more triangular than the three inner ones, quite different in shape to the long, thin trumpets of 'Fairytale'. Both the stamens and the style are red stemmed, the stamens carrying cream anthers and the style splitting at the end into three curled flourishes.

SEASON: Mid February
HARDINESS: Tender
HEIGHT: 45cm (18in)

Hippeastrum 'Chico'

In colour and form, this is similar to 'La Paz', but the narrow petals of 'Chico' twist in a way that those of 'La Paz' do not. It is a newish introduction (2002), very spidery and strange, sinister even, but in a perversely pleasurable way. Taste the drop of liquid nectar that hangs under the bottom petal. The petals, as with all hippeastrums, are divided into three that do one thing and three petals that do something slightly different. The upper three are darkish pink overlaid on green. The topmost one at 12 o'clock sweeps back, with the two lower ones curving elegantly at right angles to it. The lowest petal sheaths the stamens and style (all shiny pale lime-green) with its outriders curving out either side. 'Chico' has all the strangeness and terrifying symmetry of an orchid. It is bizarre and crushingly elegant, peering with disdain, it seemed to me, at the ancient sofa in our sitting room littered with even more bashed-up toys.

SEASON: February
HARDINESS: Tender
HEIGHT: 56cm (22in)

Hippeastrum 'Emerald'

When I grew it, 'Emerald' came through on an unusually long stem, without leaves but with long, thin buds on top. Four flowers were produced from this single stem, narrow petalled, green in tone, with the top three petals edged and streaked with deep maroon. The bottom three petals were only very faintly

edged, with no streaks. The stamens and stigma sweep forward, longer than the flower. Like *H. papilio*, this is a spidery, strange thing, not showy but deeply intriguing. Like 'Chico' it is of the type known as Cybister, bred in the USA and introduced in 1999.

SEASON: Mid April
HARDINESS: Tender
HEIGHT: 70cm (28in)

Hippeastrum 'Fairytale'

I got an astounding result the first time I grew this variety: four fat stems from a single bulb, each with six flowers. They are white and pink like 'Apple Blossom' but the colour is arranged in a completely different way, the pink laid in fine striations along the length of the white petals. The trumpets of 'Fairytale' are not as enormous as those of 'Apple Blossom' but they are exceptionally pretty, the petals more pointed, the trumpets slightly narrower. The pink veining is much stronger on the top three petals than it is on the lower ones, but each flower varies in the way that the colour is laid on and this increases their appeal enormously. The style is pink tipped, the anthers curling back on themselves in graceful, little scrolls. It was bred in The Netherlands, introduced in 1998 and is relatively quick to come into flower.

SEASON: Late January
HARDINESS: Tender
HEIGHT: 70cm (28in)

NEXT PAGE Hippeastrums make dramatic cut flowers, but if you grow your own flowers inside during late winter, the blooms will last even longer.

Hippeastrum 'La Paz'

This produces a spidery flower with petals of a strange brick-pink, drifting to pale green. As with so many hippeastrums, the colour is more intense on the top three petals than it is on the lower ones. The top petals here are slightly wider too, so the flower seems to divide itself into two halves. The long stamens and style lie flat against the channelled bottom petal, turning up at the end in an elegant backflip. The flowering stem is much thinner on these spidery types of hippeastrum, stained in this variety with bronze-red. It comes naked into growth, unaccompanied by leaves. 'La Paz' was bred in the USA and introduced in 2002, the kind of hippeastrum that fits well in a clean, pared-down interior, glass and chrome.

SEASON: Late January
HARDINESS: Tender
HEIGHT: 60cm (24in)

Hippeastrum 'Lemon Lime'

The flower stem of 'Lemon Lime' emerges before the leaves and produces up to four flowers, greenish in bud but opening to a much paler creamy mint-green with equally pale stamens and stigma hanging down against the six o'clock petal. Unlike *H. papilio* or 'La Paz', each flower opens into a balanced circle of petals. They turn evenly back on themselves to make wide open, symmetrical cups about 13cm (5in) across. 'Lemon Lime' was introduced by its Dutch breeders in 1993 and is cool, distinguished and easy.

SEASON: Mid February
HARDINESS: Tender
HEIGHT: 60cm (24in)

Hippeastrum papilio ♀

When I grew it, four strap leaves emerged before the flower stem which bore a bud larger and flatter than any I had grown before, even though it had only two flowers inside it. The flowers are narrow, when viewed from the front, the petals 11cm (4½in) long, but the mouths only 9cm (3¾in) wide. The three upper petals are wider than the three lower ones, the background colour pale creamy green, striped with maroon. The stamens and stigma hang down in a louche, self-confident way. *Hippeastrum papilio* and the varieties derived from it are quite different from the fat, rounded, more blowsy forms of hippeastrum available in the past. Both have their uses, but this species is a really beautiful thing. Gardeners must hope that more will soon be available.

SEASON: Early February

HARDINESS: Tender

HEIGHT: 55cm (22in)

HABITAT: Southern Brazil

Hippeastrum 'Picotee'

This old variety (1958) still has amazing vigour, producing, when I grew it, eight broad, strap-shaped leaves, bright green, arching out from the neck of the bulb. The flower stem, springing from the side of the bulb, was amazingly thick and strong and produced four big, fluted trumpet flowers, 14cm (5½in) across, with wide (7cm/2½in) petals arranged in two sets of three, outer and inner. All are white with a very fine picotee edge of reddish pink. The veining of the petals shows and enhances the beauty considerably. 'Picotee' is rather slow to come into flower, but is well worth the wait.

SEASON: February

HARDINESS: Tender

HEIGHT: 65cm (26in)

Hippeastrum 'Pink Floyd'

The flowers emerge as long, thin trumpets, elegant in shape but an uncompromising bright pink. They are very different in style to the wide, flat-faced flowers of 'Black Pearl' or 'Picotee'. Each trumpet of 'Pink Floyd' is 15cm (6in) long, green where it joins the stem, then flushing to deep pink, with an indistinct, white stripe down the centre of each petal. The stigma explodes in a three-curled flourish, with cream anthers ranged behind it.

SEASON: Early March
HARDINESS: Tender
HEIGHT: 60cm (24in)

Hippeastrum 'Toughie'

A so-called 'hardy' variety with handsome, bronze-coloured leaves, strap-shaped like the well-known indoor hippeastrums, but more compact. If it survives the winter, it will produce stems of deep crimson flowers in summer. For safety's sake, it is probably better to plant 'Toughie' in a pot which you can whip under cover when frost is forecast. In the ground, it is more likely to survive if you cover it with an insulating blanket of leaf mould. Plant 15cm (6in) deep and the same distance apart.

SEASON: July–September
HARDINESS: Tender
HEIGHT: 55cm (22in)

Hyacinthella (Hyacinthaceae)

Hyacinthella pallens

The hyacinthellas, once lumped in with hyacinths, now have their own club, and this member has bell-shaped, pale blue flowers in a fairly dense spike. To settle and thrive it needs warm, dryish summers. Though perfectly hardy, *H. pallens* is not likely to be happy in places where summers are predominantly cool and damp. Plant the bulbs in autumn, choosing a fertile, well-drained spot in full sun. Set them 5–8cm (2–3½in) deep and the same distance apart.

SEASON: March
HARDINESS: Fully hardy
HEIGHT: 10cm (4in)
HABITAT: Croatia (Dalmatia) where it grows on dry, rocky hillsides

Hyacinthoides (Hyacinthaceae)

Hyacinthoides italica ♀

Up to 20 small, starry flowers are held in a short, wide, conical head, pale violet-blue but stippled with darker blue stamens. They face up rather than hang down and have a spicy scent, lighter than the bluebell's. Plant *H. italica* 8cm (3½in) deep and the same distance apart.

SEASON: May
HARDINESS: Fully hardy
HEIGHT: 10–20cm (4–8in)
HABITAT: Europe (south-eastern France, north-western Italy,
Portugal, Spain) where it grows in grassy, rough places

Hyacinthoides non-scripta

ENGLISH BLUEBELL

These familiar beauties, which spread in great carpets through English woods in late spring, have had more botanical tags tied on them than any plant should have to bear. First they were labelled hyacinth, then scilla, then endymion (a lovely name). Now they are hyacinthoides, which sounds more like an affliction than a flower. The tubular bells, usually blue, occasionally white or pink, hang on one side of a drooping spike. Each bell flips back on itself at the mouth, producing six neat scrolls. They will not flower well in deep shade. They will naturalize in grass, though, as you often see them in Britain, growing on the verges or banks of lanes in the West Country. On damp, heavy clay they can spread faster than ground elder and in a garden can become invasive thugs. They are probably safest not released into a border but confined to wildish corners, planted under deciduous shrubs and trees, where they could follow on from *Allium paradoxum* var. *normale*, another appealing ruffian. The smell of English bluebells is wonderful, something that is lacking in the much reviled Spanish bluebell (*Hyacinthoides hispanica*), which is actually a good garden plant. Its bells – blue, pink or white – are held all round the stem rather than one side of it, like the English bluebell's. Ecologists, though, object to the fact that the Spanish bluebell can cross with the English one and dilute the wild stock. Plant bulbs in autumn, in moist soil in dappled shade, setting them 8cm (3½in) deep and 10cm (4in) apart.

SEASON Late April–May
HARDINESS: Fully hardy
HEIGHT: 35cm (14in)
HABITAT: Western Europe, including Britain, where it grows in woods and meadows

H

Hyacinthus (Hyacinthaceae)

Before the Dutch nurserymen got hold of it, *H. orientalis* was known only as a mostly blue-flowered wild plant, native in Turkey, north-western Syria and the Lebanon; some time after 1543, it was brought from there as a beautiful curiosity into the botanic garden at Padua, Italy. Florists soon got to work on this obliging bulb, making the flowers bigger and increasing the range of colours, so that already by 1576 the great plantsman Lobelius (Charles de l'Obel) was writing of several different kinds, referring to one in particular as 'the best hyacinth known in Holland'.

ABOVE Apothecary John Parkinson (1567–1650) had a fine garden in London's Long Acre and shared much of his knowledge of plants in his first book, the *Paradisi in Sole Paradisus Terrestris*, published in 1629.

Sweetly scented flowers were particularly prized in that age of stinking streets and few baths, so it is not surprising that by 1629 when John Parkinson published his famous *Paradisus* the hyacinth was considered 'so plentifull in all gardens that it is almost not esteemed'. It was easy to grow, too, much easier than the tulips and turban ranunculus that swept alongside it on that first great sixteenth-century influx of foreign plants into Europe. Parkinson said that the hyacinths had been 'brought out of Turkie and Constantinople'. Where their true home was 'is not as yet understood'.

The great boom in hyacinths was yet to come, though: in the eighteenth century a Dutch grower, Pieter Voerhelm, produced the first double flowers and started a craze that almost equalled tulipmania in its madness. Two hundred pounds was paid for double varieties such as 'Assemblage de Beautés', 'adorned with Bells, some of which are broader than an English crown, erect and well-reflected, displaying a large Heart, charmingly mixed with Violet, White, Scarlet, and Carnation Colours; it continues a long time in high Bloom'.

Double hyacinths are still scarce, but the number is growing, as is the range of colours. The lovely amethyst and purple varieties such as 'Purple Sensation' were scarcely heard of a few years ago but have become great favourites with gardeners. They make good cut flowers, blooming outside in March and April. Choose carefully for a cutting garden so you have a wide selection of colours and also a good spread of early-, mid-season and late-flowering varieties. 'Anna Marie' and 'Jan Bos' are very early; 'Delft Blue' and 'Purple Sensation' are early; and 'Carnegie' and 'City of Haarlem' are late. Flower arrangers say a drop of bleach in the vase helps keep the water sweet.

Keen plantsmen soon discovered that it was possible to force hyacinths into bloom earlier than Nature intended. Nehemiah Grew, secretary of the Royal Society and a pioneer in the painstaking business of finding out how plants are made, had already in 1682 observed that the hyacinth's flower buds were formed in the bulb the previous season and that it might be possible to tickle them into bloom 'by keeping the Plants warm, and

OPPOSITE The white-flowered hyacinth 'Carnegie' provides a spicy scent in the spring garden. Use it to follow on from the earlier-flowering white variety 'L'Innocence'.

thereby enticing the young lurking Flowers to come abroad'. We need to trick them into thinking they have had their winter before we force them to have their spring. Forcing winter bulbs was an important task for head gardeners of the Victorian and Edwardian eras. At Rangemore, Burton-on-Trent, in the UK, home of Mr Bass of beer fame, 1,600 Roman hyacinths, 600 Dutch hyacinths and 1,200 crocuses were forced every year.

CULTIVATION

If you are growing hyacinths outside, then cultivation is very simple. Plant in autumn in any well-drained, moderately fertile soil in sun or dappled shade. Then leave them to get on with life. The flowers produced in succeeding seasons will be smaller than the ones you got in the first spring, but in a garden setting this is not necessarily a disadvantage. The spikes, being less heavily laden, stand up properly and can take a surprising amount of rain without spoiling. Blue and white hyacinths look very pleasing set among clumps

ABOVE Nehemiah Grew (1641–1712) was one of the first people to study the anatomy of plants.

of blue cowichan primulas, woodruff and sweet cicely (*Myrrhis odorata*). If you want something less Delft in effect, add a scattering of smyrnium. Pink hyacinths work well with the purple-flowered little pea *Lathyrus vernus* or when spread under the branches of *Magnolia stellata*. If you are planting outside, set the bulbs 15–20cm (6–8in) deep and 8–10cm (3½–4in) apart.

Growing hyacinths indoors is an entirely different proposition but an essential activity for anyone who loves flowers. Nothing lifts the spirits so much on a drear January morning as to come down to a sitting room full of the spicy scent of hyacinths. They will come into flower just as the last of your paperwhite narcissi (*Narcissus papyraceus*) are finishing and, together with a clutch of different hippeastrums, veltheimia and cymbidium orchids, will see you through all those dark months from November to March, when the garden is a muddy, chilly, inhospitable place.

For forcing indoors you need to get hold of specially prepared hyacinths, usually available in garden centres from mid August onwards. These will have been given a speeded-up summer and winter so that by the time you get them they think spring is imminent and start pushing themselves up to flower. Get the biggest bulbs you can find and plant them as soon as you can. Use a layer of crocks or coarse grit at the bottom of the containers to improve drainage and set the bulbs in the compost or bulb fibre, close but not touching, with their noses just showing above the surface. Compost provides more food, bulb fibre provides better drainage. You can use bowls without holes but you need to be careful with the watering. Old china soup tureens and big china wash bowls, the kind that used to stand with a matching pitcher on Victorian dressing tables, make good containers. So do wicker baskets which you can buy ready lined with plastic (or line yourself with a plastic bag).

OPPOSITE The early-flowering hyacinth 'Ostara' pushes up between clumps of blue-flowered polyanthus.

For the next 10–12 weeks, keep the bowls of bulbs in a cool, dark place where the temperature does not rise above 7–9°C (45–48°F). Research done by the Dutch Bulbgrowers' Association shows that different varieties need different periods in the dark. 'Carnegie' is relatively slow: eleven weeks in a dark place followed by another three weeks in the light. 'Delft Blue' has a quicker turnaround time: nine weeks in the dark followed by just over three weeks in the light. Some people bury the containers outside, or heap them over with ashes, but this is a cumbersome business. Try your garage or shed instead. Or a cellar, if you have got one. Some gardeners keep old fridges plugged into their workshops and store their bulbs in that, but you must make sure the temperature never falls below 4°C (39°F). You could even dispatch the bulbs to a distant cupboard, though few houses now have the right kind of deeply, damply arctic cupboard. There are still houses, though (usually in the country rather than the town) where 10°C (50°F) is considered a positively luxurious inside temperature for November. This cold period encourages the roots to develop. Without a good root system to support and feed them, the flower spikes may abort. If the temperature creeps up above 9°C (48°F), the leaves will grow too long and lanky – a common problem. When the flower shoots are 2–3cm (¾–1in) long, bring the bowls into the light but keep them still cool (around 10°C/50°F). Check whether they need watering. The compost should be moist but never waterlogged, which will cause the bulbs to rot.

When the flower spikes are beginning to colour, bring the bowls into the warm (around 18°C/65°F). They last in good condition for at least a month. Do not bring all the bowls in from the cold at the same time. The bulbs will tick over quite happily at stage one (dark) or stage two (chilly), and if you bring them in gradually you spread the flowering over a longer period. The whole process, depending on the varieties you choose and the regime you adopt, will take 13–18 weeks. Christmas is a less realistic target than early January. Central heating shortens the life of flowers forced in bowls. If you can move them outside or on to a balcony for an occasional breath of cooler air, this will extend the show considerably. Unless you are growing a multiflowered type, you will probably need to stake the hyacinths as they come into full flower. A continuous fence of string, looped round each stem and round a few thin sticks in between is often the easiest way.

When they have finished flowering, plant the bulbs outside in the garden and allow them to die down naturally. It may take them a season to build up again to flowering size, but once they have got over the shock of being forced they settle and flower well.

Special glasses are still made (old ones are expensive collectors' pieces) for forcing hyacinths in water. These containers flare out into a wide mouth, so that you can sit the bulb in the dish shape at the top, with the roots dangling into the water below. It is not a wildly successful way to grow a bulb, though. When the flower spike gets top heavy, there is no way you can stake it. And forcing in water exhausts the bulb to such an extent that it is unlikely ever to recover enough to flower subsequently in your garden.

Hyacinthus multiflowered blue

The multiflowered hyacinths (they used to be called Roman hyacinths) are very useful for forcing because they produce several spikes of flowers from each bulb. The spikes are lighter, less densely packed with flowers than the usual heavyweights, so they are not as likely to need staking. And because several spikes come from each bulb, it does not matter that, individually, they carry fewer flowers. Five bulbs will easily fill a 30cm (12in) bowl. The blue most commonly offered in this form is a rather washed-out, greyish shade, but you can also get hold of multiflowered hyacinths in pink or white. Outdoors, plant 15–20cm (6–8in) deep and 8–10cm (3½–4in) apart.

SEASON: Late February (indoors); late March (outdoors)
HARDINESS: Fully hardy
HEIGHT: 30cm (12in)

Hyacinthus orientalis 'Anna Marie' ♀

This is one of the earliest varieties to bloom, whether you grow it indoors or out. The spike is not too big, an advantage when you are growing in bowls inside. The colour is good too – a soft, pale pink, slightly darker down the centre of each petal, but otherwise very uniform. The leaves are not too meaty and their bright, clean green sets off the colour of the flowers perfectly. Outdoors, plant 'Anna Marie' 15–20cm (6–8in) deep and 8–10cm (3½–4in) apart.

SEASON: Early January (indoors); March (outdoors)
HARDINESS: Fully hardy
HEIGHT: 30cm (12in)

Hyacinthus orientalis 'Carnegie'

This is a late variety, raised by the great Dutch bulb grower A Lefeber, and comes after the similar white variety 'L'Innocence'. If you are forcing them for the house, do not expect them to appear as soon as 'Jan Bos' or 'Anna Marie'. The white is very pure, and the foliage very bright, clean green. The individual flowers on each spike are enormous and they all come out at once. The only contrast is the faint sprinkle of cream at the centre of the flower, scarcely noticeable, where the stamens cluster together. 'Carnegie' is an easy hyacinth, tallish but strong and with a lovely scent. The smell of blue 'Delft Blue' goes 'off' very quickly; white 'Carnegie' does not. Outdoors, plant 15–20cm (6–8in) deep and 8–10cm (3½–4in) apart.

SEASON: Early February (indoors); late March (outdoors)
HARDINESS: Fully hardy
HEIGHT: 35cm (14in)

Hyacinthus orientalis 'City of Haarlem' ♀

An unusual colour, rich Jersey cream, on spikes that are not too overloaded with flower. In bud, they have a very pleasing, green tinge, lost when they open, the petals exceptionally thick and waxy in texture. This is an old variety, bred in 1893, and is usually among the last of the hyacinths to flower inside or out. The scent of 'City of Haarlem' is excellent, not inclined to go 'off' like 'Delft Blue'. The foliage is mid-green and not too broad. Outdoors, plant 15–20cm (6–8in) deep and 8–10cm (3½–4in) apart.

SEASON: Early February (indoors); early April (outdoors)
HARDINESS: Fully hardy
HEIGHT: 32cm (13in)

Hyacinthus orientalis 'Delft Blue' ♔

'Delft Blue' is an early variety and the colour is a good mid, powdery blue, soft and restful. The flower spikes are very dense and heavy, a typical spike at least 14cm (5½in) long. The flowers all come out at the same time and touch each other so you do not see stem in between. If you are forcing them, use a deep container, so that you can stake the blooms. They need it. Unfortunately 'Delft Blue' develops an unpleasant smell very quickly, even while the spikes are still young and fresh. In this respect, white 'Carnegie' and pink 'Anna Marie' are much better. Outdoors, plant 15–20cm (6–8in) deep and 8–10cm (3½–4in) apart.

SEASON: Mid January (indoors); March (outdoors)
HARDINESS: Fully hardy
HEIGHT: 35cm (14in)

Hyacinthus orientalis 'Gipsy Princess'

The thick clotted cream colour of 'Gipsy Princess' works well outside interspersed with the remains of dark slate-coloured hellebores. The colour is strange, but modified to advantage by the very slight purplish tint at the top of each bell. The flower spikes hold themselves well compared with a variety such as 'Sky Jacket', which topples under too heavy a cargo. The scent is very pleasant, though this trait is never as noticeable outside as it is indoors. Outdoors, plant 15–20cm (6–8in) deep and 8–10cm (3½–4in) apart.

SEASON: Mid January (indoors); mid March (outdoors)
HARDINESS: Fully hardy
HEIGHT: 22cm (9in)

NEXT PAGE To weather spring storms, hyacinths growing outside need stout stems as these have, rising up behind a neat row of double daisies (*Bellis perennis*).

Hyacinthus orientalis 'Hollyhock'

A double variety, just like the hyacinths you see in eighteenth-century prints, when these doubles were very fashionable and sparked a mania almost as bad as the tulip fever of the 1600s. The flat-faced flowers are a bright, deep pinkish red, and the doubling creates an entirely different effect, a dense but not clotted spike. In bud 'Hollyhock' is very green (an enchanting characteristic), and the green stays on the tips of the flowers as they open, which complicates (therefore enhances) the overall impression. It begins to look like a stock. Outdoors, plant 15–20cm (6–8in) deep and 8–10cm (3½–4in) apart.

SEASON: February (indoors);
March–April (outdoors)
HARDINESS: Fully hardy
HEIGHT: 20–30cm (8–12in)

Hyacinthus orientalis 'Jan Bos'

Being a naturally early variety, this is a good hyacinth to force in bowls inside. The colour is a dark, saturated pink, not red, as it is so often described. In bud, the flowers are greenish, but this disappears as they develop. Then the colour is fairly uniform, though slightly darker down the centre of each petal. The spikes are not too enormous, so stay upright reasonably well. 'Jan Bos' is generous too, as a second spike sometimes appears when the first one is fully out. The leaves fold together down the centre, so do not seem so overpoweringly fleshy as they do for instance on 'Anna Marie'. Outdoors, plant 15–20cm (6–8in) deep and 8–10cm (3½–4in) apart.

SEASON: Early January (indoors);
March (outdoors)
HARDINESS: Fully hardy
HEIGHT: 28cm (11in)

Hyacinthus orientalis 'Purple Sensation'

'Purple Sensation' produces compact spikes that give the impression of being exceptionally full; though this is not a true double, some of the flowers have eight petals. The colour is as good as the name suggests (unusual in an age of hyperbole), a sensational and extraordinary amethyst, developing from buds that are a weird greenish, brownish mauve. Though the overall effect is of a single shade, the petals are actually bicoloured, striped with a darker shade down the centre of each petal. This is an exceptional hyacinth with a wonderful perfume. Outdoors, plant 15–20cm (6–8in) deep and 8–10cm (3½–4in) apart.

SEASON: Early March (indoors);
mid April (outdoors)
HARDINESS: Fully hardy
HEIGHT: 26cm (10½in)

Hyacinthus orientalis 'White Pearl'

This is a good variety to force, as the bright green leaves do not seem to get as long and strappy as some other varieties. In bud, the white flowers are tinged with green – very cool and elegant. The stem opens into a head that makes a perfect, fat cylinder, the smell outstanding. As they age, the flowers start to turn creamy. 'White Pearl' produces a good, vigorous spike, compared for instance with the rather thin one of 'Woodstock'. Outdoors, plant 15–20cm (6–8in) deep and 8–10cm (3½–4in) apart.

SEASON: Early January (indoors);
March (outdoors)
HARDINESS: Fully hardy
HEIGHT: 25cm (10in)

Hyacinthus orientalis 'Woodstock'

This is a gorgeous colour, deep royal-purple, the flared inside edge of the flowers a deep amethyst, turning to purple on the outside and towards the base. But it is stringy in form and does not make the fat, compact heads that 'White Pearl' does. The flowers droop slightly rather than presenting their faces straight out to the world, and this may be why the spikes generally seem thinner and more straggly than other varieties. Outside, this does not matter as much as it does indoors. The smell is amazing and the colour sublime. Outdoors, plant 'Woodstock' 15–20cm (6–8in) deep and 8–10cm (3½–4in) apart.

SEASON: Early February (indoors); late March (outdoors)
HARDINESS: Fully hardy
HEIGHT: 30cm (12in)

Hymenocallis (Amaryllidaceae)

Hymenocallis × festalis ♀

This is a vigorous hybrid raised by crossing two Peruvian species *H. narcissiflora* and *H. longipetala*. The flowers, which look like spidery, white daffodils, all sprout from the top of the fleshy stem and are eventually taller than the shiny, strap-shaped leaves. On each stem there may be up to five scented beauties, 15–20cm (6–8in) across, the central frilly, white cup surrounded by six outrageously long, thin, curving petals. For most of us these will be plants for the greenhouse or cool conservatory as they are very tender and need a minimum of 15°C (59°F). Plant the bulbs in spring using a loam-based compost, mixed with grit or 6mm (¼in) gravel (two parts compost to one part grit). One bulb will fit comfortably in a 15–20cm (6–8in) pot; set so its shoulders and neck are above the surface of the compost. Give *H. × festalis* plenty of water while it is growing and feed every two to three weeks with a potash-rich liquid fertilizer (tomato feed is ideal). This hybrid is evergreen, but still needs a quiet resting period after flowering when the compost should be kept only just moist.

SEASON: July–August
HARDINESS: Tender
HEIGHT: 80cm (32in)

Ipheion (Alliaceae)

These South American bulbs come into leaf early in winter and give an incredible display of flowers through March and April. In summer, they lie dormant. The starry blooms are honey scented, a smell unfortunately not as strong as the allium-like onion taint that comes from the leaves if you bruise them. Where they are happy, they bulk up quickly into big clumps. Divide and replant them in late summer while they are dormant. Though technically frost tender, ipheions will take temporary plunges in temperature; prolonged frosts are a different matter. Fortunately they look wonderful in pots, and in cold areas this may be the best way to grow them, planting them in a loam-based compost such as John Innes No 2 with added grit. Feed the plants when they are growing strongly but keep them only just moist in summer when they are dormant. Outside, any lightish soil, rich in humus, is likely to suit them, moist but well-drained and in full sun. They are less likely to succeed in heavy, clay soils. Guard your plants against slugs and snails, their only enemy. The bulbs are best bought damp-packed as they hate to dry out.

Ipheion 'Alberto Castillo'

The foliage makes low mats, the leaves not quite so long nor so vigorous as those of 'Rolf Fiedler'. The flowers are gorgeous, flat, white stars, the three inner petals poised at right angles to the three outer ones. On the back of each petal is a dark, central line and the same dark purplish colour drifts down the stem. This little detail adds greatly to the pleasure of seeing a clump in bloom. This ipheion was first found by Alberto Castillo in an abandoned garden in Buenos Aires, Argentina, and was reintroduced to cultivation in the 1980s. It looks superb in a pot, particularly if you keep it sheltered in a cold frame during winter, when it is producing its foliage. Then, at flowering time, you can whisk it out, pristine and undamaged by the weather. Otherwise let it loose among your peonies, between the carmine shoots of *Paeonia lactiflora* or among the woodier stems of *P. suffruticosa* varieties. Plant 8cm (3½in) deep and 8cm (3½in) apart.

SEASON: Early March
HARDINESS: Frost hardy
HEIGHT: 15cm (6in)

Ipheion 'Rolf Fiedler' ♈

This is a wonderfully vigorous variety with clean green foliage that at first does not sprawl, but arches up and away from the starry flowers. These are sky-blue, not so deep and intense as 'Jessie', but very lovely and produced one at a time over a long period. They all face in the same direction, flaring out like ear trumpets from the stem, as if to catch the passing gossip. On the outside of each petal is a dark, central line which merges into the throat of the flower. In the centre are three dots of yellow, the stamens squeezed into the narrow base. In cold areas, it is safest to grow this in a pot so you can protect it from frost in winter (all ipheions look good in pots), but you will need to repot every year. The bulbs bulk up quickly but hate to be overcrowded; they show their displeasure by not flowering. In the garden you could plant 'Rolf Fiedler' with hostas or mix it with the cream and apricot flowers of *Tulipa linifolia* Batalinii Group 'Apricot Jewel' or 'Bronze Charm'. Plant 8cm (3½in) deep and 8cm (3½in) apart.

SEASON: March–April
HARDINESS: Frost hardy
HEIGHT: 18cm (7in)

Ipheion 'Jessie'

'Jessie' produces a broad-faced flower of a more intense blue than 'Rolf Fiedler'. The petals are not so sharply pointed and this creates the impression of a fuller, more rounded flower. The richness of the colour does not fade out towards the base, so contrasts cleanly with the yellow triangle made there by the three stamens. It is slightly shorter than 'Rolf Fiedler', and does not grow so vigorously, but has the same clear green, arching foliage. Blues such as this, not veering towards grey or purple, are rare in the spring garden. Use 'Jessie' on its own under deciduous azaleas or round the tall, upright shoots of a tree peony, which will only just be showing its bronze foliage. Plant 8cm (3½in) deep and 8cm (3½in) apart.

SEASON: March–May
HARDINESS: Frost hardy
HEIGHT: 10cm (4in)

Ipheion uniflorum 'Charlotte Bishop'

The wide spreading mats of leaves come through in autumn, narrow and glaucous grey-green, making a thick, grassy clump. In spring, solitary, star-shaped flowers shoot up from the sprawling foliage on lightly bronzed stems. When they first emerge, the petals form two triangles, one imposed on the other, but the form changes when the flower is fully open, and all six petals dive down to the vase-shaped throat. At first, 'Charlotte Bishop' is deep rich lilac, but unfortunately fades to a less attractive colour as it ages. A thin, dark line runs down the back of each petal, and the flowers are sweetly scented. This selection was introduced in 2003, an excellent addition to a family which in the past has dressed mostly in blue, white or violet. Use it to fill in bare ground under low-growing shrubs such as *Ceratostigma willmottianum* or mix it with spring-flowering *Scilla bifolia*. Plant 8cm (3½in) deep and 8cm (3½in) apart.

SEASON: Early March
HARDINESS: Frost hardy
HEIGHT: 12cm (5in)

Ipheion uniflorum 'Froyle Mill' ♀

Expect flowers in a dark purplish blue, a much deeper shade than 'Jessie'. Those flowers are rounded. These are starry. The dark line bisecting the back of the petal is a feature, as it is with all ipheions. Try it with the dwarf hoop-petticoat daffodil (*Narcissus bulbocodium*) or with clumps of the white-flowered *Anemone nemorosa* 'Lychette'. 'Froyle Mill' is named after the Hampshire garden where it was first found and is fragrant but perhaps a little more tender than other varieties. Plant 8cm (3½in) deep and 8cm (3½in) apart.

SEASON: March–April
HARDINESS: Frost hardy
HEIGHT: 14cm (5½in)

Iris (Iridaceae)

Iris was a Greek goddess, the personification of the rainbow, which she used as her pathway through the sky. And iris is a goddess among flowers, insultingly superb: seductive and yet distant all at the same time. I am certainly prepared to throw myself overboard for these flowers, but it would be so nice if they showed a few signs of being interested in me in return. Love needs a little encouragement now and again, and I have been let down by iris rather often in the past. But then, each year as they emerge, caution, prudence, and all the other things your mother reminds you about from time to time are thrown to the wind, and I am hooked all over again. It has been happening to people for centuries. Millennia even. Bearded irises were brought from Syria into Egypt by Thutmose III, who was making gardens 1,500 years before Christ was born. The flower still shines out in bas-relief on Thutmose's temple at Karnak.

The Roman author Pliny gave elaborate instructions on preparing iris roots to make medicine, and subsequent physicians endorsed its powerful qualities. It could fasten loose teeth. It could 'provoke sleepe and bringeth out teares'. It was good for 'gnawinges in the belly and for them that have taken a thorowe cold'. Early beauty counsellors of the second and third centuries promised it would scour out freckles, spots and other life-threatening blemishes.

ABOVE Clovis I (c.466–511), king of the Salian Franks, who adopted the iris as his emblem.

In the sixth century AD, the iris was adopted as an emblem by Clovis, king of the Franks. Finding himself trapped between an army of raging Goths and a dangerous bend in the Rhine near Cologne, he noticed a patch of yellow iris growing far out in the middle of the river. They were a signal that the river, at that point, would be shallow enough to ford. He led his army through the river, past the shimmering iris, to safety on the far bank. Forever after, the flower remained the badge of his descendants.

So, a powerful flower, and it knows it, looking at us, its keepers, with a wonderful, daring insolence. And it is a various one, adapted to grow as well in marshes as it does in the dry, dusty plains of central Asia. Forgetting entirely about the tall, bearded rhizomatous iris that hog most of the limelight (and are outside the scope of this book), you can have iris in bloom for eight months of the year. You would start with the small, early ones – Turkish *I. histrioides* or *I. reticulata* from Russia and the Caucasus which would see you through the first three months of the year. The Algerian iris (*I. unguicularis*) may have started even sooner, particularly if you have put it at the base of a hot, sunny wall. *I. lazica* from the Black Sea coast flowers at much the same time.

In March and April you can be hovering over gorgeous Juno iris such as *I. bucharica* and *I. aucheri*. If you are very careful and clever you might even be able to gloat over the primrose-yellow blooms of *I. winogradowii*. If you fail with that, April can still give you the delicious, plum scent of *I. graminea* and a whiff of violets from *I. kolpakowskiana*. You would coast through May with different types of Dutch iris. These are the ones that you see for sale in florists' shops as early as February, but, if you plant them in the garden in autumn, May is their most likely flowering time. They take up very little room and are extremely useful for slipping between clumps of herbaceous perennials, which at that stage are still not too leafy to overpower them. The iris foliage is thin and grassy, and when it has flowered the whole plant disappears underground, just like a daffodil.

In June you would shift over to the similar-looking Spanish iris, which generally flower three weeks later than the Dutch. After that, you would finish June with the magnificent inky blue blooms of the English iris, wider-petalled, more intensely coloured than the Dutch, but, inexplicably, much harder to find in nurserymen's catalogues. *Iris orientalis* should not really be in this book at all as it is a rhizomatous iris, not a bulbous one. But I have had it all my gardening life and it will bring you through into July with elegance and grace.

Iris flowers make a reasonable job of covering the rainbow spectrum, though they are strongest on the blue, indigo and violet end of the scale. They cannot provide a true red; the reddish-looking ones are actually tawny brown. They are models of symmetry, built in threes: three outside petals (called falls), three upright petals (called standards) and, right in the centre, three strappy petals (called style arms) protecting the anthers.

The list below contains 13 of the species iris superbly categorized and described by William Rickatson Dykes, a schoolmaster at Charterhouse, UK, in his seminal work *The Genus Iris* (1913). Because there are such vast numbers of iris, they have been divided into different groups, according to their different characteristics. Strictly, I should stick to bulbous irises, which have been sorted into three classes: the Reticulatas, the Junos and the Xiphiums. But it is impossible to be strict with these flowers, so I have also included *I. lazica* and *I. unguicularis* (both rhizomatous iris from the Unguiculares group) together with *I. graminea* and *I. orientalis* from the group of Spuria iris superbly grown by Sir Michael Foster, a Victorian professor of physiology, in his garden at Ninewalls, Shelford, Cambridgeshire, UK.

ABOVE In his spare time, Sir Michael Foster (1836–1907) was professor of physiology at Cambridge University but his true love was iris, which he grew superbly well in his Cambridgeshire garden.

OPPOSITE *Iris graminea* is not a showy iris, but it smells deliciously of ripe plums, a trait intriguing enough to endear it to all lovers of iris.

RETICULATA SECTION This includes *I. histrioides* ('Angel's Tears', 'Lady Beatrix Stanley'), *I. kolpakowskiana*, *I. reticulata* ('Cantab', 'George', 'Gordon', 'Harmony', 'J S Dijt', 'Katharine Hodgkin', 'Purple Gem') and *I. winogradowii*. The early-flowering Reticulatas generally grow best in sunny, sandy soils (*I. winogradowii* is the exception) and do not like too much moisture. In the open ground, plant Reticulata iris at least 10cm (4in) deep, which to some extent prevents the bulbs splitting up and so encourages them to flower again the following season. When shallowly planted, the bulbs divide into masses of tiny bulbils which take at least two years to grow back to flowering size and are likely to come to a disastrous end before they get there. Varieties of *I. reticulata* such as purple-flowered 'George' and blue 'Harmony' are excellent planted in shallow bowls to bring indoors – 15 bulbs will fit nicely into a container about 22cm (9in) across – but they cannot be forced hard as hyacinths can. Dykes noted that although buds are slow to develop inside the spathes, once they show, they grow at an extraordinary rate – 6cm (2¼in) in 24 hours. The name Reticulata comes from the netted tunic that covers all the bulbs of this group. Other iris do not have it.

ABOVE The dwarf iris 'Harmony' has *Iris reticulata* as one of its parents, but the flower is bigger and bolder, and settles well in sunny, sandy soils.

JUNO SECTION   This includes *I. aucheri*, *I. bucharica*, *I. cycloglossa* and *I. magnifica*. The heartland of the Junos is northern Afghanistan, a country of mountains and steppes where winters are cold and snowy and summers are hot and arid. The temperate climate of much of western Europe is not what they want: bulbs are too damp in winter and not hot enough in summer. This is why the Junos have a reputation of being the most difficult of the bulbous iris to grow. They like full sun and light, very well-drained soil that dries out in summer. Avoid acid soil and stiff clay. Plant them in autumn, setting the bulbs so that there is 5–10cm (2–4in) of soil over their heads and mulch them generously every year. Characteristic of this group are the thick, fleshy roots growing from the base of the bulb, and for commercial growers this make the bulbs less easy to manage; they hate to be out of the ground. You have to be careful when planting not to break these roots as they are very brittle. The leaves too are different from other iris: they clasp each other on the stem, as the foliage of sweetcorn does, and the standards of the flowers tend to be held outwards, rather than upright. Start with the easy ones – *I. bucharica* which settles and clumps up quite

rapidly and white-flowered *I. magnifica* which is also well mannered. The other two Juno irises in the list below may need to be grown in pots in a frame where they can bake in summer, away from the hurly-burly of the mixed border. Use clay pots if you can and plant in September using a loam-based compost (John Innes No 3) mixed with fine gravel or grit. There should be at least 4cm (1½in) of compost on top of the bulbs. Water well to kick-start growth; the plants will probably not need watering again until they are in active growth. Sink the pots in sand if you can. It prevents them drying out too quickly and provides extra insulation in freezing weather. Repot the bulbs every year (September is a good time) and feed them with a fertilizer high in potash but low in nitrogen. Stop watering when the leaves begin to turn yellow, so the bulbs can dry off for their summer rest.

XIPHIUM SECTION This includes the English iris, broad-petalled *I. latifolia*, earlier-flowering Spanish iris (*I. xiphium*) and the more common Dutch iris, which Thomas Hoog bred *c.*1900 by crossing a deep blue, early-flowering form of *I. xiphium* with a yellow-flowered form of the same species. This new strain of iris had strong stems and big flowers in shades of blue, violet, bronze, yellow and white, and they bloomed earlier than the Spanish iris. Several of the Dutch iris Hoog bred – 'Frans Hals', 'Imperator' (a prize winner in 1915) – are still available but most were superseded by the De Graff brothers, who made another leap forward by crossing the best of the Spanish irises with *I. filifolia* to produce a race of Dutch iris with long, straight standards that lasted a long time as cut flowers. The prize-winning varieties 'White Excelsior' which they bred in 1920 and 'Wedgwood' (1925) are still around today.

The hybridizers' work created good-looking flowers, but it was Dr J J Beijer at the Bulb Research Centre at Lisse, in The Netherlands, who made the market for the growers of cut flowers. By studying the iris's response to temperature, he worked out exactly how to stop and start the bulb's growing mechanisms: heat (30–35°C/86–95°F) induced dormancy; cold (5–13°C/41–55°F) kick-started growth, so the industrious Dutch quickly learned how to produce their Dutch iris all year round. The so-called Spanish and English irises had been the most important iris crops for Dutch growers, but after these breakthroughs they were quickly superseded by the Dutch irises. English iris could not be tricked into growing out of season (and I respect them all the more because of it). Bulbs of Dutch iris are usually available in several different sizes (6–7cm/2¼–2½in, 7–8cm/2½–3½in, 8–9cm/3½–3¾in, 9–10cm/3¾–4in, 10cm/4in up). It is worth paying for the best; the bigger the bulb, the better the flowers. Plant in autumn, setting the bulbs at least 10cm (4in) deep and 10cm (4in) apart. They like rich, well-drained soil. In very cold areas, they can be planted in spring for a September display. Xiphium iris of all kinds are ideal in a cutting garden. When gathering flowers, leave as much foliage behind as you can and do not cut before the first bud in the spike is beginning to open up. The Spanish iris (*I. xiphium*) flowers about three weeks later than the Dutch and is useful for extending the season. Last come the English iris, the most beautiful of all.

OPPOSITE Though commercial growers have developed Dutch iris such as 'Oriental Beauty' chiefly for the cut flower market, they make splendid garden flowers, blooming in late April and May.

Iris 'Apollo'

This fine iris, bred by G Hommes of Heiloo in the early 1970s, has yellow falls with a darker blotch in the centre, lolling under a topknot of iceberg-white, faintly tinged with blue. Use 'Apollo' with forget-me-nots or columbines, or to cheer up mounds of *Geranium* 'Brookside' which will not yet be in flower. Plant the bulbs in a well-drained position in full sun or slight shade. If the ground seems dry, water them after planting. After that, they should need little attention. Set them 10cm (4in) deep and 10–15cm (4–6in) apart.

SEASON: Late May
HARDINESS: Fully hardy
HEIGHT: 50cm (20in)
SECTION: Xiphium (Dutch)

Iris aucheri ♀

Named after Pierre Martin Aucher-Eloy, a French naturalist who settled in Istanbul in 1830, the most common form of *I. aucheri*, known since 1877, has beautifully scented flowers of pale blue with a yellow flash on the falls. In the wild, though, the colour varies considerably and some excellent named selections – 'Leylek Lilac' (mauve-blue), 'Snow Princess' (white), 'Turkish Ice' (pale glacier-blue) – have been raised from seed collected near Leylek, Diyakabir in Turkey. In favoured gardens, this iris will settle in a well-drained, sunny spot, where you can mulch it with mushroom compost after it has flowered; otherwise grow it in a pot so you can keep it dry in a greenhouse or frame during summer. It smells of violets. Water it from below, not above, so the neck of the bulb stays dry. Use it to follow on from early crocus such as *C. corsicus* or *C. etruscus*. Plant 5–10cm (2–4in) deep and 10–15cm (4–6in) apart.

SEASON: March–April
HARDINESS: Fully hardy
HEIGHT: 15–25cm (6–10in)
SECTION: Juno (Species)
HABITAT: North-western Iran, northern Iraq, south-eastern Turkey and northern Syria where it grows on rocky slopes at 550–2,100m (1,800–7,000ft)

Iris bucharica ♀

The broad, glossy green leaves come through the ground looking like the foliage of leeks, sheathed, two-dimensional, splayed out either side of the stems. The buds, long and pointed (you may get as many as seven from a single bulb), emerge from the centre and open into flowers that sit only just above the fan of leaves. Because it is so short, you should put *I. bucharica* near a path, where you can smell it and admire the pale, translucent cream standards, the falls of strong lemon-yellow and the dark beard. The throat is

marked with three dark lines, a sightline for pollinating insects. Although this iris has slightly too much foliage for the size of its flower, it is enchanting. By early June the leaves become an embarrassment, but you will have remembered the previous September to sprinkle seed of love-in-a-mist or California poppy round the iris to disguise their too-slow death. Introduced to cultivation in 1902, this is not a Juno to keep you awake at night; it settles and bulks up well provided it has sun and good drainage. The famous iris lover William Dykes, author of *The Genus Iris*, wrote that from two bulbs planted in 1906 he counted 40 flowers five years later. Plant 5–10cm (2–4in) deep and 15cm (6in) apart.

SEASON: Late March
HARDINESS: Fully hardy
HEIGHT: 15cm (6in)
SECTION: Juno (Species)
HABITAT: Central Asia, the western Pamir Alai and northern Afghanistan where it grows on stony, grassy slopes up to 2,400m (8,000ft)

Iris 'Cantab'

This is an old Reticulata iris, raised by E A Bowles in 1914, and, although it is not as showy nor as vigorous as some of the newer varieties, still has charm. The flowers are quite small (5cm/2in across), compared for instance to 'Purple Gem' (7cm/2½in). Both standards and falls are a soft, limpid mid blue, with a brilliant orange line running down the centre of the falls into the middle of the flower. It is good in pots. Try 'Cantab' mixed with *Crocus chrysanthus* 'Snow Bunting' or set between clumps of *Helleborus* × *sternii*. If you are not growing the bulbs in pots, put them in well-drained soil in full sun. Top-dress with grit to prevent rain splashing soil onto the flowers. Set 10cm (4in) deep and 5–10cm (2–4in) apart.

SEASON: Late January
HARDINESS: Fully hardy
HEIGHT: 16cm (6½in)
SECTION: Reticulata

Iris cycloglossa

A vigorous iris, introduced to cultivation in 1958 and producing up to three clove-scented flowers from each bulb. The standards of *I. cycloglossa* are unusually tall and upright for a Juno, and the wide, pale violet-mauve falls have a large, white, central blotch with an orange stripe running down into the throat of the flower. Most Junos like a dry summer rest. This one is happiest kept moist. Plant 5–10cm (2–4in) deep and 10–15cm (4–6in) apart.

SEASON: May
HARDINESS: Fully hardy
HEIGHT: 40–50cm (16–20in)
SECTION: Juno (Species)
HABITAT: North-west Afghanistan (Herat region) where it grows in damp, grassy places at 1,450–1,700m (4,750–5,750ft)

Iris 'George' ♈

The overall colour is a deep rich purple, with the three upright 'ears' in the centre and the three trumpet mouths sticking out between, making a very symmetrical flower, as all iris are. Each thin mouth is no more than 3cm (1in) long, flaring out at the end into a divided top with a tongue underneath, splashed at its throat with darker purple and white. Down the centre is a yellow landing strip, leading to the dark, mysterious interior of the flower. When the flowers die, the top three ears go first crumpling, almost melting before your eyes. At flowering time, the stiff, upright grassy leaves – there are just two or three of them – are shorter than the flowering stems, so the blooms display themselves well. Afterwards, of course, the foliage gets much longer. Charming in bowls indoors, but bring in the bowls only just before the iris are ready to flower and keep them in a cool place. Outside, mix 'George' with *Chionodoxa* 'Pink Giant' or interplant it with the autumn-flowering cyclamen *C. hederifolium* whose marbled leaves will still be looking good in late winter and early spring. Plant 10cm (4in) deep and 10cm (4in) apart.

SEASON: Early February
HARDINESS: Fully hardy
HEIGHT 12cm (5in)
SECTION: Reticulata

Iris 'Gordon'

A very sturdy, upright, little iris, with pleasing, mid-greyish blue standards, thin and only very slightly streaked with darker purple. The throat is white, veined with deep purple, and the end of the fall is the same rich, velvety colour. Down the centre of each fall is a distinctive, strong, orange stripe. Enchanting. And easy. Try 'Gordon' with *Primula vulgaris* subsp. *sibthorpii* or beside a bush of the glaucous rue *Ruta graveolens* 'Jackman's Blue'. Plant 10cm (4in) deep and the same distance apart.

SEASON: Early February
HARDINESS: Fully hardy
HEIGHT: 12cm (5in)
SECTION: Reticulata

Iris graminea ♀

The flowers, famous for their plummy scent, sit practically on the ground, too few of them, given the vast amount of foliage that the plant produces. But at least the leaves are deciduous, bright, clean green, and do not get rust, which is the downfall of the big bearded iris. So you need to get down on your knees to catch the distinctive scent of plums, and then you will see that the flowers are finely made: three pale purple 'ears' stand up in the centre, three 'arms' (the falls) stretch out horizontally between them, pinkish mauve with a deeper line of purple defining the midrib. The ends of the falls are pinched in, the mauve running out at the tips into a pale cream, deeply veined in bluish purple. Like tulips, irises are impossible to describe. The point of both is the complex overlaying of one colour on another. My clumps grow on well-drained soil in full sun, but I have seen *I. graminea* growing well in half shade. Either way, it likes plenty of humus in the soil. Split and replant clumps every three or four years to encourage better flowering (September is the time to do it). This has long been a popular plant with gardeners, cultivated already by the end of the sixteenth century. It should not be in this book, as it is a rhizomatous iris, not a bulbous one,

but its gorgeous scent wins it a place. Use it at the front of a border to break up mounds of a pink such as *Dianthus* 'Hidcote' or between clumps of *Euphorbia rigida*. Plant 5cm (2in) deep and 10cm (4in) apart.

SEASON: Late April
HARDINESS: Fully hardy
HEIGHT: 20–40cm (8–16in)
SECTION: Spuria (Species)
HABITAT: North-eastern Spain, south-eastern Europe (Romania, Bulgaria), Turkey, Russia, Caucasus and Crimea where it grows in alpine meadows

Iris 'Gypsy Beauty'

The flowers of 'Gypsy Beauty' are a strange, almost translucent pale purplish blue, a fine contrast planted with *Dicentra spectabilis* 'Alba' or *Smyrnium perfoliatum*. Set the bulbs in well-drained soil in full sun or slight shade, 10cm (4in) deep and 10–15cm (4–6in) apart.

SEASON: Late May
HARDINESS: Fully hardy
HEIGHT: 50cm (20in)
SECTION: Xiphium (Dutch)

Iris 'Harmony'

'Harmony' came from a cross between *I. histrioides* 'Major' and *I. reticulata* made by C J H Hoog in The Netherlands. The cross produced a brilliant royal-blue flower, bigger than that of either of its parents and with more compact foliage. The blue mouths are splashed with white at the throat, and have a brilliant yellow stripe down the centre. Above are jaunty, feathery blue crests. Mix it with spring-flowering *Cyclamen coum* or set it between the snaky arms of *Euphorbia myrsinites*. Plant 10cm (4in) deep and the same distance apart.

SEASON: Early February
HARDINESS: Fully hardy
HEIGHT: 10cm (4in)
SECTION: Reticulata

Iris histrioides 'Angel's Tears'

Iris histrioides is a Turkish species that, in the wild, produces flowers of quite a deep blue. 'Angel's Tears' is paler, softer in appearance, the mottled throats of the flowers bisected by thin, yellowish orange lines. Try it with *Crocus* 'Vanguard' or an early daffodil such as *Narcissus cyclamineus* or mad *N*. 'Rip van Winkle'. Set the bulbs deep to encourage repeat flowering and choose a well-drained, sunny spot where they can get a warm summer rest. Plant 10cm (4in) deep and the same distance apart.

SEASON: February–March
HARDINESS: Fully hardy
HEIGHT: 15cm (6in)
SECTION: Reticulata

SEASON: Late January
HARDINESS: Fully hardy
HEIGHT: 9cm (3¾in)
SECTION: Reticulata

Iris histrioides 'Lady Beatrix Stanley'

In every way, this is a more substantial flower than, say, 'Cantab', and a richer, more pleasing colour. It is a gorgeous iris with wide, spoon-shaped, horizontal falls. The lid above them (more properly called the stigma flap) divides in two so that each fall seems to look at you like an exceptionally alert mouse. Overall, the colour is rich blue, the throats creamy, each with a bright yellow beard running down into the centre of the flower. The cream is stippled and streaked with the same blue-purple colour. Above, strongly vertical, are three standards, narrow, the lower halves folded back on themselves so they appear even narrower there, swelling out above. At flowering time, there are just two leaves, shorter than the flower itself and slightly broader than the foliage of *I. reticulata*. 'Lady Beatrix Stanley' smells of violets. It demands good drainage, but does well outside as it likes to be cool and not too dry in summer. Introduced to cultivation *c*.1930, it is named after Lady Beatrix Stanley, the formidable editor of *The New Flora and Silva* magazine. Set it in front of the bold marbled foliage of *Arum italicum* 'Marmoratum'. Plant 10cm (4in) deep and the same distance apart.

NEXT PAGE This early iris 'Katharine Hodgkin' is only 8cm (3½in) tall, but in its markings is one of the most subtle of all dwarf iris. It flowers in late January.

Iris 'J S Dijt'

This has dark, rich, velvety falls, broken dramatically down the centre with an orange stripe. The standards are the same reddish purple, but do not seem so dark as they do not have the velvety texture of the falls. 'J S Dijt', named after the Dutch nurseryman who bred it, is a neat, handsome iris, with the narrow foliage overtopping but never getting in the way of the flowers. Try interplanting it with *Crocus etruscus* which is out at the same time. Give it a well-drained, sunny spot and top-dress the ground around with grit so the flowers do not get splashed with soil when it rains. Set the bulbs 10cm (4in) deep and the same distance apart.

SEASON: Mid February
HARDINESS: Fully hardy
HEIGHT: 13cm (5in)
SECTION: Reticulata

Iris 'Katharine Hodgkin' ♀

You can take subtlety too far and you may feel that perhaps this iris has. Close to, it is extraordinary, but in a garden you need to think carefully where to put it. It works well in a pot and certainly does not need noisy neighbours. The flowers come through without any leaves, the three falls at first folding in on themselves at the tip, so it is difficult to see the lovely markings: navy-blue feathered and spotted on a bluish cream background. It is a weird colour, only coalescing into yellow at the throat. The 'lid' (properly the stigma flap) is stained with blue down the centre, and the three upright standards are so finely veined

with blue that the background cream almost ceases to exist. Subdued and strange in its beauty, it is not difficult to grow but increases rather slowly in the garden. 'Katharine Hodgkin' was raised in 1958 by Edward Anderson of Lower Slaughter in Gloucestershire, UK, president of the Alpine Garden Society. In his spare time he was a research chemist, but what he really liked doing was breeding iris like this one, which came from *I. histrioides* 'Major' crossed either with *I. danfordiae* or *I. winogradowii*. Anderson named it after the wife of his friend Eliot Hodgkin who had an amazing collection of rare bulbs at his home near Twyford in Berkshire, UK. Plant 10cm (4in) deep and the same distance apart.

SEASON: Late January
HARDINESS: Fully hardy
HEIGHT: 8cm (3½in)
SECTION: Reticulata

Iris kolpakowskiana

This enchanting dwarf iris, named in 1877 after a governor of Turkestan, cost me £9 for a single bulb in 2006 and was worth every penny. The single flower rose between four slender, channelled leaves (more like crocus leaves than iris) and took a long time to break from its papery cased bud. The outer half of the falls are deep plum-purple, the inner half whitish, hair-streaked with purple. Yellow flashes light up the throat. The uprights are slightly frilly, pale lavender-blue. It is supposed to smell of violets, but I have never caught that. Perhaps it has not been warm enough. *Iris kolpakowskiana* needs full sun, shelter and perfect drainage. Professional growers lure it into flower with extra calcium and magnesium. Do not worry about planting companions. Concentrate instead on keeping it alive. Plant 10cm (4in) deep and (if you can afford more than one) the same distance apart.

SEASON: Mid April

HARDINESS: Fully hardy

HEIGHT: 10cm (4in)

SECTION: Reticulata (Species)

HABITAT: Central Asia, western Tien Shan and southern Kazakhstan where it grows on open grassy or stony slopes at 1,100–3,000m (3,600–10,000ft)

Iris latifolia (*Iris xiphioides*) ♀

ENGLISH IRIS

A robust and beautiful iris, first described by the Flemish botanist Rembert Dodoens in 1568. Then another Flemish botanist, Lobelius, saw *I. latifolia* flowering near Bristol, where it had probably been brought by Spanish ships from the Cordillera Cantábrica or from the Pyrenees. On the basis of this sighting, Lobelius described it as English iris, an erroneous tag that has stuck. The sixteenth-century botanist Carolus Clusius looked for it in vain when he was in England, visiting Sir Francis Drake. It is scarcely surprising he never found this species; the only iris native to Britain are the yellow flag iris (*Iris pseudacorus*) and the stinking iris (*I. foetidissima*). Already, by 1788, Haarlem bulb growers were offering 37 different kinds of 'English' iris in their catalogues, and by 1808 Van Veen & Co. of Haarlem listed 47. Now just six appear in *RHS Plant Finder* including 'King of the Blues' first introduced by the fine bulb company Barr in 1898 and purple 'Duchess of York' introduced by Barr in 1928. Grow them before they disappear altogether, for they are gorgeous things, in mottled shades of blue, mauve and purple, some as pale as a misty morning, some as dark as ink (but, unlike Dutch and Spanish iris, never yellow). As well as being beautiful, *I. latifolia* is also useful for gardeners, because it flowers later than the Dutch types with bigger flowers, sturdy and reliable. Unfortunately, it fell out of favour with commercial growers because it could not be forced out of season for the cut flower market, like the Dutch iris. Try it in dampish soil with *Lilium pyrenaicum* or *Narcissus pseudonarcissus* (they grow together in the wild), or with sanguisorba and veratrum. It is hardier than Dutch iris, and in the right conditions (damper than the ground you might generally choose for iris) will settle and increase. If you are more than usually blessed, *I. latifolia* may even naturalize in grass, provided it is not too coarse. The late Christopher Lloyd had it growing in grass in his fine garden, Great Dixter in Sussex, UK. The leaves do not come through until spring. Plant bulbs 10cm (4in) deep and 10–15cm (4–6in) apart.

SEASON: June–July

HARDINESS: Fully hardy

HEIGHT: 30–50cm (12–20in)

SECTION: Xiphium (Species)

HABITAT: Pyrenees and north-west Spain (Picos de Europa) where it grows in damp alpine meadows

Iris lazica ♀

The evergreen foliage of this species, first described in 1895, is broader and a brighter green than that of the Algerian iris (*I. unguicularis*), but it does not brown off so noisily and the habit of growth is stiffer, slightly more fan-like. The flowers are very similar to *I. unguicularis*, rather overwhelmed by the strappy leaves and perhaps best picked and enjoyed inside. They are not scented and are smaller than the best forms of *I. unguicularis*, but the falls are a darker, richer shade of purplish blue, the white throat speckled and streaked with purple. A bright orange beard runs down to the base of the flower. The standards are purple, the same size and shape as the falls. In the wild, *I. lazica* is separated from the similar *I. unguicularis* by 400km (250 miles) of bare, brown hill. There, it is a low-altitude plant found in scrub, among hazel trees and other half-shaded places. So, in the garden, you might expect it to want a similarly damp, shady spot. But before I knew much about it, I put it in gravel at the foot of a warm west wall of the house, and it grows lustily. It is often said that *I. lazica* flowers later than *I. unguicularis* but I have not found that to be true. In our garden, the two species flower together. Use it under winter-flowering jasmine or with clumps of the dwarf daffodil *Narcissus* 'Tête-à-tête'. It does not like chalk soils. Plant shallowly, with the rhizome at the same level as the soil and 10–15cm (4–6in) apart.

SEASON: December–February

HARDINESS: Frost hardy

HEIGHT: 25–40cm (10–16in)

SECTION: Beardless (Unguiculares)

HABITAT: The Black Sea coast (eastern end) from Trabzon in Turkey east to Georgia where it grows in tea plantations and among groves of hazel from sea level to 400m (1,300ft)

Iris magnifica ♀

A huge fountain of glossy green leaves
surrounds the flowers, peering out from
the leaf axils. There may be up to seven
of them on a stem, the bold, white
standards washed with the faintest hint
of lilac, the white falls splashed in the
centre with bright yellow. As its name
suggests, *I. magnifica* is one of the most
magnificent of all the Juno iris, first
described in 1935, and is not difficult
in deep, well-drained soil in full sun.
If it needs dividing, do it in early autumn.
Use it between mounds of *Geranium
maderense* or *G. palmatum*. Plant
5–10cm (2–4in) deep and 15–20cm
(6–8in) apart.

SEASON: April–May
HARDINESS: Fully hardy
HEIGHT: 40–50cm (16–20in)
SECTION: Juno (Species)
HABITAT: Tajikistan where it grows on the
rocky slopes of the Pamir Alai at around
1,600m (5,250ft)

Iris 'Oriental Beauty'

This bicoloured iris produces
enormous flowers, the yellow falls
stained with blue, which makes a
very pretty rim round the edges.
The standards are the same violet-
blue, with only the faintest staining
of yellow at the base. It is very
mysterious in bud, when the yellow
is dominant and the blue appears
almost grey. Try 'Oriental Beauty' in
front of a fountain of the giant fennel
Ferula communis or with *Lupinus*
'Polar Princess'. Plant 10cm (4in)
deep and 10–15cm (4–6in) apart.

SEASON: Late April
HARDINESS: Fully hardy
HEIGHT: 45cm (18in)
SECTION: Xiphium (Dutch)

Iris orientalis (*I. ochroleuca*) ♀

This species should not be here, as it is a rhizomatous iris, not a bulbous one. But it is a great garden plant, known in cultivation since 1768, and one of the few things that has been with me all my gardening life so I cannot bear to leave it out. It grew in a long, thin border in our first house and I brought a clump of it to the garden of the Dorset rectory, where we lived for more than 30 years. When we finally left, only snowdrops (given to me by my mother from the hills of my Welsh home) and this iris came with me. It is a Spuria type with long, strong, sword leaves that come early in the season but never look tatty. It will be the last of the iris listed here to bloom (June and early July), producing from each tall stem a succession of white, fleur-de-lis flowers with brilliant orange beards. Try it with larkspur or between clumps of *Geranium psilostemon*. It provides a good way of punctuating over-beefy clumps of hosta and looks splendid beside bronze fennel (*Foeniculum vulgare* 'Purpureum'). *Iris orientalis* does well in heavyish, damp soils, but like all the Spurias takes time to settle. September is the best time to plant, setting the rhizomes 5cm (2in) deep and 15cm (6in) apart.

SEASON: June–July
HARDINESS: Fully hardy
HEIGHT: 90cm (36in)
SECTION: Beardless (Spuria)
HABITAT: North-eastern Greece, Lesbos, Sámos and western Turkey
where it grows in ditches and marshes at 150–1,000m (500–3,300ft)

Iris 'Professor Blaauw' ♀

The flowers are smaller than those of
'Oriental Beauty', with more rounded,
more horizontal falls, but they are a
fabulous, rich gentian-blue, with only a
small, orange tongue. The standards are
neat, less tall than in 'Oriental Beauty',
and of the same saturated royal-blue as
the falls. It looks terrific with purple
aquilegias or the lime-green heads of
Euphorbia characias. For a real Monet
effect, mix it with golden-yellow
wallflowers. 'Professor Blaauw' was bred in
the late 1940s by the Zeeland nurseryman
H S van Waveren, who crossed the Dutch
iris 'White Perfection' with a Moroccan
species, *I. tingitana* var. *fontanesii*, which
nobody before had thought of using as a
parent. The Professor, blooming in a kind
of blue that had never been seen before
in these flowers, soon became one of the
most widely grown Dutch iris in The
Netherlands, planted on more than 365ha
(900 acres) of the light, sandy soils of the
cut flower nurseries. Plant 10cm (4in)
deep and 10–15cm (4–6in) apart.

SEASON: Late April
HARDINESS: Fully hardy
HEIGHT: 65cm (26in)
SECTION: Xiphium (Dutch)

Iris 'Purple Gem'

An absolutely gorgeous iris with
the narrow, reed leaves typical of
Reticulata iris. The flower is deep,
delicious purple, the tips of the three
horizontal falls seeming darker than
the rest. This is perhaps more a
question of texture than actual colour
– they are velvety. The throat is
creamy white, streaked with dark
purple, a very striking contrast.
If you lift the stigma flap you find
a bold, yellow streak running to
the centre of the flower. The three
upright standards are deep purple,
narrow and wavy edged. 'Purple Gem'
is a splendid iris, good in pots or
mixed in a gravelled area with
Crocus tommasinianus 'Roseus'.
Plant 10cm (4in) deep and the
same distance apart.

SEASON: Late January
HARDINESS: Fully hardy
HEIGHT: 12cm (5in)
SECTION: Reticulata

Iris reticulata ♀

The flower, known in gardens since 1808, is variable in the wild; the form I have grown was deep purple with much less red in it than a variety such as 'George'. In all respects it is a slighter flower with narrow standards and throats, marked with white. The central stripe is orange, compared with the yellow of 'Harmony'. It is an enchanting, finely boned flower, but whereas the falls of 'George' and 'Harmony' are almost 2cm (¾in) long *I. reticulata*'s are not much more than half that. It looks gorgeous planted in shallow earthenware bowls for early spring, but I have never had much success in getting it to settle and increase. Fortunately, it is cheap to replace. You can bring it inside in bowls when it is just about to flower, but it cannot be forced hard, as hyacinths can. Inside, though, you catch the scent more easily. Try it with *Crocus chrysanthus* 'E A Bowles'. Set *I. reticulata* in well-drained, gritty soil where it can dry out completely in summer. The bulbs have an unfortunate habit of splitting after the first season, and deep planting sometimes prevents this. Plant 10cm (4in) deep and the same distance apart.

SEASON: Mid February
HARDINESS: Fully hardy
HEIGHT: 10–15cm (4–6in)
SECTION: Reticulata (Species)
HABITAT: Northern Iran, north-eastern Iraq, Caucasus and eastern Turkey where it grows on mountain slopes at 600–2,700m (2,000–9,000ft)

Iris 'Sapphire Beauty'

An iris of showy bright purplish blue, darker in the standards than the falls, which are veined with the dark colour but on a light ground. The tongue is bright orange and the foliage thin, strappy and well behaved. Use 'Sapphire Beauty' with the dramatic lupin 'Thundercloud' or in front of the dark foliage of *Actaea simplex* Atropurpurea Group. Plant 10cm (4in) deep and 10–15cm (4–6in) apart.

SEASON: Late May
HARDINESS: Fully hardy
HEIGHT: 65cm (26in)
SECTION: Xiphium (Dutch)

NEXT PAGE The Algerian iris (*I. unguicularis*) chooses an odd time of year to produce its flowers but, because there is so little else in bloom in winter, it is a long-established favourite with gardeners.

Iris unguicularis (*I. stylosa*) ♀

ALGERIAN IRIS

This winter-flowering iris has been known to gardeners in Europe since at least 1789. You find it looking happiest at the foot of a sunny wall on limestone soil rather than acid ones; the only treat you need to give it is a top-dressing of bonemeal or potash in either autumn or spring. If you cut down the old foliage in August, then you will be able to see the flowers better, when the clump starts to bloom in November. If you do not do this, then at least pull away the old dead leaves. More sun will get through to the rhizomes and you may alarm and flush out a few slugs (a flower for breakfast in winter is their chief delight). Even if it is barbered in August, *I. unguicularis* is still an untidy thing. The evergreen foliage is narrow, dull in colour, tall and strappy, and the ends of the new leaves soon brown off. Overall, you could not call it a good garden plant, but the flowers are so welcome, coming when they do, scented as they are, we forgive the lack of any other attribute. The flowers themselves balance on top of enormously long tubes (the perianth) which in effect becomes the stem. It makes picking them a nerve-wracking business, since the tubes snap very easily. Gather them as furled buds rather than as open flowers. The tube splays out into the three falls, characteristic of all iris, but the crests are insignificant. This is a tolerant species, though it prefers limy soil if it can get it. In season, guard it zealously against slugs and snails. Why won't the wretched things eat ground elder instead? After a hot, dry summer, *I. unguicularis* comes into flower early. After a damp, cool one, it may not get going until February. It hates being moved. If you have to disturb it, lift it in big clumps in spring after it has flowered and be prepared for it to sulk before it starts flowering again. Plant it so the rhizomes are just below the surface of the soil and 10cm (4in) apart.

SEASON: November–March

HARDINESS: Fully hardy

HEIGHT: 30cm (12in)

SECTION: Beardless (Unguiculares)

HABITAT: Algeria, Tunisia, Greece, western and southern Turkey and western Syria where it grows in light scrub, open pine woods and rocky places

Iris unguicularis 'Mary Barnard' ♀

The foliage seems to be neater and more upright than most types of *I. unguicularis*, which is a distinct advantage. The flower is a lovely, velvety blue-purple, a much more intense colour than the species. The falls, purplish at the edges, become royal-blue at the centre, where the gold beard dives down the white-streaked throat. The standards are tinged at the base with a strange reddish bronze. 'Mary Barnard' is a very lovely variety, collected in 1962 outside Algiers by the iris-lover E B Anderson. Plant it so the rhizomes are just below the surface of the soil and 10cm (4in) apart.

SEASON: February–March
HARDINESS: Fully hardy
HEIGHT: 30cm (12in)
SECTION: Beardless (Unguiculares)

Iris unguicularis 'Walter Butt'

A pale selection, ghostly grey-blue, but with a heavenly scent. The flowers are bigger than most of this tribe and usually earlier too. 'Walter Butt' is easy, free-flowering and wonderful to pick; the scent is more pronounced indoors than out. Pair it with the cheerful, little *Crocus tommasinianus*. Plant it so the rhizomes are just below the surface of the soil and 10cm (4in) apart.

SEASON: November–February
HARDINESS: Fully hardy
HEIGHT: 30cm (12in)
SECTION: Beardless (Unguiculares)

Iris winogradowii ♕

The soft primrose-yellow flowers, finely dotted with purple-brown, seem very large on so dwarf a plant, but are gorgeous. A faint, orange line marks the falls. In the right spot, *I. winogradowii* has the potential to become a good perennial plant, as the bulbs do not split up after flowering, in the manner of other irises from the Reticulata section. But it does have very particular requirements. Give it damp, peaty but well-drained soil (definitely not chalk) in full sun or semi-shade, and it may clump up for you. Do not let it dry out entirely in summer. It hates to be transplanted. If you are lucky enough to have to split it, do this as soon as possible after the leaves have died down, before new root growth begins. It was introduced to cultivation in 1914 and named after the man who found it, P Z Winogradow-Nikitin. We are fortunate he did not insist on Nikitin being part of the name, too. Plant 8cm (3½in) deep and 10cm (4in) apart.

SEASON: March–April
HARDINESS: Fully hardy
HEIGHT: 6–10cm (2¼–4in)
SECTION: Reticulata (Species)
HABITAT: Southern Caucasus (Tbilisi region) where it is a rare native of alpine meadows

Iris xiphium
SPANISH IRIS

First described in *Rariorum Aliquot Stirpium* (1576) by the French botanist Carolus Clusius after his journeys through Spain and Portugal in 1564. Shortly after, these iris arrived in The Netherlands, where Clusius grew them in the botanic garden at Leiden University. The so-called Spanish iris became very popular because it produced so many different colours of flower – blue, violet, bronze, white, orange, yellow – and it was deliciously scented. It is thought that the species originated in the Maghreb in north Africa and drifted over to the Iberian peninsula during the Tertiary Period. Sir Cedric Morris found a particularly beautiful form of *I. xiphium* with violet falls and bronze standards in the Monchique valley inland from the Portuguese Algarve coast. Has anyone found it since? Or are they all now buried under the concrete foundations of the Algarve's holiday villas? If you are growing *I. xiphium* in a cutting garden, gather the flowers when the first bud on the stem is just beginning to open. It needs a good summer baking if it is to flower in subsequent seasons. Either lift and dry off the bulbs, as you might the corms of gladiolus, or plant fresh bulbs each September. Use them as you might the Dutch iris, set in swathes between musk roses, peonies, variegated honesty and *Mathiasella bupleuroides* 'Green Dream'. Plant 10cm (4in) deep and 10–15cm (4–6in) apart.

SEASON: June
HARDINESS: Fully hardy
HEIGHT: 40–60cm (16–24in)
SECTION: Xiphium (Species)
HABITAT: Southern Europe (south-west France, Corsica, southern Italy, Spain, Portugal) and northern Africa (Morocco, Algeria, Tunisia) where it grows in grass on sandy soils

I

Ixia (Iridaceae)

Ixia cultivars
CORN LILY

Named varieties are available (purplish 'Blue Bird', creamy white 'Hogarth', deep pink 'Mabel', yellow 'Marquette'), but ixias are most often sold as mixtures for growing under cover as cut flowers. Their home is South Africa, where they grow in sandy grassland and that is why they do so well in Australia, where the loveliest spreads I have ever seen were flowering in the light soil under fruit trees in an old orchard near Melbourne. The starry flowers (up to 20 on a stem) often have dark centres, and the stems are wiry, like those of freesia. Being South Africans, they grow during winter to be ready for their spring flowering and for gardeners in the chillier parts of Europe this cycle is difficult to break. Some suppliers keep corms in cold storage and offer them for spring planting to flower later in summer. This trick works once, but afterwards ixias revert to South African time. Otherwise, you have to plant in October at the front of a very sunny border, and give the corms a covering of ashes or bracken to protect them against frost. Or you can grow them in pots in a greenhouse or conservatory, using a loam-based compost (John Innes No 3) mixed with grit. Give them as much light as possible (without sun the flowers will not open) but not too much water until the first flower spikes appear. Thereafter, the ixias will need much more to drink, with a high-potash fertilizer added every two weeks. The flowers come out in succession, so the plants look good for a month or more. Stop watering when the foliage begins to die back. Repot the corms the following autumn in fresh compost (or start again with fresh ones – they are not expensive). Outside, set the corms 12cm (5in) deep and about 7cm (2½in) apart.

SEASON: May–June
HARDINESS: Half hardy
HEIGHT: 40cm (16in)

Ixiolirion (Ixioliriaceae)

Ixiolirion tataricum
Ledebourii Group

This is rather a wispy thing, similar to *Triteleia*, with thin, grassy, grey-green leaves; it will not be able to hold its own in rough company. Up to five trumpet flowers emerge from the same point at the top of the stem, sky-blue, with the petals turning back on themselves. Down the centre of each petal is a conspicuous, raised stripe, leading the eye to the bunch of pale cream stamens. Ixiolirion are not difficult to grow, but like so many bulbs from central Asia they will flower best after a really hot, dry summer. They are good flowers to cut, and this may be the best way to grow them, lined out on their own in a cutting garden, without too much competition. Otherwise combine it with autumn-flowering *Zephyranthes candida* and nerines in the kind of narrow, sunny border you sometimes find under a greenhouse wall. Plant the bulbs in rich, well-drained soil in full sun, where they will be damp in autumn and winter but completely dry in summer. Set them 10cm (4in) deep and 7cm (2½in) apart.

SEASON: Late May
HARDINESS: Fully hardy
HEIGHT: 30cm (12in)

Lachenalia (Hyacinthaceae)

Perhaps the closest thing to lachenalia in Europe is the Spanish bluebell, but these South African plants, named after Werner de Lachenal, an eighteenth-century professor of botany at Basel University, are very much more complex and interesting. Most of us will have to grow them in pots, for they are not hardy, but in a cool environment the flowers last a long time (more than six weeks) so a potful of bulbs makes a good display. Use a loam-based compost (John Innes No 3) mixed with grit or gravel and water only moderately until growth starts. The leaves emerge long before the flowers. Reduce watering as the foliage fades, and keep the bulbs dry until fresh growth starts again in autumn. Feed every two weeks while the plants are in active growth. Six bulbs should fit comfortably into a pot 15–25cm (6–10in) across.

Lachenalia pustulata ♛

The two leaves come through early in autumn and are very weird: stiff, thick, fleshy, and covered on the upper surface with bumpy, little lumps like frogspawn. Between them rises the flower stem, very stout and covered in a soft greyish bloom. The bell flowers (there may be up to 20 of them) are held in a spike 9cm (3¾in) long and come out alternately around the stem, each supported by a strange, little bracket jutting out from the main stem. They are intricately marked, the ground colour white with a hint of pale blue which becomes deeper at the base of the flower. The top two petals of *L. pustulata* fold back to display the knobby, little stamens and style, which jut out precociously. The lower petal curls down and away from the centre. Each one is tipped with a purple line. Plant 5cm (2in) deep, 3–5cm (1–2in) apart.

SEASON: April
HARDINESS: Half hardy
HEIGHT: 17cm (7in)
HABITAT: South Africa (Western Cape) where it grows on grassy slopes

Ledebouria (Hyacinthaceae)

Ledebouria cooperi (L. *adlamii*)

The foliage, dark green boldly striped with purplish brown, is rather more eye-catching than the heads of purplish pink flowers, which are striped with green and purple down the middle of the tiny petals. By nature this ledebouria is almost evergreen. Grow it in a loam-based compost, mixed with grit and give it plenty of light. Water L. *cooperi* well when it is growing strongly, but give less water in winter so that the plant just ticks over. Set the bulbs with their noses just above the soil and 5cm (2in) apart.

SEASON: June
HARDINESS: Half hardy
HEIGHT: 5–10cm (2–4in)
HABITAT: South Africa (Eastern Cape), Swaziland
and Lesotho where it grows in light grassland

Leucojum (Amaryllidaceae)

SNOWFLAKE

It is all too easy to think of snowflakes as padding plants. In some seasons, though, they flower so profusely that they turn themselves into stars. Superficially, they look like stretched snowdrops, growing on stems sometimes 45cm (18in) long. But when you look at the flower closely, you can immediately see the differences. Snowdrops have three long outside petals that hang down over three short inner ones. The snowflake has six petals all of the same length, each with a bright green spot on the end. The plant is often taller than a snowdrop, and the foliage is bright green rather than greyish. The flower stems of snowflake are flattened; since each of them carries several flowers, a single clump lasts a long time. Its ability to thrive in shade is one of its great assets, pushing through a mat of ivy, or leavening a planting of Mrs Robb's bonnet (*Euphorbia amygdaloides* var. *robbiae*). Try it with hellebores or between clumps of spotty-leaved, blue pulmonarias. Let it stride behind winter-tinted bergenias or leap out of a mound of variegated periwinkle. Ferns are good companions too, since they enjoy the same kind of cool, damp growing conditions. The ferns will not necessarily be there to set off the snowflakes in winter, but this does not matter. Deciduous ferns lie like small animals on the ground at this winter season, covered in tawny ginger fur, but you can see the tightly curled points where the new fronds will unfurl to take over the space where the snowflakes formerly were.

CULTIVATION

The best time to move snowflakes is just after they have flowered. If this is not possible, buy bulbs in autumn and grow them on in pots before setting them out in spring. Dig leaf mould or compost into the place where you intend to plant them, especially if you garden on dry, sandy soil. Humus helps soils such as these to retain moisture. Snowflakes will also grow in damp grassland, which is where they are found in the wild. They favour heavy, clay soil, which is kind of them, since so few bulbs do.

LEFT The enchanting chubby flowers of the spring snowflake (*Leucojum vernum*) are a welcome sight in the early spring garden.

Leucojum aestivum 'Gravetye Giant' ♀

SUMMER SNOWFLAKE

From the foliage, you might think that this was a daffodil, but each flowering stem, flattened to make two quite sharp edges, bears a head of pretty, white bell flowers, up to six to a stem. They droop down on long stalks, each petal marked at its tip with a neat, lime-green spot, very restrained and effective. Inside are narrow, orange stamens. 'Gravetye Giant' was selected as a particularly good form by the splenetic Edwardian gardener William Robinson and named after his garden in Sussex, UK. *Leucojum aestivum* naturalizes anywhere that is not too hot or dry and lasts a long time in flower. Set the bulbs 10cm (4in) deep and 10–15cm (4–6in) apart.

SEASON: Early April
HARDINESS: Fully hardy
HEIGHT: 50cm (20in)

Leucojum vernum ♀

SPRING SNOWFLAKE

The flowers often arrive before the glossy leaves – thick, juicy stems bearing one, occasionally two flowers on each, white tipped with green. They are wider, fatter than the flowers of *L. aestivum*. In the damp, heavy, rich ground they prefer, *L. vernum* clumps up quite quickly. The best form is var. *vagneri*, originally from Hungary, which nearly always has two flowers to a stem. Plant in sun or light shade setting the bulbs 10cm (4in) deep and 10–15cm (4–6in) apart.

SEASON: March
HARDINESS: Fully hardy
HEIGHT: 15–20cm (6–8in)
HABITAT: Southern and eastern Europe where it grows in woods and other shady places

Lilium (Liliaceae)

LILY

Lilies provide everything that the heart could desire in a garden plant: fine form, grace, elegance, an extraordinary, complex range of colours and sometimes swoony scent as well. They come at a good time too, when gardeners, having done all the early summer stuff, are casting about for ways to continue the show through July and August. The choice is vast, but gardeners in love with lilies soon discover that lilies may not be in love with them. On the west coast of Scotland, you see them at their best, because gardeners there can give them the cool, acid soil, moist but well-drained, that so many lilies choose for themselves in the wild. Though there are about a hundred different species (and more than twice as many garden hybrids listed in *RHS Plant Finder*), few of them are happy on stiff, alkaline soils. If that is what you have got, the safest option is to grow lilies in pots so you can at least provide a better-drained home.

ABOVE *Lilium speciosum* var. *album* does not produce its flowers until the end of summer, but they are well worth waiting for.

Getting a lily to flower in its first year is no problem; the bulb suppliers will have seen to that. Bad drainage and underground slugs will probably be the chief causes of failure in successive seasons. But, if your morale is fragile, start with the easy ones: species such as *L. lancifolium*, *L. martagon*, *L. pyrenaicum*, *L. regale*, and hybrids such as 'Black Beauty' or the vigorous Citronella Group. Well-known *L. regale* is an undemanding flower, always anxious to do its best. It has a powerful sweet scent – better than that of the martagon, which smells worse than a badger's sett. But the martagon has a wonderfully wild soul and looks glorious at the edges of a garden, where you want it perhaps to meld into the wider scene beyond.

Scent is an important reason to plant lilies, especially if they are in pots close to where you sit out on a summer evening. Scent first attracted me to the African Queen Group, sweet-smelling trumpet lilies of soft apricot-orange, and to 'Casa Blanca'. If scent is an important attribute, you should also surround yourself with *L. candidum*, *L. cernuum*, *L. regale* and *L. speciosum*. The trumpet lily 'Black Dragon' smells gorgeous. So do lilies of the Pink Perfection Group.

Lilies are wonderful flowers to cut, and if you cannot bear the thought of raiding your borders plant some in rows in a cutting garden. Here *L. lancifolium* and *L. longiflorum* come top of the list, but *L. pardalinum* and *L. speciosum* also make wonderful cut flowers, as do 'Black Beauty' and *Lilium* × *dalhansonii* 'Mrs R O Backhouse'. If possible, cut halfway up

OPPOSITE The martagon lily grows wild in much of Europe and is not a difficult lily to establish in sun or half shade.

the stem, so that the bottom half (with its leaves) can continue to make food to pump back into the bulb for the following season. Without this, bulbs may not be able to bulk themselves up sufficiently to flower again. The best time to gather lilies is when the first flower in a spike is just beginning to open. The rest will open in the vase. Strip the leaves from the part of the stem that will be in the water. If you do not do this, the leaves rot and the water stinks.

In many bulb catalogues you will find lilies classified in one of nine divisions, depending on their parentage. The classifications bring order to *The International Lily Register*, though to the lilies themselves, of course, it is a meaningless exercise. For gardeners, the divisions provide a rough shorthand as to whether the lily is likely to be scented (lilies from Division VI are often well endowed in this respect), to need very acid soil and whether it is stem rooting or not. Stem-rooting lilies, such as *L. cernuum* and *L. davidii*, need to be planted deeper than other types.

DIVISION I Early flowering Asiatic hybrid lilies derived from *L. amabile*, *L. bulbiferum*, *L. cernuum*, *L. concolor*, *L. davidii*, *L.* × *hollandicum*, *L. lancifolium*, *L. leichtliniii*, *L.* × *maculatum* and *L. pumilum*. The flowers, rarely scented, are born in elegant umbels.

DIVISION II Hybrid lilies of the martagon type, which have one parent as *L. hansonii* or *L. martagon*. The flowers are of the Turk's cap type, sometimes scented, with leaves held in whorls up the stem.

DIVISION III Hybrid lilies derived from *L. candidum*, *L. chalcedonicum* and other related European species (but not *L. martagon*). The flowers are usually of the Turk's cap type, sometimes scented, and the leaves are not held in whorls but spiral their way up the flowering stems.

DIVISION IV Hybrid lilies derived from American species. The flowers may be funnel-shaped but are usually of the Turk's cap type, occasionally scented. Leaves are held in whorls up the stem.

DIVISION V Hybrid lilies derived from *L. formosanum* and *L. longiflorum*. The flowers are big, often sweetly scented, trumpet- or funnel-shaped. Narrow leaves are scattered up the stem.

DIVISION VI Hybrid trumpet lilies derived from Asiatic species such as *L. henryi* and *L. regale* (but excluding *L. auratum*, *L. japonicum*, *L. rubellum* and *L. speciosum*). The flowers are usually scented but can be trumpet- or bowl-shaped, sometimes almost flat, occasionally recurved.

DIVISION VII Oriental Hybrid lilies derived from Far Eastern species such as *L. auratum*, *L. japonicum*, *L. rubellum* and *L. speciosum*. The flowers are often sweetly scented and may be trumpet- or bowl-shaped, sometimes flat, occasionally recurved. Leaves are held alternately up the stem.

DIVISION VIII All hybrids that do not fit anywhere else.

DIVISION IX All species lilies together with their forms and varieties.

OPPOSITE Flowering in early June, *Lilium* × *dalhansonii* 'Mrs R O Backhouse' is a beautiful thing, named after its creator, a lily enthusiast of Sutton St Nicholas in Herefordshire.

The letters that follow the division number attempt to describe the habit of the flowers and their shape. The flower habit letters indicate:

a/ upward-facing flowers;

b/ outward-facing flowers;

c/ downward-facing flowers.

The letters that come after the slash relate to the flower shape:

/a trumpet-shaped flowers;

/b bowl-shaped flowers;

/c flat flowers;

/d recurved flowers.

Many lilies, of course, will not fit in to these man-made boxes, and defy the conventions. The result is a log jam of numbers and letters, as with 'Sweet Surrender', which is **Ib-c/c-d**.

In the lilies listed below, you will not find any of the new, dwarfed kinds (which I think are foul – lacking in any of the grace and elegance with which nature endowed the family). There is also a clear prejudice against lilies with upward-facing flowers. These have chiefly been bred to suit the needs of commercial growers (they are easier to cut and pack than lilies with outward- or downward-facing flowers) but are not half so pleasing to look at in a garden. Unfortunately, lily breeding is fuelled by the cut flower industry, not by the delights and desires of gardeners. We have to put up with the unfortunate consequences of a worldwide trade in flowers, which sees lilies grown in South America flown in to the international market at Aalsmeer and then flown on to a florist's shop on Fifth Avenue in New York. Lilies that pack well cost less to transport. In the list below there is also a bias towards lilies with reflexed flowers, which I think is the loveliest of all the different forms that lily blooms can take.

Of the almost three dozen lilies listed, half are species. For grace, form and heart-stopping loveliness, they cannot be bettered. Unfortunately, the supply of lilies seems a particularly volatile business, and hybrids suddenly disappear from nurserymen's lists. (Here I am thinking especially of 'Limelight' with its trumpets of a gorgeous pale greenish yellow, which I loved but lost and have not been able to find again.) Though there are always plenty of 'novelties' on offer you cannot depend on old favourites being there too.

CULTIVATION

Is it best to plant lilies in autumn or in spring? Both have their dangers. Autumn-planted bulbs may rot in soil that is too cold and too damp. Inquisitive animals may dig them up or eat them. Underground slugs party to devastating effect among the scales. You may forget where you have put the bulbs and cut right through them with a spade as you attempt to plant something else right on top of their heads. I have done it.

The guilt is terrible, even worse than the wasted opportunity of sticking your nose into the oriental white trumpet of 'Casa Blanca' and swaying drunkenly on the smell.

The difficulty in spring is that bulbs may have shrivelled away some of their health and vigour. Unlike daffodils, they have no outer protective coat. It is pathetic in a garden centre to see displays of lily bulbs in boxes of wood shavings spurting out forests of sickly white shoots, desperately trying to keep to the timetable devised for them by nature rather than some godforsaken marketing department. You must buy them before they start sprouting. And spring-planted bulbs, even good, sound ones, scarcely have time to get themselves settled before they have to start growing. The precious resources they have built up are drained while the roots scramble to settle themselves and haul in the necessary food and drink. Though you will get a show, it is not always as good as it could be and the following season might be worse, as the bulbs struggle to build themselves up to strength again. Once settled though, lilies are not difficult and slowly clump up to explode dramatically among spent euphorbias and clouds of summer fennel.

I have tried both seasons. Since our weather is so unpredictable, neither can safely be said to be better than the other. September is supposed to be the best month of all to shift and plant lilies, but that does not suit bulb merchants, since the top growth has not died down and they are difficult to pack and post then. But, like the bulbs of snowdrops, lilies

ABOVE Perhaps the most popular lily of all, *Lilium regale* casts its scent over a June garden. It is pictured here growing with the feathery umbellifer *Ammi majus*.

hate to dry out completely. Whenever you get them, plant them as quickly as you can, spreading the roots out carefully over the compost.

Though they hate drying out, lilies also demand good drainage. On heavy ground, you need to incorporate bags and bags of leaf mould and grit. Lay each lily bulb on a bed of sharp sand and sprinkle more sand into the mixture that you use to fill up the planting hole. Sharp sand is the term for a particularly rough, gritty sand on sale at garden centres: ordinary builder's stuff will not do. Most lilies prefer a soil that is just the acid side of neutral. *Lilium auratum*, *L. pardalinum*, *L. speciosum* and its cultivars are the fussiest in this respect. Martagon lilies, however, are perfectly happy on limy soils, as are *L. candidum*, *L. henryi* and *L. pyrenaicum*.

In open ground, lilies like the clematis formula: feet in shade, head in sun. They are ideal for growing through the low branches of shrubs that can provide a parasol of leaves to keep the sun off their roots. Low shrubby growth will also help to anchor lilies safely, though they should never be planted where they will catch the worst of the prevailing wind. Some, such as the easy-going martagons, thrive in the light dappled shade cast by taller shrubs. Deep shade suits none of them. The greatest treat, especially for stem-rooting lilies, is a yearly mulch of leaf mould.

On heavy clay soils, the easiest way to grow lilies is in pots, either smart ones to display on a terrace or big, cheap, black plastic ones which you can drop into borders wherever you want a boost. The pots themselves will not be seen as by high summer there is plenty of foliage – geranium, iris, fennel, euphorbia – to disguise them. The underground slugs that do so much damage to lilies will not find bulbs in pots so easily as they do when they are in the open ground, and you can mix up a fast-draining compost, as acid as might be necessary, made to suit whichever lilies you want to grow. Use a heavy, loam-based compost with added grit, and when you have potted up the lilies (plenty of crocks at the bottom of the pot) keep them under cover in a shed or cold frame through winter, so that the compost does not get too wet. If the pot is too big to move, cover it with a dustbin liner to keep out rain.

Big tubs, with seven or ten bulbs in them, will give a better effect than three tiddlers with three bulbs in each. In small pots, lilies are more likely to dry out in summer and freeze in winter, neither of which is good for them. They like to be fed while they are growing. I use a combination of slow-release fertilizer, scattered on top of the compost (and topped off with grit to stop birds throwing the compost about) and liquid feeds every two weeks (tomato food is ideal, as it is high in potash).

Lilies, which can already demonstrate plenty of ways of dying, now have a newish enemy, the lily beetle. The beetle itself is bright red, slow and not hard to catch. The larvae, greyish yellow, look like bird droppings and are more difficult to spot, until you have got your eye in. The adult beetles burrow into the soil for winter and are most active, feeding on lily foliage and flowers, between May and August. You need to make regular patrols, wearing your very best beetle-squashing boots.

OPPOSITE Exuberant trumpet lilies of the Pink Perfection group add glamour to a late June border.

Lilium African Queen Group ♀

A vigorous, beautifully scented strain of lilies, first introduced in 1958, bearing up to six trumpet flowers on a stem (they need staking) clothed with narrow, green leaves. Each flower is carried on a longish stalk and opens from a yellowish bud, dark flushed with red, into a flared trumpet, the petals flexing only at the tips. It is a good colour, soft buttery orange, with a dark reddish line down the centre of the backs. Prominent ginger anthers range round a three-knobbed stigma. African Queen Group lilies will grow in sun or partial shade and look good with the old-fashioned *Helenium* 'Moerheim Beauty'. Plant bulbs 20cm (8in) deep and 35–40cm (14–16in) apart.

SEASON: Mid July
HARDINESS: Frost hardy
HEIGHT: 1.2m (4ft)
DIVISION: VIb-c/a

Lilium 'Anglia'

Broadish leaves are produced alternately up the stem getting smaller as they reach the upward-facing flowers. These are sweetly scented and make open, flattish stars. The petals are white, with a dark pink streak up the centre. The middle of each flower is speckled with the same dark pink. The tall upright style ends in a purplish stigma and around it are rather mean, narrow ginger anthers. Try 'Anglia' with selinum, or between aquilegias, whose foliage is looking good now (if you remembered to cut the plants down after flowering…). Failing this, plant it with acidanthera (*Gladiolus murielae*), which comes on later and so will extend the interest right into October. Plant bulbs 15cm (6in) deep and 30cm (12in) apart.

SEASON: Mid August
HARDINESS: Fully hardy
HEIGHT: 80cm (32in)
DIVISION: VIIa-b/b

Lilium 'Black Beauty'

A fine, strong lily, raised in Oregon in 1957 from a cross between *L. speciosum* var. *rubrum* and *L. henryi*. Broad, green leaves are set alternately up the stem and the flowers (up to 24 on a stem) are held on long, stiff, outward-facing stalks. Many of the stalks divide to produce two flowers. They are strongly reflexed, the petals curving back to touch each other at the back round the stalk. The petals are dark wine-red, very finely edged in white, with darker puckering on the inner surface. The stamens, of course, are very prominent (which is one of the reasons I love lilies with reflexed flowers), dark ginger in colour. Usefully, 'Black Beauty' inherited lime tolerance from *L. henryi* (one of its parents), which makes it an undemanding lily for gardeners to grow. Plant bulbs 20cm (8in) deep and 35–40cm (14–16in) apart.

SEASON: Early August
HARDINESS: Fully hardy
HEIGHT: 1–1.8m (3–6ft)
DIVISION: VIIIb-c/d

SEASON: Mid July
HARDINESS: Fully hardy
HEIGHT: 1m (3ft)
DIVISION: IX
HABITAT: Eastern North America from Quebec, New Brunswick and Nova Scotia south to Maine and North Carolina where it grows in dampish woodland among ferns and along the banks of streams

Lilium canadense

In terms of form, *L. canadense* is one of the most elegant of all lilies, the flowers (up to 20, but more likely three or four) held out on long stalks (14cm/5½in) at the top of fine, strong stems; they dangle and move individually in the breeze. In the form I grow, var. *coccineum*, the flowers are a rich, fiery red (yellow is more common) slightly darker at the top, flipping out at the bottom to reveal a complex interior. Here, the red at the ends of the petals drifts into orange at the centre, darkly freckled with maroon. The flowers are not big (7cm/2½in across at the mouth) but they last a long time and carry themselves so gracefully that they take your breath away. Smallish leaves whorl round the stems at regular intervals. This was the first American lily ever to find its way over the sea to Britain (*c.*1629) and, though capricious, is an astonishing thing, worth any amount of trouble. Give *L. canadense* deep, acid, leaf-mouldy soil and a position where it never dries out. It prefers a little shade, perhaps between azaleas or rhododendrons that enjoy the same kind of conditions. It is difficult to keep for long in a pot because the running stolons poke themselves out from the holes at the bottom and then have nowhere to go. Plant bulbs 10cm (4in) deep and 35–40cm (14–16in) apart.

Lilium candidum ♀

MADONNA LILY

The Madonna lily is smaller, purer than
L. regale, the flowers, all white, opening
wide into stars rather than trumpets.
There may be anything from five to a
dozen of them in a head, but only a few
are out at any one time. The rest wait.
The buds at the top of the stem are held
very upright, but as they develop they
drop to the horizontal and the flowers
face outwards. Brilliant orange anthers
and a pale green style curve out beyond
the petals. The scent is delicious: lighter,
more complex than that of *L. regale*. It is
unusual among lilies in producing a new
basal tuft of leaves at the end of summer
(no other lily does this). By the time
L. candidum comes into flower, this basal
clump is looking tattered, so you need to
disguise it with catmint, delphiniums,
tobacco plants or campanulas. These
stalwarts of the cottage garden are
natural companions for the Madonna
lily. Unfortunately, it is a martyr to
botrytis; the leaves wither and the bulbs
consequently cannot gather in the
nourishment they need to produce
decent flowering spikes. Fungicides will
help, but they are preventatives rather
than cures. You need to start spraying
before you see the problem, not after.
Most of us are not that prescient.
Unlike other lilies, *L. candidum* likes
to be baked. Give it a bright, sunny
spot (it does well on chalky, alkaline
soils – another atypical trait) and plant
shallowly, no more than 3cm (1in) deep,
and 20–25cm (8–10in) apart.

SEASON: Late June

HARDINESS: Fully hardy

HEIGHT: 1.2m (4ft)

DIVISION: IX

HABITAT: Perhaps centred in the
Caucasus, but now widespread in south-
eastern Europe where it grows in scrub and
on rocky slopes up to 600m (2,000ft)

Lilium 'Casa Blanca' ♀

A pure white lily, derived from *L. auratum* and introduced in 1984. It is fabulously scented, particularly at night. Narrow, dark green leaves are held alternately up the stem with up to five flowers (18–20cm/7–8in wide) clustered at the top. The petals are broad and slightly reflexed, making a wide-faced flower of great charm. There is a faint, green flash up the midrib (the lower part only) of the three inner petals, and the inner surface is slightly puckered, the flesh standing up like little thorns. The style with its tripartite knob curves out and up, with six ginger-topped stamens (not so long) around it. 'Casa Blanca' is a showy beauty. Use it to take over from clumps of *Helleborus argutifolius* or *Iris siberica*. Plant bulbs 15cm (6in) deep and 30cm (12in) apart.

SEASON: Mid July
HARDINESS: Fully hardy
HEIGHT: 85cm (34in)
DIVISION: VIIb/b-c

SEASON: Mid June
HARDINESS: Fully hardy
HEIGHT: 60cm (24in)
DIVISION: IX
HABITAT: North-east Siberia through to Korea

Lilium cernuum

First discovered in 1900, this is a finely made and beautifully scented lily, which generously gave its pinkish purple colouring to many later Asiatic cultivars. There may be six or more of the nodding Turk's cap flowers on a single stem, the curved petals spotted all over with a deeper purple. The habit is enchanting, the reflexed, dangling flowers showing off the inside of the flowers with their prominent, ginger anthers. Each flower is held on its own long (14cm/5½in) stalk, all of them breaking together from the top of the flowering stem. The stem itself is narrow and wiry, clothed to the halfway point with very fine leaves. *Lilium cernuum* is a delicate, elegant lily and needs suitably restrained companions – *Blechnum spicant*, perhaps, or *Polypodium vulgare* 'Elegantissimum'. It is stem rooting and, though it will put up with limy soils, prefers something peatier and moist. Unfortunately it never seems to stay long in a garden, but that is not a reason to do without it altogether. Plant bulbs 20cm (8in) deep and 30cm (12in) apart.

SEASON: Mid July

HARDINESS: Fully hardy

HEIGHT: 1.5m (5ft)

DIVISION: Ic/d

Lilium Citronella Group

A splendid group of lilies, first introduced in 1958, with dark stems topped by up to 20 hanging, reflexed flowers of a most brilliant chrome-yellow. They are held out on long stalks, so the head becomes rather imposing, each flower gorgeously turning back its petals to display the dark spots on their insides. At the point where they meet the stalks, the backs of the petals are stained with red. Most often you see the ginger-brown-topped stamens in profile, like lizard's tongues looping out to pick up flies. Dark green leaves clothe the stem all the way up to the flowerhead. Citronella Group lilies are a vigorous gang, long-lasting in the garden, and lovely with *Euphorbia griffithii* or pushing through fronds of *Dryopteris erythrosora*. Plant bulbs 20cm (8in) deep and 35–40cm (14–16in) apart.

Lilium × *dalhansonii* 'Mrs R O Backhouse'

One of a series of fine, old lilies which arose from a cross between *L. martagon* and *L. hansonii* made by Robert and Sarah Backhouse, who lived at Sutton Court, Sutton St Nicholas in Herefordshire, UK. This lovely hybrid had already, by 1921, won an Award of Merit from the Royal Horticultural Society. It produces smallish, reflexed flowers, up to 16 in a head, opening in turn from the bottom upwards. In general habit it is very much like its parent, *L. martagon*. In bud, 'Mrs R O Backhouse' is pinkish, but it opens to a flower of a gorgeous, soft colour, not quite brown, not quite apricot, not quite yellow, freckled in the centre with dark purplish spots. The spots are carefully arranged, big towards the centre, but scarcely a dust-covering at the outer edges of the petals. Lovely, orange anthers dangle down from the centre of each flower. The leaves are held in whorls at regular intervals up the stems. This is a beautiful and unusual lily, splendid with *Onoclea sensibilis* or *Adiantum venustum*. Give it a sheltered site with some shade where the soil stays moist but is never waterlogged. As well as draining adequately, the soil needs to be rich in humus. If it is heavy, add grit to the planting hole. Remember to protect the emerging shoots from slugs. Plant bulbs 12–15cm (5–6in) deep and 30–35cm (12–14in) apart.

SEASON: Early June

HARDINESS: Fully hardy

HEIGHT: 75cm (30in)

DIVISION: IIc/d

Lilium davidii

This species is named after the famous plant hunter Abbé David, who first found it in 1869, though it was another plant hunter, Ernest Henry Wilson, who introduced it into the UK at the beginning of the twentieth century. Though the bulbs are small, the flowerhead sometimes contains as many as 20 orange-red blooms, sharply reflexed and darkly spotted. Each flower is held out on its own long stalk. They open from the bottom of the head upwards, so the display lasts a long time. *Lilium davidii* is a very handsome creature, stem rooting; it needs to be mulched with plenty of leaf mould each year. Though tolerant of lime, it much prefers neutral or acid soil. Plant it between low-growing shrubs which will shade its roots while allowing the flowers to shoot out in full sun. Plant the bulbs 20cm (8in) deep and 35–40cm (14–16in) apart.

SEASON: July
HARDINESS: Fully hardy
HEIGHT: 1m (3ft)
DIVISION: IX
HABITAT: Western China (Sichuan, north-west Yunnan)

Lilium duchartrei

First discovered by Abbé David in 1869 but not introduced until 1903, when Ernest Henry Wilson, plant hunting for the famous Veitch nursery in Devon, brought it to the UK from China. Its name, though, commemorates Pierre Étienne Duchartre, the nineteenth-century author of a classic monograph *Observations on the Genus Lilium*. The tall, slender stems, quite sparsely leaved, are topped by up to ten flowers (sadly, often less) on long, separate stems.

They are extravagantly reflexed, the petals doubling back on themselves to touch base at the back of the flower. The flowers are only 5cm (2in) across, so this is not a showy variety, but it is staggeringly lovely, the white blooms heavily stippled with deep purple halfway along the petals, to the point where they begin to double back. Ginger anthers are ranged round a long, exploratory style, topped with a purple, three-cornered stigma. *Lilium duchartrei* is lightly scented, stoloniferous and stem rooting, happiest in places like the west of Scotland where there is plenty of rain (there has to be some compensation for the weather) and no shortage of damp, peaty soil. Plant bulbs 10cm (4in) deep and 20cm (8in) apart.

SEASON: Early July
HARDINESS: Fully hardy
HEIGHT: 90cm (36in)
DIVISION: IX
HABITAT: China (north-western Yunnan, Gansu, western Sichuan) where it grows in damp places in scrub and alpine meadows

NEXT PAGE *Lilium henryi* is named after Augustine Henry, who first saw it growing on limestone cliffs above the Yangtze river in China.

Lilium 'Gran Cru' ♔

Though its bright brashness needs toning down with something like bronze-leaved *Carex buchananii*, 'Gran Cru' is an eye-catching lily, introduced in 1991. Its wide, gold petals are splashed at the base with deep reddish mahogany. The anthers are an even darker colour, deep furry brown, standing up around a ginger-topped style. Plant bulbs 15cm (6in) deep and 25–30cm (10–12in) apart.

SEASON: July
HARDINESS: Fully hardy
HEIGHT: 40cm (16in)
DIVISION: Ia/-

Lilium henryi ♔

Named after the plant-hunting Professor Augustine Henry, who in 1888 saw this species growing on the limestone cliffs of the Yichang gorge on the banks of the Yangtze river. A lime-tolerant lily, producing 4–20 apricot-orange Turk's cap flowers held on long stalks (sometimes two on a single stalk) away from the main stem. The surface of each curled-back petal is covered with little eruptions, like the hairs of a stiff brush. *Lilium henryi* is an excellent garden lily and fairly persistent, which is a relief given the death wish so deeply embedded in lilies such as beautiful *L. duchartrei*. It is stem rooting and easy to grow in part shade in soil that is alkaline or neutral. The bulbs are big and growth starts very early in the year, so the shoots may need some protection against frost. Though apparently a carrier of virus, *L. henryi* does not show its effects, as so many other lilies do. Plant bulbs 20cm (8in) deep and 35cm (14in) apart.

SEASON: August
HARDINESS: Fully hardy
HEIGHT: 2m (6½ft)
DIVISION: IX
HABITAT: China (western Hupei, Guizhou) where it grows on limestone in scrub up to 1,100m (3,600ft)

Lilium lancifolium 'Splendens' ♀

TIGER LILY

A fine, eye-catching lily, in bloom for a long time as the flowers (up to 20 in a head) open from the bottom upwards in turn, no more than four out at the same time. They are a clear, soft, almost luminous orange, the petals curling back extravagantly so they meet each other round the stem at the back of the flower. Large, dark spots, purplish in tone, cover the petals. The wonderfully elegant stamens, with the anthers, dark plush brown, are held at right angles to the filament. The style is knobbed in the same plushy colour. No scent, which is a pity, but this is a strong, handsome lily to grow between clumps of *Dryopteris wallichiana* or *D. tokyoensis*. *Lilium lancifolium* first appeared in England at the beginning of the nineteenth century, sent from Canton to the Royal Botanic Gardens at Kew by William Kerr, who in 1803 went to east Asia to look for new plants. Sir Joseph Banks, then unofficial director of Kew, saw it flower and immediately arranged for it to be propagated. Ten thousand bulbs of *L. lancifolium* were eventually distributed from Kew. It is not difficult to propagate as it produces small, dark bulbils in the angles where its leaves are joined to the flowering stems. It is stem rooting and will tolerate alkaline soils but is happiest in damp, acid ones in sun or part shade. Plant bulbs 20cm (8in) deep and 35–40cm (14–16in) apart.

SEASON: Early August
HARDINESS: Fully hardy
HEIGHT: 1.2m (4ft)
DIVISION: IX
HABITAT: Eastern China, Korea and Japan

Lilium leichtlinii

This is a very beautiful creature with fine, strong, black stems, covered in equally fine, narrow leaves. The flowers are borne on stalks (at least 14cm/5½in long) at an angle to the main stem and are a rich, deep yellow, deeper than *Lilium* 'Yellow Star'. They are deeply reflexed and dark spots cover nearly the whole of the petal. On the backs of the petals is a reddish stain, particularly noticeable at the uppermost end. Stamens, very prominent, are held out at right angles to the nodding flowers, with dark, gingery anthers balancing on top of the filaments. The style, upward-facing, ends in a three-cornered, brownish stigma. *Lilium leichtlinii*, named after the German plantsman Max Leichtlin (1831–1910), was introduced to cultivation by accident when it was found in a consignment of *L. auratum* sent to Veitch's nursery in Devon, UK. It looks lovely thrusting out from the tangled branches of *Rubus* 'Benenden' or interplanted with red hot pokers. Try it, too, with various types of deschampsia. By nature, this lily is stem rooting and where it is happy spreads by rhizomes to make quite large clumps. It prefers acid soil, part shade and almost pure leaf mould. Plant bulbs 20cm (8in) deep and 35–40cm (14–16in) apart.

SEASON: Mid July
HARDINESS: Fully hardy
HEIGHT: 1.3m (4½ft)
DIVISION: IX
HABITAT: South Korea and Japan (Honshu, Shikoku, Kyushū) where it grows in damp but well-drained ground by streams at 300–600m (1,000–2,000ft)

SEASON: Late July
HARDINESS: Half hardy
HEIGHT: 80cm (32in)
DIVISION: Vb/a

Lilium longiflorum 'White Heaven'

A gorgeously scented lily, more common in florists' shops than in gardens, with long (15cm/6in), elegant trumpet flowers, white very faintly tinged with green, especially when they are still in torpedo-shaped bud. The trumpets flare out softly at the end, but the central arrangement of stamens and stigma – pale, bleached cream – is not as showy as in many lilies. The shape of the flowers is wonderful, each trumpet (there can be six on a stem) carried on its own fat, juicy stalk. Short, broad leaves clothe the stem all the way up to the flowerhead. Use 'White Heaven' with green *Paris polyphylla* or between the swirling, spreading fronds of *Polystichum setiferum* 'Herrenhausen'. It also looks good with lime-green alchemilla or lime-green tobacco plants. Though only rated half hardy, I have grown it successfully out of doors in my cool-temperate garden, though, of course, recent winters have been relatively mild. It is stem rooting. Plant bulbs 20cm (8in) deep and 35–40cm (14–16in) apart.

Lilium mackliniae

MANIPUR LILY

Named after his wife, Jean Macklin, by the plant hunter Frank Kingdon Ward who in 1946 discovered *L. mackliniae* growing among rocks near Ukrhul on the border between India and Burma. He had actually been sent to look for crashed American warplanes, not plants, but, luckily for gardeners, could not resist gathering a seedhead he did not recognize. *Lilium mackliniae* has enchanting cup-shaped flowers (7cm/2½in across), up to six of them on a stem, not showy, but very charming, wide faced and pale pink, though darker in bud, when the dark purple at the tips of the outer petals looks like colour that has run and coagulated in the rain. The same deep purple stains the petals inside at the base. Small, neat stamens have dark orange-brown anthers, but unfortunately there is no scent. This is a stem-rooting lily that prefers leafy, well-drained, neutral or acid soil in dappled shade and seems to do better in high, cool, damp places than in low, hot, dry ones. Plant bulbs 20cm (8in) deep and 30cm (12in) apart.

SEASON: Mid May
HARDINESS: Fully hardy
HEIGHT: 42cm (17in)
DIVISION: IX
HABITAT: North-eastern India (Assam) where it grows on grassy and rocky slopes at 2,100–2,600m (7,000–8,500ft)

Lilium martagon ♀

In the wild, *L. martagon* has a more extensive range than any other lily on earth, so gardeners can rely on it as an adaptable species. Where it is happy, it grows vigorously and makes large clumps, taller and more floriferous than the white form (see p.334). Whorls of leaves are set up the stems, with smaller, more scattered leaflets directly under the flowering spike, which stretches over the top 30cm (12in) or so of the dark, purplish stems. The flowers are a kind of crushed raspberry, deeper than pink, but not quite purple. In a good spike there may be 30 of them, opening from the bottom up. They are lightly spotted, but the chief delight comes from the contrast made by the ginger anthers, dangling around the dark style. The flowers are set all the way round the stem, so it is not one-sided. This is a tough lily, naturalizing well and seeding itself about liberally where it is happy. It is stem rooting and equally happy on acid and alkaline soils, in sun or semi-shade. Plant bulbs 20cm (8in) deep and 35–40cm (14–16in) apart.

SEASON: Mid June
HARDINESS: Fully hardy
HEIGHT: 1.1m (3½ft)
DIVISION: IX
HABITAT: Europe, western Siberia and the Caucasus where it grows in alpine meadows and scrub

Lilium martagon var. *album* ♈

The foliage is pale and sparse, topped by wonderful stems of Turk's cap flowers, rarely more than ten in a head, sticking out on short stalks from the main stem and facing down. When you look into the hanging flowers you see the curious, long, green style, like a hunting horn, and the six golden anthers wobbling on their stalks round it. The flowers reflex gradually, so the older ones are tightly curled back, the young ones only just beginning the journey. The buds are white, stained with green at the base. Unfortunately slugs seem to adore *L. martagon* var. *album* and demolish shoots before you have even noticed them. It is stem rooting. Plant bulbs 20cm (8in) deep and 35–40cm (14–16in) apart.

SEASON: Late June
HARDINESS: Fully hardy
HEIGHT: 60cm (24in)
DIVISION: IX

Lilium martagon var. *cattaniae*

Found in the wild in south-eastern Europe, this is the most desirable of all the forms of the martagon lily. The flowers are so dark as to seem almost black and the petals have a glossy sheen, quite absent in ordinary *L. martagon*. The buds are hairy, like poppies. The best group I have ever seen grows in shade in a Scottish garden where the flowering stems push through a beach of pebbles alongside a stream. They are swamped every winter by floods, but it does not seem to bother them. *Lilium martagon* var. *cattaniae* is a stem-rooting lily, and like all of this tribe is best bought damp-packed as the bulbs hate to dry out. Plant 20cm (8in) deep and 35–40cm (14–16in) apart.

SEASON: Late June
HARDINESS: Fully hardy
HEIGHT: 60cm (24in)
DIVISION: IX

Lilium nepalense

A fabulous lily producing huge, elegantly reflexed flowers that dangle downwards, showing just a glimpse of the richly maroon interior. There are sometimes four to a stem, more usually just one. It is variable in its colouring: the interior can be heavily or lightly shaded, the outside may be a weird lime-green, sometimes yellowish, sometimes pale celadon-green. From the centre dangle the anthers, laden with dark brown pollen, a perfect complement to the maroon interior. *Lilium nepalense* is not easy, but worth any amount of trouble. As it is not reliably hardy, this acid-lover is probably best grown in a pot of ericaceous compost and plunged outdoors when all danger of frost has passed. Water well when in growth, but keep dryish during the winter. In the garden, because it is stoloniferous and stem rooting, *L. nepalense* needs to be set deep in cool, really well-drained, acid soil and partial shade. Protect it in winter with bracken or leaf mould. In the wild, the stems creep about underground quite far from the mother bulb. If you choose to do without the pot, plant bulbs 20cm (8in) deep and 35–40cm (14–16in) apart.

SEASON: June–July
HARDINESS: Half hardy
HEIGHT: 60–100cm (24–39in)
DIVISION: IX
HABITAT: Himalayan regions of northern India into Nepal and Bhutan where it grows among limestone rocks on steep slopes at 2,300–3,000m (7,500–10,000ft)

SEASON: Mid July
HARDINESS: Fully hardy
HEIGHT: 55cm (22in)
DIVISION: Ia/b-c

Lilium 'Netty's Pride'

By modern standards, 'Netty's Pride' produces smallish flowers (9cm/3¾in across), five or six on a stem, the petals deep ox-blood-maroon with ivory at their tips. The dark colour fades out at the end in a series of small dots. Dahlias do this, but in lilies the colours are more often arranged the other way around, pale at the centre, the colour darkening as it reaches the edges of the petals. Here, ginger-topped stamens stand up straight in the centre of the flower around the purple knob of the stigma. The stems are very dark, which increases its allure as does the lush foliage – the leaves reaching right up to the flowerhead. The unusual colour makes 'Netty's Pride' a quirky, bizarre flower, excellent for pots in a cool conservatory, though unfortunately it is not scented. Outside it makes an eye-catching companion for *Sanguisorba officinalis* or the dark foliage of *Actaea simplex* Atropurpurea Group. Plant bulbs 15cm (6in) deep and 30–35cm (12–14in) apart.

SEASON: July

HARDINESS: Fully hardy

HEIGHT: 1m (3ft)

DIVISION: IX

HABITAT: Western USA (Oregon, California) where it grows in marshy land and scrub

Lilium pardalinum ♀

LEOPARD LILY

First described in 1859, this lily carries orange Turk's cap flowers on top of stems of whorled leaves. Yet 'orange' is too simple a description: the top half of each petal is orange-red, the bottom half yellow, covered with large, dark spots – hence the leopard. On a well-established plant, there may be ten or 20 flowers in a head, opening from the bottom upwards, each on its own long stalk. Unfortunately there is no scent. Try *L. pardalinum* with shaggy *Inula magnifica* or with clumps of *Miscanthus sacchariflorus* or *Molinia caerulea* 'Transparent'. The bulbs spread out by way of rhizomes and in time will make huge clumps where they are happy. This species tolerates alkaline soils but is happiest in damp, acid ones rich in humus. Give it light shade and plant bulbs 10cm (4in) deep and 30–35cm (12–14in) apart.

Lilium Pink Perfection Group ♀

The colour of the large, scented, trumpet flowers – a deep purplish pink – contrasts strongly with the orange anthers in the centre, a combination very typical of the 1960s, when this strain was launched by the De Graaf nursery in Oregon, USA. The ends of the petals curl back very determinedly, which gives the stamens and style more prominence than they would otherwise have. Pink Perfection Group lilies are vigorous, sometimes bearing more than 20 flowers on a single stem, and are excellent in a herbaceous border with delphiniums or larkspur and clouds of the elegant annual *Ammi majus*. They are as happy in part shade as they are in sun. Plant bulbs 20cm (8in) deep and 35–40cm (14–16in) apart.

SEASON: Late June

HARDINESS: Fully hardy

HEIGHT: 1.5m (5ft)

DIVISION: VIb/a

Lilium 'Pink Tiger'

These are imposing lilies of a very pleasant habit. The stem is strong with narrow, dark green leaflets up to and beyond the flowering head. There are up to nine flowers, gently reflexed, of an easygoing, dirty salmon-pink (nicer than it sounds), darkly speckled inside, with the speckles reaching out over half the petal. Bright ginger anthers surround a strange style with a dark purple stigma. What sacrilege to cut them out, as florists do. Use 'Pink Tiger' to rear up between clumps of *Euphorbia characias* subsp. *wulfenii*, now just mounds of grey-green foliage. It is a good lily, though it has no scent and the flowers fade as they age. Plant bulbs 15cm (6in) deep and 35–40cm (14–16in) apart.

SEASON: Mid July
HARDINESS: Fully hardy
HEIGHT: 1.6m (5½ft)
DIVISION: Ib/c

Lilium pumilum
(*L. tenuifolium*) ♛

First discovered by Peter-Simon Pallas in 1773 and introduced to Western gardeners in the early nineteenth century by way of the botanic garden in St Petersburg, Russia. *Lilium pumilum* makes thin, upright stems, with narrow leaves climbing up to the head of up to 15 small (3cm/1in), extravagantly reflexed flowers in brilliant orange-red. It is good in pots though only slightly scented. This is a stem-rooting species, so it needs to be planted deep in well-drained, fairly acid soil. It is happiest in full sun. Cut off the seedheads (a good practice with all lilies) to allow as much as possible of the plant's strength to return to the bulbs. These are very small and need building up if they are to flower well the following season. Plant them 20cm (8in) deep and 10–15cm (4–6in) apart.

SEASON: Late June
HARDINESS: Fully hardy
HEIGHT: 45cm (18in)
DIVISION: IX
HABITAT: Siberia to Mongolia, north-eastern China and northern Korea where it grows in grass and scrub at 400–900m (1,300–3,000ft)

Lilium pyrenaicum

An easy lily, and one of the earliest to flower, producing hanging Turk's caps (up to 12 on a stem) of greenish yellow, heavily spotted and flecked with maroon. Ginger anthers hang like bell clappers from the bottom of the flower, not held at right angles to the filament (like most lilies). Close-spaced, narrow leaves are massed up the stems. Where it is happy, *L. pyrenaicum* spreads into huge clumps and, if you are lucky, will naturalize in grass. It is stem rooting and happiest in soils that are alkaline or neutral in sun or part shade. Plant bulbs 15cm (6in) deep and 30cm (12in) apart.

SEASON: June
HARDINESS: Fully hardy
HEIGHT: 30–50cm (12–20in)
DIVISION: IX
HABITAT: France and Spain (Pyrenees) where it grows in alpine meadows and light woodland

Lilium regale ♀

Famously discovered in 1903 by Ernest 'Chinese' Wilson, who later said he 'would proudly rest his reputation with the Regal Lily'. He had been sent to China by the Veitch nursery to look for the fabled handkerchief tree (*Davidia involucrata*) and came across the lilies by accident, flowering in the inaccessible Min valley in western China: 'There', he wrote, 'in narrow, semi-arid valleys down which thunder torrents, and encompassed by mountains composed of mudshales and granites, whose peaks are clothed with snow eternal, the Regal Lily has its home. In summer the heat is terrific, in winter the cold is intense, and at all seasons these valleys are subject to sudden and violent windstorms against which neither man nor beast can make headway. There, in June, by the wayside, in rock crevices by the torrent's edge, and high up on the mountainside and precipice, this lily in full bloom greets the weary wayfarer. Not in twos or threes but in hundreds, in thousands, aye, in tens of thousands.' Wilson dug up some of the bulbs, but on the way out of the valley was caught in a landslide and broke his leg. He lay immobilized on the mountain track as each of the mules in the 40-strong mule train carefully stepped over him, spreadeagled over the path. When the mules were out of the way, Wilson's porters used the legs of his camera tripod to make rough splints and carried him all the way to a medical mission. The leg set rather badly and for the rest of his life Wilson had what he called his 'lily limp'.

But a consignment of three thousand bulbs had reached Veitch's nursery by the autumn of 1904, and the lily bloomed in Britain in 1905, the first time away from its native home. Once so hidden in its wild valley, *L. regale* is now the most ubiquitous of garden lilies, good in pots, either outside or used to scent a cool conservatory. Narrow leaves climb all the way up the stem, which is darkish and slightly grey-bloomed. There may be up to 16 white trumpet flowers on a stem, heavily flushed on the backs of the petals with raspberry-red. In bud, the reddish pink is all you see. Inside, at the throat, the trumpets are yellow. The flattened, orange stamens are contained within the narrow trumpets, and do not hang out as is the enchanting way with some lilies. *Lilium regale* has a heavenly, sweet scent and is easy with alchemilla, or used to take over from tulips or Dutch iris. It is particularly happy on chalk soils – a boon for those who cannot provide the acid soil, rich in leaf mould, that so many lilies seem to demand – and prefers full sun. The scaly bulb is wine-coloured and the lily stem rooting. Wilson warned 'all who possess this treasure not to ruin its constitution with rich food'. Plant bulbs 20cm (8in) deep and 35–40cm (14–16in) apart.

SEASON: Late June

HARDINESS: Fully hardy

HEIGHT: 1.15m (3¾ft)

DIVISION: IX

HABITAT: South-west China (a very limited area in the Min valley, western Sichuan)

NEXT PAGE The splendid scented trumpets of *Lilium regale* push through *Verbena bonariensis* and the pear-shaped heads of *Allium sphaerocephalon*.

Lilium speciosum var. *album*

A vigorous lily with purple-flushed stems bearing up to 12 big, reflexed flowers, white, sometimes spotted inside with pink. The surface of the petals is pulled up into strange, sharp, little points, giving a rough texture. The points are longest towards the centre of the flower and fade out altogether towards the edges of the petals. Give *L. speciosum* var. *album* well-drained but moist, acid soil, lots of leaf mould and some shade. It is a stem-rooting lily, and in cold areas the flowers may come too late to escape the first frosts. Plant bulbs 20cm (8in) deep and 35–40cm (14–16in) apart.

SEASON: Late August
HARDINESS: Fully hardy
HEIGHT: 1m (3ft)
DIVISION: IX
HABITAT: Japan

Lilium 'Sterling Star'

An exceptionally strong, sturdy lily with upward-facing flowers of ivory white, four to a stem, each 11cm (4½in) across. The petals are very thick and waxy, stiffly splayed round the central crown of ginger anthers. Apart from the deep purple spots in the centre, they are plain. 'Sterling Star' was introduced in 1973 and is a useful, rather than heart-wrenchingly lovely thing, but dependable among clumps of *Iris siberica* which will have flowered earlier in the summer or with the supremely beautiful fern *Polystichum setiferum* 'Pulcherrimum Bevis'. Leaves clothe the whole of the dark-spotted stem. Plant bulbs 15cm (6in) deep and 35–40cm (14–16in) apart.

SEASON: July
HARDINESS: Fully hardy
HEIGHT: 80cm (32in)
DIVISION: Ia/b

Lilium 'Sweet Surrender'

Up to 16 beautiful flowers are borne on each stem, creamy coloured, with a dark flush on the backs of the petals. That makes it sound like 'Royal Fantasy' but 'Sweet Surrender' does not have upward-facing flowers. These are slightly reflexed – a very pretty habit – and have dark spots in their throats. Orange anthers balance like boats on the stamens, held out at right angles to the flower. The fine leaves grow all the way up to the top of the stem, even between the individual flowers that make up the head. Plant bulbs 15cm (6in) deep and 35–40cm (14–16in) apart.

SEASON: July
HARDINESS: Fully hardy
HEIGHT: 1.15m (3¾ft)
DIVISION: Ib-c/c-d

Lilium Triumphator

The flowers make huge trumpets, white painted over with maroon in the centre, with long (16cm/6½in), broad petals, flipping out at the mouth. A faint pinkish wash stains the backs of the petals, with the midribs of the inner ones marked in a dark pink line. Six gingery anthers wobble on top of the stamens set around a long style, bright orange-yellow at the end and three-knobbed like the ace of clubs. Triumphator is not a lily with any finesse, but it is scented and showy under mallow, underplanted with forget-me-nots. The stems are stout, with broadish leaves held alternately up them. Plant bulbs 15cm (6in) deep and 35–40cm (14–16in) apart.

SEASON: Mid August
HARDINESS: Fully hardy
HEIGHT: 1.35m (4½ft)
DIVISION: VIIIb/a–b

Lilium 'White Tiger'

A very easy-going lily, introduced in 1970, with small, bright green leaves all the way up the stem. The hanging trumpet flowers (four to six on a stem) are creamy white, only lightly reflexed, but elegantly held on their own small stalks. Outside there is a dark red flush at the base of each petal (it shows on the buds, too), but inside the flowers are cream, freckled with dark purple spots. The gingery brown anthers dangle, balanced on stamens that reach out from the flower, around the style. 'White Tiger' looks good with deschampsia or among mounds of *Euphorbia oblongata*. Plant bulbs 15cm (6in) deep and 35–40cm (14–16in) apart.

SEASON: Early July
HARDINESS: Fully hardy
HEIGHT: 90cm (36in)
DIVISION: Ic

Lilium 'Yellow Star'

The flowers (up to 11 in a head) open to big, flat-faced stars, 15cm (6in) across, outward facing and slightly reflexed. The petals are longer and narrower than those of 'Pink Tiger', bright yellow, spotted around the centre with dark maroon. Each flower is held away from the central stem on a longish (17cm/7in) stalk. In the centre is a curving style, with a dark maroon, knobby stigma at its end. Ginger anthers wobble around it, balanced at right angles on their filaments. It is a showy lily but unfortunately has no scent and will need to be staked as the dark maroon-brown stems are very tall, with bright green leaves all the way up to the flowerheads. Dark, little bulbils sit in the axils of the leaves. 'Yellow Star' looks good next to *Euphorbia mellifera* or coming up between the lax branches of *Rubus* 'Benenden'. Plant bulbs 15cm (6in) deep and 35–40cm (14–16in) apart.

SEASON: Mid July
HARDINESS: Fully hardy
HEIGHT: 2m (6½ft)
DIVISION: Ib/b-c

Maianthemum (Convallariaceae)

Maianthemum bifolium

What a difference scent makes. Lily-of-the-valley has it. Maianthemum, so similar in its habits and so useful as ground cover, does not, so tends to be forgotten. Like lily-of-the-valley it grows by way of creeping rhizomes and produces sheaves of broad, heart-shaped leaves that wrap around the fluffy spikes of white flower. It likes moist, leafy soil in half shade and makes an excellent companion for ferns such as *Blechnum nudum* and *Adiantum aleuticum* 'Imbricatum'. You are more likely to find *M. bifolium* in growth as a plant in a pot than as a dried-off rhizome and it is perhaps best bought like this. Either way, plant about 7cm (2½in) deep and the same distance apart.

SEASON: May
HARDINESS: Fully hardy
HEIGHT: 10cm (4in)
HABITAT: Western Europe to Japan

Merendera (Colchicaceae)

Merendera montana

Merendera looks like a colchicum with narrow, purplish pink petals and calls for similar treatment in a garden. As with colchicum, the leaves come after the flowers. Like a colchicum, too, it sits on the ground, a beacon for all slugs in the neighbourhood. Be prepared. Plant the corms of *M. montana* in autumn, setting them 5–7cm (2–2½in) deep and the same distance apart.

SEASON: September–October
HARDINESS: Fully hardy
HEIGHT: 7cm (2½in)
HABITAT: Pyrenees, Portugal and Spain where it grows in sub-alpine meadows

Moraea (Iridaceae)

Moraea huttonii

The moraeas are the iris of South Africa, with similarly built flowers, made in threes, though they grow from corms, not bulbs or rhizomes. They were initially named after an eighteenth-century gentleman botanist, Robert More of Shropshire, UK, but the name was sneakily tweaked by the Swedish botanist Carl Linnaeus to honour his wife, Elisabeth Moraea. Though individual flowers are short-lived, there are plenty of them on a spike, so the display goes on for some weeks. This species has scented flowers of golden-yellow, with brown eyelashes towards the centre. In cold areas, the safe option is to plant moraeas in pots using a loam-based compost (John Innes No 3) mixed with grit or sharp sand. Water after planting but keep the compost only just moist until growth begins. Then you can water more freely. Allow the foliage to die down naturally after flowering. Species from the Eastern Cape are slightly hardier than those from the Western Cape, so these are the ones to look for if you want to experiment with growing moraeas outside, which in mild areas is well worth risking. Give *M. huttonii* rich, well-drained ground in full sun, but where it will not entirely dry out in summer. Plant 10–15cm (4–6in) deep and the same distance apart.

SEASON: June
HARDINESS: Frost hardy
HEIGHT: 70–90cm (28–36in)
HABITAT: South Africa (Eastern Cape, KwaZulu-Natal) and Lesotho where they often grow alongside streams

Muscari (Hyacinthaceae)

GRAPE HYACINTH

Muscari are for painting big pools of blue in wildish parts of the garden. There are better things to use in key positions, but there is a jauntiness, a jolly gaiety, to grape hyacinths that makes them impossible to leave out of a spring scene. You can use them to make carpets under trees and shrubs, or try naturalizing them in grass, which is a good way of disguising the foliage. There is always too much of it and, depending on the species; it can be around for almost nine months of the year. In the right conditions grape hyacinths self-seed with happy enthusiasm. When they become congested, you can lift, split and replant the bulbs as you might snowdrops. Plant in autumn in large, informal groups, setting the bulbs 10cm (4in) deep and 5cm (2in) apart.

ABOVE *Muscari neglectum*, the commonest of the grape hyacinths, seeds about vigorously in a garden. It is perfectly happy in the half shade cast by overhanging trees.

Muscari armeniacum ♀

The leaves are through by mid October and lie in a lax mat over the ground, the proportion of leaf to flower always the wrong way round. Nevertheless, *M. armeniacum* is a strong, dependable grape hyacinth, invasive even, if it is in ground that suits it. It is excellent for naturalizing in short grass, the domed spikes a rich mid blue, with a very narrow, white rim round the edge of each tiny bell. The spikes get wider as they age and are lovely to pick (pull the stems rather than snapping them), with polyanthus, leucojum or dwarf daffodils. Plant this grape hyacinth round the stems of the dwarf almond *Prunus tenella* or spread it in sheets under spring-flowering magnolias. It was introduced to cultivation in 1878. Now, commercial growers, intent on grooming grape hyacinths to become perfect spring plants for garden centre display, often keep the bulbs in cold storage for a long time before planting them. When they are finally allowed to grow, the flowering spikes zoom up and bloom while the leaves are still quite short. This is not their normal habit but it certainly makes them look better in a pot. The following season in your garden, of course, they will revert to character and produce far too much foliage in relation to the flowers. Plant the bulbs 10cm (4in) deep and 5cm (2in) apart.

SEASON: Early March
HARDINESS: Fully hardy
HEIGHT: 16cm (6½in)
HABITAT: Balkans, Greece and Turkey east to the Caucasus where it is widespread in meadows and woodland up to 2,000m (6,500ft)

Muscari armeniacum 'Blue Spike'

'Blue Spike' is a showy double, with very full, broad spikes, pyramid-shaped and wide at the base. They give the impression of having twice as many flowers in them as ordinary grape hyacinths. They are a very brilliant clear blue, slightly dusty green in bud, when the spikes feel as hard as stone. Plant the bulbs 10cm (4in) deep and 5cm (2in) apart.

SEASON: Early April
HARDINESS: Fully hardy
HEIGHT: 16cm (6½in)

Muscari armeniacum 'Fantasy Creation'

Outrageously large, fluffy heads, not controlled enough to be called spikes, rise from the usual, untidy mats of foliage. They are so mad and congested it is difficult to see what is going on with the flowers, which are clean lavender-blue. Each little stalk rising from the main stem bears a clutch of double flowers, pinched in at the mouth. When the heads first emerge, tight-packed, they have the texture of moss, slate-blue with a smattering of lichen grey-green. The greenness in bud is very appealing. 'Fantasy Creation' was introduced to cultivation by a Dutch grower, Jan van Bentem, and is a dottier version of 'Blue Spike'. Plant the bulbs 10cm (4in) deep and 5cm (2in) apart.

SEASON: Early April
HARDINESS: Fully hardy
HEIGHT: 12cm (5in)

Muscari armeniacum 'Valerie Finnis'

Pale glacier-blue spikes rise from the untidy, sprawling mat of foliage that is the curse of all grape hyacinths from the *M. armeniacum* stable. As they are developing, the spike is topped with a darker blue whorl that looks almost as though it is going to develop into a topknot in the manner of *M. aucheri*. But it does not. Instead, the green buds in between these two bands of blue gradually colour up, and at maturity 'Valerie Finnis' is the same pale blue all over, making a thinner spike than *M. armeniacum*, less pyramidal. It first appeared in the Northamptonshire garden of Sir David and Lady Scott (the fine plantswoman Valerie Finnis), who gave a clump of it to Wayne Roderick of California. He passed it on to the Dutch nurseryman, Wim de Goede, who bulked it up and introduced it in the 1990s. Plant the bulbs 10cm (4in) deep and 5cm (2in) apart.

SEASON: Mid March
HARDINESS: Fully hardy
HEIGHT: 17cm (7in)

Muscari azureum ♀

Muscari azureum, introduced to cultivation in 1859, produces shortish, dense spikes of pale purplish blue with a darker stripe running down the centre of each petal. The bell-shaped flowers are not pinched in at the mouth in the manner of *M. armeniacum*. It is a compact, little plant, an excellent follow-on for *Cyclamen hederifolium* or companion for pale hellebores. The foliage is thin, strappy and greyish green, not so long and untidy as the leaves of *M. armeniacum*. It does not like to be baked in summer. Plant the bulbs 10cm (4in) deep and 5cm (2in) apart.

SEASON: Early April
HARDINESS: Fully hardy
HEIGHT: 15cm (6in)
HABITAT: Northern and eastern Turkey where it grows in alpine meadows

351

Muscari botryoides 'Album'

I like my grape hyacinths blue, not white, and this albino makes thin spikes of a rather dirty white that scarcely sing out at all. But The White Garden is still a potent dream for some gardeners and here is an obliging tenant. The individual bells in each spike are rather small but at least the foliage is shortish, as, unlike so many other grape hyacinths, *M. botryoides* 'Album' does not begin to develop until spring. And it is not invasive. Plant the bulbs 10cm (4in) deep and 5cm (2in) apart.

SEASON: Early April
HARDINESS: Fully hardy
HEIGHT: 12cm (5in)

Muscari comosum 'Plumosum'

The big spikes of *M. comosum* 'Plumosum' are made up from sterile 'flowers' of purplish blue, the purple-tinged stalks weaving and intertwining to give the effect of a piece of knitting, unravelling fast. It is a wonderfully dotty plant (dottiness always to be encouraged) but unfortunately it dies noisily, the leaves sprawling all over the place. Plant the bulbs 10cm (4in) deep and 5cm (2in) apart.

SEASON: Late April
HARDINESS: Frost hardy
HEIGHT: 30–40cm (12–16in)

OPPOSITE *Muscari armeniacum* 'Valerie Finnis' is the palest of the blue grape hyacinths and produces its iceberg-coloured spikes in the middle of March.

Muscari latifolium ♀

This tall, showy muscari has one (rarely two) sheath leaf, like a lily-of-the-valley, and the single flower spike emerges on its stem from the base of the sheath. It is very nice indeed, much less weedy looking than *M. armeniacum*. The spike itself is about 5cm (2in) long, with a dark, blackish blue spire of bells topped with a paler blue topknot. This two-tone trick is a surprise and, for me at least, makes *M. latifolium* perhaps the best of the muscari. It was introduced to cultivation in 1858 and is easy, provided you put it in a place where it will not dry out too much in summer. Plant the bulbs 10cm (4in) deep and 5cm (2in) apart.

SEASON: Late March

HARDINESS: Frost hardy

HEIGHT: 22cm (9in)

HABITAT: Southern and western Turkey where it grows in open pine forests and light woodland at around 1,000m (3,300ft)

Muscari macrocarpum

This species was well known to John Gerard who had heard it grew 'beyond the Thracian Bosphorus and from about Constantinople'. He describes it at length in his *Herball* of 1597, the leaves 'hollowed alongst the middle like a trough', the fat, juicy stems 'set from the middle to the top on every side with many yellow floures, everie one made like a small pitcher or little box', the seed 'inclosed in puffed or blowne up cods'. He says the name, *Muscari*, comes from the musk-like smell of the flowers, which is extraordinarily rich and powerful. The leaves are much longer than the flowering stems, and though arching at first lie in the end on the ground, untidy as is the foliage of all muscari. The little flowers, 25 or so in a spike, open from the bottom upwards, colouring from bronze to yellow as they develop. Each tiny bell (Gerard's pitcher) is rimmed at its narrow mouth with purple. Plant with care as *M. macrocarpum* has thick, fleshy roots and needs a long, hot, dry rest in summer if it is to flower well the following spring. Set the bulbs 10cm (4in) deep and 5cm (2in) apart.

SEASON: Mid March

HARDINESS: Frost hardy

HEIGHT: 13cm (5in)

HABITAT: Greece (Aegean islands) and western Turkey

Muscari neglectum

This is the 'common' grape hyacinth, which can sometimes be invasive, helping itself to ground you would prefer to keep for other, rarer creatures. It is a variable plant, but the flowers are most often a blackish blue, with white markings round the mouth of each little bell. The leaves are thinner than most, but still very long, and they start growing in autumn. *Muscari neglectum* naturalizes easily as the flowers seed about, and the bulbs produce masses of offsets. It is the best choice for semi-shaded positions in the garden. Use it with wild primroses and to follow on from spreads of the common snowdrop (*Galanthus nivalis*). Set the bulbs 10cm (4in) deep and 5cm (2in) apart.

SEASON: Late March
HARDINESS: Fully hardy
HEIGHT: 13cm (5in)
HABITAT: Widespread in Europe, north Africa and
south-western Asia where it grows in grass or light woodland

Narcissus (Amaryllidaceae)

DAFFODIL

There are at least 50 wild species of narcissus (more if you are a 'splitter' rather than a 'lumper'), and many of them grow in the Iberian peninsula, an important centre of distribution. With so many building blocks available, it is not surprising that breeders have been busy and that daffodils have become phenomenally popular as show flowers, with growers gathering from Australia, America and Europe to stage blooms of terrifying size and substance in world-class competitions. Compared with the wondrous tulip though, daffodils, poor things, are rather limited in what they can provide – whitish, yellowish, orange and a hint of pink (there was huge excitement when this colour first appeared in the trumpet daffodil 'Mrs R O Backhouse' in 1923), but you cannot have

ABOVE Working with her husband, Robert, Sarah Backhouse (1857–1921) bred some wonderful narcissi at her home, Sutton Court in Herefordshire.

spring without them and they are much easier to establish than tulips, which belong to hotter, drier lands farther east than the daffodil's European home. Most daffodils are fully hardy (the exceptions are some of the Tazetta types gathered in Division 8) and are easy-going garden plants, happy in dappled shade, good for naturalizing in grass or among trees. The miniatures such as 'Little Beauty' are particularly enchanting, excellent in a gravel bed or to grow in containers. The well-known paper-white narcissi (*N. papyraceus*) are the easiest of all bulbs to force and will provide you with a gorgeous, sweet-smelling bowl of flowers just six weeks after they have been planted.

Sweetly scented paper-white narcissi provided an unexpected link between three disparate events in my life. It started in Montreal, where I was talking about my book *The Naming of Names*. In the questions afterwards, we got on to the subject of forcing bulbs for winter, where I heard the latest advice on planting paper-white narcissi, which had just been published in the magazine *Canadian Gardening*. This is what it said,

A horticultural student at New York's Cornell University accidentally spilled some of his alcoholic beverage into a pot of paper-whites that had just sprouted. A few weeks later, his fellow students noticed that plants that had imbibed were shorter than others, even though the blooms were the same size. Four months and three trials later, the findings were announced: a few drops of alcohol result in stalks that are 40 per cent shorter, which means that they do not flop over.

The best way to ply your paper-whites with liquor is to place pebbles in a container, add water just to the top of the pebbles and rest the bulbs on the pebbles so they are not touching the water. Once sprouts are 5cm (2in) tall, carefully pour out the water and replace with a mixture of nine parts water to one part alcohol. Keep in mind that paper-whites prefer hard liquor: rum, gin, tequila and vodka have all proved effective. Wine or beer can damage the bulbs, so choose your potent potable responsibly. Cheers!

I would have liked some explanation from the Cornell students as to why booze should have this effect, but if the technique works as well as they say it could be a huge advantage. When they first come out, paper-whites bloom at a manageable height, around 30–40cm (12–16in). But they go on growing, and by the time the flowers finish the stems can be 75cm (30in) long. As the flowers themselves do not get any bigger, this makes them disproportionately tall. And means you have to stake.

Paper-whites had been much on my mind when I left for Canada because two days after my return our youngest daughter was getting married at home. She had asked for the church (fortunately a small country one) to be filled with paper-white narcissi, growing in the old zinc tubs (roughly 20cm/8in tall and 30cm/12in across the top) in which I usually force our winter bulbs.

Paper-whites are reliable creatures and usually bloom six weeks after planting. But, taking no chances, I planted the first batch eight weeks

ABOVE In a Greek alpine meadow, the poet's narcissus (*Narcissus poeticus*) sends its delicious scent into the evening air.

before the wedding, in case the run-up was unusually cold. Temperature has more effect on their development than any other factor. Each week after that, I planted another half dozen tubs. Unfortunately, the autumn was unusually mild and the first batch of flowers was up and out within a month, far too soon for the wedding. I quickly came to the end of the paper-whites I had ordered, and scavenged in every garden centre within a 100km (60 mile) radius, buying every last, tired bulb I could find even if they were sprouting out of their packaging. Then the weather turned very cold – brilliant sunny days, fabulous starry nights, but zero growth on flowers. The leaves of the final batches emerged and then stuck at 10–15cm (4–6in), unwilling to go further.

All the bulbs were raised on shelves in our workshop, where it is cool and there is plenty of light. The night before I left for Canada, I brought the last batch of eight tubs into the house and lined them out on the landing windowsill, which faces south. The smell in the house as I walked in three weeks later was a reassuring sign that Tilly would have her flowers. The warmth had unlocked them and they were at perfect pitch. Phew! I thought. That was a close one.

We even got the paper-whites up to the church without breaking the stems. They were staked firmly for the ride, then unstaked and staked again (less obviously) once they were in position. On the wedding day, as the brass quartet belted into the opening bars of 'Guide me O thy Great Redeemer' I breathed in a great lungful of the paper-whites' glorious scent, flickering round hundreds of candles, and felt like bursting. It was an emotional moment.

After the wedding, we went away – the first Christmas I have ever spent away from home – and holed up in Florence for a few days. It was dangerously liberating to divorce Christmas from the turkey and the anxious hours that precede its coming to the table

ABOVE For most of us, the 'Paper White' narcissus (*N. papyraceus*) will be a bulb to grow indoors, to fill chill November with its delicious scent.

with all its trimmings. Instead, we went to the Uffizzi and wandered through galleries entirely empty of visitors. Masaccio, the Florentine painter of the early fifteenth century, was my Christmas treat, first at the Uffizzi, then in the Romanesque church at Cascia, just outside Reggello to the east of Florence, where his altarpiece glows against a stark stone wall.

Masaccio was with us again at mass on Christmas morning in Santa Maria Novella where, before the service, operatic arias sung by an unseen soprano ('Canned', said my husband, suspiciously) curled high into the painted curves of the nave. In the evening, we swapped Masaccio for Giotto at a service in Gothic Santa Croce before going for a stupendous Christmas dinner at La Vedetta, a small hotel near the Piazzale Michelangelo, south of

OPPOSITE The distinguishing feature of miniature *Narcissus cyclamineus* is the way the yellow petals sweep back from the long, narrow trumpet.

the Arno: a set menu of intricate treats with not a scrap of turkey or Christmas pudding anywhere in sight. Nothing like it has ever come my way before.

But what about the paper-whites? Yes, they were in Florence, too. From the idiosyncratic Renaissance villa the Torre di Bellosguardo, where we were staying (no restaurant, but a parrot in the vestibule and a piano in our bedroom), an old stone-lined track leads from the garden down through terraces of olives. There are incredible views through cypresses and umbrella pines to the domed roof of the Duomo on the other side of the river.

ABOVE The title page of John Parkinson's book *Paradisi in Sole Paradisus Terrestris*, published in 1629.

But my eye was held at ground level, where blooming in the rough grass between the olive trees were clumps of paper-white narcissi, growing just as nature intended, the stems not too tall, the flowers slightly larger than the type we generally see. It is a native of these parts and is most often to be found in grassy, cultivated land, like the Bellosguardo olive grove. Our wedding paper-whites were good. But these wild flowers, surrounded by the lush foliage of arum and the first celadon-green buds of wild hellebore, were better. In fact, the best.

The Roman author Pliny said that the narcissus got its name from the narcotic nature of its scent 'of *Narce* which betokeneth nummednesse or dulnesse of sense, and not of the young boy Narcissus, as poets do feign and fable'. Scent, most obvious in the Jonquils and the Tazettas, such as *N. papyraceus*, is an important reason for gardeners to grow narcissus, but also accounts for their popularity as cut flowers. In early seventeenth-century Britain, the market women of Cheapside sold Lent lilies (our wild daffodil, *Narcissus pseudonarcissus*) in huge bunches, but at that time it still grew wild in many places round London. Gerard listed a dozen different kinds of daffodil in the first edition of his *Herball* (1597) including the bold, golden-trumpeted Spanish species *N. hispanicus*, which he grew in his garden at Holborn, also in London. Thirty years later, 78 different kinds appeared in John Parkinson's *Paradisus*, including some of the doubles which were particularly popular at that time: 'John Tradescant his great Rose Daffodil' and 'Mr Wilmer's Great Double Daffodil'. George Wilmer had tried to take credit for the flower, explained Parkinson, 'as if he were the first founder thereof', but it was actually raised by a Fleming, Vincent van Sion, in whose London garden it first bloomed in 1620. It is still around now, either under the name 'Van Sion' or 'Telamonius Plenus', and in parts of Ireland it grows as freely along hedge banks as though it were a true wild daffodil.

OPPOSITE 'Bravoure' is a flower for those who like their daffodils big. The trumpet is long, straight and plain, the surrounding white petals exceptionally wide.

By 1870, daffodils had become an important crop in the Scilly Islands after a grower called Trevellick sent to market a box of 'Scilly White', half-wild daffodils of the Tazetta type, and made far more money than he had ever expected from their sale. The Tazettas are not reliably hardy in most of Britain but the mild climate and the light soils of the Scillies suited them admirably and other farmers quickly followed Trevellick's example and learned how to grow early daffodils for the mainland market, where they were shipped in the old *Scillonian* steamboat.

Serious interest in breeding daffodils grew out of the work done by the Victorian pioneer William Herbert, dean of Manchester, who began to cross various wild species of daffodils, exploiting their different colours, shapes and sizes to make hybrids with great vigour and staying power. 'It is desirable', he wrote in 1837, 'to call the attention of the humblest cultivators, of every labourer indeed, or operative, who has a spot of garden, or a ledge at his window, to the infinite variety of narcissi that may thus be raised and most easily in pots at his window, if not exposed to too much sun and wind, offering him a source of harmless and interesting amusement, and perhaps a little profit and celebrity.' Herbert inspired later nurserymen such as William Backhouse of Darlington and Peter Barr, whose headquarters were in Covent Garden, to search again for the wild species of Spain and southern Europe and introduce them to British gardens. Growers may still be waiting for the profit and celebrity promised by Dean Herbert, but 'infinite variety' there certainly is and perhaps the best way to choose varieties you would like to grow is to visit the extraordinary collection established by daffodil grower Ron Scamp, at Trevarno gardens, near Helston in Cornwall, UK, where you can find the best of the modern varieties growing alongside old daffodils such as the beautiful, small-cupped 'White Lady', introduced in 1898 and 'Horace', a Poeticus daffodil bred by the great Reverend Engleheart and honoured as the best seedling of 1894.

In most bulb catalogues, you will find daffodils separated into different divisions, the differences based largely on the form of the flower.

DIVISION 1   Trumpet daffodils with one flower to a stem and trumpets (strictly known as coronas) as long as or longer than the petals (or perianth segments as they are known to daffodil experts).

DIVISION 2   Large-cupped daffodils with one flower to a stem and a cup (corona) more than one-third but less than equal to the length of the petals. Some are scented.

DIVISION 3   Small-cupped daffodils with one flower to a stem and a cup not more than one-third the length of the petals.

DIVISION 4   Double daffodils with one or more flowers on a stem where either the cup or the petals (or both) are doubled.

DIVISION 5 Daffodils of the Triandrus type, which clearly show the characteristics of *N. triandrus*: stems of two or more hanging flowers each of which has reflexed (swept-back) petals.

DIVISION 6 Daffodils of the Cyclamineus type, which clearly show the characteristics of *N. cyclamineus*: one flower held at an acute angle to the stem, with a short neck and very swept-back petals.

DIVISION 7 Daffodils of the Jonquil type, which clearly show the characteristics of *N. jonquilla*: rush-like foliage and one to five sweet-smelling flowers on a stem, with petals that can be either spreading or reflexed round a cup (either funnel-shaped or flared) that is usually wider than it is long.

DIVISION 8 Daffodils of the Tazetta type, which clearly show the characteristics of *N. tazetta*: from three to 20 sweet-smelling flowers on a thick stem, the petals spreading rather than reflexed.

DIVISION 9 Daffodils of the Poeticus type, which clearly show the characteristics of *N. poeticus*: usually one scented flower on a stem, with pure white petals and a very short cup, which might be green or yellow (or both), usually with a red rim.

DIVISION 10 Daffodils of the Bulbocodium type, which clearly show the characteristics of *N. bulbocodium*: usually one flower on a stem with the petals much less important than the trumpet or cup and the filaments and style curved.

DIVISION 11 Daffodils with cups that are split for more than half their length, both Collar types (11a) and the Papillons (11b).

DIVISION 12 Daffodils that do not fit anywhere else.

DIVISION 13 Daffodils that are true species.

As there are so many different kinds of daffodil (more than 2,000 in the *RHS Plant Finder*), specialists have evolved a strange kind of shorthand to describe them. This code encapsulates the type, colour (and sometimes the flowering time) in a string of numbers and letters: for example, 'Acropolis' is 4W-R(LM); 'Actaea' is 9W-YYR(M). The first number refers to one of the divisions listed above. After that is a letter that tells you what colour the petals are, W for white, Y for yellow. After the dash is a second letter or letters, which refer to the colour of the cup or trumpet, R for red, O for orange, P for pink. Finally, in brackets, is the flowering time, divided into VE (very early), early (E), M (mid-season), L (late) and VL (very late). But though this shorthand has its uses, you do not generally hear ordinary gardeners congratulating each other on their 9W-YYR(M)s. So in this book, I have not used it.

CULTIVATION

Some daffodils, such as *N. bulbocodium*, *N. cyclamineus*, *N. triandrus* and their cultivars prefer soil that is on the acid side of neutral. The Jonquils (Division 7) and Tazettas (Division 8) like slightly alkaline soil and need full sun where they can bake in summer. Most other daffodils like soil that is well-drained but not too dry in summer. As a general rule, daffodils prefer moisture to drought, but the Jonquils and Tazettas provide the exceptions that are an inevitable corollary to any garden rule. Poeticus daffodils will most resent being out of the ground as the bulbs are rarely without working roots.

The longer the rooting time, the better the bulbs will grow and flower, so with daffodils it pays to plant as soon as you can: September is good, late August is even better. The later you plant, the more likely the flowers are to have short stems and flowers less robust than they could be. A cool slope may suit them better than a sunny one that dries out in summer. Mulching with very well-rotted compost (never fresh farmyard manure) after the leaves have died down boosts the fertility of the soil and helps to keep the daffodil bulbs cool.

The leaves of daffodils contain minute but razor-sharp crystals of calcium oxylate, which is why grazing animals, such as deer and rabbits, leave them alone (why have so few bulbs developed this useful defence?),

so they are good for naturalizing, especially if you use them in an area where you can leave the grass to grow long before a late summer cut. The grass disguises the unsightly death of the daffodil foliage and allows species such as *N. bulbocodium*, *N. cyclamineus* and *N. pseudonarcissus* to ripen their seed and cast it about (in the wild, most species increase by seeding rather than by producing offsets). But wherever daffodils are planted, the leaves must be allowed to die down naturally, a process that can take at least six weeks. Where daffodils are planted in a lawn, itchy gardeners are usually longing to mow the whole lot down too soon.

Choose light-limbed daffodils for naturalizing, species such as the Lent lily (*N. pseudonarcissus*) or *N.* 'Actaea', which looks wonderful planted in great swathes under apple trees. In fine turf, you might succeed with the hoop-petticoat daffodil (*N. bulbocodium*) or try the easier *N. cyclamineus*, which has petals swept back like the ears of a piglet fronting a storm. It is a very appealing trait. In general, most Division 6 daffodils derived from *N. cyclamineus* ('February Gold', 'Itzim', 'Jack Snipe', 'Jenny') do well in grass. They like growing cool, not hot. Avoid mixtures, which may be cheap, but are jangly to look at when the flowers come out in spring. Use masses of a few different kinds, not a few of masses. Select varieties that follow on from one another and give you a long period of flowers.

ABOVE The hoop-petticoat daffodil (*Narcissus bulbocodium*) will naturalize in turf that is damp during the spring growing season, but dries out in summer. Here, *N. bulbocodium* grows with purple *Crocus vernus*.

The whole point of naturalizing bulbs is that they should get on with life without too much fuss on your part. But you must put some initial effort into planting them properly. For planting in turf, you need a sharp spade or a long-handled bulb planter, not one of the short, wrist-wrecking kind that looks like a modified trowel. By the time you plant in September, turf or meadow areas should have been cut quite close, so it is not difficult to cast your bulbs about and plant them where they fall. Do not dot them about with the same distance between each. Think of groups of daffodils as separate clouds, more densely spaced at the centre than they are at the edges. Leave space between groups for other bulbs such as camassias or *Gladiolus communis* subsp. *byzantinus* to come on later in the season.

If you are using a spade, chop out three sides of a rough square, ease up the turf and put in two or three bulbs, pointed ends up, before dropping the divot back in place. If you are using a bulb planter, plunge it into the ground, draw out the plug of soil, drop in a single bulb, and replace the plug. Some gardeners prefer to top up the holes with compost and leave the plugs on the ground to break down naturally. Where the grass is very coarse and hungry and where daffodils have spread into congested clumps, they may flower less or stop flowering altogether. In this case, lift the clumps, break them up into smaller pieces, and replant them in fresh ground with some bonemeal added for encouragement. You can either do this after they have finished flowering, which is the easier option because you can still see where they are, or in late August, which is better for the bulbs, as they will probably still be dormant.

In a mixed border, plant at least 13–15cm (5–6in) deep, even deeper in light soils that tend to dry out in summer. This helps to prevent daffodil bulbs from splitting into too many non-flowering offsets and also means you are less likely to spear bulbs on your fork when you are weeding your borders later in summer. Avoid daffodils with very beefy foliage. 'Bravoure', for instance, has leaves so massive they could easily fell a passing gnome. The monsters are perhaps best lined out in a cutting garden where they can be picked and displayed without their leaves. Daffodils make very good cut flowers, and you can gather them in bud, just after the upright sheath has dropped to the horizontal, the 'goose-neck' stage. Some types, notably the Tazettas and the Jonquils, are particularly sweetly scented. Unless you are encouraging species such as *N. cyclamineus* or *N. pseudonarcissus* to self-seed, deadheading daffodils is a good idea. It allows them to put all their effort into fattening up their bulbs, rather than setting seed. It is an easy job to do while you wander round in an evening, glass of wine in hand, revelling in the first light evenings of spring.

Daffodils look good planted in pots outside, but choose big ones (pots not daffodils). If you use a pot 20cm (8in) across, you will only be able to fit between three and six bulbs in it. That is not enough for a decent display. Make sure that you use a multipurpose compost and keep the containers well watered. Squirrels and mice do not attack daffodils as readily as they do crocus and tulips, but if they are troublesome put a cover of chicken wire over the pot and keep it there until the shoots come through in the spring.

Narcissus can also be grown in bowls for the house, and sweet-smelling ones are the most obvious choice. *Narcissus papyraceus* is the simplest and most commonly offered type to flower in bowls during Christmas and the New Year. With these you just plant them up (I use compost rather than bulb fibre or pebbles), water them and wait for them to grow. They generally flower within six weeks and do not need to be put in the dark to root. Similar types are 'Scilly White' and 'Avalanche' which have cups of pale lemon, rather than white. 'Soleil d'Or' is also a Tazetta but has brilliant blooms of small, gold and orange flowers, six or eight in a head. 'Cragford' with cream and orange flowers is another Tazetta hybrid that can be easily forced. For early spring flowers inside, you might try two Cyclamineus hybrids, the well-known 'Tête-à-tête' and its sister, 'Jumblie'. Both have Tazetta grandparents, but these need to be kept in a cool place outside for eight to ten weeks so that the bulbs develop good roots before they try to flower. Move them gradually in weekly stages from cold to warm, about 12°C (54°F) at first, then 15°C (59°F), then finally the full blast of a heated sitting room. Do not ever let the bulbs dry out, but do not swamp them either. And give them as much light as you can. Without it, the stems will grow unmanageably long.

ABOVE Massed daffodils spread over the hillside of a Gloucestershire garden.

Narcissus 'Acropolis'

The flower is a full double, rich lemony cream when it first comes out but settling as it develops into a paler, more ivory colour. Sometimes when I have grown 'Acropolis', buds have had a strong, green tinge on one side, which slightly distorts the eventual shape of the bloom. Flecked between the bunch of cream petals at the centre are very much smaller, orange petals. This is a strong, robust narcissus, raised in 1955 by Lionel Richardson of Waterford in southern Ireland by crossing 'Falaise' with the small-cupped 'Limerick'. Try it between the rosettes of foxgloves which will come up to bloom in early summer. Plant 13–15cm (5–6in) deep and the same distance apart.

SEASON: Mid April
HARDINESS: Fully hardy
HEIGHT: 48cm (19in)
DIVISION: 4 (Double)

Narcissus 'Actaea' ♛

An enchanting variety, raised in 1927 by the Dutch bulb growers G Lubbe & Son of Oegstgeest and one of the best of the narcissus that flower in early April. Broad, white, overlapping petals, markedly rounded, surround a tiny cup which is yellow, edged with orange. 'Actaea' is especially good in grass where it mixes easily with cowslips but is equally at home in a border among dark hellebores, which at this time are just beginning to need a boost. Like all this tribe, it has a wonderful scent. Plant 13–15cm (5–6in) deep and the same distance apart.

SEASON: Early April
HARDINESS: Fully hardy
HEIGHT: 40cm (16in)
DIVISION: 9 (Poeticus)

Narcissus 'Bell Song'

A charming, light-limbed narcissus with
a creamy, papery frill of petals round a
short, slightly frilly cup. When this first
comes out it is a pale yellowish apricot,
but it darkens as it matures and becomes
a solid pink-apricot colour, very easy and
pleasing. There are one or two flowers
on each stem and they smell gorgeous,
sweeter and lighter than many other
narcissus. This is a free-flowering variety
with a graceful habit, raised in 1971 with
N. jonquilla as one of its parents. The
first ever 'pink' daffodil was 'Mrs R O
Backhouse', named after Mrs Backhouse
of Sutton Court, near Hereford, UK, who
was an enthusiastic amateur breeder of
daffodils. Though it is derided now by
daffodil fanciers because of its windmill
petals, it was a sensation when it was
introduced in 1923. Spread 'Bell Song'
under spring-flowering amelanchier or
use it as a foreground to silver-leaved
Artemisia 'Powis Castle'. Plant 13–15cm
(5–6in) deep and 10–12cm (4–5in) apart.

SEASON: March–April
HARDINESS: Fully hardy
HEIGHT: 38cm (15in)
DIVISION: 7 (Jonquil)

Narcissus 'Bowles's Early Sulphur'

An enchanting little dwarf with
narrow, bright green foliage, generous
in the number of flowers it produces.
Some flowers have seven petals
round the central trumpet but they
are the same colour all over, a
delicate, pale, sharp yellow. Try
'Bowles's Early Sulphur' with *Crocus*
'Vanguard' or allow it to grow under
a wild-looking camellia such as
'Cornish Snow'. Plant 10cm (4in)
deep and the same distance apart.

SEASON: Late February
HARDINESS: Fully hardy
HEIGHT: 10cm (4in)
DIVISION: 1 (Trumpet)

Narcissus bulbocodium Golden Bells Group

The species is native in Spain, Portugal and south-western France, and this is a charming selection, the thin leaves (darkish green) lying out on the ground rather than upright. Three or four short, strong stems rise from each bulb and bear narrow, pointed buds. As they drop to open, the bud seems sage-green, but then the petals become a warmer yellow and flare out to make a miniature ruff round the yellow, cone-shaped trumpet. The proportion of one to the other is very different in this species: the frill is minimal, the cone-cup entirely dominant. In the wild, *N. bulbocodium* seems to favour acid soil and turf which is very damp during its spring growing season. It does brilliantly well at the Royal Horticultural Society's Wisley garden in the UK, where it seeds about very happily in thin grass on sandy soil. Try this hoop-petticoat daffodil with snake's head fritillaries or mix it with pale blue *Ipheion* 'Rolf Fiedler'. Plant 10cm (4in) deep and the same distance apart.

SEASON: Mid March
HARDINESS: Fully hardy
HEIGHT: 13cm (5in)
DIVISION: 10 (Bulbocodium)

SEASON: Mid March
HARDINESS: Fully hardy
HEIGHT: 20cm (8in)
DIVISION: 8 (Tazetta)

Narcissus 'Canaliculatus'

This charming miniature is a late-blooming, dwarf type of *N. tazetta* with rather narrow, dull green leaves which at first are slightly shorter than the flower. There can be up to seven flowers on a single stem, ranged so that they all have their own space and all look out in the same direction. Each tiny cup of orange-yellow has a little frill of white petals round it, slightly swept back from the cup. The smell is strong and spicy. 'At the fragrant odour thereof', wrote Homer of the Tazettas, 'all the broad heaven above and all the earth laughed, and the salt wave of the sea.' If it is to continue to flower well, 'Canaliculatus' needs deep planting and a hot, sunny place in the garden, as unlike most daffodils the bulbs need to bake during their summer dormancy. Use it with sun-loving iris such as *I. bucharica* and plum-scented *I. graminea*, or slip it between low mats of sweet-scented thyme. Plant 10cm (4in) deep and the same distance apart.

Narcissus 'Cheerfulness' ♀

'Cheerfulness' first appeared in 1923, a sport of the single Tazetta 'Elvira' and is an outstanding, sturdy narcissus, with up to four double, richly scented blooms borne on each thick, strong stem. From fat, greenish buds come muddled but pretty flowers with six wide cream petals surrounding a froth of cream and yellow. The centre is a contained explosion, not mixed with the surround, and the effect is rather good. The scent is excellent, spicy like that of 'Geranium'. Remember, when you are planting it, that in the wild Tazettas favour well-drained, rocky places in the central and western Mediterranean where they get well baked in summer. Without this baking, 'Cheerfulness' may dwindle to the point where all you see is a few pathetic leaves, weeping for their rocky hills. Try it in front of *Elaeagnus* 'Quicksilver' or with the perennial wallflower *Erysimum* 'Bowles's Mauve'. Set the bulbs 12–15cm (5–6in) deep and 10–12cm (4–5in) apart.

SEASON: April
HARDINESS: Fully hardy
HEIGHT: 40cm (16in)
DIVISION: 4 (Double)

Narcissus cyclamineus ☸

The species is now rather rare in the wild but N. *cyclamineus* was evidently known to gardeners in 1608 when it was first illustrated in Pierre Vallet's *Jardin du Roi Henry IV*. Sometime after that it was lost to cultivation, and Dean Herbert in 1836 declared it a figment of Vallet's imagination, 'an absurdity which will never be found to exist'. It did exist, though, and was rediscovered by the wine exporter Alfred Wilby Tait, Baron de Soutellhino, near Oporto, Portugal in 1885. The distinguishing feature is the way the petals sweep back from the long, narrow tube-trumpet, 'like the laid back ears of a kicking horse', wrote the Edwardian plantsman E A Bowles. So petals and trumpet, both a rich intense yellow, are all in a line, all in one plane. The flower from petal to the frivolously frilly end of its trumpet is no more than 4–5cm (1½–2in) long, and the whole thing is light-limbed, wild-looking. At flowering time, the leaves are about the same height as the flowers, bright green, very narrow and grassy. *Narcissus cyclamineus* likes cool, leafy, moist soil, slightly acid rather than alkaline, and will happily grow in dappled shade or in grass, provided it is not too coarse. Once settled, it is more likely to increase from seed than by offsets. Of all daffodils, it is perhaps the one that most resents being out of the ground, because left to itself it has a very short dormant period. Months spent languishing on a garden centre shelf do not suit it at all. At the Royal Horticultural Society's garden at Wisley, UK, it makes a surprising companion for the royal fern (*Osmunda regalis*), both of them growing in damp, leafy soil at the edge of a pond. If you do not have a pond, plant it to follow on from snowdrops and aconites. The flowers last a long time. Plant 10cm (4in) deep and the same distance apart.

SEASON: Late March
HARDINESS: Fully hardy
HEIGHT: 12cm (5in)
DIVISION: 13 (Species)
HABITAT: North-western Portugal and north-western
Spain where it grows in damp mountain pastures

OPPOSITE The hoop-petticoat daffodil (*Narcissus bulbocodium*) growing
in the wild in the Estrella Mountains, Portugal.

Narcissus 'Dickcissel' ♀

'Dickcissel' is not so strongly scented as the species Jonquil, but it is splendidly vigorous, bred in 1964 from the lemon-cupped Jonquil 'Binkie' and producing two or three stems from a bulb with two or three flowers on each stem. They are a good size: not too overpowering. The frilly cup is the same colour as the pointed, lemon-gold petals, but the petals fade to white at the base, which is a feature (though not everyone thinks it a good one). Behind is a long, greenish throat. Try it with dark *Euphorbia* × *martini* or use it to fill in round the bare feet of *Fuchsia magellanica* var. *gracilis* 'Tricolor'. Plant bulbs 13–15cm (5–6in) deep and the same distance apart.

SEASON: Early April
HARDINESS: Fully hardy
HEIGHT: 30cm (12in)
DIVISION: 7 (Jonquil)

Narcissus 'Eystettensis'
(N. Queen Anne's double daffodil)

A charming flower though the stems are not quite strong enough for their cargoes and tend to be pulled over towards the ground. The flowers themselves fall very clearly into the shape of six-pointed stars, very double, with narrow, pointed petals in several shades of yellow, smaller and darker towards the centre. 'Eystettenis' is an old daffodil, known since 1601, and is thought to be a hybrid of *N. triandrus*. The foliage is relatively self-effacing for a daffodil. Use it between the dark, ferny, just-emerging foliage of *Anthriscus sylvestris* 'Ravenswing'. Plant 10cm (4in) deep and the same distance apart.

SEASON: Early April
HARDINESS: Fully hardy
HEIGHT: 20cm (8in)
DIVISION: 4 (Double)

Narcissus 'February Gold' ♀

In colouring this is very similar to 'Tête-à-tête' but of course it is twice the size. Nevertheless, 'February Gold' is a very elegant flower and usefully early, though much more likely to appear in March than February. The foliage is not too beefy and the flower petals flare back slightly, away from the trumpet, an elegant pose. The trumpet is only slightly darker than the surrounding petals and is long (3cm/1in) and relatively narrow. This is an easy daffodil, a hybrid between *N. cyclamineus* and *N. pseudonarcissus* raised in 1923 by the Dutch nurserymen De Graaf. It has a musky scent and is good for naturalizing, providing an early wave of yellow before *N. pseudonarcissus* or *N. poeticus* var. *recurvus*. Give it cool, rich soil in sun or part shade, and let it loose in grass or use it in a border with the lime-green spurge *Euphorbia polychroma*. Set the bulbs 12–15cm (5–6in) deep and 10–15cm (4–6in) apart.

SEASON: Late February–March
HARDINESS: Fully hardy
HEIGHT: 40cm (16in)
DIVISION: 6 (Cyclamineus)

Narcissus 'Geranium' ♀

Introduced in 1930, 'Geranium' is a vigorous, showy narcissus with up to four flowers on a head borne on a thick, fleshy, strong stem. They are deliciously scented, the flat, frilly, orange cups surrounded by wide, papery petals. Each flower is careful not to get in the way of others in the head, a necessary stratagem because for a time they are all out together. In bud, they are the colour of Jersey cream, but the colour lightens as the flower opens. Use 'Geranium' to underplant your roses, still hideous sticks in March, or let it rise between clumps of a robust pulmonaria such as 'Lewis Palmer'. Plant bulbs 13–15cm (5–6in) deep and the same distance apart.

SEASON: Late March
HARDINESS: Fully hardy
HEIGHT: 42cm (17in)
DIVISION: 8 (Tazetta)

Narcissus 'Hawera' ♀

'Hawera' is a cross between
N. jonquilla and *N. triandrus*, raised
before 1928 by Dr William Thomson
of Hawera, New Zealand. From
N. jonquilla came the small cup;
N. triandrus contributed its reflexed
petals. There may be six or eight
flowers on a stem, each just 3–5cm
(1–2in) across and all deliciously
scented. The colour is a soft pale
yellow with the cup perhaps just a
whisper lighter than the petals. The
flowers in each head come out in
succession so each stem seems to
last a long time. It is a dear thing,
with thin, rush-like foliage – a great
advantage. Put 'Hawera' somewhere
warm, where it can be reasonably
damp in spring but dry in summer.
It looks good with *Muscari
armeniacum* 'Valerie Finnis' or soft
blue chionodoxa but is also vigorous
enough to naturalize in grass,
provided it is not too coarse. Plant
the bulbs 10cm (4in) deep and the
same distance apart.

SEASON: Mid March
HARDINESS: Frost hardy
HEIGHT: 30cm (12in)
DIVISION: 5 (Triandrus)

Narcissus 'Ice Wings' ♀

This is a graceful, light-limbed narcissus, with two
or three ivory-coloured flowers on a stem. The long,
straight trumpets are gently crinkled at the edge
and have a slight greenish tinge which is very
attractive. The petals sweep back a little from the
centre, a pleasing trait. 'Ice Wings' was raised in
1958 by Cyril Coleman of Cranbrook, Kent, UK,
from a cross between the large-cupped daffodil
'Ischia' and *N. triandrus*. Use it with the ground-
covering *Veronica umbrosa* 'Georgia Blue', or to
leaven dark clumps of *Helleborus foetidus*. Plant
13–15cm (5–6in) deep and the same distance apart.

SEASON: Mid March
HARDINESS: Fully hardy
HEIGHT: 45cm (18in)
DIVISION: 5 (Triandrus)

Narcissus 'Itzim' ♀

'Itzim' is not as prolific as 'February Gold' nor as large, but the flowers are made in the same way, the petals swept back away from the trumpet in a charming fashion. If anything, they are more reflexed than those of 'February Gold', especially when they first open. The petals are yellow, the narrow trumpets a rich shade of orange. It is a charming daffodil, raised in 1982 by Grant Mitsch of Oregon, USA. 'Itzim' will cope with light shade as well as sun but needs decent, moisture-retentive soil. You could use it in front of evergreen *Mahonia × media* 'Charity' or to light up the foliage of *Pinus mugo*. Plant the bulbs 10–12cm (4–5in) deep and the same distance apart.

SEASON: Late February
HARDINESS: Fully hardy
HEIGHT: 32cm (13in)
DIVISION: 6 (Cyclamineus)

Narcissus 'Jack Snipe' ♀

A small flower emerges on a longish stem, presenting a neat, short trumpet of bright, clean yellow surrounded by flat petals. When these first emerge, they are stained greenish yellow, but they fade to white as the flower develops. The leaves are narrow, always an advantage with narcissus. 'Jack Snipe' is an old variety, raised by Michael Williams of Saint Keverne, Cornwall, UK, before 1951. It will thrive in any decent soil in sun or part shade. Try it between blue cowichan primulas, or use it to fill in ground between dark-leaved cranesbills such as *Geranium* 'Dusky Crûg'. Plant the bulbs 10–12cm (4–5in) deep and the same distance apart.

SEASON: Early March
HARDINESS: Fully hardy
HEIGHT: 28cm (11in)
DIVISION: 6 (Cyclamineus)

Narcissus 'Jenny' ♀

This is an elegant daffodil, one of the best of the Cyclamineus seedlings raised in the 1940s by Cyril Coleman of Cranbrook, Kent, UK. The pointed, pale cream petals sweep back around a pale lemon-coloured trumpet, darker when it first emerges but gradually fading to the colour of the petals. In bud, the flower seems quite green. 'Jenny' looks charming spread under a white-flowered cherry such as *Prunus* 'Taihaku', which will come into flower just after the daffodils have finished, or used in front of *Ruta graveolens* 'Jackman's Blue'. Set the bulbs 13–15cm (5–6in) deep and 10cm (4in) apart.

SEASON: Mid March
HARDINESS: Fully hardy
HEIGHT: 30cm (12in)
DIVISION: 6 (Cyclamineus)

Narcissus × johnstonii
(N. 'Queen of Spain')

Narcissus × johnstonii is a charming variety, very simple and plain, thought to have arisen from a naturally occurring cross between the trumpet daffodil *N. pseudonarcissus* and *N. triandrus*. The petals are very pale yellow, the long, stove-pipe trumpet a slightly deeper shade and slightly frilled at the end. It is an unassuming flower with relatively little foliage, an easy companion for border plants such as pinks which will flower later in the season. Plant 13–15cm (5–6in) deep and the same distance apart.

SEASON: Mid March
HARDINESS: Fully hardy
HEIGHT: 38cm (15in)
DIVISION: 5 (Triandrus)

Narcissus jonquilla ♛
JONQUIL

A wonderful scent comes from this flower, light and sweet with none of the hefty, slightly narcotic overtones of some narcissus. There may be up to four flowers on a stem, and they are the same clear, bright yellow throughout, with short, stubby trumpets and plain, unfrilled petals. It is an enchanting species, unfussy and clean. The name comes from the Spanish *junquillo* (a rush) and refers to the leaves which are bright green and quite narrow. They usually appear in the autumn and are only a little taller than the flowers. Although daffodil expert John Blanchard has seen *N. jonquilla* submerged in the river Douro in Portugal, with its topmost flower floating on the surface of the water, it is probably best to give it the lightest soil you have got, where it can bake in summer. It seems to be happiest on chalk and other alkaline soils. Mix it with earlier-flowering *Iris histrioides* 'Lady Beatrix Stanley' or with *Crocus sieberi* subsp. *sublimis* 'Tricolor'. Plant bulbs 13–15cm (5–6in) deep and the same distance apart.

SEASON: Late March
HARDINESS: Fully hardy
HEIGHT: 38cm (15in)
DIVISION: 13 (Species)
HABITAT: Central and southern Spain and southern and eastern Portugal where it grows in damp meadows and along river banks

Narcissus 'Jumblie' ♛

'Jumblie' was introduced some time before 1952 by Alec Gray who bred it on his Cornish daffodil farm, using a pod of seed which arose from a cross between *N. cyclamineus* and *N. tazetta* 'Soleil d'Or'. 'Tête-à-tête' and 'Quince' (introduced 1953) came from the same sowing. Some pod. 'Jumblie' has more reflexed petals and a longer trumpet than 'Tête-à-tête' and is a fine, easy garden daffodil, excellent in pots outside. Plant 10cm (4in) deep and the same distance apart.

SEASON: March
HARDINESS: Frost hardy
HEIGHT: 17cm (7in)
DIVISION: 12 (Miscellaneous)

NEXT PAGE Delicate *Narcissus* 'Hawera' holds its lemon-yellow flowers above massed ranks of bluebells in blue, pink and white.

Narcissus 'Little Beauty' ♥

Though early, 'Little Beauty' is a sturdy, little thing with creamy white petals round a well-proportioned, yellow trumpet. In form, it is a perfect miniature trumpet daffodil, bred by the Dutch nurserymen J Gerritsen & Son. Although known since the 1950s, it is still a favourite with gardeners. It is excellent in pots outside, naturalized in short grass, or scattered between wood anemones and the rounded, evergreen leaves of *Saxifraga stolonifera*. Plant 10cm (4in) deep and the same distance apart.

SEASON: March
HARDINESS: Fully hardy
HEIGHT: 14cm (5½in)
DIVISION: 1 (Trumpet)

Narcissus 'Little Gem' ♥

When it is fully grown, the flower points itself slightly skywards with both trumpet and petals small, but well proportioned; the gold trumpet is very slightly darker than its surround. The foliage is broader than you might expect on such a small variety, but at flowering time is no more than 15cm (6in) tall. Use 'Little Gem' between the marbled foliage of autumn-flowering *Cyclamen hederifolium*, mix it with the bright blue flowers of *Scilla bifolia* or let it loose in short grass. Plant 10–12cm (4–5in) deep and the same distance apart.

SEASON: Late February
HARDINESS: Fully hardy
HEIGHT: 20cm (8in)
DIVISION: 1 (Trumpet)

Narcissus 'Lothario'

A strong, vigorous daffodil with a wide, overlapping frill of flattish, pale yellow petals round a nicely shaped, crinkled orange trumpet. 'Lothario' is upright, well proportioned and provides a useful boost between clumps of the Lenten rose (*Helleborus orientalis*), which by late April are beginning to look tired. Plant 13–15cm (5–6in) deep and the same distance apart.

SEASON: Late April
HARDINESS: Fully hardy
HEIGHT: 47cm (19in)
DIVISION: 2 (Large-cupped)

Narcissus 'Minnow' ♛

This charming miniature, introduced in 1962 by Alec Gray, bears two or three flowers on a stem, very small and dainty. A tiny, circular cup of soft yellow is surrounded by a neat halo of cream petals. It is a charmer, with not too much leaf, but you need to be close to appreciate it. Unlike other Tazettas, 'Minnow' will settle in grass, provided it is not too coarse. Plant 10–12cm (4–5in) deep and the same distance apart.

SEASON: Early April
HARDINESS: Fully hardy
HEIGHT: 20cm (8in)
DIVISION: 8 (Tazetta)

SEASON: Early March
HARDINESS: Fully hardy
HEIGHT: 35cm (14in)
DIVISION: 1 (Trumpet)

Narcissus 'Mount Hood' ♛

The foliage is beefier than one might wish (though not so terrifying as that of 'Bravoure') which is scarcely surprising as this is a strong daffodil, classically shaped, with a pale frill of petals round a trumpet that, when it first emerges, is a cool, pleasing lemon. As the flower ages, it fades to the same ghostly colour as the petals. They, though, do not lose the strong yellow that washes over their backs at the point where the flower joins the stem. This big, well-formed bloom was raised by P van Deursen of The Netherlands before 1938, but needs good soil to perform well. Use 'Mount Hood' with *Tellima grandiflora*, trilliums or *Dicentra formosa alba*. Plant 13–15cm (5–6in) deep and the same distance apart.

Narcissus × *odorus* 'Double Campernelle'

An enchanting, eggy, messy, double flower with a full, rich centre and star-like outer petals. 'Double Campernelle' has an unusually lovely scent (as you would expect from the species name), sweet and not overpowering. It is a nice, funny thing with reed-thin foliage and is very good for cutting. *Narcissus × odorus* originated as a hybrid between *N. pseudonarcissus* and *N. jonquilla,* but in this form the flower has doubled. Plant 10–12cm (4–5in) deep and the same distance apart.

SEASON: Late March
HARDINESS: Fully hardy
HEIGHT: 25cm (10in)
DIVISION: 4 (Double)

SEASON: October–December (indoors);
late February–March (outdoors)
HARDINESS: Frost hardy
HEIGHT: 50–75cm (20–30in)
DIVISION: 13 (Species)
HABITAT: Northern Africa, southern Spain and
southern France, where it grows in stony places
and grassy, cultivated land

Narcissus papyraceus
(N. 'Paper White')
PAPER-WHITE NARCISSUS

For most of us, this will be a flower to grow inside
rather than out, though in very warm, sheltered
areas it is worth trying N. *papyraceus* in a sunny,
protected spot outside. The flowers are small,
little more than 2cm (¾in) across, but the effect
en masse is terrific as there are up to 15 flowers in
a head. White petals surround a minute white cup,
with a pale creamy 'eye' created by the stamens.
The flowers come out in turn, so the display lasts a
long time – up to a month in a cool room. Though
they stand up straight at the beginning, they
eventually get too long to remain upright and need
staking. The smell is gorgeous and does not go off
like hyacinths. Bulbs are usually available by the
end of August. Buy the biggest, fattest ones you
can find; then you get two stems of flower from
each one. Generally, you can depend on the bulbs
flowering just six weeks after you have planted
them, though early batches may take a little longer.
In bowls, you can plant the bulbs almost touching,
but they perform better in deep containers than
shallow ones. Outdoors plant 15cm (6in) deep
and the same distance apart.

Narcissus 'Passionale' ♥

Now more than 50 years old, this is still a great
favourite, with wide, triangular, whitish petals, the
texture of crepe, and a trumpet-shaped cup of soft,
pale rose-pink. The colouring is similar to 'Bell
Song' but 'Passionale' is considerably taller. If you
like pink daffodils, this is an easy, reliable one
raised by Guy Wilson in 1956 from a 1930s'
daffodil, 'Rose of Tralee'. It flowers generously
in the garden. Use it in front of the hairy-leaved
Papaver orientale 'Patty's Plum', which will come
up to flower later, or set it between pink-toned,
deciduous azaleas such as *Rhododendron*
'Exquisitum'. Plant 13–15cm (5–6in) deep
and the same distance apart.

SEASON: April
HARDINESS: Fully hardy
HEIGHT: 50cm (20in)
DIVISION: 2 (Large-cupped)

Narcissus 'Petrel'

Though short, 'Petrel' gives good value in a garden as there are up to five, slightly scented blooms on each stem. The narrow foliage is also an advantage. Buds are an acid greenish cream, but open out into much paler flowers, with oval, overlapping petals of creamy white around a small, neat, thimble-like trumpet. 'Petrel' is perhaps at its best before all the flowers have opened and the richer colour of the buds is most evident, but it is a charming variety, introduced in 1970 by Grant Mitsch of Oregon, USA, the result of a cross between *N. triandrus* and the Jonquil hybrid 'Quick Step'. Try it with dwarf spurges, such as *Euphorbia* 'Copton Ash', or the navelwort *Omphalodes cappadocica*. It needs to be in the foreground of any planting. Plant 10–12cm (4–5in) deep and the same distance apart.

SEASON: Mid April
HARDINESS: Fully hardy
HEIGHT: 28cm (11in)
DIVISION: 5 (Triandrus)

Narcissus 'Pipit' ♛

A light-limbed variety, producing from two to four flowers in a head. When the flowers first come out, the cup is a little darker than its surround, but it soon fades to the same rather sharp sulphurish yellow. The petals fade to white at their junction with the cup, which is not an advantage, though it obviously pleased Grant Mitsch of Oregon, USA, who raised 'Pipit' in 1963 by crossing the large-cupped daffodil 'Binkie' with *N. jonquilla*. The daffodil looks good rising from a cloud of forget-me-not or the Virginia cowslip (*Mertensia virginica*). It is also tough enough to settle in grass. Plant 13–15cm (5–6in) deep and the same distance apart.

SEASON: Early April
HARDINESS: Fully hardy
HEIGHT: 35cm (14in)
DIVISION: 7 (Jonquil)

Narcissus poeticus var. *recurvus* (N. old pheasant's eye) ♀

An enchanting narcissus, later than 'Actaea', which is useful for a gardener wanting to extend the daffodil season. The flower is tall and elegant, though relatively small for the height of the stem (certainly not as substantial as 'Actaea') with white petals surrounding a tiny, yellow eye ringed with red. The scent is gorgeous, rich and nutmeg-spicy. Grow *N. poeticus* var. *recurvus* as it grows in the wild, in meadows above Lake Garda in Italy, mixed with *Muscari botryoides*. Patrick Synge wrote of seeing it in a meadow in the Pyrenees, mixed with purple orchis, which is much more exotic but a fantastic combination to try if you have the right kind of meadow. Either way, a dampish, grassy situation in dappled shade will suit it much better than a hot, dry place in full sun. In dry conditions flower buds tend to abort, though; even when suited it can be shy to flower. It is not always easy to establish as it hates being lifted and dried off, which is what bulb growers have to do to get bulbs to us, their customers, in late summer. If it settles in your garden, leave it alone and let it get on with its life undisturbed. Plant 20cm (8in) deep and the same distance apart.

SEASON: May

HARDINESS: Fully hardy

HEIGHT: 55cm (22in)

DIVISION: 13 (Species)

HABITAT: *Narcissus poeticus* is widespread in eastern and central France south to central Spain, southern Italy and north-western Greece where it grows in alpine meadows. Var. *recurvus* is thought to have come originally from the Valais district of Switzerland where it grows at 1,500–2,200m (5,000–7,225ft)

Narcissus pseudonarcissus ♀

LENT LILY

These are Wordsworth's daffodils, but in the wild the species is very variable: some flowers are all cream, some all yellow, some have a yellow trumpet surrounded by a white frill of petals. The ones I have are the same sharp yellow throughout (though bought as *N. pseudonarcissus* perhaps it is actually the Tenby daffodil, *N. obvallaris*), with cups slightly too large for the surrounding petals. *Narcissus pseudonarcissus* is good for naturalizing in semi-shaded grass where you might combine it with the smallish, bright blue *Camassia quamash*. The best wild ones I know favour hedge bottoms in West Dorset pastures, in the UK, where they fight for living room against the bluebells. Plant 13–15cm (5–6in) deep and the same distance apart.

SEASON: Late March

HARDINESS: Fully hardy

HEIGHT: 30cm (12in)

DIVISION: 13 (Species)

HABITAT: Western Europe, including Britain, where it grows in woods and meadows

Narcissus 'Quail' ♀

A very robust and easy variety, raised in 1974 by Grant Mitsch of Oregon, USA, from the large-cupped daffodil 'Daydream' crossed with *N. jonquilla*. Each stem of 'Quail' bears two or three smallish but well-proportioned flowers, both trumpet and the surrounding frill of petals the same clear bright yellow. The scent is gorgeous, a feature of all the Jonquils. Use it as a curtain raiser to wallflowers, which it can rival for perfume, or plant it between clumps of the bronze-leaved fennel, *Foeniculum vulgare* 'Purpureum', still low at this stage but a wonderful foil for the vivid yellow blooms of the narcissus. Plant 13–15cm (5–6in) deep and the same distance apart.

SEASON: Early March
HARDINESS: Fully hardy
HEIGHT: 45cm (18in)
DIVISION: 7 (Jonquil)

Narcissus 'Rijnveld's Early Sensation' ♀

This looks just like a normal, yellow daffodil, but it chooses an extraordinary time to come into bloom. And whereas most daffodils flower when their foliage is full grown, 'Rijnveld's Early Sensation' pushes up flower stalks while the leaves are still less than half their height. The petals are a pleasing pale yellow with a nice greenish backing to their outer surfaces. The trumpet, medium sized, is a deeper shade, just frilly enough to be interesting, but not over fussy. A clump of these flowers is a very generous sight at the nadir of the year, and they seem remarkably resistant to bad weather, even withstanding hard frosts. Plant them where the flowers will get plenty of light. Among daffodils, 'Rijnveld's Early Sensation' is on its own at this time of year, so planting possibilities are unlimited. Try it in front of *Mahonia* × *media* 'Lionel Fortescue' or underplant it with the dark-leaved celandine, *Ranunculus ficaria* 'Brazen Hussy'. Set the bulbs 13–15cm (5–6in) deep and the same distance apart.

SEASON: Mid December
HARDINESS: Fully hardy
HEIGHT: 30cm (12in)
DIVISION: 1 (Trumpet)

NEXT PAGE Two or three spicily scented flowers are produced on each stem of the easy-going *Narcissus* 'Suzy'.

Narcissus 'Rip van Winkle'

A wonderfully mad, very double flower, known since 1884, with plenty of green on the backs of the narrow petals. It opens flat and starry, with no hint of a trumpet, of course, because of the doubleness. The outer petals are pale; the ones in the middle pale and dark yellow mixed together. The green makes this flower particularly charming, but in heavy rain the stems are not capable of holding it upright. Even so, I am very fond of 'Rip van Winkle' and use it between the arms of a prostrate rosemary which it can use as a prop. It would also be good with the spring vetchling (*Lathyrus vernus*). Plant 10cm (4in) deep and the same distance apart.

SEASON: Early March
HARDINESS: Fully hardy
HEIGHT: 20cm (8in)
DIVISION: 4 (Double)

Narcissus 'Saint Keverne' ♈

Bred in 1934 by the Cornish grower Michael Williams, this is still a terrific daffodil, all deep golden-yellow, the long, slender trumpet with its frilled edge perfectly balanced in relation to the surrounding, thickly textured petals. Commercial growers find 'Saint Keverne' usefully resistant to basal rot. Line it out in a cutting garden (daffodils look good in a jug with catkins), or set it between bronze-purple clumps of *Euphorbia dulcis* 'Chameleon'. Plant 13–15cm (5–6in) deep and the same distance apart.

SEASON: Early March
HARDINESS: Fully hardy
HEIGHT: 48cm (19in)
DIVISION: 2 (Large-cupped)

Narcissus 'Segovia' ♥

A small, dainty daffodil, in form rather like 'Xit' but with a little, flat, lemon cup in the centre of the pure white, rounded petals. 'Segovia' was raised in 1962 by Mrs F M Gray of Camborne, Cornwall, UK. Plant 10cm (4in) deep and 8–10cm (3½–4in) apart.

SEASON: April
HARDINESS: Fully hardy
HEIGHT: 15cm (6in)
DIVISION: 3 (Small-cupped)

Narcissus 'Silver Chimes'

A vigorous variety, now that it has been cleaned of the virus that once plagued it, with broad, bright green foliage (slightly too beefy to be ideal). There may be up to seven flowers in a head, opening out in turn from the enclosing papery sheath. Each has a tiny, creamy white frill surrounding an even tinier, very pale yellow cup. It is strongly scented, with a hint of apple hidden somewhere deep within. 'Silver Chimes' is an old flower raised before 1914 by the Martins (father and son) of Truro, Cornwall, UK, from the Tazetta 'Scilly White' and *N. triandrus*, but it was an excellent new find for me, the first time I grew it. Mix it with grape hyacinths, or use between feathery clumps of *Ferula communis*. The gorgeous foliage of this giant fennel erupts very early in the year and makes a fine companion for many of the taller narcissi or tulips. The Tazettas need a warmer and sunnier spot than other kinds of daffodils. Plant the bulbs in well-drained soil where they can bake in summer, setting them 13–15cm (5–6in) deep and the same distance apart.

SEASON: Early April
HARDINESS: Fully hardy
HEIGHT: 40cm (16in)
DIVISION: 8 (Tazetta)

Narcissus 'Sun Disc' ♀

An enchanting, rounded, flat-faced little flower, introduced before 1946 by the famous Cornish daffodil grower Alec Gray. It has wide, overlapping petals of soft butter-yellow and a frilly, flat disc of darker yellow in the centre. You can scarcely call it a cup, as it is pressed right back against the surround. The whole flower is barely 5cm (2in) across, but it is a dainty thing and a good, not harsh, yellow. The foliage is narrow, in keeping with the general scale of the flower. Use 'Sun Disc' with *Corydalis flexuosa* 'China Blue' or between violas such as 'Belmont Blue' or 'Eastgrove Blue Scented', which will later make mats of flower and leaf to fill the spaces where the daffodils were. It bulks up very quickly. Plant 13–15cm (5–6in) deep and 10cm (4in) apart.

SEASON: Mid April
HARDINESS: Fully hardy
HEIGHT: 30cm (12in)
DIVISION: 7 (Jonquil)

Narcissus 'Suzy' ♀

A charming, light-limbed narcissus, which occasionally produces more than one flowering stem from a bulb, with two or three flowers on each stem. The wide, pointed petals are golden-yellow but fade slightly as they age. A nice scent, lightly spicy, comes from the short, wide, frilly trumpet of bright orange. 'Suzy' is a cross between the large-cupped daffodil 'Hades' and *N. jonquilla*, raised before 1954 by the Cornish grower Dr R V Favell. It bulks up quickly and looks terrific with the queen of umbellifers, *Selinum wallichianum*, or when its bright golden flowers bob in front of a sober stand of *Euphorbia amygdaloides* var. *robbiae*. Plant 13–15cm (5–6in) deep and the same distance apart.

SEASON: Mid March
HARDINESS: Fully hardy
HEIGHT: 38cm (15in)
DIVISION: 7 (Jonquil)

Narcissus 'Tête-à-tête' ♀

'Tête-à-tête' (together with 'February Gold', 'Jumblie' and 'Jack Snipe') derives from the species *Narcissus cyclamineus*, which grows in moist alpine meadows in Portugal and Spain. It is a bossy little thing with brilliant buttercup-yellow flowers, bred before 1949, and destined to become the most famous of the many miniature daffodils introduced by enthusiast Alec Gray (1895–1986) of Camborne, Cornwall, UK. This one variety alone accounts for a third of all daffodils raised in The Netherlands. A double 'Tête-à-tête' arose there a little while ago, and a consortium of growers paid a fortune to acquire a monopoly of the stock. You recognize it immediately because of its bright green leaves, surrounding equally bright stems which bear from one to three flowers, very narrow in bud. The frill is yellow, the cup verges on orange and is slightly waved. The colour is not harsh, almost exactly the same as 'February Gold', and the flower well proportioned, held at a pleasing, slightly drooping angle to the stem. It is a very prolific variety compared with 'Little Gem' and amazingly durable in the garden. Although 'Tête-à-tête' has *N. tazetta* as its other parent, it does not mind having damp feet and, being so small, is easy to accommodate. It will do in any reasonable soil. Try it with deep blue cowichan primulas or among soft blue *Anemone blanda*. It is also a popular variety for forcing, but unlike *N. papyraceus* it will need a long, cool period in the dark before coming up to flower. When you have finished with it inside, you can plant it out in the garden. Set the bulbs 10cm (4in) deep and the same distance apart.

SEASON: Late February
HARDINESS: Fully hardy
HEIGHT: 22cm (9in)
DIVISION: 12 (Miscellaneous)

Narcissus 'Trevithian' ♀

An extremely pretty flower, with the surround and the cup both the same clear buttercup-yellow. It is not too frilly or over-complicated – smallish, neat, rounded and very sweetly scented. The cup is simple and shapely, neither too large nor too long and the petals lie relatively flat. 'Trevithian' was bred before 1927 by the Cornish grower Percival Dacres Williams of Saint Keverne, UK. Plant it next to the extraordinary dragon arum (*Dracunculus vulgaris*) – it may help to drown the arum's smell – or use it as a forerunner to the yellow, scented blooms of *Rhododendron luteum*. Plant 13–15cm (5–6in) deep and the same distance apart.

SEASON: Late March
HARDINESS: Fully hardy
HEIGHT: 40cm (16in)
DIVISION: 7 (Jonquil)

Narcissus 'White Lady'

A sweet, old-fashioned thing, with creamy white petals and a small, pale yellow cup, introduced before 1897 by the Reverend George Engleheart of Dinton, Hampshire, UK. It is one of my favourite daffodils, with a light, flimsy texture that makes it a natural for semi-wild situations. Set 'White Lady' in large drifts between clumps of brunnera or contrast it with the evergreen fronds of *Polystichum setiferum* 'Pulcherrimum Bevis'. Plant 13–15cm (5–6in) deep and the same distance apart.

SEASON: April
HARDINESS: Fully hardy
HEIGHT: 45cm (18in)
DIVISION: 3 (Small-cupped)

Narcissus 'Xit'

It seems extraordinary that the same genus can produce members as disparate as 'Bravoure' and 'Xit', which is so small, so pure, you think it might really be at heart a snowdrop but was given the wrong clothes. The all-white frill is quite big in relation to the flat-faced, frilly cup, which presses itself back against the petals, afraid to go ahead. The stamens are minuscule things of creamy white, though stamens are never an outstanding feature of narcissus as they are with crocus. The leaves are reedy thin, a good thing, or else they would overwhelm the fragile flower. This is yet another of Alec Gray's introductions, raised some time before 1948. 'Xit' is charming with *Ipheion* 'Jessie' or combined with the strange khaki blooms of *Fritillaria acmopetala* or *F. assyriaca*. Plant 13–15cm (5–6in) deep and the same distance apart.

SEASON: Late March
HARDINESS: Fully hardy
HEIGHT: 30cm (12in)
DIVISION: 3 (Small-cupped)

Narcissus 'White Lion' ♥

A very vigorous variety with broad foliage and cheerful, messy flowers. The pointed outer petals are creamy white, the centre a blobby mixture of largish white petals mixed with shortish yellow ones. Behind is a long, green throat which holds the flowers some distance from the stems. 'White Lion' was raised before 1949 by the Dutch nurserymen De Graaff-Gerharda from a cross between the old double 'Mary Copeland' and the large-cupped daffodil 'John Evelyn'. Plant 13–15cm (5–6in) deep and the same distance apart.

SEASON: Late March
HARDINESS: Fully hardy
HEIGHT: 40cm (16in)
DIVISION: 4 (Double)

Nectaroscordum (Alliaceae)

Nectaroscordum siculum (*Allium siculum*)

A tall, pointed bud wrapped in a papery sheath breaks open to reveal the cluster of flowers inside. The foliage, though long (55cm/22in), is lax and soon collapses on the ground. It is strap-shaped, mid-green and thoughtfully does not get in the way. If you crush it, it gives off a strong smell of garlic. The flowering stem is strong and straight (though tall, they do not need staking), and the cluster of buds opens into a drooping umbel of up to 30 flowers, striped in maroon and cream. They are small, but because there are lots of them the head lasts a long time (they open in succession). Right in the centre of each flower is a shiny ring of lime-green. The long stalks on which the flowers hang are a dull bronze-green. The seedpods are a great feature, for they turn upwards, so the plant rises like a chandelier between hostas such as 'Krossa Regal' or hellebores. Combine *N. siculum* with the dark red flowers of a peony or use it between grasses such as *Deschampsia cespitosa* and *Molinia caerulea* 'Transparent'. It seeds itself about very readily and sits as happily in semi-wild shaded parts of a garden as it does in grass. Remember though that if you plant it in grass, you will not be able to mow until late July. Plant the bulbs in any reasonable soil in sun or shade, setting them 15cm (6in) deep and 25cm (10in) apart.

SEASON: Early May
HARDINESS: Fully hardy
HEIGHT: 85cm (34in)
HABITAT: Southern France and Italy, including Sicily

Nerine (Amaryllidaceae)

Nerines have flowers that seem almost to be lit up from within. They are in a way, for the surfaces of their petals are made up of curiously shaped cells which concentrate any available light onto the pink sap inside them. Icing-sugar pink is the standard colour but wonderful new shades are emerging, particularly from seedlings of tender *N. sarniensis*. All nerines make excellent cut flowers, though if you grow them in pots you will not need to cut. You can bring the pots inside instead. *Nerine bowdenii* is hardy, but will grow best at the base of a sunny, south-facing wall. A good summer baking encourages plenty of flowers through autumn. In cold areas, mulch clumps when they have finished flowering to give extra protection against frost. If you think the flower-power is dwindling, try feeding in summer with a fertilizer high in potash (tomato feed is ideal). Being more tender, *N. filifolia*, *N. flexuosa* 'Alba' and *N. undulata* are best grown in pots, planted so that the tips of the bulbs just show above the surface of the compost. Use a loam-based one, such as John Innes No 2, and give the bulbs plenty of water when they are growing strongly. In winter, when they have finished flowering, they need to be kept somewhere warm and dry. Do not be in a hurry to pot them on. They flower better when the bulbs are rather cramped in the pot. If you feel you must meddle, do it in August, but it should not be necessary more than once every five years.

ABOVE The frilly pink petals of *Nerine undulata* create an ethereal effect in the autumn garden.

Nerine bowdenii ♡

The bulbs as they multiply almost push each other out of the ground, but this does not stop them flowering. Indeed they seem to like it and flower best when slightly congested. Long, thin, pointed buds, sheathed in green and very elegant, rise up from the naked bulbs on stems of an equally bright green. Then the bud explodes into a roundel of bright pink flowers, nine or so in a head, coming out in turn. The petals are long and thin and curl back on themselves as the flower develops. Close to, you see they are almost striped, with a deep pink line down the centre of each, paler stripes either side. The stamens curl out and up, like a lily's. A well-established clump of *N. bowdenii* is a lovely sight and they come at a good time of the year, when you think there are not many treats left. The bright green, strappy leaves follow the flowers and do most of their growing in spring before the whole plant shuts down for its summer rest. The species is named after the Cornishman Athelstan Bowden, who found it in 1903 growing in the mountains near King William's Town in the Eastern Cape and sent bulbs to his mother who lived at Newton Abbot in Devon, UK. Set the bulbs 6cm (2¼in) deep and 25cm (10in) apart.

SEASON: Late September
HARDINESS: Fully hardy
HEIGHT: 70cm (28in)
HABITAT: South Africa (Eastern Cape, KwaZulu-Natal, Free State) where it grows on cliffs and rocks up to 3,000m (10,000ft)

Nerine filifolia

This species is virtually evergreen, with grassy, new leaves produced just as the old ones are dying. The flowers can be pink or white but have petals that are astonishingly frilly and carefree. In a cool room, a plant in a pot makes a beautiful and long-lasting display. *Nerine filifolia* was first collected in the Free State in 1879 by Thomas Ayres, a Herefordshire man who settled in South Africa and was appointed naturalist to the Matabeleland expedition of 1880. In pots, plant so the nose of the bulb is just above the surface of the compost.

SEASON: October–November
HARDINESS: Half hardy
HEIGHT: 30cm (12in)
HABITAT: South Africa (Free State) where it grows in damp meadows or on rocks by (sometimes even in) streams

Nerine flexuosa 'Alba'

A spray of thin, bright green leaves (23cm/9in long) surrounds a strong, equally bright green stem, thicker than that of *N. undulata*. A dozen white flowers break out of a long, pointed sheath to make an attractive, flattish head. The petals are only slightly frilled, and they arrange themselves in a fan over the top three-quarters of an arc, leaving the creamy stamens to hang down in the gap. This is a very attractive, pure, clean flower, which still looks splendid all through November. *Nerine flexuosa* 'Alba' is not fully hardy so it is safest to grow it in a pot which you can whisk under cover on a frosty night. Plant so the nose of the bulb is just above the surface of the compost.

SEASON: Mid October
HARDINESS: Half hardy
HEIGHT: 45cm (18in)

Nerine undulata

Four strappy leaves, thin and rather lax, rise alongside the flowering stem, which is topped with a head of frilly-petalled flowers. Individually, they are smaller than those of *N. flexuosa*, but there are more of them (14 in a head). The petals are narrow and made to seem all the more so because of their wavy edges. The flowers have the habit of arranging their petals in a three-quarter circle, leaving a space at the bottom for the style and stamens to hang down, all tipped with dark purple. This is a charming species, much more ethereal than *N. bowdenii*, and it stays looking good all through November. It has been known in gardens since 1767. *Nerine undulata* is safest in a pot, planted so the nose of the bulb just shows through the surface of the compost.

SEASON: Mid October
HARDINESS: Half hardy
HEIGHT: 50cm (20in)
HABITAT: South Africa (Eastern Cape)

Nomocharis (Liliaceae)

SEASON: June
HARDINESS: Fully hardy
HEIGHT: 60–80cm (24–32in)
HABITAT: Western China (south-western Sichuan, north-western Yunnan) where it grows in mountain pastures up to 4,300m (14,000ft)

Nomocharis aperta

On each stem are five or six slightly drooping, saucer-shaped flowers of pale purplish pink, spotted at the base with dark crimson. *Nomocharis aperta* was first collected by the plant hunter Abbé Delavay in 1889 near Tali in north-western Yunnan and was subsequently found both by George Forrest (in south-western Sichuan) and by Reginald Farrer (at the Chawchi Pass on the border of China and Tibet). Even Farrer, not usually lost for words, struggled to pin down the precise appeal of the nomocharis. 'It is like some hybrid of a minor Lily with *Odontoglossum rossi*', he wrote, 'combining the perverse and sinister spottings of the one with the frank and graceful loveliness of the other, alike in proud, meek port and delicacy of shell pink colouring.' When you have seen these growing in the wild, he continued, 'there is nothing very much left for you to look on'. Farrer also said that he looked forward to a happy future for nomocharis 'on well-drained grassy banks in English gardens', but they are much more likely to be happy in Scotland than they are in the south of England. *Nomocharis aperta* is a natural companion for rhododendrons since it enjoys the same cool, moist woodlandy conditions. The bulbs hate to dry out so are best bought damp-packed in autumn and planted in soil that is rich in humus and on the acid side of neutral. Even better is to wait till spring and buy a plant already growing in a pot. It prefers shade to full sun. Plant bulbs 15cm (6in) deep and 20cm (8in) apart.

Notholirion (Liliaceae)

Notholirion bulbuliferum

From a clump of basal leaves, tall stems rise up, studded with up to 30 trumpet-shaped flowers, pale blue-mauve tipped with green. Like nomocharis, *N. bulbuliferum* grows best in areas where summers are cool and damp; give it partial shade. Like cardiocrinums, notholirions are monocarpic, which means that they die after they have flowered, leaving behind a cluster of offsets which take at least three years to build up to flowering size. It is not easy to establish but is lovely with ferns such as *Blechnum spicant* and *Dryopteris wallichiana*. Buy bulbs damp-packed in autumn as they hate to dry out. Plant in deep, well-drained, humus-rich soil which is on the acid side of neutral, setting the bulbs 15cm (6in) deep and 40cm (16in) apart.

SEASON: July–August
HARDINESS: Frost hardy
HEIGHT: 60–90cm (24–36in)
HABITAT: Nepal to western China (Shaanxi, Gansu) where it grows in alpine meadows at 3,000–3,750m (10,000–12,400ft)

Ornithogalum (Hyacinthaceae)

Ornithogalums seem rather despised by gardeners, perhaps because the best known of them – the star of Bethlehem (*O. umbellatum*) – is invasive if you give it full sun and good ground, but keeps its flowers sulkily shut if you try and curb it with poorer ground and shade. But the family has some surprising members, such as *O. dubium* with flowers as orange as a marigold's and some of superstar status, such as the gorgeous *O. arabicum*. Unfortunately the most interesting ones are also the most difficult to grow, at least for those who garden in temperate climates with rather cool, dampish summers. Pots may be a better alternative than the open ground. Then the bulbs can get the summer baking they need, in a cold frame or greenhouse. The flowers of many ornithogalums (especially those of *O. arabicum* and *O. dubium*) are slow to develop but, once they come out, last an amazingly long time. That is why chincherinchee (*O. thyrsoides*) has become such a successful crop for growers of cut flowers. The foliage is flaccid and untidy but fortunately is all produced at ground level. So although (like alliums) the leaves are at their worst when the flowers are at their best, they are relatively easy to disguise. *Ornithogalum arabicum*, *O. dubium*, *O. magnum* and *O. thyrsoides* need as much sun as you can give them, while *O. nutans* and *O. umbellatum* will settle in partial shade, though the flowers will be more reluctant to open.

LEFT The star of Bethlehem (*Ornithogalum umbellatum*) can be invasive in a garden, but naturalizes well in grass.

Ornithogalum arabicum

Grown in gardens since 1629, *O. arabicum* is a great surprise to those who do not know it and one of the loveliest members of this diverse tribe. The strong stems have up to a dozen wide-petalled, ivory-white flowers (6cm/2¼in across) clustered at the top. Each flower emerges from a hooked sheath, white tipped with green. Alternate petals are also lightly tipped with green, but there is no green stripe up the back of the petals, a feature of so many of the ornithogalums. In the centre of each flower is an astonishingly shiny, round, black button eye; ranged around it are fat, white filaments each topped with a golden knob, the whole thing just like a miniature crown. *Ornithogalum arabicum* makes a superb cut flower (scented), which lasts a long time in a vase. The strappy foliage is already dying off as the flowers begin to open. In cold areas, it may be best to grow half-hardy species such as this in pots of loam-based compost so that they can be kept frost-free in winter. While the plants are growing give them full light and plenty of water. Let them dry off after flowering, before repotting in fresh compost in autumn. Five bulbs should fit in a pot 10–15cm (4–6in) across. You can keep them in the pot or plant the whole potful outside when the first tips of growth show through. Either way, the bulbs need a thorough baking in summer. If you are planting outside in spring, set the large, pear-shaped bulbs 10cm (4in) deep and 15cm (6in) apart.

SEASON: Late May
HARDINESS: Half hardy
HEIGHT: 48cm (19in)
HABITAT: Mediterranean

Ornithogalum dubium ♀

This surprising ornithogalum is slow to develop from bud to flower then bursts out in dayglo-orange – nicer than it sounds because the centre is stained with a bronze blotch and the stamens make pricks of light round a small, dark bulbous eye in the centre. The buds are tinged with green, but this is nowhere apparent in the flower when it opens. There are about 16 flowers in each head, small (3cm/1in across) but so vivid they cannot be overlooked. The spike at first is slim, but the flowers low on the stem have longer stalks than those higher up so as the spike develops it becomes broader based, less narrow. At flowering, the leaves which have already been around a long time are mostly withered away. Try *O. dubium* with the dark leaves of *Geranium sessiliflorum* 'Nigricans'. Plant it where it will be dry and baked after flowering, setting the bulbs 10cm (4in) deep and 10cm (4in) apart.

SEASON: Mid June
HARDINESS: Half hardy
HEIGHT: 25cm (10in)
HABITAT: South Africa (Western Cape, Eastern Cape)

Ornithogalum nutans ♀

This is a curiously ghostly, ethereal plant, not in its form or habit, which is fleshy and robust, but in its colouring – white and a curious grey-green, the colour of lichen. The foliage, which comes through early, is long, lank and untidy, like a bluebell's, with fat, fleshy flower stems rising from it. Each stem carries about 12 star flowers, which develop from the bottom up, so that no more than five are fully open at any one time. At the centre of each star is a white tube containing the stamens. Each white petal has a lichen-coloured stripe down the centre and a darker, greener shade washes over the backs as well. *Ornithogalum nutans* is too untidy (the foliage too flaccid) for a border but would fit in the sort of place where you might use bluebells – a semi-wild part of the garden, where it might grow with brunnera, primroses and oak fern (*Gymnocarpium dryopteris*). Though it may become invasive, *O. nutans* is a very nice thing, understated and soothing. Plant in light shade, setting the bulbs 10cm (4in) deep and 10cm (4in) apart.

SEASON: Late March
HARDINESS: Fully hardy
HEIGHT: 40cm (16in)
HABITAT: Bulgaria, Greece and Turkey (but widely naturalized) where it grows in fields and waste places

Ornithogalum thyrsoides ♀
CHINCHERINCHEE

For many years this has been a favourite cut flower as it lasts such a long time in bloom. Picked in bud, the stems waxed, chincherinchees (the common name is supposed to echo the sound that the stems make when they rub together) were robust enough to survive a sea crossing from South Africa to the Covent Garden flower market in London. Now they are freighted round the world by air. Each long, narrow spike can bear 20–30 white flowers. The spikes widen as the flowers begin to open and show off their prominent, yellow stamens. In coolish areas, it may be safer to grow *O. thyrsoides* in pots in a conservatory or greenhouse. You can keep them in pots permanently or plant them out when they are just poking through the surface of the compost. By this time the worst of the cold weather should be behind them. Outside, a sandy, well-drained loam will suit them best. They must have sun and, while they are growing, plenty to drink. Outdoors, plant in spring, setting the bulbs 10cm (4in) deep and 10cm (4in) apart.

SEASON: June
HARDINESS: Half hardy
HEIGHT: 40cm (16in)
HABITAT: South Africa (Western Cape) and Namibia (Namaqualand)

SEASON: Early May
HARDINESS: Fully hardy
HEIGHT: 25cm (10in)
HABITAT: Europe, Turkey, Syria, Lebanon and northern Africa; naturalized in parts of Canada and USA.

Ornithogalum umbellatum
STAR OF BETHLEHEM

If you have not been brainwashed to think of it as a thug, *O. umbellatum* will appear unexpectedly charming, with wide, spreading heads of flowers like a triteleia, light, feathery and airy. The white star flowers are held on long stalks away from the stem; the stalks on the lowest flowers are the longest, so the head makes a broad-based pyramid, wider than it is tall. Typically, each head bears 6–9 flowers, the backs of the petals striped with pale grey-green, like so many of this tribe. The flowers have very precise habits, opening at eleven o'clock and closing at three in the afternoon. The foliage is thin, grassy and lax, the tips of the leaves beginning to yellow at flowering time, which is a pity. Disguise it with the arms of a silvery artemisia. *Ornithogalum umbellatum* is a good flower to naturalize in meadow grass or under shrubs such as philadelphus or lilac, though it may become invasive. If it is too shady, though, the flowers will not open at all. Plant in well-drained soil 10cm (4in) deep and 10cm (4in) apart.

Pancratium (Amaryllidaceae)

Pancratium maritimum

SEA DAFFODIL

This makes a wonderfully showy indoor plant for late summer, if you can persuade it to bloom. The big, long-necked bulbs produce umbels of sweet-smelling, white flowers, up to 10cm (4in) across, the sharply toothed central cones surrounded by six white petals, in the manner of Peruvian daffodil (*Hymenocallis narcissiflora*). There will most probably be a flower packed inside the bulb when you first buy it. Getting it to perform in subsequent years is more difficult. It needs a summer baking. This can be most easily arranged if you grow *P. maritimum* in a deep pot in a greenhouse or conservatory, using loam-based potting compost (John Innes No 2) with added grit (two parts compost to one part grit). Water freely once the bulb is growing well and feed once a month with tomato fertilizer. Keep the plant in growth until the grey-green leaves start to die down at the beginning of the following summer. Then the bulb needs to be really warm and dry if you are ever to see another flower. But as its own natural habitat is increasingly suffocated by concrete condominiums, this bulb is worth some trouble. If you want to risk it outside, plant bulbs 25cm (10in) deep and 30cm (12in) apart.

SEASON: August–September
HARDINESS: Half hardy
HEIGHT: 30cm (12in)
HABITAT: Mediterranean areas of south-west Europe where it grows in sand dunes by the sea

Paris (Trilliaceae)

Paris polyphylla ♈

Paris polyphylla grows from a creeping rhizome, in this case a very thick, fleshy, brown one, and produces a pale green flower; the construction of the bloom is so extraordinary that it does not need colour. The name comes from the Latin word *par* meaning 'equal' and that is the essence of its charm. It is symmetrical, poised and beautifully balanced. Clasping the strange flower is a skirt of shiny, green leaves. Above that another ruff of pale green petals, from which spill thread-thin stamens, like spiders' legs. Crowning the middle is the knobby ovary with a purple stigma as the final element of the whole fantastic edifice. Why, you might ask? But don't. Just admire. In autumn, it will present you with capsules of red berries. Trilliums are natural companions as are erythroniums and wood anemones. Buy *P. polyphylla* damp-packed in autumn, plant it in a cool, damp, shady place in the garden and then leave it alone. Set the rhizomes 10–12cm (4–5in) deep and 30cm (12in) apart.

SEASON: April–June
HARDINESS: Fully hardy
HEIGHT: 60cm (24in)
HABITAT: Himalayas to Burma, Thailand and western China
where it grows in woods at 1,700–3,500m (5,750–11,700ft)

Polianthes (Agavaceae)

Polianthes tuberosa

TUBEROSE ♈

For most of us now these will be plants to scent a greenhouse or conservatory, as they hate to be chilly and demand a minimum temperature around 15°C (59°F). But they are worth some trouble as the heads of white, waxy, tubular flowers look spectacular and smell even better. 'The Pearl' has flowers that are almost double. The tuberose, already known to the great plantsman Carolus Clusius in 1594, has long been popular as a cut flower, and early accounts show that it was once widely grown in market gardens, 1,500 roots packed into 0.1ha (0.25 acre) plots, planted in spring and lifted in autumn before the first frosts. Some growers left the tubers in the ground and thatched over their plots with straw instead. In pots outside, tuberoses look good with cannas, castor oil plants and other exotica. Plant in a loam-based compost and give the plant as much light as possible. Three tubers should fit in a deep pot about 15cm (6in) across. Feed every two weeks during the growing season. When the display is over, gradually reduce the amount of water you give so the leaves die down. The tuber then needs a dry dormant period. If you plant outside, do it in spring. Choose a rich but well-drained piece of ground in full sun and give *P. tuberosa* plenty of water. Lift the tubers before the first frost and store them in sand until planting time the following season. Set the noses of the tubers just under the surface of the soil and 20cm (8in) apart.

SEASON: Late June
HARDINESS: Tender
HEIGHT: 1m (3ft)
HABITAT: Mexico (though it has never been recorded in a wild habitat)

Puschkinia (Hyacinthaceae)

Puschkinia scilloides var. *libanotica*

Foliage and flowers push through together, the two leaves arranged one either side of the flowering stem. This is a wispy, ethereal flower and needs a place to itself in the garden, where, doing its quiet, little thing, it will not be overwhelmed by noisy neighbours. As its name suggests, it is similar in appearance to a scilla, up to ten small, starry flowers (more usually six) ranged in a spike at the top of a rather thin stem. The flowers are milky white with a thin, blue line down the centre of each petal. It is named not for the poet Aleksander Pushkin but after a Russian botanist of the early nineteenth century, Count Apollo Puschkin, who made many plant-hunting trips in the Caucasus. Try *P. scilloides* var. *libanotica* with *Anemone nemorosa* 'Robinsoniana' or *Ipheion* 'Rolf Fiedler', or use it to fill the spaces between clumps of autumn-flowering *Cyclamen hederifolium*. Left alone, it will naturalize under trees, and this is perhaps the best way to use it, provided the ground is not too dry. Puschkinias are equally happy in sun or light shade. Plant bulbs in autumn, setting them 5cm (2in) deep and 10cm (4in) apart.

SEASON: Mid March
HARDINESS: Fully hardy
HEIGHT: 14cm (5½in)
HABITAT: Turkey and Lebanon where it grows in grassland made damp by melting snow at 1,900–3,700m (6,250–12,250ft)

Ranunculus (Ranunculaceae)

Ranunculus ficaria 'Brazen Hussy'

CELANDINE

This form of yellow-flowered celandine has deep bronze-chocolate leaves and was discovered in 1976 by the late Christopher Lloyd in a wood near his home, Great Dixter at Northiam in Sussex, UK. Gardeners are conditioned to look on celandines with hatred as they multiply more rapidly than weeders can cope with. But established between the pink-bronze shoots of an herbaceous peony, scattered between the arthritic crowns of *Crambe cordifolia* or under the pale stems of the golden-leaved *Rubus cockburnianus* 'Goldenvale', this celandine can make good use of ground that would otherwise be bare. Just as you think 'Brazen Hussy' is getting above itself, it dives underground and you forget about it completely. Plant tubers 5cm (2in) deep and 20cm (8in) apart.

SEASON: March
HARDINESS: Fully hardy
HEIGHT: 10cm (4in)

Romulea (Iridaceae)

Romulea bulbocodium

In both leaf and flower, romuleas most resemble crocuses, the funnel-shaped blooms rising up from a tuft of fine, grassy foliage. But these have proper stems, crocus do not; what seems to be the stem of a crocus is actually the throat of the flower itself. *Romulea bulbocodium*, introduced to gardeners in 1739, is lilac-purple, cream-coloured or yellow at the throat, with yellowish or creamy stamens bunched in the centre. The flowers rarely open before midday (and then only if it is sunny) and shut up again firmly in the evening. Plant corms in autumn, setting them in well-drained soil in full sun, 5cm (2in) deep and 8cm (3½in) apart.

SEASON: March–April
HARDINESS: Frost hardy
HEIGHT: 5–10cm (2–4in)
HABITAT: Mediterranean, Portugal, north-west Spain and Bulgaria where they grow in rocky, sandy places or in scrub up to 1,000m (3,300ft)

Roscoea (Zingiberaceae)

When young, roscoeas do not seem to have enough flower in relation to the overall bulk of the plant, but the flowers get bigger as the plant becomes more established. Although they are firmly placed in the ginger family, they look as though they really want to be orchids and have that hooded look, made up from a strange configuration of petals, each adapted in the very particular way that is characteristic of many of the orchid family. Two ears flop down, completely covered by one big, fan-shaped petal, sometimes entire, sometimes divided. Above stands a rounded, pointed petal, strongly folded in on itself. In the centre, two small, cowl-shaped petals protect the stamens and style. It is wildly complicated. Roscoeas are named after William Roscoe who founded the Liverpool Botanic Garden in 1802. They like cool woodland, damp and shady, the kind of spot they might share with trilliums, bloodroot (*Sanguinaria canadensis*) and ferns. A thick winter mulch will provide extra protection against frost.

Roscoea auriculata

From a very stout ribbed stem, leaves sheath off at intervals all the way up to the flowers at the head. In *R. auriculata* they are rich, clear purple, poking out in succession from the top of the stem. In the very centre, two small, white cowl-shaped petals hover over the stamens and style. Plant the fleshy rhizomes in leafy, humus-rich soil, setting them 15cm (6in) deep and 20cm (8in) apart.

SEASON: Mid July
HARDINESS: Borderline hardy
HEIGHT: 40cm (16in)
HABITAT: Nepal, Sikkim and Tibet where it grows in woods and meadows

Roscoea 'Beesiana'

From a strong, thick, ribbed stem, leaves peel off at regular intervals, as in a hedychium. The flower may be white or pale primrose-yellow suffused with purple and made in the complex way of all roscoeas: two ears, a wide fan, a pointed hood and two much smaller, inner cowls protecting the stamens and style. 'Beesiana' is good with *Polystichum setiferum* 'Pulcherrimum Bevis' and lilies such as 'Anglia' or 'Casa Blanca'. Buy it damp-packed in spring as the tubers hate to dry out. Plant in good, moisture-retentive soil, in part shade or sun, setting the tubers 15cm (6in) deep and 12cm (5in) apart.

SEASON: Early July
HARDINESS: Borderline hardy
HEIGHT: 44cm (18in)

Roscoea cautleyoides ♔

Introduced in 1912 and one of the earliest roscoeas to flower, with neat, upright growth, the leaves sheathed round the strong flowering stem. On top are white or light sulphur-yellow flowers, not quite important enough for their position but beautifully formed, with six petals, each developed for its own function. Two outer petals droop down either side of a divided central petal, another stands like a hood at the top, with two smaller hooded petals inside sheltering the stamens. Set *R. cautleyoides* alongside the grey-blue flowers of *Campanula portenschlagiana* or use it to follow on from *Corydalis flexuosa* 'China Blue'. It is best bought damp-packed as the fleshy tubers hate to dry out. Plant in sun or dappled shade, setting the tubers in good, moisture-retentive soil 15cm (6in) deep and 12cm (5in) apart.

SEASON: Early June
HARDINESS: Borderline hardy
HEIGHT: 30cm (12in)
HABITAT: Western China (Sichuan, Yunnan) where it grows in wooded areas with rhododendrons and pines

Roscoea cautleyoides 'Kew Beauty' ♀

'Kew Beauty' is a selected form of *R. cautleyoides* with leaves that are a darker green and flowers that are a slightly lighter, richer yellow. Use it with the feathery fronds of *Dryopteris felix-mas* 'Crispa' and surround it with snowdrops, which will use the ground to good effect before the roscoeas get going in late spring. 'Kew Beauty' is best bought damp-packed as the fleshy tubers hate to dry out. Plant it in sun or dappled shade, setting the tubers in good, moisture-retentive soil 15cm (6in) deep and 12cm (5in) apart.

SEASON: Early June
HARDINESS: Borderline hardy
HEIGHT: 30cm (12in)

Roscoea purpurea

A strong-growing species, introduced in 1820, producing tufts of narrow, folded, rich green foliage. Large, hooded flowers of dark purple, rather like orchids, appear between the axils of the leaves. Plant *R. purpurea* with a greyish-leaved hosta such *H.* 'Blue Blush' or with elegant *Lilium cernuum*. It is best bought damp-packed as the tubers hate to dry out. Plant in good, moisture-retentive soil in part shade or sun, 15cm (6in) deep and 12cm (5in) apart.

SEASON: July–August
HARDINESS: Borderline hardy
HEIGHT: 30cm (12in)
HABITAT: Himalayas (Nepal, Bhutan, northern India)

Scadoxus (Amaryllidaceae)

Scadoxus multiflorus subsp. *katherinae* ♀
BLOOD LILY

Lunatic puffballs (12–15cm/5–6in across) explode barely above ground with as many as a hundred spidery, salmon-red flowers interlocking to make a head like a psychedelic dandelion clock. When the flower is fully opened, the leaves start to grow, fleshy and wavy edged. It is the waviness of the foliage that distinguishes this subspecies from its parent. *Scadoxus multiflorus* subsp. *katherinae* provides a spectacular, though bizarre, late summer surprise, the flowers bristling with yellow-tipped stamens. Orange berries follow later. Scadoxus will not survive frost so for most of us this will be a flower to grow (or at least start off) in a greenhouse or conservatory where the temperature is 13–16°C (55–61°F). Use a loam-based compost and plant the bulb in spring so that its neck is level with the surface of the compost. You will need a pot at least 25cm (10in) across. When the first growth comes through, water freely and feed once a month. After flowering (the bloom will last for at least five weeks), allow the bulb to dry off for a winter rest. Do not be in a hurry to repot it. The roots are very brittle and scadoxus flowers best when it is slightly pot bound.

SEASON: Mid August
HARDINESS: Tender
HEIGHT: 14cm (5½in)
HABITAT: South Africa (Eastern Cape, KwaZulu-Natal)
where it grows in the shade of trees and shrubs

Schizostylis (Iridaceae)

KAFFIR LILY

Though these are South African plants, natives of stream banks and damp meadows, they settle in more temperate gardens with little fuss. The species *S. coccinea* produces brilliant red, bowl-shaped flowers, but selected varieties may be pale pink or, like 'Jennifer' and 'Sunrise', push towards salmon. Schizostylis is happiest in a damp, peaty, sandy loam in full sun. It hates to dry out and will happily grow at the margin of a pond, with its feet actually in the water. The sword-shaped leaves are practically evergreen. They make good cut flowers, especially if you grow them in a greenhouse border where the extra protection will extend the flowering period through November.

ABOVE The brilliant red flowers of the Kaffir lily, *Schizostylis coccinea* 'Major', make a striking foreground to autumn asters.

Schizostylis coccinea 'Jennifer' ♀

A robust variety with mid-pink flowers, verging towards salmon. Plant the rhizomes 5–8cm (2–3½in) deep and 10cm (4in) apart.

SEASON: September–November
HARDINESS: Frost hardy
HEIGHT: 45cm (18in)

Schizostylis coccinea 'Major' ♀

Bigger and better in every way than the straight species, 'Major' has brilliant red flowers. It will do well in good, rich soil in full sun and requires plenty of water during summer. Combine it with the variegated, ground-hugging *Cotoneaster atropurpureus* 'Variegatus' or the delicate hanging flowers of *Fuchsia magellanica* var. *gracilis* 'Tricolor'. Plant the rhizomes no more than 5cm (2in) deep and 10cm (4in) apart.

SEASON: September–November
HARDINESS: Frost hardy
HEIGHT: 45cm (18in)

Schizostylis coccinea 'Sunrise' ♀

Big, salmon-pink flowers, each 5–6cm (2–2¼in) across, are typical of this variety. Try 'Sunrise' under a salmon-tinted fuchsia such as 'Salmon Cascade' or with hare's tail grass (*Lagurus ovatus*) and purple-flowered liriope. Plant the rhizomes 5–8cm (2–3½in) deep and 10cm (4in) apart.

SEASON: September–November
HARDINESS: Frost hardy
HEIGHT: 45cm (18in)

Scilla (Hyacinthaceae)

SQUILL

Squills provide much of spring's blue, though there is a welcome nonconformist, *S. autumnalis*, that flowers from late August until October. They are mostly small, biddable things, though again there is an exception: *S. peruviana* is a sumo wrestler compared with the rest of the tribe. You have to have lots of squills and they look best where they are comfortable enough to seed themselves about, either in thinnish grass or under trees and shrubs that in spring may still be leafless. 'They have a genteel appearance when in blow', wrote the Rev. William Hanbury in 1770, 'without the rambling look of many of the sorts of perennial flowers.'

Scilla autumnalis
(*Prospero autumnalis*)

The flowers come before the narrow leaves and are rather a wispy colour, the lilac side of blue; if this scilla was competing alongside its cousins in spring, we would probably think it not worth having. But there is a touching quality about bulbs that choose to flower in autumn, when the gardener's horizon is closing in. Because there is less about to claim our attention we lavish love on the few things that choose this season for their performance. Use *S. autumnalis* among autumn-flowering *Cyclamen hederifolium* or colchicums. Plant the bulbs 8cm (3½in) deep and 8cm (3½in) apart.

SEASON: August–October
HARDINESS: Fully hardy
HEIGHT: 10cm (4in)
HABITAT: Southern Britain, southern Europe east to the Caucasus in sandy, rocky places near the sea

Scilla bifolia ♔

This species is called *bifolia* because it is supposed to have just two leaves arching up and away from the shorter flower stem set between them. The ones I have grown as often as not had three leaves rather than two, but to a gardener this scarcely matters. The rich violet-blue flowers are this scilla's *raison d'être*: up to 20 in a spike, developing slowly from the bottom up and each holding a circlet of mauve stamens in the centre. Individually, though, the flowers are nowhere near as big as those of, say, *Chionodoxa luciliae*, nor is it as vigorous as *S. siberica*. As John Gerard noted, the seedpods are surprisingly big and darkly lustrous, 'so ponderous or heavie, that they lie trailing upon the ground'. Try it with the luminous foliage of *Valeriana phu* 'Aurea' or use it to underplant shrubs such as philadelphus or lilac where it can multiply undisturbed. *Scilla bifolia* will survive and seed about in grass, provided it is not too beefy. Plant 8cm (3½in) deep and 8cm (3½in) apart.

SEASON: Early March
HARDINESS: Fully hardy
HEIGHT: 9cm (3¾in)
HABITAT: Central and southern Europe and Turkey where it grows in mountain meadows not far from the snow line

OPPOSITE A river of blue *Scilla siberica* flows in an elegant swirl through spring woodland.

Scilla litardierei ♀

It is a surprise this scilla, a really lovely species, introduced to gardens in 1827, with broad-based heads of flowers in a mid-blue that just verges on purple. In bud, S. *litardierei* looks like a grape hyacinth with the same mossy greenness to the tight, knobbly, unopened flowers. But in bloom, it is more feathery; the flowers are open, not constricted, showing a fluff of dark-tipped stamens. The foliage is narrow, dark green and, as it emerges only just before the flowers, is still in good shape at flowering time. The colour stays in the flowers after they have withered – a strong, clear blue. It is very worthy of a place in the garden. Give S. *litardierei* full sun and plant the bulbs 8cm (3½in) deep and 8cm (3½in) apart.

SEASON: Late April

HARDINESS: Fully hardy

HEIGHT: 26cm (10½in)

HABITAT: Croatia and Montenegro where it grows in meadows and among limestone rocks

Scilla mischtschenkoana
(S. 'Tubergeniana') ♀

The flower spikes try to bloom before they are properly through the ground, but the stem goes on growing and then the leaves arrive, both of which make the flower look less anxious. *Scilla mischtschenkoana* has large flowers, compared with other scillas, pale iceberg-blue with a line of darker blue running down the middle of the backs of the petals, pale stamens in the centre. It is very elegant, not showy but enchanting. The stem, which is green at the base, darkens at the top, making a good contrast with the pale flowers. This scilla is a fairly recent arrival in western Europe, introduced to gardeners in 1931 by the Dutch firm of Van Tubergen after six bulbs turned up unexpectedly in a consignment of *Puschkinia scilloides* sent by the German consul and plant hunter Georg Egger from Tabriz in north-west Iran. It will be happy in dappled shade. Plant 8cm (3½in) deep and 8cm (3½in) apart.

SEASON: Early February

HARDINESS: Fully hardy

HEIGHT: 12cm (5in)

HABITAT: Georgia, Armenia, Azerbaijan and Iran where itgrows in mountain meadows close to the snow line

Scilla peruviana

In the wild S. *peruviana* has been found in several different colours: dark purple, brownish purple (in northern Africa) and white, but the form usually offered to gardeners is a darkish blue. In the early stages, the centre of the flower is just a small, greenish hump. Gradually the head spreads to make a broad pyramid about 12cm (5in) across with the flowers at the bottom edge coming out first. These first ones, at the lower end, are dead before the final ones at the top emerge. The buds are dark purplish blue, but when they open the flowers are slightly paler, 40 at least in the head. Each is carried on a longish (7cm/2½in) stalk and is dark at the centre, where the stamens make six cream dots. The leaves are quite broad and fleshy, practically evergreen when (and where) winters are not too cold. The flowerhead is held above this strap-shaped, shiny green foliage, rather like bluebell foliage but coarser and thicker. This species was one of the first scillas to be widely cultivated by gardeners in sixteenth-century Europe, and the mistake about its name was stitched in right from the beginning when the keen plantsman Everard Munichoven sent a picture of the plant to Carolus Clusius, then collecting plants for a new botanic garden at Leiden, with a note that it came from Peru. Soon after, plantsmen realized that in fact it was a European native and grew profusely in Spain, but by then it was too late. The wrong name stuck. Choose a warm, sunny place for S. *peruviana* where the bulbs can ripen in summer. They need to be divided regularly. Without this attention, they stop flowering. Plant no more than 5cm (2in) deep and 15cm (6in) apart.

SEASON: Mid May

HARDINESS: Frost hardy

HEIGHT: 40cm (16in)

HABITAT: Not from Peru at all, but found in the western Mediterranean (Portugal, Spain, Italy, northern Africa) where it often grows in marshy ground that dries out in summer

Scilla siberica ♀
SIBERIAN SQUILL

Glossy green leaves and flowers come through the ground together, the flowers bright blue with four or five on each stem. *Scilla siberica* is a generous plant, often producing more than one stem of flowers from each bulb. Give it moist but well-drained soil. It does best in light shade, but will put up with sun, provided the soil does not dry out completely. Give it a treat each year by top-dressing with leaf mould. Use S. *siberica* to carpet the ground under spring-flowering magnolias and viburnums. It is perhaps the best species for naturalizing and if you are lucky may even settle in grass, provided it is not too lush. Set the bulbs 8cm (3½in) deep and 8cm (3½in) apart.

SEASON: March–April
HARDINESS: Fully hardy
HEIGHT: 15cm (6in)
HABITAT: Ukraine, Russia, Georgia, Azerbaijan and northern Iran where it grows in mountain meadows not far from the snow line

Scilla siberica 'Spring Beauty'

The bright, slightly glossy green leaves are longer than the flowers, but these are such a good bright blue they are in no danger of being overwhelmed. The flowers of 'Spring Beauty' are darker on the outside than the inner and darker overall than those of S. *siberica*. The stem too is dark, where the flowers are borne, though it drifts to green at the base. Spread 'Spring Beauty' under the variegated coronilla C. *valentina* subsp. *glauca* 'Variegata' or among epimediums such as E. × *youngianum* 'Niveum'. Set the bulbs 8cm (3½in) deep and 8cm (3½in) apart.

SEASON: Late March
HARDINESS: Fully hardy
HEIGHT: 10cm (4in)

Sparaxis (Iridaceae)

HARLEQUIN FLOWER

Sparaxis grandiflora ♛

From a fan of leaves rise wiry stems of funnel-shaped flowers (5–6cm/2–2¼in across) which may be cream, yellow, orange or various shades of purple with contrasting blotches in the centre. Its South African clock tells it to start growing in late autumn, which is fatal where winter means frost. In cool climates, therefore, S. *grandiflora* is best grown in pots in a greenhouse or conservatory, using a loam-based compost mixed with coarse sand or leaf mould. Do not overwater and keep the plants cool. Dry off the corms as the flowers fade and keep them completely dry during their resting time. Outdoors, treat S. *grandiflora* as an annual (it is not expensive), choosing a sunny site under the shelter of a wall. It makes an excellent cut flower. Plant in spring 10cm (4in) deep and 10cm (4in) apart.

SEASON: April–May (indoors); August–October (outdoors)
HARDINESS: Half hardy
HEIGHT: 20cm (8in)
HABITAT: South Africa (Western Cape) where it grows on clay soils in damp rocky places

Sprekelia (Amaryllidaceae)

Sprekelia formosissima
JACOBEAN LILY

The leaves are still short when the flower spike spears through alongside them – a deep pink stem, with the flower folded on top of it like a complicated grasshopper. When it opens, it is the same height as the leaves and produces a single, wonderful bloom of dull red. The top three petals bend back on themselves at three, nine and twelve o'clock, the two horizontal petals curving back round like a ram's horns. The lower three petals act quite independently, dropping and sweeping away to five, six and seven o'clock, but not reflexing in such a noticeable way. Long, elegant stamens are tipped with golden anthers. Sprekelias, named after the eighteenth-century German botanist J H von Sprekelsen, are eye-catchers, to be used inside, like hippeastrums, but unfortunately the flowers do not last much more than a week. But such poise, such drama. Nothing I ever did inside the house was as good as a windowsill one May, where five sprekelias, each one growing in an old clay pot, were lined up like guardsmen. Start S. *formosissima* off in a greenhouse or conservatory where the temperature does not drop below 7–10°C (45–50°F). Use a pot at least 13cm (5in) across and a loam-based compost (John Innes No 3), and set the bulb so that its neck and shoulders are just above the surface of the compost. Water moderately and feed once every two weeks. From a planting in late February, you can expect blooms in late May. Keep the foliage growing after the flower has finished, as you would with a hippeastrum, and allow it to die down in autumn. During winter, the bulb needs to be kept quite dry, or it rots. Do not be in a hurry to repot sprekelias. The roots hate to be disturbed.

SEASON: Late May
HARDINESS: Tender
HEIGHT: 17cm (7in)
HABITAT: Guatemala and Mexico where it grows on rocky slopes

Sternbergia (Amaryllidaceae)

Sternbergia lutea

The best sternbergias I have ever seen were growing on a rubbish dump in Elba, the crocus-like flowers (4cm/1½in across) pushing in brilliant gold through rusty tin cans and shards of bathroom tiles; like so many autumn-flowering bulbs, they come as a surprise. Away from their Mediterranean home they are happier on light, chalky soils than they are on heavier, cooler ones. Though they take time to settle, they will, if happy, build up into large colonies. Sternbergias, named after the eighteenth-century plantsman Count Kaspar van Sternberg of Prague, like to be baked during their summer dormancy, so plant them in good, fast-draining soil, in full sun, setting the bulbs 10–15cm (4–6in) deep and 10cm (4in) apart.

SEASON: September–October
HARDINESS: Frost hardy
HEIGHT: 15cm (6in)
HABITAT: Southern Europe, Turkey and central Asia
where it grows on rocky hillsides or in sparse scrub

Tecophilaea (Tecophilaeaceae)

Tecophilaea cyanocrocus ♀

The blue seems scarcely possible, searingly clear and bright, in the manner of some gentians. The flowers are made rather like crocuses, but of course no crocus can produce a bloom of this colour. Tecophilaea was introduced in 1836 and is unusual in being named after a woman, Tecophila Billotti, the flower-painting daughter of a professor of botany in Turin, Italy. The variety 'Leichtlinii' has paler blue flowers with white centres. *Tecophilaea cyanocrocus* is not fully hardy (and is too expensive to lose), so it is probably best to grow it in a greenhouse or cold frame where it has a little protection against frost and can get the dry summer dormancy it craves. Plant 5cm (2in) deep in a pot of loam-based compost mixed with an equal amount of sharp sand. After flowering, gradually water less until the leaves die down and the corms settle into their summer dormancy. Outside, plant in well-drained, sandy soil in full sun and mulch with llama manure for luck… Set the corms 5–8cm (2–3½in) deep and 8cm (3½in) apart.

SEASON: March–April

HARDINESS: Frost hardy

HEIGHT: 10cm (4in)

HABITAT: Chile (the slopes of the Andes above Valparaíso at around 3,000m/10,000ft), but probably now almost extinct in the wild

Tigridia (Iridaceae)

Tigridia pavonia
PEACOCK FLOWER

Prized by the Aztecs, not for their flowers but for the mealy bulbs which provided an important source of food. The flowers are short-lived, but there are so many of them you do not notice their going. The colours are vivid and various – white, pink, red, orange, yellow – with the petals arranged as two flat, superimposed triangles, the inner one much smaller than the outer, which can be 10cm (4in) across. The centres are strangely mottled, and ringed with a contrasting colour. John Gerard published a goodish picture of tigridia – The floure of Tigris – in his *Herball* (1597) but had never seen it himself and did not believe it existed. 'Meere fictions', he wrote dismissively. But more than 200 years later it appeared in an early edition of Curtis's famous *Botanical Magazine* (1801) praised for its 'splendid beauty', which surpassed 'every competitor'. *Tigridia pavonia* is tender and needs a winter temperature that does not dip much below 8°C (46°F). Grow it in a pot of loam-based compost mixed with sharp sand. Give plenty of water while it is growing, but allow it to dry off after flowering. Outside, it is a natural companion for *Anthemis tinctoria* 'Sauce Hollandaise' or for succulents such as aeoniums and echeveria that have been bedded out for summer. Do not plant before the end of April and give the bulbs light, gritty, well-drained soil in full sun. Protect them during winter with dry bracken fronds or something similar. You can also lift and store them inside to use the following season. Plant 10cm (4in) deep and 10cm (4in) apart.

SEASON: August

HARDINESS: Tender

HEIGHT: 50cm (20in)

HABITAT: Central (Mexico on the Sierra Madre) and South America where it grows in oakwoods and on verges at 2,000–3,000m (6,500–10,000ft)

Trillium (Trilliaceae)

WAKE ROBIN

ABOVE The dark spotted leaves of the wake robin (*Trillium sessile*) are combined with *Narcissus* 'Thalia' in a planting by Carol Klein at Glebe Cottage in Devon.

The name suggests what to expect: a thing of threes, three elegant leaves held out flat at the top of a fleshy stem, three sepals, three petals, and multiples of three of everything that is held inside them. Sometimes, as with *T. erectum,* the flowers are held on stalks; sometimes, as with yellow, scented *T. luteum,* they are not. Advanced gardeners call the first bunch pedicellate, the second sessile. Trilliums are distinctive rather than showy (*T. grandiflorum* is the exception) and in a garden need a very particular kind of background – wildish, woody, dappled. This is a superb group of plants, but they do not like bossy, competitive neighbours; they associate well with other woodlanders such as azaleas, hepaticas, *Anemone nemorosa* 'Robinsoniana' or epimediums. Be patient. Trilliums need a season or two to establish themselves, and in their first year, while they are building up a good root system, may not make any growth above ground at all. As with iris, new roots grow every year along the fresh piece of rhizome close to the terminal bud. If you can resist poking and prodding them to see what is going on, in time they should make good clumps, long-lived and trouble-free. Give them light shade and damp, woodlandy, humus-rich soil. They like rich ground, and some are perhaps happiest on soil that is on the acid side of neutral. They generally emerge some time in March, flower during April and May, and then die down from July onwards. The longer you can keep them growing, the fatter the rhizome underground will be and the better the chances of a good flower display the following year. Mulch trilliums with leaf mould or very well-rotted manure so that they do not dry out, and try to keep them in leaf until the end of summer. The easiest way to acquire them is to buy plants already growing in pots. If you buy rhizomes in autumn, make sure they are sent damp-packed. They hate to dry out.

OPPOSITE The arresting flowers of the American species, *Trillium erectum*, shine out alongside Lowes Path in New Hampshire, USA.

Trillium catesbyi

This American species, named after the American naturalist and explorer Mark Catesby, has nodding, reflexed flowers with white, often flushed pink petals and long, curved, green sepals over plain, deeply veined leaves. The stems are stained a reddish pink. Combine it with the dark feathery foliage of *Corydalis flexuosa* 'Purple Leaf' or spreads of lily-of-the-valley. *Trillium catesbyi* prefers a humus-rich, acid soil that is well drained but never dries out. The rhizomes are best bought damp-packed in autumn and planted 10cm (4in) deep and 30cm (12in) apart.

SEASON: May
HARDINESS: Fully hardy
HEIGHT: 50cm (20in)
HABITAT: South-eastern USA (North Carolina to Georgia and west to Alabama and Tennessee) where it grows in acid soil on hillsides and in open thickets of mountain laurel in sun or shade

Trillium erectum ♀

An easy, vigorous, upright trillium introduced to gardeners in 1759 and called wet dog in some parts of America, because of its characteristic smell. The most common form of *T. erectum* has polished mahogany-red petals clasped by purplish green sepals, but f. *albiflorum* has flowers of white or pink with deep purple centres. In both cases, the leaves are plain mid-green. By August, its fruit develops into a big, round, dark berry surrounded by the three sepals. The rhizomes are best bought damp-packed in autumn and planted 10cm (4in) deep and 30cm (12in) apart.

SEASON: Late April
HARDINESS: Fully hardy
HEIGHT: 30cm (12in)
HABITAT: Canada (Quebec to Ontario) and eastern USA (Michigan to Pennsylvania, Kentucky, Georgia) where it grows in acid soil in deciduous forest and under rhododendron and mountain laurel

Trillium grandiflorum ♀

This is one of the easiest trilliums to grow but is also one of the best, generous with its flowers which it holds showily above its dark green leaves. The white petals (up to 9cm/3¾in long) make broad, slightly reflexed triangles, furrowed with veins, drifting into a dull purplish pink as they age; under them, and poking out between the petals, are three narrow, green sepals. Standing in the centre are the soft gold stamens. 'The most beautiful hardy woodlander that I know,' wrote Col. Grey, who knew a lot. Like all trilliums, this is slow (much slower than you would wish) but capable in time of giving a superb display. The double form, 'Flore Pleno' is even slower. How much time have you got? Try *T. grandiflorum* with *Dicentra spectabilis* 'Alba', smilacina or martagon lilies, which are very happy in dappled shade. It is not fussy about soil, flourishing on alkaline ground as well as acid. The rhizomes are best bought damp-packed in autumn and planted 10cm (4in) deep and 30cm (12in) apart.

SEASON: April–May

HARDINESS: Fully hardy

HEIGHT: 40cm (16in)

HABITAT: Canada (Quebec) and eastern USA (Michigan, Wisconsin as far south as Arkansas and Georgia) where it grows on well-drained soils in woods of beech and sugar maple

Trillium kurabayashii

A very handsome and robust trillium, named after the Japanese botanist Masataka Kurabayashi, who first noted the species growing on the west coast of the United States. The three softly triangular leaves are at least 12cm (5in) across; they are lightly mottled and carried at the top of a thick stem flushed at the bottom with purple. A deep purple flower (a hellebore colour) rises stemless from each ruff of leaves, three narrow upright petals enclosing the equally upright, floury stamens. For a deeply mysterious partnership, plant *T. kurabayashii* with *Fritillaria persica* 'Adiyaman'. Alternatively, leaven the trillium's dark colours with a smattering of pale erythroniums such as *E. californicum* 'White Beauty' or *E. revolutum* 'Plas Merdyn'. The rhizomes are best bought damp-packed in autumn and planted 10cm (4in) deep and 30cm (12in) apart.

SEASON: Early April

HARDINESS: Fully hardy

HEIGHT: 22cm (9in)

HABITAT: West coast USA (north-western California, Sierra Nevada, south-west Oregon) where it grows in conifer forests and in alder thickets along streams

Trillium luteum ♔

Collected in 1886 by a Mr Harbison in the Cherokee country of North Carolina, this is a reasonably easy trillium to establish; your reward will be elegant, lemon-scented, greenish yellow flowers. The petals of *T. luteum* are narrow compared, say, to those of *T. grandiflorum*, but the colour and the smell compensate for the lack of substance. The leaves are wide and ornamental, blotched all over with a pale silvery green. Rhizomes are best bought damp-packed in autumn and planted 10cm (4in) deep and 30cm (12in) apart.

SEASON: April
HARDINESS: Fully hardy
HEIGHT: 40cm (16in)
HABITAT: South-eastern USA (North Carolina, northern Georgia, eastern Tennessee, southern Kentucky) where it grows on chalky soils in deciduous forests

Trillium recurvatum

Mottled leaves underpin long-lasting flowers with narrow, reddish purple petals and downward-curving, green sepals. This is one of the latest of the trilliums to open, found in the wild with camassias and *Mertensia virginica*. In gardens *T. recurvatum* is a good companion for *Arum italicum* 'Marmoratum' or dark-stemmed *Polygonatum* × *hybridum* 'Betberg'. The brittle rhizomes are best bought damp-packed in autumn and planted 10cm (4in) deep and 30cm (12in) apart.

SEASON: April–May
HARDINESS: Fully hardy
HEIGHT: 30cm (12in)
HABITAT: Central USA (south-west Michigan to Iowa and Missouri, south to eastern Texas, northern Louisiana, northern Mississippi and northern Alabama) where it grows in woods and on the rich, clay soils of flood plains

Trillium sulcatum

In many ways this is similar to *T. erectum* but *aficionados* will point out that *T. sulcatum* is taller and has much larger leaves than *T. erectum*. And *T. sulcatum* smells of mushrooms, rather than wet dog. Both though have broadish petals, the maroon colour perhaps darker in this species than in *T. erectum*. The edges of the pale maroon sepals curl in on themselves in a distinctive way. In the wild it grows with dicentra and Jack-in-the-pulpit (*Arisaema triphyllum*). In the garden, try it with bloodroot (*Sanguinaria canadensis* 'Plena') – another natural companion – or with the toad lily (*Tricyrtis formosana*). The rhizomes are best bought damp-packed in autumn and planted 10cm (4in) deep and 30cm (12in) apart.

SEASON: April
HARDINESS: Fully hardy
HEIGHT: 40cm (16in)
HABITAT: USA (north-eastern Alabama, Tennessee, eastern Kentucky, north-western North Carolina, south-western Virginia) where it grows on neutral or slightly acid soil on wooded slopes and alongside streams

T

Triteleia (Alliaceae)

Think agapanthus, shrunk in the wash, and you will have some idea what triteleia (formerly brodiaea) look like. They are long-lasting and come at a good time to fill the gaps left by spring-flowering bulbs. They also make good cut flowers.

ABOVE The charming creamy flowers of *Triteleia ixioides* 'Starlight' hover above ferns and aquilegias in the National Trust's garden at Hidcote, Gloucestershire.

Triteleia 'Corrina'

All the buds shoot out from the same point at the top of the strong, wiry stems. There may be 18–20 flowers in each head, funnel-shaped, each opening into a star of gorgeous blue. A dark stripe (very narrow) runs down the back of each petal, neat and correct. The wispy stamens are a slightly paler blue. The lax, flaccid, bluebell-like foliage is already dying off as the triteleia comes into flower. Give 'Corrina' a foreground of pinks such as *Dianthus* 'Hidcote' or *D.* 'Fair Folly' in well-drained soil in sun or light shade. Plant 8cm (3½in) deep and 8–10cm (3½–4in) apart.

SEASON: Early June
HARDINESS: Frost hardy
HEIGHT: 45cm (18in)

Triteleia ixioides 'Starlight'

This bears wide-spaced heads of creamy flowers similar in form to its blue relative, *T. laxa*. There may be more than 20 flowers in each head waiting to emerge in turn. It is gorgeous in bud when the flowers are waspishly striped with a dark chocolate line down the back of each petal. The lines then all clasp together at the top, very natty, dark brown on cream. When the flower opens, the stripe does not show so much on the upper side; all is richly clotted Cornish cream. The foliage is thin and strappy, not at its best by flowering time, but 'Starlight' pays rent in the garden as it is in flower for such a long time. The colour is distinctly odd, but try it with the bronze foliage of the hardy hippeastrum 'Toughie' or among small-leaved hostas such as 'Blue Blush' and 'Devon Green'. Plant in well-drained soil in full sun, setting the corms 8cm (3½in) deep and 8–10cm (3½–4in) apart.

SEASON: Early May
HARDINESS: Frost hardy
HEIGHT: 15cm (6in)

Triteleia laxa 'Koningin Fabiola'

Loose clusters of rich purplish blue flowers spring from the top of strong stems and, flowering in mid-summer, bring a pleasing waft of blue into the garden, before the agapanthus arrive. Try 'Koningin Fabiola' with cerinthe and the hosta 'Lemon Lime'. Being a native of California, it likes a warm, sunny spot, where you can plant the corms about 8cm (3½in) deep and 8–10cm (3½–4in) apart.

SEASON: June
HARDINESS: Frost hardy
HEIGHT: 45cm (18in)

Triteleia 'Rudy'

The flowers are striped in white and purplish blue, a surprising effect. The blue is in the centre of each petal, darkest in the central rib down each petal; the white fades out either side to the edges. The flowers are very pretty, opening up like the flared mouth of a tuba. 'Rudy' makes a good cut flower, if you can bear to cut any. Give it a sunny site and well-drained soil. Plant the corms 8cm (3½in) deep and 8–10cm (3½–4in) apart.

SEASON: June
HARDINESS: Frost hardy
HEIGHT: 45cm (18in)

Tulbaghia (Alliaceae)

Tulbaghia violacea 'Silver Lace'

Tulbaghias are South African plants, named after the Dutchman Ryk Tulbagh, an eighteenth-century governor of the Cape of Good Hope. This variegated version is an enchanting plant, with flowering stem and leaves of the same soft grey-green as the species, but the leaves are margined with cream, narrowly strap-shaped and only about 18cm (7in) long. Even on its own, the foliage would be an asset. From mid-summer onwards, the tall, strong flowering stems produce heads of violet flowers, 15 or more, all emerging from the same point, like an allium. The flowers come out in turn, so the effect of a single head is long-lasting. 'Silver Lace' is lovely in a pot, which is the safest way to grow it, as it is not reliably hardy. Use a loam-based compost and give the plant plenty of water while it is growing. Reduce watering after the plant has finished flowering and keep it almost dry during its winter dormancy. Outdoors grow in well-drained soil in full sun and mulch to protect against winter frost. Plant the rhizomes in spring 5cm (2in) deep and 20cm (8in) apart.

SEASON: Late June–September
HARDINESS: Frost hardy
HEIGHT: 45cm (18in)

Tulipa (Liliaceae)

Tulips are Old World rather than New World flowers. Their heartland is in central Asia, close to the great mountain ranges of the Tien Shan and the Pamir Alai. In this remote, wild area, far from the cities of men, you will find more wild tulips than anywhere else on earth. Though the flower has now been introduced very successfully into parts of the world where Nature never intended it to grow, central Asia is still the cradle of this enormous genus. It is the queen of all bulbs, producing the sexiest, the most capricious, the most various, subtle, powerful and intriguing flowers that any gardener will ever set eyes on.

Tulip bulbs are solid things, covered with a brown or black skin, called the tunic. We are used to seeing quite big, chunky tulip bulbs for sale in late summer. The bulbs of wild tulips are much smaller, and the colours of the tunics are more various, some almost red, others gorgeous rich chestnut. Some wild tulips produce bulbs with a hairy coat just under the tunic, with tufts of hair sticking out at the top.

Tulips can reproduce themselves in two ways. The mother bulbs produce offsets – baby bulbs that grow alongside the parent bulb and take a few years to grow on to flowering size. The flower also sets seed in a distinctive, three-sided seedpod, but, if you want to grow a tulip from seed, you will have to wait five to seven years for a flowering-size bulb. Offsets always show the same characteristics as the parent. Tulips raised from seed may not. So, by crossing certain wild tulips and sowing their seed, breeders could produce new tulips quite easily. But you need to be patient.

Some tulips have only two leaves, but usually there are more, and they vary widely in width, length and colour: some are bright, shining green, some almost grey, some striped and speckled in patterns like snakeskin, or trimmed with neat edges of cream or silvery white. Some tulips, especially the small, wild ones have leaves with waved and crinkled edges which lie on the ground like drunken starfish.

But the point of a tulip, of course, is its flower, more gorgeous, more capable of variation, than any other flower on earth. They display themselves on sturdy, upright stems, most often just one flower on each, though some wild tulips such as T. turkestanica and T. biflora carry several flowers at once. So do garden tulips such as 'Georgette'. The shape of the flower and its petals varies widely. Some make rounded bowl shapes, others splay open into stars. Some have long, narrow petals, others have broad, generous ones. Lily-flowered tulips such as 'Sapporo' flip out from the waist and, in terms of form, are wildly elegant.

From the first, gardeners appreciated the tulip's extraordinary ability to break from a plain colour into a brilliant *mélange* of flamed and feathered colours, rose on white, dark brown on mustard-yellow, purple on red, each pattern, each petal, as complex as a fingerprint. These selections, rather than the wild originals, were the tulips that were most prized in early oriental gardens. Certain colour combinations – rose and white, brown and yellow – were always highly desirable, and still are, though they are not as easy to find as the combinations of red and yellow which characterize so many of today's tulips. Old paintings show how taste in tulips changed in the centuries after they were first introduced to Europe: Eastern-style flowers with crisp outlines, pointed tops and sharply defined waists gave way to tulips that had larger, more rounded flowers in a wider range of colours. The subtlety of the markings became increasingly important.

Wild tulips generally have six petals, though some garden tulips such as 'Blue Diamond' are blowsy double flowers, full of petals. Though they do not always stand up to bad weather, they are very showy. It is always worth peering into the centre of a tulip, because so much of its beauty lies in the contrast between the colour of the petals and the colour of the base. Sometimes this basal blotch is no more than a smudge. Sometimes it makes a distinct star or a perfect circle, rimmed perhaps with another contrasting colour. The colour of the pollen varies too: olive-coloured, orange, deep purple. Each centre is a miracle of complexity.

The number of tulips available to gardeners exploded in the nineteenth century when growers in Europe first got hold of the spectacular wild tulips

ABOVE Wild tulips grow in their natural habitat, the
Tien Shan mountains of Kazakhstan.

of central Asia. Dutch bulb firms such as Van Tubergen quickly recognized that these new beauties had great commercial potential and began to send their own collectors out onto the rocky hillsides of the Tien Shan. With great skill and expertise, Dutch growers in the Haarlem bulb fields learned how to bulk up these exotic newcomers and then how to use them to breed new varieties. The dazzling panache of the tulip tribe, its variety, its range and its beauty, makes it indispensable to gardeners and it will provide spectacular colour for three months, from late February to late May. The only difficulty is choosing between varieties.

By the end of the nineteenth century, when Dutch growers increasingly dominated the market, the names of garden tulips were in a great muddle. Identical tulips were being grown under half a dozen different names. Gradually order was retrieved from chaos and a preliminary list of tulip cultivars was published in 1917. New lists have been published regularly since then, the most recent of which lists more than 5,600 tulips. New varieties are constantly being introduced as breeders try to improve the colour, size, form and stamina of the flowers. Length and strength of stem are also important in garden varieties; so is immunity to disease. But many of the most beautiful of the 'broken' tulips are no longer available. Since it was discovered that colour-breaking was caused by a virus, tulips such as the fabulous Rembrandts have been withdrawn by Dutch growers, who do not want the virus to spread to and infect their single-coloured stock. This is a great and important loss to gardeners.

Bulb catalogues generally list tulips in 15 different groups, divided according to flowering time or the form of the flowers. You will find some of the earliest March-flowering tulips among the Kaufmanniana and Greigii tulips – spectacular, low-growing tulips bred from central Asian species. April can be filled with Fosteriana tulips such as 'Flaming Purissima', Single Earlies like old 'Generaal de Wet' gorgeously veined and netted, red on orange, and outrageous Double Earlies such as 'Alice Leclerq'. As April drifts into May a torrent of tulips comes into flower: Triumph tulips, the green-streaked Viridifloras and the Darwin Hybrids. In May you can choose Single Late types or outrageous Parrots, as beautiful still as anything you will see in an Old Master painting. In May, fat Double Late tulips such as fabulous 'Black Hero' will also be in their prime, with delicate Fringed tulips and elegant Lily-flowered varieties such as 'Maytime' to set beside them. Among the miniature wild tulips you can find flowers that span the whole spring season from *T. biflora*, which is often open by the middle of February, to *T. sprengeri*, which is the last of all tulips to flower, often continuing its blaze into the beginning of June.

DIVISION 1 (SINGLE EARLY) This is a relatively small group of tulips, which flower in late March and early April on short, sturdy stems, rarely reaching 40cm (16in), more commonly half that height. Most are on the red-orange-yellow side of the spectrum, but 'Purple Prince' is a notable exception.

DIVISION 2 (DOUBLE EARLY) These generally flower in early or mid April.

OPPOSITE 'Better dead' said Daniel Hall of Double
Late tulips such as 'Blue Diamond.' But doubles last a
long time in flower and are superb used in pots.

They are often taller (30–40cm/12–16in) than the Single Earlies, with flowers wider than they are high, packed with petals. Many come from the mid-nineteenth-century tulip 'Murillo' which gives the group an unusual homogeneity in terms of height and flowering time. 'The doubling of a flower is always a doubtful blessing', said the Edwardian tulip supremo Sir Daniel Hall, 'but to double a tulip is to destroy the finest and most distinctive qualities that it should possess. It may be argued that double tulips are more lasting, but it is no gain that a nightmare should endure for two nights instead of one.' Long life makes them a favourite for forcing in pots indoors. Outdoors, in bad weather, they may suffer more than singles.

DIVISION 3 (TRIUMPH) The name was invented in 1923 by Dutch breeder N Zandbergen of Rijnsburg, and Dutch growers used it to describe the tulips they raised by crossing Single Earlies with Darwin tulips. In flowering time (late April till early May) they usefully span the gap between their two parents. They include a very wide range of colours from ivory-white 'Shirley' to the deep claret of 'Jan Reus'. Height is generally 45–50cm (18–20in).

ABOVE The magnificently whiskered Sir Daniel Hall (1864–1942) was director of the John Innes Horticultural Institute as well as the author of two fine books about tulips.

DIVISION 4 (DARWIN HYBRID) Introduced in 1943 by D W Lefeber of Lisse, who crossed Darwin tulips with species such as the brilliant *T. fosteriana* to produce a race of tulips that cover the yellow-orange-red spectrum. The single flowers are among the tallest of garden tulips (60–70cm/24–28in), flowering in May. The group is an important commercial crop in The Netherlands where the old tulip 'Apeldoorn' and its many sports are still widely grown.

DIVISION 5 (SINGLE LATE) The forerunners of the Single Late tulips were originally gathered from gardens where they had hung on for generations, delighting gardeners with their extraordinary range of colours and fine, strong flowers. Now the Single Late tulips are made up of an amalgamation between these old Cottage types and the newer Darwins; years of cross-breeding gradually blurred the distinctions between the two groups. Of all garden tulips, these are perhaps the best at settling in a garden and returning year after year. This attribute alone makes them worth growing. Some such as orange 'Dillenburg' are scented. Scent, in tulips, is most often associated with yellow and orange varieties. This group will perhaps appeal particularly to those who love the tulips of Dutch flower paintings, for the Cottage tulips still have the blood of old tulips running in their veins. This stretches in an unbroken line back to the garden tulips first cultivated in Eastern gardens. Of all types, they are also the most prone to 'break' in the garden, producing flowers mottled and striped and flamed in contrasting shades. They have kept their vigour too, growing to 60–75cm (24–30in) and flowering in May.

DIVISION 6 (LILY-FLOWERED) This beautiful group of tulips was introduced by Rengert Cornelis Segers who started his breeding work in 1919, using an old Darwin called 'Bartigon' as one of the parents. By the 1950s, lily-flowered tulips, especially elegant 'China Pink' and 'White Triumphator', had become established favourites with gardeners. The group is still deservedly popular, as no other kind of tulip has such perfect form, producing long, waisted flowers with petals pointed and sharply reflexed. In style they are similar to the Ottoman tulips so favoured by the sultan's court in Constantinople (now Istanbul). They are the ones you see on glazed tiles in the mosques of that beautiful city. They grow to 45–60cm (18–24in) and flower in May.

DIVISION 7 (FRINGED) This is a relatively modern grouping, first proposed in 1981. The earliest fringed flowers such as 'Sundew' (found in 1917 as a sport of the Darwin 'Orion') were originally placed in the same division as Parrot tulips, but the Fringed tulips are not so madly wayward. The flowers have delicately fringed petals, the fringing sometimes of the same colour as the petals, as in yellow 'Maja', sometimes of a contrasting colour as in 'Burgundy Lace' where a white fringe edges claret-coloured petals. Although the slippery genes typical of the tulip produced this modification in 1917, it was more than 40 years before breeders began to capitalize on the new characteristic, when the Knijn brothers of Spierdijk

ABOVE A bouquet of brilliant tulips from the *Hortus Eystettensis*, a record of the flowers in the Bishop of Eichstatt's garden, made in 1613 by Basilius Besler.

introduced red 'Arma', a fringed sport of 'Couleur Cardinal'. This is now a fast-expanding group, the tulips growing to 30–50cm (12–20in), flowering in May.

DIVISION 8 (VIRIDIFLORA) These are not entirely green-flowered, as the name suggests, but a group of tulips with flowers that are streaked or mottled with green. Like the Cottage tulips, this is an ancient race: the tendency of the petals to retain green markings was already noted by the artist who painted the beautiful tulips shown in the famous flower book *Hortus Eystettensis* published in 1613. 'Spring Green' is one of the most popular of this tribe, lovely with cow parsley and bluebells. Tulips in this group can be 35–60cm (14–24in) tall and flower in May.

DIVISION 9 (REMBRANDT) True Rembrandt tulips with the characteristic feathers and flames caused by a virus infection; they are no longer commercially available.

NEXT PAGE Tulips, including lily-flowered kinds such as orange 'Ballerina', 'China Pink', 'Red Shine' and yellow 'Westpoint', shine against mounds of spurge and honesty.

DIVISION 10 (PARROT) These arose as 'sports' or mutations from perfectly well-behaved tulips such as the old Single Late tulip 'Clara Butt', known since 1899. In 1910, this sported to produce the Parrot tulip 'Fantasy'. The soft rose of the original became crested and striped with green; the petals, instead of being smooth and round, became deeply slashed at the edges, curling and twisting in all directions. These puckered, laciniated petals are the distinguishing feature of the Parrots. The name comes from the appearance of the flower in bud, which looks a bit like a parrot's beak. In the Parrot group are some of the showiest and most daring of garden tulips, bred now with stems more capable of carrying their cargo than were the early cultivars of this class. The tulip's propensity to 'sport' was discovered almost as soon as it was introduced from the East; Parrots appear in many early flower paintings. They were all red and yellow types until in 1907 the famous Covent Garden bulb merchant Barr & Son introduced the purple and white Parrot 'Sensation', a sport discovered in a bed of the old purple tulip 'Reine d'Espagne'. These are perhaps the most flamboyant tulips you can have in your garden, height 40–60cm (16–24in), flowering in May. Some such as 'Orange Favourite' are scented.

DIVISION 11 (DOUBLE LATE) 'Better dead', said the tulip aficionado Sir Daniel Hall, who never disguised his prejudices. These tulips, sometimes called 'paeony-flowered', have huge heads of flower, bursting in an untidy way with petals. Like the Double Early tulips, they do not stand up well to bad weather, but look wonderful in pots in cool conservatories. Although tulip fanciers such as Hall considered them deeply unrefined, the Double Late tulips last an astonishingly long time in the garden. Some such as 'Black Hero' and 'Blue Diamond' will stand in good fettle for nearly a month. They look terrific planted together in a border. The Double Late tulips are 45–60cm (18–24in) tall and bloom from early to late May.

DIVISION 12 (KAUFMANNIANA) The Kaufmanniana tulips have been bred from the wild *T. kaufmanniana*, a native of central Asia, where it grows on the stony slopes of the Tien Shan mountains. It is called the waterlily tulip because of the way it opens flat in the sun. The petals of the Kaufmannianas tend to be long and thin, and the leaves are sometimes mottled with dark purplish brown. The flowers are early (mid March onwards) and generally short (at 15–25cm/6–10in).

DIVISION 13 (FOSTERIANA) *Tulipa fosteriana* from the mountainous region of Bukhara, crossed with other species such as *T. greigii* and *T. kaufmanniana*, produced this useful group of garden tulips. The foliage may be greyish or a clear glossy green as in the outstanding scarlet 'Cantata'. Fosterianas generally flower from early April onwards and are often taller (20–45cm/8–18in) than the Kaufmannianas.

DIVISION 14 (GREIGII) The strongly mottled and striped, ground-hugging foliage of the species *T. greigii* is one of the outstanding characteristics of this group. The leaves often have wavy edges. The inner petals of the

OPPOSITE In full flower, the Darwin Hybrid tulip 'American Dream' is a dazzling sight, brilliant orange and red.

flowers tend to remain upright while the outer ones splay out extravagantly. D W Lefeber raised some of the most outstanding early cultivars by crossing *T. greigii* with Darwins to get extra large blooms on tall stems. Like the Kaufmanniana tulips, these are low growing (20–30cm/8–12in) and generally flower in late March or early April.

DIVISION 15 (SPECIES) In this division are the rest of the wild tulips, the original building blocks from which the vast collection of garden tulips was gradually constructed. From their original mountain homes in central Asia, they were carried west along the old trade routes until, in the middle of the sixteenth century, they made the great leap into Europe, smuggled in a diplomatic bag out of Constantinople by the Flemish ambassador Ogier de Busbecq. Gradually, some tulips found that life in France and Italy was not too bad an alternative to life on the stony Tien Shan mountains of central Asia. They settled and became naturalized, often on vine terraces or in olive groves, where the ground was not disturbed too often. This is where you might find pinkish red *T. didieri* (now known as *T. passeriniana*) or scented, yellow *T. australis*. If you go to Crete, you might see the elegant, pink flowers of *T. saxatilis* Bakeri Group growing with mourning widow iris and anemones on the Omalos plain. But nothing in Europe can compare with the sight of tulips growing wild in Kazakhstan, where whole hillsides are covered in *T. greigii* in savage sunset colours. Between them, the wild species tulips provide an incredibly long season of flowering, and if you take the trouble to put them in the right place in the garden they will not only come back year after year but will also increase. Some of the most useful for garden planting are *T. linifolia* Batalinii Group and its offspring, *T. humilis* Violacea Group, and *T. orphanidea* Whittallii Group. *Tulipa sprengeri* is markedly late flowering, appearing usually in June. In Britain, where tulips are at the furthest western edge of their preferred range, it is the only tulip that self-seeds with any success in gardens. Surprisingly large spreads of *T. sylvestris* will naturalize, though, where they find conditions that suit them: ground that drains like a sieve and plenty of sun in summer. They like places where there is a clear separation between summer heat and winter cold.

When you buy tulip bulbs, you will probably be thinking of colour – moody 'Black Hero', orange 'Prinses Irene' the flowers mottled over in complex webs of green and purple, zinging red 'Cantata' with a heart as black as coal. Few other flowers can produce such a range of alternatives, and since colour is what first comes to mind the tulips listed below are sorted into five different colour groups, rather than listed alphabetically as most other bulbs in this book are. Whatever your colour scheme, there will be a tulip to fit it. But in making your choices, you also need to consider height and flowering time.

Tulips can provide you with flowers that practically sit on the ground, as well as ones that wave to the clouds. You would not want to put tall tulips in a window box, because, from inside, all you will see is stem and leaf. Raised up from the ground, flowers will also be more exposed. In a window box, or any other windswept situation, you want strong-stemmed, fairly

OPPOSITE The species tulip *T. sprengeri* is the latest of all tulips to flower. It does so with pointed petals in an uncompromising pillar box red.

short tulips with heads that will not snap off in rough weather. But it is useful to be offered so many options, in terms of height, from little *T. polychroma* only 10cm (4in) tall to 'Beau Monde' which has pink-veined flowers on stems 65cm (26in) tall. As a rough guide, expect the early-flowering tulips to be fairly short, the late ones much taller. Most hover in the middle, at 40–60cm (16–24in) tall.

You can exploit these different heights in the way you plant tulips. Set three pots in a group together, two pots packed full of medium-height tulips arranged in front of one filled with taller types. This triangular grouping fits well into a corner, made perhaps where your house wraps round a terrace, or where the wall of a balcony wall meets the wall to which it is fastened. In a scree, or some other gravel-covered area, low-growing tulips look best. This kind of setting mimics the scenery of the Asian steppes where wild tulips such as those of the magenta-pink *T. humilis* Violacea Group grow. In a mixed bed or border, you can use tall tulips towards the back of a scheme (or at the centre of an island bed) with shorter tulips growing towards the front of the border. In a windy garden, experiment carefully. It may be that you must leave tall varieties for gardeners in less exposed situations.

By choosing carefully, you can have tulips in bloom outside from February until early June, though the main flowering season will be April and May. For an early glimpse of spring, plant wild (species) tulips such as *T. humilis* Violacea Group from the Taurus mountains in Turkey. Their brilliant magenta-pink flowers are only 15–20cm (6–8in) high. Tiny *T. polychroma*, with iceberg-white flowers washed over with grey-blue, is scarcely 10cm (4in). Both are capable of flowering in February, though they will hold back if the season is particularly harsh. For a mid-March display you might choose tulips such as lemon-yellow 'Berlioz' or one of the types of *T. greigii* with foliage mottled like snakeskin. By April you will be spoilt for choice: purple 'Negrita', gorgeous flame-coloured 'Prinses Irene', sumptuous 'Couleur Cardinal', a colour too sexy for even the most daring cardinal. At the beginning of May you can indulge in mad, magnificent Parrot tulips, the kind that Dutch artists loved to paint. With tulips such as 'Rococo' and 'Weber's Parrot', you can create your own Dutch still life.

CULTIVATION

When you buy a tulip bulb, the flower will already be stored away at its heart. It is the ultimate designer package, pared down, functional, beautiful in its chestnut-coloured coat. All you have to provide is a little food and drink and a home that is not too soggy. The reward will be an explosion of colour: brilliant reds and oranges, dark subtle purples, pale porcelain-precious pinks or minimal white. Though bulbs are available from late summer, the best planting time is late October or early November.

In the wild, tulips choose homes on ground that drains as fast as an emptying bathtub. To make them happy in your garden, you have to provide something similar. If you garden on light, fast-draining soil, you are already halfway to making tulips (and many other bulbs) happy. If you have only

OPPOSITE 'Rococo' is one of the craziest of the Parrot
tulips, with petals twisting and turning in all directions.
They make superb cut flowers.

heavy, sticky clay to offer them, add grit or gravel to the planting hole and mulch heavily with grit when you have finished planting. Gradually, this will work its way down into the soil and improve drainage. Choose an open, sunny situation for planting, one which will not be swamped with foliage from surrounding plants before the tulips have died down themselves.

The general guide for planting bulbs is to put them three times deeper than the height of the bulb itself. With species tulips, which have small bulbs, this means setting them so that there is 10–12cm (4–5in) of soil on top of their heads, more with bigger bulbs. In mixed plantings, you can go deeper than that, to avoid disturbing them when you are weeding or dealing with other plants growing nearby. But the nature of your soil makes a difference too. Gardeners on heavy, clay soil may choose to plant more shallowly than those who garden on fast-draining, sandy soil. Set tulip bulbs 10–20cm (4–8in) apart, depending on the effect you are trying to create. The smallest species tulips can go right at the front of a border, top-dressed with gravel, which mimics the kind of conditions they choose in the wild: open, sunny slopes covered with stone and shale. A light-limbed geranium such as 'Ann Folkard' can spread its arms to cover the space later, or you can sprinkle seed of annuals such as love-in-a-mist or California poppy directly onto the gravel as the tulips are dying down. Enough of the seed will germinate to give you a good show through summer.

Tulips look magnificent in tubs and other containers, and if you garden on heavy, damp clay this is the best way to grow them. In a pot, you can create a home that drains decently, even if you cannot arrange the summer baking that is the other thing they need. Check that all containers have drainage holes at the base and put a layer of 'crocks' at the bottom. For tulips I favour a fast-draining potting mix that is two-thirds John Innes No 3 soil-based compost and one-third 6mm (¼in) gravel. Do not use composts made with peat. Tulips like alkaline conditions, not acid ones. When the container is half full, set out the tulip bulbs on top of the compost, flat end at the bottom, pointed end at the top. To get a good show in tubs, you should plant bulbs more closely than you might in open ground. A container 25cm (10in) across will take seven bulbs. One 35cm (14in) across will accommodate about 12. In a 60cm (24in) tub you can plant at least 22 tulip bulbs.

Fill up the container with more compost, firming it gently down so that there is about 3cm (1in) free space at the top of the container. Top off the pots with a layer of gravel. This looks sharper than compost, keeps down weeds and also dissuades birds from excavating in your pots. It keeps the neck of the tulip clean and dry when it comes through in spring and also means that you will not get compost splashing onto the backs of the petals when the tulips come into flower. Write the name of the tulip you have planted on a label and bury it at the side of the container. You may want to plant it again. If it is 'Magier' you certainly will.

Water the container well, and leave it until it has almost dried out before watering again. When the tulips are in active growth they will need a steady supply of moisture. Stick your finger in the compost to test whether it is drying out. If the bulbs are short of water while they are developing, the flower buds may abort. Reduce watering when the leaves start to die down, as the bulb draws all their goodness back into itself to support the subsequent season's growth. As for feeding, you can either sprinkle a slow-release fertilizer on top of the compost after planting, or use a low-nitrogen, high-potash feed (the kind you might use for tomatoes) while the plant is in growth, adding it to the watering can when you water.

What happens next to the tulips in your garden depends on your temperament. In perfect conditions, tulip bulbs get baked in summer and that is what they need if they are to flower the following season. The hot, dry summers they experience in their wild habitats prompt new flower buds to form deep in the hearts of the bulbs. In gardens, they do not always get that essential hot, dry spell, and many gardeners find that tulips do not flower as well in subsequent years as they do in their first.

We cannot do much to change our weather, but we can choose tulips that try their best to accommodate it. Species tulips will often settle and increase, in ground that drains well and dries out in summer. I have seen terrific spreads of T. sprengeri under cherry trees, where during summer the trees suck all moisture out of the ground. Tulips of the Single Late type are also tenacious, but no tulip can survive an automatic irrigation system that keeps the ground permanently damp in summer.

There is, though, an unreal expectation on the part of gardeners that every tulip bulb should produce a flower every year. This is not how they perform in the wild. Even though you may see hillsides covered with flower, only perhaps one in ten of the bulbs present underground will be producing a bloom. Tulips will flower in their first year, certainly. The clever growers see to that. But flowering is an exhausting business for them. They need to build themselves up to strength again. If they are left undisturbed, in the right kind of ground, they will do this.

You can save tulip bulbs by cleaning them when the foliage has died down and then storing them in the dry. It is unlikely, however, that all the bulbs you save will flower again the following spring. They may have exhausted themselves and need building up. They may have split into several 'daughter' bulbs, which will need time to build up to flowering size. For a container, buy fresh bulbs each season to be sure of a good performance. Old bulbs can be lined out in a spare piece of ground and used as cut flowers.

The worst thing that can attack tulips is a type of botrytis, commonly called tulip fire, which stunts and distorts growth. Leaf tips look as though they have been scorched, and the leaves and flowers are covered with brown spots. Shoots usually collapse and are swallowed up by mould. In damp weather, spores quickly travel from one plant to the next, so you must dig up and destroy infected plants as quickly as you can. If you have a bad attack, leave the ground free of tulips for at least five years so that the spores die out. Your best defence against this debilitating disease is to provide good drainage for your tulip bulbs and to put them in a place where air circulates freely around the flowers. Think hillside. Think central Asia.

White/Pastel

SEASON: Late March–early April

HARDINESS: Fully hardy

HEIGHT: 10cm (4in)

DIVISION: 15 (Miscellaneous)

HABITAT: Macedonia across to the Black Sea, south-western Russia, eastern Turkey, Iran, Turkmenistan, Afghanistan, Pakistan and western China where it grows on high plateaux and stony hillsides

Tulipa biflora (*T. polychroma*)

For a long time there has been controversy about the correct name for this species. *Tulipa biflora* may be the 'official' name but gardeners need to know that the best forms will probably still be listed as *T. polychroma*. In the wild, the differences between the two are unclear because this tulip has a huge range, from Macedonia to western China. Though small, it is profuse, bearing four to six flowers on each stem. The pointed buds begin to open while they are almost sitting on the ground and make small, spreading, cup-shaped flowers dead white, rather than ivory. The outsides of the petals are flushed with green and a strange greyish lavender. The big basal blotch is bright yellow; so are the stamens. The leaves are pale grey-green, longer than the flower stems, but they are not overpowering. Try *T. biflora* with little crocus such as *C. chrysanthus* 'Blue Bird' and mounds of small alpine pinks for summer. Plant 10–12cm (4–5in) deep and the same distance apart.

Tulipa 'Blushing Girl'

This tulip is exceptionally tall and the flower enormous, at least 10cm (4in) across. It is particularly beautiful in bud, when it is egg-shaped with the petals wrapping neatly to a fine point. It opens into an ivory-white bloom with a very narrow rim of deep pink round the edges of the petals. The colour does not flush down through the flower, as it does in 'Magier'. Fortunately, the foliage is not too heavy, but the flower does not weather as well as some other pale tulips, such as 'White Parrot'. In 'Blushing Girl' there is no contrasting basal blotch; the anthers are pale mustard-cream. Use it with mahogany wallflowers and a lowish spurge such as *Euphorbia rigida*. Plant 15cm (6in) deep and the same distance apart.

SEASON: Early May

HARDINESS: Fully hardy

HEIGHT: 65cm (26in)

DIVISION: 5 (Single Late)

Tulipa 'Flaming Purissima'

'Flaming Purissima' is an enchanting tulip because it is so variable. It makes long, thin, pointed buds, the petals hooking round slightly at the top. The petals (finely textured) are pale primrose, washed over and 'flamed' with a soft red. The intensity of the wash varies from flower to flower. Some are deeply infused, others are scarcely marked at all. It is spectacularly lovely, much creamier than 'Purissima'. Wide, rounded petals – generous – open out in the sun showing a very small, indeterminate blotch of yellow at the base, thin, dark stamens and a twisted stigma. The foliage is broad, pale greyish green. The stem is slightly hairy, furry, the top half flushed with a reddish glow. Plant 15cm (6in) deep and the same distance apart.

SEASON: Late March
HARDINESS: Fully hardy
HEIGHT: 45cm (18in)
DIVISION: 13 (Fosteriana)

Tulipa 'Magier'

'Magier' is an astonishingly lovely tulip, especially when combined with bluebells. It bears an elegant flower of pale creamy white, finely edged in purple. As the flower ages, which it does gracefully and well, the purple leaches through the petals, gradually staining and darkening them. In a big group, you get flowers at all stages which looks gorgeous. This is an old tulip, introduced in 1951, but it is strong as well as subtle, various in its make-up, one of the all-time greats. 'Magier' has a snow-white base and dark purple anthers, which drop their pollen like soot. Sprinkle seed of love-in-a-mist round the bulbs to provide a later show of summer flowers. Plant 15cm (6in) deep and the same distance apart.

SEASON: May
HARDINESS: Fully hardy
HEIGHT: 60cm (24in)
DIVISION: 5 (Single Late)

Tulipa 'Salut'

This amazingly showy tulip was introduced in 1955 by the Dutch firm Hybrida. The wide pale green leaves are slightly taller than the flowers which are at first urn-shaped, but very ready to splay out in the sun, if it comes. Flat out like this, the flower is at least 15cm (6in) across. The petals are creamy, the three outer ones with a splash of soft pink up the centre. In proportion to the overall size, the flowers are huge and the flush of pink on the outside gives an enchanting effect even before the flower opens. Inside is a very pronounced, dramatic blotch of dark velvety brown, with a faint halo of yellow round the outside. Occasionally the yellow is faintly splashed with red. The anthers are inconspicuous – deep yellow. Because 'Salut' is such a drama queen, it is an ideal tulip to grow by itself in a pot. If that is not enough for you, try it with the bright green feathery foliage of the giant fennel *Ferula communis*. Plant 15cm (6in) deep and the same distance apart.

SEASON: Late March
HARDINESS: Fully hardy
HEIGHT: 30cm (12in)
DIVISION: 13 (Fosteriana)

Tulipa 'Sapporo'

'Sapporo' was initially raised for forcing, but it makes a wonderful garden tulip. The two are not always compatible. The form is elegantly and lightly waisted and the petals beautifully pointed. As the flower opens out, it makes an enchanting, vase-like shape. Initially, 'Sapporo' is sulphur-yellow, but it fades as it ages to pale ivory. The later stage is better than the early, and it is better open than closed. There are no contrasting markings on the petals, and only faint dark stains at the base. The stamens, too, are creamy. The value of this tulip lies primarily in its form. The foliage is greyish. Try it with a grey-leaved hosta such as 'Halcyon' or set it between clumps of *Helleborus* 'Silver Dollar' or *H. argutifolius* 'Silver Lace'. Plant 15cm (6in) deep and the same distance apart.

SEASON: Mid April
HARDINESS: Fully hardy
HEIGHT: 35cm (14in)
DIVISION: 6 (Lily-flowered)

Tulipa 'Snow Parrot'

This produces an exceptionally pretty flower with ragged petals, but it keeps its general form, unlike madder, more puckered Parrots. Here the distortion of shape is minimal. The flower is a soft, greyish white, the outsides of the petals washed over with grey, blue and mauve. The blue is most heavily accented at the base of the flower. At the edges, the colour drifts into a pinkish mauve, all very light and delicate. 'Snow Parrot' is extremely elegant, but in a fluffy rather than a cool way. There is a tiny basal blotch of dirty yellow; the anthers are also yellowish. Plant 15cm (6in) deep and the same distance apart.

SEASON: Early April
HARDINESS: Fully hardy
HEIGHT: 40cm (16in)
DIVISION: 10 (Parrot)

Tulipa 'Spring Green' ♀

Many people would put 'Spring Green' at the top of their top ten tulips as it goes with anything, and also has a slightly wild, fey look about it. In fact it is a strong tulip, very resistant to wind and grows bolt upright on a thick stem. The flower is smallish, compared to many more modern tulips ('Spring Green' was raised in 1969), but that is why it looks so good with other wildish plants – *Smyrnium perfoliatum* or sweet cicely. The flowers are creamy white with a broad, green flame up the centre of each petal; the flame shows both on the inside and the outside of the flower. Each petal has a slightly sideways twist. It is reluctant to open up in sunshine so you are less aware of its weaknesses: that it has no contrasting basal blotch and the anthers are an uninteresting greenish grey. Plant 15cm (6in) deep and the same distance apart.

SEASON: Late April
HARDINESS: Fully hardy
HEIGHT: 48cm (19in)
DIVISION: 8 (Viridiflora)

Tulipa 'Weber's Parrot'

The flower of 'Weber's Parrot' is like a fop's handkerchief, the huge, crinkled petals gently streaked with pale pink on a creamy white ground, formless, even for a Parrot, but fun. The difficulty is that it collapses in the rain, as the stem is not strong enough to carry the vast weight of the flower. But it is worth the risk and is such a wonderfully ludicrous sight you cannot help but love it. Use it in between bearded iris whose foliage will help prop up the flowers. The tulips will not get in the irises' way as they dive underground in summer. Plant 15cm (6in) deep and the same distance apart.

SEASON: Mid May
HARDINESS: Fully hardy
HEIGHT: 50cm (20in)
DIVISION: 10 (Parrot)

Pale/Deep Pink

Tulipa 'Angélique' ♀

The pretty, double flowers of apple-blossom-pink gradually darken as they age so you get varying intensities of colour in the same group (good). 'Angélique' is a boudoir tulip, very frilly and feminine, with petals edged and streaked in a lighter tone. The central ribs of the outer petals are flushed with green. The central blotch is very small, pale yellow but, since this is a double, scarcely visible. The foliage is pale too, greyish and narrow. 'Angélique' is a showy tulip, slightly scented and it develops well, unlike 'Carlton'. It is a sport of 'Granda', raised in 1959 by D W Lefeber. Try it with pink and white double daisies (*Bellis perennis*) and lime-green *Smyrnium perfoliatum*. Plant 15cm (6in) deep and the same distance apart.

SEASON: Early May
HARDINESS: Fully hardy
HEIGHT: 45cm (18in)
DIVISION: 11 (Double Late)

Tulipa 'Apricot Parrot' ♀

This is a fabulously outrageous Parrot with mad petals, puckering out from a central, smooth, tight midrib. The backs of the petals are almost white, feathered at the edges with pink. On the backs are occasional streaks of green. The flowers (unusually large) open wide and madly in the sun, when they show much more pink on the inside. The basal blotch is an indeterminate creamy white, flushing up the centre midrib. The stamens appear rather dark, arranged in the yellowish epicentre. 'Apricot Parrot' was introduced in 1961 by H G Huyg, a sport of 'Karel Doorman'. Plant 15cm (6in) deep and the same distance apart.

SEASON: Mid April
HARDINESS: Fully hardy
HEIGHT: 50cm (20in)
DIVISION: 10 (Parrot)

Tulipa 'Beau Monde' ♀

'Beau Monde' is an old-fashioned-looking tulip with a smallish flower, creamy buff in bud, the buff changing to pink as the flower develops. It opens to a pale, delicate bloom of off-white, with a pale pink flush up the centre of the petal. At the base is an indeterminate, yellow blotch, pale stamens and stigma. The stem is quite thin for such a tall tulip and in rain it tends to flop, but it is excellent in a cottage garden setting with traditional companions such as forget-me-nots and white honesty. Plant 15cm (6in) deep and the same distance apart.

SEASON: Mid April
HARDINESS: Fully hardy
HEIGHT: 65cm (26in)
DIVISION: 3 (Triumph)

Tulipa 'Big Chief' ♀

The leaves are very broad and untidy, which is a disadvantage, but in bud this is a thrilling tulip raised in 1960 by A Frijlink & Sons. The buff-cream on the back of the closed petals is gradually edged with a soft orange-red, and then the flower colours very slowly as it develops. At maturity there is still a faint creamy buff overlay on the backs of the petals. 'Big Chief' makes a big, triangular flower, very impressive, though the colour is not easy. There is an indistinct basal blotch of canary-yellow which extends a good way up the inner petals. Use it between low mounds of catmint or let it rise from a carpet of mahogany-coloured pansies. Plant 15cm (6in) deep and the same distance apart.

SEASON: Early April
HARDINESS: Fully hardy
HEIGHT: 60cm (24in)
DIVISION: 4 (Darwin Hybrid)

Tulipa 'Capri'

This strongly upright, thick-stemmed tulip has fine, clean, greyish foliage slightly on the broad side. The flowers are a rich, deep pink, big and showy, though not the best in terms of form. But each flower has a very surprising and splendid navy-blue base, edged with white, which is the making of this tulip, as the base is large and very dramatic. A pale cream stigma sits in the centre of very dark stamens, increasing the complexity of the interior. This is a fine tulip, given that it is a single-coloured one, without the intricacy of a bloom such as 'Magier'. 'Capri' is a favourite among Dutch growers for forcing, but in the garden makes a good companion for *Alchemilla mollis* and *Geranium palmatum*. Plant 15cm (6in) deep and the same distance apart.

SEASON: Late April
HARDINESS: Fully hardy
HEIGHT: 48cm (19in)
DIVISION: 3 (Triumph)

Tulipa 'Douglas Bader'

The greyish foliage is not too dominant, always an advantage with tulips. The flower is flat-bottomed and makes a triangular shape. It is a strange colour, a kind of dirty pink, not uniform, but netted over a paler underlay. Though it is small, it is complex enough to be interesting, good for those who do not like bright lipstick-pinks. The small, white basal blotch adds very little; the stem though is dark and gives the flower much more drama than it would otherwise have. The stamens are also a surprise: deep plum-purple. 'Douglas Bader' was introduced in 1976 by J F van den Berg & Sons. Try it with the dark foliage of *Actaea simplex* 'Brunette' or *Cirsium rivulare*. Plant 15cm (6in) deep and the same distance apart.

SEASON: Late April
HARDINESS: Fully hardy
HEIGHT: 45cm (18in)
DIVISION: 5 (Single Late)

Tulipa 'Estella Rijnveld'

One of the showiest of the Parrot tulips, 'Estella Rijnveld' produces large flowers with petals that are deeply cut and waved. They are striped like raspberry-ripple ice cream – rich red on a white ground. Occasionally you will find flecks of green with the red. This is an old tulip, introduced by Segers in 1954, and almost too outrageous to combine with other plants in the garden. Put it on its own in a pot and make sure you are at home for the performance of its opening. Plant 15cm (6in) deep and the same distance apart.

SEASON: Mid May
HARDINESS: Fully hardy
HEIGHT: 60cm (24in)
DIVISION: 10 (Parrot)

Tulipa 'Fantasy' ♀

This huge, superb, blowsy tulip splays open in sunshine to show mad petals of soft rose, crested and striped with green. It is wildly formless, but showy and fun, the petals having a rich, satiny sheen, paler on the outside than within. 'Fantasy' arose as a sport from the old pink tulip 'Clara Butt' and has been around since at least 1910. Use it to liven up a rose bed or combine it with silvery *Salvia argentea* and biennial verbascums. Plant 15cm (6in) deep and the same distance apart.

SEASON: Mid May
HARDINESS: Fully hardy
HEIGHT: 56cm (22in)
DIVISION: 10 (Parrot)

Tulipa 'Groenland'
(*T.* 'Greenland')

'Groenland' is one of the best of the Viridiflora tulips, a pale, old-fashioned dirty pink, the flat-topped petals flared up the centre with a broad, green stripe edged in cream. Pale green flushes up from the centre on the inside and is very prominent on the outside up the central beam. The petals are pointed, slightly puckered as the edges tend to draw in together. Though the flower of 'Groenland' is relatively small, the growth is strong and upright, the flower held on an elegant stem that is not too thick. The foliage, too, is well-behaved. This is another old tulip, introduced in 1955 by J F van den Berg & Sons. Plant 15cm (6in) deep and the same distance apart.

SEASON: Late April
HARDINESS: Fully hardy
HEIGHT: 63cm (25in)
DIVISION: 8 (Viridiflora)

Tulipa humilis Violacea Group
(*T. pulchella* 'Violacea', *T. violacea*)

An enchanting tulip, tiny but unmissable. From a narrow, funnel-like base, the flower opens into a goblet of rich rosy-mauve, the backs of the outer petals washed over with green or grey. The inner petals, fatter than the outer ones, have dark veins down the midribs. All six are pointed, not rounded. The basal blotch is black (or yellow) while the filaments may be white or yellow at the base, navy-blue at the tip and the anthers deep purple. The leaves are long, thin, channelled, somewhat glaucous and closely set on the stem. This is one type of a variable species which has lived with several different labels. For the moment, the namers of names have decided to lump all these similar types of tulip together under the heading *T. humilis*. There are at least a dozen named types of *T. humilis* and there is not a dud among them. Writing in the *Gardeners' Chronicle* of 1934, E K Balls, who saw it growing on Mount Elwend, said, 'Among the rocks I found quantities of *Tulipa violacea* (which now seems likely to be synonymous with *T. humilis* and *T. pulchella*). My first view of the tulip was from below, with the sunlight shining through it. The flower is rather larger than that of *T. polychroma*, and does not open so wide to the sun, but keeps its cup-like shape. Of a bright claret colour, with a greenish base to the petals, and black anthers, it grows four to six inches high and on 26th May I found the last colonies of it flowering at about 12,000ft. I had found quantities of bulbs so low down as 10,000ft but they were long out of flower. It grows in a moist, sandy loam, among the rocks, chiefly on the west and south-west slopes.' Use it with later-flowering *Allium cernuum* and a smattering of California poppies, the seed scattered round the tulip flowers in early spring. Plant 10–12cm (4–5in) deep and the same distance apart.

SEASON: March
HARDINESS: Fully hardy
HEIGHT: 10–15cm (4–6in)
DIVISION: 15 (Miscellaneous)
HABITAT: Northern Iran, especially around Mount Elwend, northern Iraq and south and east Turkey

OPPOSITE Viridiflora tulips, such as 'Groenland', all have petals variously striped and patterned in green.

Red

Tulipa 'Alice Leclercq'

'Alice Leclercq' is an absolutely gorgeous tulip, excellent in pots, introduced in 1952 by the Dutch grower P Dames of Lisse. The showy flowers are bright orange-red with a very narrow, yellow edge round each of the petals. It is well-balanced too, with a stem that is not too tall for its cargo of petals. Plant 15cm (6in) deep and the same distance apart.

SEASON: Mid April
HARDINESS: Fully hardy
HEIGHT: 30cm (12in)
DIVISION: 2 (Double Early)

Tulipa 'American Dream'

In bud, 'American Dream' is creamy yellow, with petals finely edged in orange-red. It opens to a dazzling, orange-red flower, with the cream still dominating on the outside surface of the three outer petals. The base is yellow with a very clear, interesting, petal-shaped blotch in black. The dark anthers make this an intriguing flower, with its cool, clotted-cream petals and vibrant interior. When you have planted the tulip bulbs, poke some nasturtium seeds in between them to cover the ground in summer and autumn when the tulips have gone. Plant 15cm (6in) deep and the same distance apart.

SEASON: Late April
HARDINESS: Fully hardy
HEIGHT: 55cm (22in)
DIVISION: 4 (Darwin Hybrid)

Tulipa 'Arma'

'Arma' is a very good tulip of cardinal-red, the edges of the petals frilled and fringed. It makes a short, dumpy flower, which shows an excellent tendency to succumb to virus. Among the red flowers you may find some fabulous ones, striped with red on a yellow ground, or yellow flowers very lightly feathered in red. Some petals have a strong, green mark up the centre (tulip fanciers call it the 'beam'). The small basal blotch is bright yellow and the anthers dark purplish black. The flower is not big, but it is showy, and the dark anthocyanin-red drifts down the stem from the flower. 'Arma' is an excellent choice for window boxes, mixed perhaps with the rounded leaves of *Saxifraga stolonifera*. It is a sport of 'Couleur Cardinal' and was introduced in 1962 by Knijn Bros. Plant 15cm (6in) deep and the same distance apart.

SEASON: Early May
HARDINESS: Fully hardy
HEIGHT: 35cm (14in)
DIVISION: 7 (Fringed)

Tulipa 'Cantata'

The colour – an astonishing orange-red – is beautifully set off against the glossy, mid-green foliage. Pale buff-cream flares up the backs of the outside petals, which twist and flare in an intriguing way. The flower is triangular in outline, but instead of lying flat the broad petals pinch in their edges to face each other and then flip out at the top, though not in the controlled way of the lily-flowered tulips. The basal blotch on 'Cantata' is arrow-shaped, black with a neat, yellow rim. Plant 15cm (6in) deep and the same distance apart.

SEASON: Late March
HARDINESS: Fully hardy
HEIGHT: 30cm (12in)
DIVISION: 13 (Fosteriana)

Tulipa 'Couleur Cardinal'

The flowers of 'Couleur Cardinal' are large and form a good cup, of brilliant cardinal-red, with a marvellous, dark blush, a plum-coloured bloom up the backs of the petals. The colour is wonderfully lustrous, like the most expensive satin, dull on one side, gleaming on the other. The base is a perfect disc of yellow, very neat, very orderly, pierced by narrow, black stamens. It is an old tulip, known since 1845, and stands up well to bad weather. In 1911, Walter Wright, founder and editor of *Popular Gardening*, described this tulip 'shining with the dusky splendour of old wine' when it was planted either side of the Broad Walk at Kew Gardens, in the UK. It is a beauty. Try it with seedlings of bronze fennel or mix it with equally lustrous wallflowers. Tulips and wallflowers complement each other brilliantly. Plant 15cm (6in) deep and the same distance apart.

SEASON: Late April
HARDINESS: Fully hardy
HEIGHT: 30cm (12in)
DIVISION: 3 (Triumph)

Tulipa 'Doorman's Record'

'Doorman's Record' produces excellent, mad flowers of rich damask-red, twisted with yellow and green. There is a fine outline of yellow crinkling around the edges of the petals. These are very large and puckered, with strange, little horns on the backs of the outer ones. Sometimes the backs are heavily plated with green. The base is yellowish green, the stamens purple, dusted with creamy pollen, and the foliage broad, clean and a pale greyish green. It is a very good tulip to use in a pot, as long as it is not hit by hail or strong wind. Plant 15cm (6in) deep and the same distance apart.

SEASON: Early April
HARDINESS: Fully hardy
HEIGHT: 33cm (13in)
DIVISION: 10 (Parrot)

Tulipa 'Dyanito'

'Dyanito' is an elegant tulip with tall, narrow buds that open to pointed flowers of a good, soft, glowing red, a pleasing, more complex colour than for instance 'Brilliant Star'. Some have a hint of green or yellow on the outsides of the petals. The blooms are not wildly waisted, compared with some other lily-flowered varieties such as 'West Point', but the deep yellow base is prettily arranged with a streak up the midrib of each petal, giving a crown-like effect of points. The anthers are dark purplish black. Use it against a backdrop of lime-green *Euphorbia* × *martinii*, mixed perhaps with the lily-flowered tulip 'Ballerina'. Plant 15cm (6in) deep and the same distance apart.

SEASON: Late April
HARDINESS: Fully hardy
HEIGHT: 55cm (22in)
DIVISION: 6 (Lily-flowered)

Tulipa 'Jan Reus'

'Jan Reus' is a strong, straight tulip with classic, square shoulders and rounded petals, named after one of the pioneers of bulb growing in the clay area of northern Holland. It is an extraordinarily good colour: a deep red, the colour of claret, not a common shade among tulips. The yellow basal blotch is overlaid

with a smaller disc of blackish yellow. The foliage is broad, but the flowers are held well above it. It doesn't get in the way. Plant 15cm (6in) deep and the same distance apart.

SEASON: April
HARDINESS: Fully hardy
HEIGHT: 50cm (20in)
DIVISION: 3 (Triumph)

Tulipa 'Rococo'

'Rococo' is baroque in the extreme, a madly Parroty tulip with fringed edges to its petals. The petals themselves wind about in all directions. The colour is a superb, rich damask-red with the backs of the petals washed over in purple. The base is bright yellow, with a pale green stigma in the centre of a clutch of dark anthers. If you have a hedge of copper beech, this is the tulip to put in front of it, to flower sumptuously while the young beech leaves are still soft, lustrous bronze. If you do not have a hedge, try interplanting with *Carex buchananii*. Plant 15cm (6in) deep and the same distance apart.

SEASON: Mid May
HARDINESS: Fully hardy
HEIGHT: 43cm (17in)
DIVISION: 10 (Parrot)

Tulipa sprengeri ♀

Tulipa sprengeri was first found in 1892 by a German botanist, living at Amasya, who sent bulbs to Damman & Co.'s nursery near Naples, Italy. It was named after Carl Sprenger, who worked at the company and introduced it into cultivation in 1894. Its habit is markedly upright, the flower appearing well above the thin, glossy, green leaves. The oval bud opens to a star made up of narrow, pointed petals, a clear reddish orange or bright scarlet. There is sometimes a buff coat on the backs of the outer petals (they are thinner than the inner ones), suffused with olive and green. It is the latest of all tulips to flower. It is a very distinct

tulip, not only in its time of flowering, which is well after all others have died down, but also because it seems to enjoy shade and does not mind moist soil. It is one of the few tulips that can be persuaded to naturalize far from its natural habitat and will even grow in grass, provided it is not too coarse. You sometimes find *T. sprengeri* flourishing in surprisingly shady positions under shrubs. I have seen wonderful spreads of it under a cherry tree, most of its growth accomplished before the tree fully leafs up. It is easy to increase from seed, and will make a flowering-size bulb within five years – most tulips take seven years to develop from seed to viable bulb. When happy, it will seed itself about in a garden. Set in good soil in part shade where the bulbs need not be disturbed and where seedlings can settle and thrive. It does not need companions. Plant 10–12cm (4–5in) deep and the same distance apart.

SEASON: Mid–late May
HARDINESS: Fully hardy
HEIGHT: 40cm (16in)
DIVISION: 15 (Miscellaneous)
HABITAT: Pontic mountains, near Amasya, Turkey

Purple/Mauve

Tulipa 'Black Hero'

A stunning tulip, tall for a double and strong. The stems do not snap easily. The flowers are very dark, at least as dark as 'Queen of Night' (of which 'Black Hero' is a sport) and very double, making a short, stubby, round ball. There is quite a lot of green on the outside petals, but this enhances the appeal rather than otherwise. The foliage is greyish and not overpowering – another bonus. Mix it with *T*. 'Blue Diamond' for a knockout spring container. Plant 15cm (6in) deep and the same distance apart.

SEASON: Late April
HARDINESS: Fully hardy
HEIGHT: 60cm (24in)
DIVISION: 11 (Double Late)

Tulipa 'Attila'

Strong stems carry long-lasting, pale purplish violet flowers, rounded in form, with thick, substantial petals. The colour fades off very slightly at the edges of the petals, which gives the flower added complexity. The base is white, streaked with blue, and spotted with pollen from the dark aubergine anthers. 'Attila' is a lovely tulip, very elegant, very classy, a blue-rinse flower raised in 1945 by F van der Mey of Lisse. Use it with forget-me-nots and pale lemon wallflowers. Plant 15cm (6in) deep and the same distance apart.

SEASON: Mid April
HARDINESS: Fully hardy
HEIGHT: 50cm (20in)
DIVISION: 3 (Triumph)

Tulipa 'Bleu Aimable'

'Bleu Aimable' produces a wide, spreading flower, not blue – one of the few colours that a tulip cannot produce – but a soft, gentle, dull mauve-purple, the complexities of which improve as the flower ages. It is a fine colour, one of the best in this range, unsurpassed since the flower was first introduced almost a hundred years ago. Use it with sweet cicely and the elegant hosta 'Krossa Regal'. Plant 15cm (6in) deep and the same distance apart.

SEASON: Early May
HARDINESS: Fully hardy
HEIGHT: 60cm (24in)
DIVISION: 5 (Single Late)

Tulipa 'Blue Diamond'

This is a wonderful tulip, greenish bronze in bud, which makes a stubby, thickly petalled flower like an overblown ranunculus. It is formless, of course, but very showy and a lovely, old-fashioned purple. Hidden in the muddle of petals is a surprising blue base, the purple and the blue an excellent foil for the grey-green foliage. Double Late tulips make a showy display in a tub, ideal either outside or in a cool conservatory. Outside, try 'Blue Diamond' against a bank of lavender. Plant 15cm (6in) deep and the same distance apart.

SEASON: Mid April
HARDINESS: Fully hardy
HEIGHT: 40cm (16in)
DIVISION: 11 (Double Late)

Tulipa 'Blue Parrot'

The petals curl in on themselves, making a congested but not wildly parroty flower. They are Victorian purple, a gorgeous, off-beat colour, which also runs down the top part of the stem. The base (hidden) is peacock-blue flooding round a strange, curled stigma. 'Blue Parrot' is a classy tulip, both handsome and elegant. It is a sport of 'Bleu Aimable' and was introduced in 1935 by John F Dix of Heemstede. Use it among clumps of old-fashioned *Paeonia officinalis* and grey-toned teucrium. Plant 15cm (6in) deep and the same distance apart.

SEASON: Early May
HARDINESS: Fully hardy
HEIGHT: 55cm (22in)
DIVISION: 10 (Parrot)

Tulipa 'Maytime'

The mid-green foliage is slightly crinkled, wide, but not long, so the exaggerated vase-shaped flowers are held well above it. The petals are long (at least 9cm/3¾in) but thin; although very handsome in bud, when its narrow waist is most effective, 'Maytime' looks thin and straggly when it opens in the sun, which it does very readily. Then the advantage of the extravagant lily-flowered form is lost. The petals, rich magenta-purple, fold their edges together slightly and twist at the top. The basal blotch is white with an indeterminate, mauveish ring round it. This is another old flower, raised in 1942 by De Mol & A H Nieuwenhuis. Use it between banks of rosemary and *Artemisia* 'Powis Castle'. Plant 15cm (6in) deep and the same distance apart.

SEASON: Late April–early May
HARDINESS: Fully hardy
HEIGHT: 34cm (14in)
DIVISION: 6 (Lily-flowered)

NEXT PAGE In terms of shape, lily-flowered tulips such as 'Maytime' are among the most elegant of all tulips, with pointed petals and slim, nipped-in waists.

471

Tulipa 'Negrita'

The flowers of 'Negrita' are a good, rich purple, veined with seams of an even darker colour. At the base is a clear blue blotch, edged in cream. It is very beautiful in bud, when the flower makes a broad-based, three-sided pyramid, the petals joining in a point at the centre. It has a habit of throwing more than the usual six petals, so the resulting flowers are astonishingly full and blowsy. It will always be a favourite of mine as I planted it in quantity to provide flowers for the wedding of our middle daughter. She had the great good sense to get married in the tulip season. Plant 15cm (6in) deep and the same distance apart.

SEASON: Late April–early May
HARDINESS: Fully hardy
HEIGHT: 45cm (18in)
DIVISION: 3 (Triumph)

Tulipa passeriniana (T. didieri)

The tulip supremo Sir Daniel Hall considered this species a stray from cultivation, one of the most common and typical forms of the so-called neo-tulipae. The leaves are upright, lance-shaped, glaucous, the upper stem leaves more narrow and pointed than the lower. It is an enchanting tulip, similar to *T. platystigma* (another of the neo-tulipae). The form is comparable, but even better, the petals less rounded, more pointed. Although white and yellow kinds have been found in the wild, *T. passeriniana* is usually a rich, deep pink with none of the red of *T. platystigma*. The stamens and anthers are large and dark, and the basal blotch black with a clear, well-defined edging of cream. The foliage is greyer than that

of *T. platystigma*, the leaves folded together and slightly crinkled. This is a very elegant tulip, opening from narrow, pointed buds, a beautiful thing. It was first described in 1846, and John Baker, the keeper of the Herbarium at Kew Gardens, UK, was one of several who noted the variability of this tulip, 'Came last year from wild Italian stock in Upper Savoy,' he wrote in 1890. 'Flowered the first year – was pure yellow. This year the flowers took on a reddish tinge.' He thought the variability might have something to do with the age of the bulb, yellow in its first flowering season, settling then to the more usual red. Use it between mounds of *Dianthus* 'Hidcote' and *Tulbaghia violacea* 'Silver Lace'. Plant 10–12cm (4–5in) deep and the same distance apart.

SEASON: Mid April
HARDINESS: Fully hardy
HEIGHT: 40–50cm (16–20in)
DIVISION: 15 (Miscellaneous)
HABITAT: St Jean-de-Maurienne in Savoy, France, and northern Italy

Tulipa 'Recreado'

'Recreado' produces rich, dark plum-purple flowers, much deeper and more saturated in colour than the Triumph tulip 'Blue Ribbon'. The bloom sits on a strong, straight stem, with the dark colour drifting down the top half of it. The petals are well-shaped, quite broad, and softly pointed, making a flower that is rectangular rather than triangular in form. There is little variation in colour between the inner and outer surface of the petals, though the texture is different; the inside is shinier, glossier. At the base is the faintest dark smudge, surrounding dark purple anthers. A fine tulip, which looks good with *Ipheion* 'Alberto Castillo' or *Iris chrysographes* 'Ellenbank Nightshade'. Plant 15cm (6in) deep and the same distance apart.

SEASON: Late April
HARDINESS: Fully hardy
HEIGHT: 50cm (20in)
DIVISION: 5 (Single Late)

Tulipa 'Purple Prince'

'Purple Prince' is a plain rich, light reddish-purple tulip with crinkled petals, narrower in outline than the similar Triumph tulip 'Purple Star'. At the base of the flower is a pale yellow blotch in the shape of a Maltese cross. The stigma is weird and twisted. You do not need to grow many different tulips before realizing that what goes on inside the flower is even more interesting than its outside appearance. Use 'Purple Prince' with the old-fashioned wallflower *Erysimum* 'Bowles's Mauve' and clumps of *Erigeron karvinskianus*. Plant 15cm (6in) deep and the same distance apart.

SEASON: Late March
HARDINESS: Fully hardy
HEIGHT: 30cm (12in)
DIVISION: 1 (Single Early)

Yellow/Orange

Tulipa 'Annie Schilder'

'Annie Schilder' is a lovely, old-fashioned, egg-shaped tulip in gorgeous toffee-orange, slightly paler round the edges of the petals. On the back there is a curious pinkish/purplish sheen which takes the edge off the orange. These are not markings, as you find on the Triumph tulip 'Prinses Irene', but a more muted series of colour washes. The base is lemon-yellow, edged with green. It is gorgeous with the rich green early foliage of *Geranium maderense*. A fine tulip. Plant 15cm (6in) deep and the same distance apart.

SEASON: Late April
HARDINESS: Fully hardy
HEIGHT: 45cm (18in)
DIVISION: 3 (Triumph)

Tulipa 'Ballerina' ♀

This is an elegant, rather small-flowered tulip with pointed petals in lovely sunset shades of orange and red, netted together in an indistinguishable way. Outside, the flowers seem to be flamed with blood-red on a lemon-yellow ground with orange-yellow veining at the edges; inside, they are feathered marigold-orange and bright red. The petals tend to roll in on themselves. At the base is a buttercup-yellow star with smudges of pale green. 'Ballerina' makes tall, thin, very beautiful buds, soaring above the greyish foliage. It is a fabulous tulip, fine-boned and complex, though at first glance you might dismiss it as plain orange. It is scented, a light evanescent scent like primroses, and is the only orange lily-flowered tulip, raised in 1980 by J F van den Berg & Sons. Plant 15cm (6in) deep and the same distance apart.

SEASON: Early May
HARDINESS: Fully hardy
HEIGHT: 55cm (22in)
DIVISION: 6 (Lily-flowered)

Tulipa 'Bestseller'

'Bestseller' produces huge flowers of lovely, soft orange, not solid colour but paler towards the bottom of the petal, then darkening into a scarcely distinguishable, arrow-headed blotch. The backs of the petals are washed over with rose. It is an extraordinary tulip, but because the blooms are so big stems tend to snap in bad weather. Set it between the spearing foliage of *Iris orientalis* and generous *Geranium* 'Brookside'. Plant 15cm (6in) deep and the same distance apart.

SEASON: Late April

HARDINESS: Fully hardy

HEIGHT: 45cm (18in)

DIVISION: 1 (Single Early)

Tulipa 'Fringed Elegance'

This is a showy tulip, lightly and quite elegantly fringed in a sharp, pale acid-yellow. The backs of the petals are very slightly paler than the insides. The flowers are enormous, opening out in the sun to a bloom 15cm (6in) across. The stems bend slightly under the weight, but this gives them a charming, informal aspect. There is a slight hint of red in some of the flowers, either finely edging the petals or streaking up their backs. At the base is a pronounced, arrow-shaped, black blotch round a clutch of coal-black anthers. The foliage is broad and so rather coarse, but this is not surprising given the size of the blooms on 'Fringed Elegance'. Plant 15cm (6in) deep and the same distance apart.

SEASON: Late April

HARDINESS: Fully hardy

HEIGHT: 60cm (24in)

DIVISION: 7 (Fringed)

NEXT PAGE 'Ballerina' is the only orange lily-flowered tulip and has a wonderful light scent, as do many orange and yellow tulips.

Tulipa 'Für Elise'

'Für Elise' is a charming tulip with good foliage, streaked longitudinally with maroon on a greyish green background. The original two basal leaves are broad, the rest narrower. In outline, the bud is neatly triangular, making a three-sided pyramid. The flower, much taller than broad, is a pleasant apricot-cream and has neat, pointed petals. There is a faint, pink flush up the outside of the flower. It shows on the inside too, but as an orange glow around the yellow basal blotch. This is an excellent choice for pots, as 'Für Elise' is early and not too tall. In a border, try it with the curry plant (*Helichrysum italicum* subsp. *serotinum*) and *Gillenia trifoliata*. Plant 15cm (6in) deep and the same distance apart.

SEASON: Late March
HARDINESS: Fully hardy
HEIGHT: 28cm (11in)
DIVISION: 14 (Greigii)

Tulipa 'Generaal de Wet'

'Generaal de Wet' is an old, sweetly scented tulip, known since 1904. It produces a variable crop of flowers with red netted in various quantities and strengths over an orange ground. The red, as well as veining over the backs of the petals, tends to gather in a very fine fringe on their edges. Variability is always to be encouraged, and this is a wonderful tulip, light limbed, thin stemmed, the petals finely textured compared with modern varieties. There is an indistinct blotch of yellow at the base of the flower, dark anthers in the centre. The petals are slightly untidy, which in this variety is charming. Plant 15cm (6in) deep and the same distance apart.

SEASON: Early April
HARDINESS: Fully hardy
HEIGHT: 40cm (16in)
DIVISION: 1 (Single Early)

Tulipa 'Georgette'

This is a multiflowered tulip of enormous charm, bearing three or four flowers on a strong stem. When the flower first emerges it is plain yellow, a good, soft, clean colour. Then gradually a narrow, red rim, characteristic of this variety, develops round the edges of the petals. It is enchanting, the red gradually feathering in on the sides as the flower ages – a very classy act. The flower is neat and well-formed, generally egg-shaped. There is no contrasting basal blotch, and the anthers are the same soft yellow as the flowers. 'Georgette' is excellent in pots, as the overall effect is very full. Conversely, the foliage is relatively narrow and unobtrusive. In a border, use it with *Convolvulus cneorum* and astelia. Plant 15cm (6in) deep and the same distance apart.

SEASON: Late April
HARDINESS: Fully hardy
HEIGHT: 50cm (20in)
DIVISION: 5 (Single Late)

Tulipa 'Gudoshnik'

'Gudoshnik' is an outrageous tulip with huge blooms and fat, rounded petals. The flowers are very varied: shades of pale peach-orange, streaked finely with red. Each is slightly different. A few may be plainish red. At the base are smudgy, black arrows, not as clearly defined as in 'Fringed Elegance'. When the flowers are red, the black base is much more clearly marked and also edged with pale yellow. It is a showy mix of flowers, carried on good, strong stems and I will always love it because it was the first tulip I ever grew. Use it with *Stipa tenuissima* and *Euphorbia seguieriana*. Plant 15cm (6in) deep and the same distance apart.

SEASON: Late April
HARDINESS: Fully hardy
HEIGHT: 55cm (22in)
DIVISION: 4 (Darwin Hybrid)

481

Tulipa 'Orange Favourite'

A gorgeous Parrot tulip of bright, rich orange-red with green flecks flaming out from the backs of the petals. The buds are exceptionally long and open into really stupendous, scented flowers. Though it does not have the excessively wild form of, say, 'Weber's Parrot', 'Orange Favourite' is one of the best of all tulips, but not for the faint-hearted. It is a sport of 'Orange King' and was introduced in 1930 by K C Vooren of Limmen. Plant 15cm (6in) deep and the same distance apart.

SEASON: Early May
HARDINESS: Fully hardy
HEIGHT: 50cm (20in)
DIVISION: 10 (Parrot)

Tulipa 'Prinses Irene' ♀

'Prinses Irene' is a sport of the equally excellent Triumph tulip 'Couleur Cardinal' and was introduced in 1949 by Van Reisen & Sons of Voorhout. It is a remarkable tulip of soft orange, flamed on the outside of the outer petals with purple and hints of green, exceptional because of these complex flushes of subdued colour on the bright orange ground. The inside of the flower is plain, rich orange, with no basal blotch. Use it with *Sedum telephium* 'Purple Emperor' and *Euphorbia polychroma* 'Major'. Plant 15cm (6in) deep and the same distance apart.

SEASON: Late April–early May
HARDINESS: Fully hardy
HEIGHT: 35cm (14in)
DIVISION: 3 (Triumph)

Dwarf Tulips

Tulipa 'Berlioz'

The flowers of 'Berlioz' have slightly pointed petals of lemon-yellow, the base on the inside a golden-yellow. The outsides of the petals are flushed with red. The foliage is distinctly mottled with purplish brown. This is an excellent tulip to use in pots. It was introduced in 1942 by Van Tubergen Ltd, one of an orchestra of Kaufmanniana tulips that includes 'Chopin', 'Glück' and 'Giuseppe Verdi'. Plant 15cm (6in) deep and the same distance apart.

SEASON: Mid March
HARDINESS: Fully hardy
HEIGHT: 20cm (8in)
DIVISION: 12 (Kaufmanniana)

Tulipa clusiana
LADY TULIP

Neatly furled buds open to white flowers, tall and thin, widening in sunshine to make a star. They are usually borne singly, occasionally two to a stem, the stem itself reddish where it joins the flower. The flower sits bolt upright with narrow, tapering petals; the backs of the outer ones are washed with crimson, leaving a clear, white edge round the margins. The great beauty of the flower lies inside, where the white is set off against a basal blotch of deep purple. The anthers are the same rich purplish black. Once introduced into Europe, *T. clusiana* quickly adapted and became naturalized particularly in dampish fields in southern Europe, where it wandered freely by underground stolons. For a while in the 1920s and 1930s it was cultivated as a popular cut flower along the French Riviera. Carolus Clusius, the famous seventeenth-century botanist after whom this tulip is named, reported that this tulip had been sent to Florence from Constantinople in 1606. He himself got it from a Florentine called Matthaeus Caccini, and it flowered for him in April 1607. Even then, it was called the 'Lady Tulip'. The English plant lover John Parkinson wrote of it as 'this rare Tulipa, wherewith we have beene but lately acquainted', but gives an accurate description. 'The root hereof is small, covered with a thicke, hard blackish shell or skinne, with a yellowish woollinesse both at the toppe and under the shell… bearing one flower… and is wholly white, both inside and outside of all the leaves [petals], except the three outermost, which have on the backe of them, from the middle towards the edges, a shew of a brownish blush or pale red colour, yet deeper in the midst, and the edges remaining wholly white: the bottoms of all these leaves are of a darke or a dun tawnie colour and the chives [stamens] and tippes of a darking purple or tawnie also. This doth beare seed but seldom in our countrie.' This is a delicate-looking and most attractive tulip, but it can be shy flowering. You need to plant it deeply in a warm, sheltered corner. For a while it may produce only leaves and spread, because of its habit of forming new bulbs at the end of long stolons. After a warm summer it may decide to flower. Several cultivars were raised by Van Tubergen Ltd in 1959 including 'Cynthia', which has creamy yellow flowers, the outsides of the petals flushed red with a green edge. 'Lady Jane' has soft pink flowers, the petals margined in pale ivory. Use it between low mats of thyme, acaena and De Caen anemones. Plant 10–12cm (4–5in) deep and the same distance apart.

SEASON: Mid April

HARDINESS: Fully hardy

HEIGHT: 30–45cm (12–18in)

DIVISION: 15 (Miscellaneous)

HABITAT: Iran, near Shiraz, eastwards to the Himalayas and Tibet

Tulipa humilis

The flowers are cup-shaped, but open to a star in sun, the inner petals longer and wider than the outer ones. There are several selected forms, varying in colour from white to pale pink, crimson and purple. The basal blotch can be yellow, blue or purple and covers at least a third of the petals, with anthers of yellow or purple, matching the base. The name *humilis* means 'low growing' and it is, with the thin, slightly glaucous leaves taller than the flowers. 'Persian Pearl' has flowers of a bright cyclamen-purple, each with a yellow base. The outsides of the petals are washed over with pale greenish grey. 'Eastern Star' has magenta-rose flowers with yellow centres. The first bulbs of this species were sent to England in 1838 by the Austrian explorer Theodor Kotschy, who gathered them above Derwend in the Elbur mountains north of Teheran. They arrived at the home of the Reverend William Herbert, a botanizing parson, who gardened at Spofforth, near Harrogate, Yorkshire, UK. He was responsible for popularizing many of the bulbous plants then being introduced from western Asia, and *T. humilis* flowered in his garden in April 1844. This is an easily grown tulip, excellent for pots and gravelled areas, though the buds will not develop if the bulbs are starved of moisture in spring. Grow it through the sprawling arms of *Euphorbia myrsinites*. Plant 10–12cm (4–5in) deep and the same distance apart.

SEASON: Late March
HARDINESS: Fully hardy
HEIGHT: 10cm (4in)
DIVISION: 15 (Miscellaneous)
HABITAT: South-eastern Turkey, north and west Iran, northern Iraq and Azerbaijan, growing on rocky slopes or thin alpine turf just below the snow line at 1,000–3,500m (3,300–11,700ft)

Tulipa linifolia Batalinii Group 'Bright Gem'
(*T. batalinii* 'Bright Gem') ♛

'Bright Gem' is one of several enchanting, little tulips (others are 'Apricot Jewel', 'Bronze Charm', 'Yellow Jewel') which arose from crosses between red and yellow forms of *T. linifolia*. The foliage is narrow, and the first leaves lie over the ground like starfish. Neat, triangular pyramids of bud open into flowers of rich yellow, with a hint of bronze ('Yellow Jewel' is a paler lemon-yellow). There is a warm, though faint reddish flush on the outsides of the outer petals, which intensifies the colour. The outer petals are slightly longer than the inner ones, and as they age they curl back on themselves. The basal blotch is just a small, round disc of smudgy grey with dark anthers at the centre. These tulips not only return each year but also increase to make a rich mat. Follow them with California poppies sown direct on the ground, then covered with gravel. Plant 10–12cm (4–5in) deep and the same distance apart.

SEASON: Late April
HARDINESS: Fully hardy
HEIGHT: 20cm (8in)
DIVISION: 15 (Miscellaneous)

Tulipa 'Little Beauty' ♛

The foliage is long (up to 19cm/7½in), narrow, channelled and very slightly wavy. It lies flat on the ground in a straggly way. The flower, rich pink-purple, emerges from the centre and sits, like a waterlily, practically on the ground. Even at maturity, 'Little Beauty' is no more than 15cm (6in) tall. But this tulip often has eight petals rather than six, which gives the impression of a full flower, even though it is only 5cm (2in) across. It opens wide to make a beautiful, upright bowl in the sun. The petals are very pointed, and the outer ones are washed on the back with a dull green. At the centre is an indeterminate, white blotch, overlaid with dark, rich blue. The stamens, very dark blackish purple, seem huge in relation to the size of the flower. The colour is startling, and the form very beautiful, as is the case with so many of the species tulips and their offspring. 'Little Beauty' makes an enchanting garden flower, but being so short it needs its own space in the foreground of a bed, or on a scree, perhaps with stokesia behind and dwarf agapanthus. Plant 10–12cm (4–5in) deep and the same distance apart.

SEASON: April
HARDINESS: Fully hardy
HEIGHT: 15cm (6in)
DIVISION: 15 (Miscellaneous)

Tulipa orphanidea 'Flava'

Tulipa orphanidea is a very variable species, found in Greece, Bulgaria and Turkey where it grows among stands of *Pinus nigra*, in cornfields and on stony, mountain slopes up to 2,000m (6,500ft). It is named after Theodoros Orphanides, professor of botany at Athens University, who found it in 1857, growing on Mount Malevo in the Greek Peloponnese. It has narrow foliage and beautifully shaped flowers: very neat and sharp when in bud, the pointed petals opening into a poised bloom of enormous charm. Some flowers of this species are bright red or orange-brown, but 'Flava' is yellow, the petals narrowly edged and feathered with red. They seem paper thin, showing the green veins that run down the length of each petal. Some flowers are yellower than others. There is a smudgy, dark blotch at the base of each flower and dark, almost purple stamens dusted with yellowish pollen. It is a real beauty, in form as well as colour. Plant 10–12cm (4–5in) deep and the same distance apart.

SEASON: Late April
HARDINESS: Fully hardy
HEIGHT: 21cm (8½in)
DIVISION: 15 (Miscellaneous)

Tulipa orphanidea
Whittallii Group
(*T. whittallii*) ♀

An outstanding tulip with neat, pointed petals of burnt orange-caramel, very distinct and unusual. The outer petals are smaller than the inner ones and are flushed with a pale creamy buff on the reverse. A sharp, thin buff line is drawn, as with a ruler, up the midribs of the inner petals. The flower makes a perfect bud with all the petals meeting at a sharp point in the middle. At the base is a smoky, indeterminate blotch, greenish black with a yellow halo, the dark colour drifting slightly up the veins of the petals, like watercolour paint on wet paper. The filaments are dark green or olive, the anthers almost black. The margins of the leaves are sometimes tipped with deep red, and the stem is also dark at the top, where it meets the flower. Though small, this is an excellent garden tulip, growing well and increasing freely. It is a native of the eastern Mediterranean, found especially round Izmir (Smyrna) in western Turkey and was introduced from the wild by Edward Whittall (1851–1917), a descendant of an English family who had settled in Izmir and founded an export company, Whittall & Co. As a result of hunting trips, Whittall became interested in the flowers of western Anatolia, and eventually horticulture became his main business. His own garden at Bornova near Izmir was filled with rare plants. Whittall first sent bulbs of what was then called *T. whittallii* to Henry Elwes (1846–1922), a keen amateur botanist who gardened at Colesborne in Gloucestershire, UK (he is better known for his snowdrops than for tulips). Thank heavens he did. This is my all-time favourite tulip. Years and years of growing has not yet brought in front of me anything I like better. Set it in front of mounds of *Euphorbia pithyusa* or *E. cyparissias* 'Fens Ruby'. Plant 10–12cm (4–5in) deep and the same distance apart.

SEASON: Late April–early May
HARDINESS: Fully hardy
HEIGHT: 30cm (12in)
DIVISION: 15 (Miscellaneous)

Tulipa saxatilis Bakeri Group (*T. bakeri*)

The leaves are bright green and slightly shiny. From them arises a slender stem carrying a single, erect, mauve-purple flower (very occasionally two flowers), which is bell-shaped, the petals long and curved in on themselves. The backs of the outer petals are stained green, while the inner petals have a well-defined green rib up their backs. There is an unusually large basal blotch which covers the bottom third of the petals with bright yellow, circled by a ring of muddy white. The stamens are orange. It is a Cretan endemic, found on the high flat Omalos plain, in old vineyards and olive terraces, and also on rocky cliffs and screes. It is named after George Percival Baker of Sevenoaks in Kent, UK, the man who first showed it at the Royal Horticultural Society in 1895. It is not flamboyant, compared with the huge, wild beauties of central Asia, but it is a charmer. The best form is called 'Lilac Wonder', which is prolific and easy. Plant 10–12cm (4–5in) deep and the same distance apart.

SEASON: Mid April
HARDINESS: Fully hardy
HEIGHT: 15cm (6in)
DIVISION: 15 (Miscellaneous)

Tulipa sylvestris

This is a leafy species, the foliage long, narrow, grey-green and vigorous, though the general habit of the plant is somewhat straggling. The golden, scented flowers open from slightly drooping buds, held at right angles to the stem, so you can understand why early growers thought that this was not a tulip but a strange kind of daffodil. The outer petals are netted over with green, with a touch of maroon at each tip. They turn back on themselves, even when the flower is in bud. All the petals are long and narrow, very pointed, and there is a pronounced, green midrib up the outside of the inner petals. The stem is slender, but surprisingly strong, tinged sometimes with red where it joins the flower. From early times, *T. sylvestris* was known as a weed of cultivated land, especially vineyards, described as early as 1576. It has a strongly stoloniferous habit, and may have spread with the movement of vine stock. It has been found in northern France, Germany, Switzerland, Belgium, Holland, Sweden and England, usually in places that suggest it has escaped from gardens. The nurseryman Claridge Druce remembered seeing it in the Thames valley in southern England where it had become naturalized. 'It occurs in Christ Church meadows – I have seen a flower', he wrote, 'but it was doubtless originally planted. So, too, at Besilsleigh, where it flowered last year (1927) and there is a relic of Speaker Lenthall's garden. So, too, in a coppice at Charlbury where

it is a relic of Lord Jenkinson's Pleasaunce and in Sarsdon where it is in Lord Dacre's park.' It often persists in grassy places where it is not noticed, for the leaves are thin and grassy themselves, but after a good hot summer flowers will appear, as they do at several sites in Britain. I have seen wonderful great spreads in Cambridgeshire, Lincolnshire and Nottinghamshire, where *T. sylvestris* grows in grassy meadows, and more surprisingly I have also seen it poking out from hedgerows in Dorset. As its name suggests, it does not mind light shade. It is tempting to suggest planting it in grass, but it will only survive where the grass is not too coarse and overwhelming. Otherwise, give it a space of its own, with *Euphorbia cyparissias* or dwarf iris for company. Plant 10–12cm (4–5in) deep and the same distance apart.

SEASON: Mid April
HARDINESS: Fully hardy
HEIGHT: 30cm (12in)
DIVISION: 15 (Miscellaneous)
HABITAT: Nobody is sure where this species originated, but it is quite widely naturalized in Europe, western Anatolia, north Africa, central Asia and Siberia

Tulipa vvedenskyi

The showy, cup-shaped flower is bright crimson-red, a bulky bloom with broad, pointed petals, all of which have a twist in them. The outer petals curl away from the centre and are flushed on their backs with purple. The backs of the inner petals are washed with yellow. There is an indeterminate, plain yellow blotch at the base of the petals, which streaks up into the red, but it does not extend far. The leaves are in proportion to the flower, broad, glaucous and closely set on the stem. *Tulipa vvedenskyi* is one of the central Asian tribe of tulips and is named after the Russian botanist A I Vvedensky. 'Tangerine Beauty' is a form with flowers that are more orange than red. Plant 10–12cm (4–5in) deep and the same distance apart.

SEASON: Late April

HARDINESS: Fully hardy

HEIGHT: 25cm (10in)

DIVISION: 15 (Miscellaneous)

HABITAT: Valley of the river Angren in western Tien Shan, Uzbekistan

NEXT PAGE From *Tulipa linifolia*, with its brilliant red flowers, comes a whole host of excellent dwarf tulips such as 'Bright Gem' and 'Bronze Charm'.

Uvularia (Convallariaceae)

MERRYBELLS

Uvularia grandiflora ♔

Merrybells is an odd name as this is rather a recessive plant, quiet and woodsy. The top of each stem droops over soft yellow, tubular flowers; they also droop, so you could never call this a show-stopper. Give *U. grandiflora* the companions it has in the wild: disporums, erythroniums, osmundas and *Trillium grandiflorum*. It needs shade and cool, damp, humus-rich soil. Set the rhizomes 8–10cm (3½–4in) deep and 30cm (12in) apart.

SEASON: April–May
HARDINESS: Fully hardy
HEIGHT: 38cm (15in)
HABITAT: North America (Quebec south to Georgia and west to Kansas)

Veltheimia (Hyacinthaceae)

Veltheimia bracteata ♀

Lush, shining leaves (10cm/4in long, 5cm/2in wide when young) appear in a basal cluster long before the flowers. The stem, darkly spotted, starts to grow in mid-winter but the flower spike develops incredibly slowly, after six to eight weeks finally making a head like a miniature red hot poker, just 10cm (4in) long. It is a pretty, greyish kind of pink, the spike made up from up to 50 long, narrow tubes which hang down round the stem. At first the tubes are closed at the bottom; when they open, neatly frilled, they look greenish because of the stamens crowded in the mouth of the tube. Veltheimias, named after an eighteenth-century German botanist, August von Veltheim, were favourite pot plants for nineteenth-century gardeners, decorating Victorian parlours along with aspidistras and asparagus fern. Now, inexplicably, they seem less popular. They are tender plants so need to be grown where winter temperatures do not drop below 5°C (41°F). For most of us that will mean a greenhouse or conservatory – though, like hippeastrums, they can be raised quite satisfactorily on a cool windowsill indoors. They do not need heat or full sun. Just give them plenty of light. Use a loam-based compost mixed with sharp sand (two parts compost to one part sand) and set the bulb with its neck just above the surface of the compost. Feed and water well while the plant is in active growth, but during its summer resting period (it is practically evergreen) keep it barely moist. Gradually, *V. bracteata* will develop into a fat clump and will need repotting, but do not be in too much of a hurry to move it on. The roots are fragile and hate being disturbed.

SEASON: Late February
HARDINESS: Tender
HEIGHT: 48cm (19in)
HABITAT: South Africa (Eastern Cape) where it grows on rocky hillsides

Watsonia (Iridaceae)

This genus gets its name from Sir William Watson (1715–87), a physician and apothecary at London's Foundling Hospital. The showy spikes of tubular flowers are certainly worth having, but watsonias, being half hardy, are risky things to grow outdoors (though this has never stopped gardeners growing gladiolus, which have the same needs). It is probably safer to start off the corms inside in pots of loam-based compost mixed with sharp sand. Either keep them permanently in pots in a greenhouse or conservatory, or transfer them outside when all danger of frost has passed. In a pot you can plant the corms more closely than you would outside.

Watsonia borbonica 'Arderne's White'

This is a white-flowered form of *W. borbonica* found in the 1880s in the Worcester division of the Western Cape by H M Arderne, an enthusiastic collector of South African plants. It is now naturalized in parts of California, where it was first introduced as a garden plant. There may be up to 20 flared, long-tubed flowers on each branched spike, rising out of clumps of sword-shaped leaves. Outdoors, plant the corms of 'Arderne's White' 10–15cm (4–6in) deep and 30cm (12in) apart.

SEASON: July–August
HARDINESS: Half hardy
HEIGHT: 1m (3ft)

Watsonia pillansii
(*W. beatricis*)

Collected in the Montagu Pass by the botanist Neville Pillans, who worked in the herbarium at the Kirstenbosch Botanic Garden in Cape Town, this is a slow-growing, elegant plant producing unbranched spikes of perhaps 30 terracotta-coloured flowers from sheaves of sword-shaped leaves. In ideal conditions *W. pillansii* is evergreen – a natural companion for cannas and other exotic plants such as *Beschornia yuccoides*. Outdoors, plant the corms 10–15cm (4–6in) deep and 30cm (12in) apart.

SEASON: July–August
HARDINESS: Half hardy
HEIGHT: 60cm (24in)
HABITAT: South Africa (Western Cape, Eastern Cape, KwaZulu-Natal, Mpumalanga) where it grows on grassy slopes

OPPOSITE Watsonias are only half hardy, but if carefully overwintered, *Watsonia pillansii* makes an elegant summer companion for exotic cannas.

Zantedeschia (Araceae)

ARUM LILY, CALLA LILY

Zantedeschia aethiopica ♀

Zantesdeschias, named after the nineteenth-century Italian physician and botanist Giovanni Zantedeschi, are handsome enough to grow for their foliage alone; in a mild winter it is almost evergreen. The leaves are huge, tough, arrow-shaped beauties at least 40cm (16in) long and 25cm (10in) wide, the ends curling over each other where the leaf joins the stem. The spathes of the spectacular, white flowers can be up to 15cm (6in) long, thick and fleshy, with a creamy yellow spadix poking up from the centre. The blooms unroll from tightly scrolled stems of pale green. Flowering occurs over several months, and each bloom lasts for at least three weeks; they are lovely at all stages of their development, giving, at the end, an insouciant twist to their pointed spathes. They are naturals for streamside planting, where they look excellent with yellow flag iris and Bowles's golden sedge (*Carex elata* 'Aurea'); if you want to plant them at the side of a pond, use a planting basket 25–30cm (10–12in) across filled with soil and sink the basket up to 30cm (12in) deep in the water.

SEASON: Late April–July
HARDINESS: Fully hardy (borderline)
HEIGHT: 90cm (36in)
HABITAT: South Africa and Lesotho where it grows in wet, marshy places

Zantedeschia aethiopica 'Crowborough' ♀

'Crowborough' is a splendidly accommodating arum lily, white-flowered, discovered in a Sussex garden, where it was growing happily in a mixed herbaceous border. Until then, gardeners had supposed that all arum lilies needed a bog, if not a streamside, if they were to flourish. Established plants make strong, weed-suppressing clumps, good with *Iris sibirica* and bronze fennel. Give them good, rich, damp ground in sun or dappled shade, and in chilly areas protect the rhizomes with a thick winter mulch. Plant the rhizomes 15cm (6in) deep and 60cm (24in) apart.

SEASON: Late April–July
HARDINESS: Fully hardy (borderline)
HEIGHT: 90cm (36in)

Zantedeschia aethiopica 'Green Goddess' ♀

'Green Goddess' has long (20cm/8in), drooping, white spathes tipped and veined with green. Flower arrangers love it (and arum lilies make wonderful, long-lasting cut flowers), but in a garden setting 'Crowborough' has more clout. Try 'Green Goddess' with the yellow flag (*Iris pseudacorus*) or contrast the fine, arrow-shaped leaves with the deeply cut foliage of dark-stemmed *Ligularia przewalskii*. Plant the rhizomes 15cm (6in) deep and 60cm (24in) apart.

SEASON: Late April–July
HARDINESS: Fully hardy (borderline)
HEIGHT: 90cm (36in)

Z

Zephyranthes (Amaryllidaceae)

RAIN FLOWER

Zephyranthes candida

The rushy foliage, bright shining green, like a tussock of grass, is almost evergreen. Then, late in August, the first bud pushes up on a bright green stem that, at first, looks as though it is going to be another leaf. It bursts from its papery sheath to produce a flower of pristine whiteness, in form rather like a crocus. The base is tinged with lime-green, inside and out; otherwise the whole bloom is pure, shining white with six bright gold stamens standing up in a central crown. *Zephyranthes candida* is an enchanting thing, its name meaning 'flower of the west wind' for in its home it comes into bloom in response to the first of the late summer rains. The best display I have ever seen was in a narrow border under the vinery wall at West Dean garden in Sussex, UK, where, with its short, grassy, well-behaved foliage, it was still in bloom in the middle of November. In a border no more than 30cm (12in) wide, Z. *candida* grew with hermodactylus and nerines, an excellent combination. Give it rich, moist, well-drained ground in full sun. Plant in spring, setting the bulbs 10cm (4in) deep and 10cm (4in) apart.

SEASON: Late August

HARDINESS: Frost hardy

HEIGHT: 30cm (12in)

HABITAT: Argentina (especially in marshy areas along the river Plate) and Uruguay

Zigadenus (Melanthiaceae)

SEASON: Mid June
HARDINESS: Frost hardy
HEIGHT: 50cm (20in)
HABITAT: USA (Tennessee west to Texas
and Kansas) where it grows in open
woods and grassland

Zigadenus nuttallii

From grassy, grey-green leaves rise tall, wiry stems, covered in a greyish bloom. The stems divide into branches, which sometimes bear just a single flower, sometimes more. They are tiny, each one creamy green with a distinct grey-green wash on the backs of the petals. The most surprising feature of the flower is the glistening, lime-green blotch (the nectary) at the base of each of the petals clustered round the domed centre with its curling stamens. *Zigadenus nuttallii* could never be called a showy thing, but it is airy and elegant – also extremely poisonous. Excellent in a pot, where you can give it the close attention it deserves. Otherwise give *Z. nuttallii* good, rich soil with plenty of leaf mould. It is most frequently sold already growing in a pot, but if you acquire bulbs plant them 10cm (4in) deep and 10cm (4in) apart.

How to grow bulbs

LEFT TO RIGHT *Tulipa* 'Bleu Aimable', *Tulipa sprengeri*, *Tulipa* 'Ballerina', *Tulipa* 'Spring Green', *Tulipa* 'Generaal de Wet', *Tulipa* 'Snow Parrot'

Growing bulbs

Gardeners might seek rules. Plants do not know they exist, but in this chapter you will find some general guidelines on planting bulbs, corms, tubers and rhizomes. To get the best results, however, you need to understand your own patch and what it can offer, then match those offers with the plants that can make best use of them. That is why it is so important to know something about where bulbs grow in the wild and what kind of conditions they find there. Sometimes, bulbs demand special treatment, and this chapter also explains how you can grow bulbs in frames and cool greenhouses, even indoors. No other group of plants is so staggeringly beautiful; they are worth any amount of trouble.

The first thing to be said is that it is unrealistic to expect every bulb you plant to produce a flower every year. Certainly each newly bought bulb should flower – the clever producers will have seen to that – but afterwards flowering will depend entirely on the growing conditions you have provided. In the wild, even in the conditions that most suit them, only a proportion of any group of bulbs (a different portion each year) will actually be in flower each season. The rest will be building up to what for them is an extraordinary expenditure of resources. They have to flower, because producing seed with its infinite capacity for slight difference offers future generations the best chance of survival. When you think about where to put bulbs in your garden, you must bear in mind their natural habitats, which are provided for all the species included in this book. It is your job as a gardener to try and persuade these treasures that they are at home, persuade them that a bed of damp clay and a summer of cloud and drizzle are a fair exchange for life out on the shale-strewn slopes of the great Tien Shan mountains where their winters are spent under a deep blanket of snow and summers are hot enough to burst a thermometer. Gardeners expect a lot of bulbs. Why, for instance, should a gladiolus, born to be dashed with the spray of an African waterfall, settle into an allotment in Yorkshire? I don't know why. I am just thankful there is enough elastic built into the plant's genes to allow it to make the transition.

The second thing you need to understand about cultivating bulbs is that no garden will provide exactly the same growing conditions as any other garden. If you know your garden well, you can already distinguish between its various microclimates. Bulbs will make those distinctions even more delicately. They will do their best to please, but if you have been crass enough to think of your own needs before theirs ('I must, I simply MUST have just that shade of blue in my shady corner…'), they may die. Some will die however much you try to please them. When you have killed the same thing three times in succession, it is probably best to give up trying to grow it. One day, you will realize what it was you were doing wrong. In the meantime, gather as much knowledge as you can of where each bulb lives. This is the best indication of what it will be looking for in your garden.

OPPOSITE Lily bulbs do not have any kind of protective coat to cover their scales and need to be handled carefully.

Because no one garden is like any other, it is perhaps worth pointing out that I garden in the south-west of Britain, a fairly soft part of the country, close enough to the sea to ensure that frosts rarely come in September. My experience of bulbs is coloured by the place in which I have grown them, where the climate is damper than they like, and cold frames have been useful to aid the summer baking. For most of my gardening life, I have worked with a clay soil, stiff and badly drained. In these conditions, growing bulbs in pots is often a more viable alternative to growing them in the ground. Now I have friable, nutritious, fast-draining greensand, which gardeners are not supposed to get until they go to heaven. It is not by chance that commercial bulb growers are to be found in the eastern counties of Britain (Lincolnshire, Cambridgeshire) where there is less rain and the soils are light and well-drained, like the ground that the Dutch growers have brought into such profitable production in The Netherlands. Many bulbs will be dreaming of a home on fertile, alkaline soil, well-drained but also moisture-retentive.

Soil matters, because by far the greater proportion of bulbs prefer to grow in a bright, sunny situation on light ground that warms up quickly in spring. Good drainage is vital. On heavy soils you may have to work hard to provide suitable conditions, and the work will involve monumental quantities of grit, under the bulb, over the bulb and on top of the ground in which the bulb is growing. But requirements differ, as you would expect, and you will find specific cultivation details included with each entry in this book. Suggestions are given, too, for planting depth and distance, but these are no more than guides. On heavy soils you may find it better to plant more shallowly. On light soils you can plant more deeply. In the wild, tulip bulbs may be sitting 25–30cm (10–12in) deep, but on the inhospitable mountains on which they often grow they need that insulating layer of rock and shale to protect them from the worst extremes of heat and cold. Some bulbs produce 'droppers', small bulblets that drop down into the soil beneath the parent bulb and effectively pull the whole growing unit deeper into the ground, no matter where you first set it. *Tulipa sprengeri* is notorious for pulling itself down into the depths of the earth. It is expensive to buy, not because it is difficult to grow, but because it is laborious to harvest. Conversely, most rhizomes like to be set rather shallow in the soil.

The best time to plant bulbs is when they are dormant. So spring-flowering bulbs are usually planted in autumn, crocus and daffodils first (from September onwards), tulips last (not before early November). Summer-flowering bulbs such as crinums, eucomis and galtonias are usually planted in early spring. The trickiest subjects for suppliers to deal with are the late summer- and autumn-flowering bulbs such as amaryllis, colchicum, cyclamen and autumn-flowering crocus. They are not sufficiently dormant to be sent out in spring, but too advanced to go out with the spring-flowering bulbs in autumn. Suppliers will often offer a separate delivery of autumn-flowering bulbs to arrive in the second half of August. Some plants such as cyclamen hate to be dried out completely, and you will get much better results from buying a growing plant than you will from planting a dry tuber. Snowdrops also hate it, and for years the advice has been to acquire them 'in the green', that is straight after they have finished flowering but while they are still in leaf, when clumps can be split up and the bulbs replanted. Now, some suppliers prefer to wait until the foliage has died down and send out snowdrop bulbs in summer, packed in damp compost. Some bulbs (the smaller alliums, in particular) have such a short dormant period that they will often still be in leaf when they are sent out, but reputable suppliers try to send these damp-packed too.

Size matters. The best flowers generally come from the biggest bulbs, but if you are buying hyacinths to grow outside then the biggest will be the most easily blown over. Here, the most sensible purchase will be a bulb less than 18cm (7in) around the waist. Bulbs of all kinds must be sound, though, and you can test this by pressing gently on the basal plate to check that it is firm. Bulbs of dwarf iris should be a clean creamy white. Black streaks may indicate that the bulbs have the dreaded inkspot disease, which will prevent them flowering well. The bulbs of lilies and fritillaries are not protected by any kind of tunic, so you should check that they are still plump. Reputable bulb suppliers will send them out packed in wood shavings or something similar to prevent them drying out.

When you are planting, you need to set bulbs the right way up, which is obvious if you are handling a daffodil bulb but not always so obvious with a cyclamen (roots often grow from the top of their tubers). It is positively tricky with things such as *Anemone coronaria* whose tubers look like dried-up gobbets of dung. If in doubt plant the bulb on its side (if it has one).

Planting depths are suggested for each bulb in this book, but depth is a variable measure and will depend to some extent on the kind of soil you have. Experiment (and note down the results. If you don't, you will have forgotten by the time the next season comes around). As a rough guide, set the bulb in a hole three times deeper than the bulb's height (remembering that cyclamen and many rhizomes prefer to be shallowly planted).

Take time to prepare the planting ground, loosening the soil, taking out weeds, adding grit to very heavy, sticky clay. Unless you are saving seed, remember to deadhead. If you do, the plant will be able to use all its resources to prepare the bulb for another season, rather than ripening its seedpod. For the same reason, you should never cut down the foliage or flowering stems of bulbs. All the goodness they contain must be reabsorbed by the bulb if it is to survive. If you use fertilizers, stick to ones that are high in potash and phosphate (which encourage flowers and roots) and low on nitrogen. Nitrogen encourages leafy growth, and although bulbs need their leaves it is best not to get foliage too lush and soft as it is then more prone to aphid attack and fungal disease. Lilies in pots will probably need feeding every two weeks. Small bulbs, growing in the open ground, can be given a feed when they first emerge. Bulbs growing in turf should not be fed at all as fertilizer will boost the growth of the grass which may then overwhelm the bulbs. All bulbs, though, can be planted with bonemeal, a slow-acting,

long-lasting treat to help them on their way. The only disadvantage of bonemeal is that foxes think it may signify a meal and dig up the bulbs before discovering they have been cheated.

The length of time that your bulbs stay in flower will be entirely dependent on weather conditions. Long, cool springs extend the flowering period. If there is a sudden, hot spell in early May, tulips will bolt through their routine at top speed and there is absolutely nothing you can do about it. Just enjoy them while they are there.

The simplest route to happiness is to work out what likes you (scillas and camassias for instance both thrive on heavy soil) and then grow a lot of it. But gardeners are not content with that. They like to push the boundaries, grow things with which they are unfamiliar. And your garden may provide many different possibilities for displaying bulbs: in beds and borders, at the foot of a sunny wall, naturalized in grass, used as ground cover between trees and shrubs, on a gravelled scree, in pots, in a greenhouse or bulb frame and indoors.

Beds and borders

Instinctively the gardener will think of showy subjects to use in beds and borders: hyacinths, tulips, crown imperials (*Fritillaria imperialis*), alliums, iris, galtonias, gladioli (especially the elegant *Gladiolus murielae*, which used to be called acidanthera), zantedeschia, lilies. These nine between them will furnish a bed in splendour for at least seven months from March until September. The chief difficulty is remembering where you have put them. Gardeners all know they are supposed to keep records of these things, but do they? It is

enchanting to have the surprise of forgotten lily shoots spearing up alongside your columbines. Hideous, though, to spear bulbs that are still underground on the end of your fork while you are weeding. So the safest thing in beds and borders is to plant deep rather than shallow and to mulch the beds thickly to suppress annual weeds and cut down on the amount you need to disturb the soil. On heavy soils, excavate a decent hole for each bulb, put a hummock of grit at the bottom of the hole, perch the bulb on the hummock and put more grit on top of it. Backfill the hole with earth mixed with a handful of bonemeal and firm down gently. This sounds a bore, and is, but the grit improves drainage round the bulb and also goes a little way to deter the small, black underground slugs that inhabit heavy, clay soils. They are very partial to tulip and lily bulbs. As well as suppressing weeds, the mulch will provide food

ABOVE Tulips grow with *Anemone coronaria* in mixed colours beside a wall at The Old Rectory, Duntisbourne Rous, Gloucestershire. Design by Mary Keen.

OPPOSITE Soft pink spikes of gladiolus are combined here with gypsophila, white cosmos and the purple heads of *Verbena bonariensis*.

for the bulb. The bonemeal will, too, and slowly, which is what they need. I use a lot of bonemeal when planting bulbs, a handful in each hole. Although planting distances are given for each bulb in this book, for the most eye-catching effects in beds and borders you may want to plant more closely.

Hot spots

Many plants will be competing for a garden's hot spots, those places (always too few) where you can risk growing bulbs, corms, tubers and rhizomes that you know are not fully hardy. There will always be an element of gamble in this. There may be a run of eight mild winters then suddenly a monstrous one, with prolonged, deep-seated frosts that will seek out and destroy these seemingly established treasures. But the joy of the eight seasons of success will persuade you to try again. Optimism is built into a gardener's soul.

The most likely hot spot for bulbs will be at the base of a sunny wall, but you will already have bagged some of the available space for your tender climbers. Fortunately bulbs do not seem to mind sharing space. My best clump of belladonnas (*Amaryllis belladonna*) grows at the foot of a vine trained out against the south-facing front of the house. Belladonnas, along with freesias, *Iris unguicularis*, ixias, nerines, *Ornithogalum arabicum*, *Pancratium maritimum*, schizostylis, sternbergias, tigridias and *Zephyranthes candida*, might be among your first choices for such a situation, though each of the above will have slightly different cultural requirements. The zephyranthes, for example, needs a moister soil than *Iris unguicularis* (see individual entries for notes on cultivation). But reserve your hot spots for bulbs that either need extra shelter during winter or as much baking as possible in summer. Or both. Start with the easy ones: belladonna and Algerian iris.

ABOVE Magenta-coloured *Gladiolus communis* subsp. *byzantinus* is a European native and naturalizes surprisingly well in grass, provided it is not too coarse.

Naturalizing bulbs in grass

The vogue for 'wild' gardening has led inevitably to an increased interest in naturalizing bulbs in grass, an attempt to re-create the flower-rich meadows that are such a potent part of the romantic's dream of how things used to be. Unfortunately it is not as easy to do as it seems. Although a bulb's natural habitat may be alpine pasture, there is a world of difference between the fine, thin grass you find on a mountain slope and the lush, rich turf that is typical in the well-fed soil of most gardens. Even fields of un-improved pasture are fairly rare. A bulb

OPPOSITE Mixed plantings of anemones and narcissi fill the ground under trees in an Oxfordshire woodland.

that is perfectly able to fight for living space on the Karatau mountains of Kazakh-stan may be completely overcome by the opposition in more temperate areas, where growth of all things is lusher and more dominant. But in a general sense you should (always depending on local conditions) be able to naturalize camassias, crocus, some fritillaries (including the reasonably robust *Fritillaria pyrenaica*), *Gladiolus communis* subsp. *byzantinus* (which I had growing among cow parsley in a patch of rough grass in our old rectory garden), leucojum, a few lilies such as *L. martagon* and *L. pyrenaicum*, some ornithogalums and *Scilla bifolia*. And daffodils, of course, which will grow anywhere. Avoid mixtures of daffodils, and instead plant separate spreads of just a few different kinds. It is a mistake to use huge, beefy daffodils if you are trying to create a wild-looking scene. Stick to light-limbed types such as late-flowering old pheasant's eye (*Narcissus poeticus* var. *recurvus*) or species such as *N. obvallaris* – the Tenby daffodil. I planted the Tenby daffodil for patriotic reasons, but it is a good plant, and would probably behave as well even in an Englishman's garden. It grows about 30cm (12in) high on stiff stems and has trumpets and petals of bright golden-yellow. Until the middle of the nineteenth century the Tenby daffodil grew in vast quantities around Tenby in Pembrokeshire, Wales. Then an agent from Covent Garden appeared on the scene and encouraged local collectors to bring him bulbs which he sent by the truck load to London. One farmer, Rees of Holloway Farm, sold every wild bulb in his fields for £80. Forgive him. It is a whole lot more than he would have earned that year from his sheep.

Remember that the later the flowers come into bloom, the longer you will have to wait before you can cut the grass. Some gardeners cannot stand looking at the blown-over messy aspect that uncut grass presents any time after late June. Bear this in mind when you are choosing what to plant. If you are a tidy-minded soul, stick to early-flowering bulbs. Crocus are enchanting in grass, as long as the turf they are growing in is short enough. To provide the best conditions for these earliest flowers, you need to mow late in the autumn season, so the bulbs can spear through grass that is tight and low and does not get in their way. By late May, crocus leaves will have died down and it will be safe to mow again. As a very rough rule, you need to leave at least six weeks after flowering before you mow.

Planting in grass can be done in two ways. A long-handled bulb planter (do not buy any other kind) pulls up a plug of earth intact so you can pop a bulb into the hole and jam the plug on top. Each time you make a new hole, the plug is pushed up out of the top of the planter, so in a relatively short time you can make a lot of holes, with the plugs lying conveniently alongside. Or you can strip the turf from an area by marking it into parallel strips with the edge of a sharp spade. Use the spade to lever up the turf along the strip, rolling it up as you go, like a piece of carpet. When you have cleared the area you want to plant, loosen the surface of the soil, sprinkle it with bonemeal and plant as normal with a trowel. When you have finished, unroll the strips of turf back over the bare earth and lightly tamp them down to fit. Some lawnmowers do quite a good 'rolling' job, if you raise the blades high enough and run the mower over the disturbed area.

Bulbs as ground cover between trees and shrubs

The ground beneath trees and shrubs is often under-used in a garden but there are plenty of bulbs that will thrive in these conditions, particularly if the trees and shrubs are deciduous. The early bulbs can charge up into the light and flower before leaves develop on the canopy above them. By the time the ground is shaded out, they will have done their thing and be ready to disappear below ground again. Some bulbs positively enjoy dappled shade (think of a bluebell wood in England or trilliums growing in the wild in the States). And although you may think of the ground under trees and shrubs as being rather a hungry and thirsty place to grow, some bulbs benefit from the fact that the ground is kept extra dry in summer by their companion's hungry roots. The best spread of *Tulipa sprengeri* I ever saw grew under the wide canopy of an old flowering cherry. Generations of self-seeding had spread the original planting into a vast pool of red lapping out into the surrounding grass, usefully thin there because it was starved by the tree's roots.

For planting beneath trees and shrubs you might think of aconites, anemones such as *A. blanda* and *A. nemorosa* (natural woodlanders), arisaemas, arums such as *A. italicum* (which is particularly good in heavy soils, with its beautiful, marbled leaves), chionodoxa, colchicums, lilies-of-the-valley, cyclamen (especially autumn-flowering *C. hederifolium* because its leaves are so handsome and last so much longer than its flowers), erythroniums, snowdrops, some shade-loving lilies (especially species such as *L. canadense*), grape hyacinths, paris, scillas in quantity and trilliums (though you need to remember that some are happier on soil that is acid rather than alkaline). Bulbs or tubers with good foliage (I am thinking particularly of arums and cyclamen) are especially useful because the leaves are around so much longer than the flowers and make superb ground cover. Specific growing instructions are given with each entry in this book. Be aware which of your chosen subjects prefer alkaline conditions and which acid. The latter benefit from a yearly mulch of leaf mould.

Gravelled areas and scree beds

Of all growing areas in a garden this is perhaps the one that most closely mimics the kind of habitat that bulbs from the Mediterranean areas eastwards into Turkey and central Asia will understand. Those gardening west and north of these fabled areas will rarely be able to give bulbs the baking that they long for in summer, but cloches help. If that proves to be not enough, shift the sulky bulbs to a frame, where you can manipulate growing conditions in a more radical way.

The best garden screes are on open, sunny, sloping sites, the poorer the ground the better. If the slope is on raised ground with a retaining wall, the flowers will be closer to you as you bend to admire them. You will pick up any scent more easily, too. Plenty of clinker under the topsoil will aid drainage, and when you have planted your bulbs you can top-dress the area

with 6mm (¼in) gravel. This keeps the necks of the bulbs dry when they come through the ground and prevents soil splashing up to dirty the petals. In summer, gravel sops up heat and keeps the ground underneath warmer than it might otherwise be.

But old areas of yard or gravelled drive, not regularly used by cars, also make good growing areas for some bulbs. In our old garden, *Crocus tommasinianus* 'Whitewell Purple' refused to settle in the clay soil of the bank where I originally put it, but somehow got its seeds down onto the old driveway in front of the house and grew there magnificently, with absolutely no help from me. In our new garden, *Crocus tommasinianus* 'Roseus' has settled very successfully in a pebbled area under some lollipop bay trees.

Crocus, particularly treasures such as *C. malyi* or *C. imperati*, are naturals for a scree bed. So are some of the smaller alliums such as *A. narcissiflorum* and *A. cernuum*, the dwarf eucomis *E. vandermerwei*, dwarf iris such as the heartbreaking *I. histrioides* 'Lady Beatrix Stanley' or *I. kolpakowskiana*, *Triteleia ixioides* 'Starlight' or some of the dwarf tulips: *T. orphanidea* Whittallii Group (my all-time favourite tulip) or the usefully late *T. linifolia* Batalinii Group 'Bright Gem'. You may need occasionally to top up the gravel on top of the scree, but generally these areas are low-maintenance. If you are lucky, your bulbs will begin to seed about, and the less disturbed the seedlings are the better. If the area needs to earn its keep during summer, scatter seed of light-limbed annuals (California poppy, love-in-a-mist) directly onto the gravel in early autumn or spring. They, too, will begin to seed themselves, so eventually you establish a completely self-sustaining patch.

Bulbs in pots

Gardeners usually use pots in rather prominent situations, so whatever is growing in the pot needs to be able to stand the spotlight. You might have a pair of tubs either side of your front door. You might line some handsome terracotta pots out on a terrace. You might use an important urn or edgily rusted steel box at the end of the garden, framed in an arch, to tempt the eye away from something you would rather not see beyond. So when gardeners choose bulbs for pots, they tend to go for showy subjects such as tulips and lilies, with smaller, shallower pots earlier in the season filled with dwarf *Iris reticulata* or sumptuous crocus such as *Crocus sieberi* subsp. *sublimis* 'Tricolor'.

For an effect you can depend on, you will usually need to replant every year. Only lilies seem happy to settle permanently in

ABOVE *Crocus tommasinianus* 'Whitewell Purple' is an excellent subject for pots as it is early flowering and neat in habit.

OPPOSITE Many Central-Asian bulbs, including tulips, are used to growing on shale-strewn slopes. For them, gravel is a natural environment.

pots where they will clump up and flower as well in subsequent seasons as they do their first. Tulips certainly will not. The best thing to do with tulips once they have flowered is to line them out in a cutting garden or spare piece of ground where they may or may not flower again. Then plan a different show for your pots the following season.

There are a few general points to bear in mind. First, size. The bigger the container, the happier your bulbs will be and the greater the effect of your planting. One big container massed with one (at most two) kinds of bulb will make an unforgettable splash. Three smaller pots scattered in different places can be overlooked. A big container provides a more stable planting environment than a small one. The potting compost does not heat up nor cool down so fast. Watering and feeding are easier (provided there are plenty of 'crocks' at the bottom to allow excess water to drain away).

In exposed situations, use a loam-based compost rather than a multipurpose or coir-based one. Loam-based composts (John Innes No 3 or similar) are heavy. If you have to lug bags upstairs to a balcony or terrace, this is a disadvantage, but a loam compost adds weight to tubs and pots and makes them more stable. A heavy container will be lighter to move round if you use polystyrene chips instead of crocks at the bottom, for drainage. In a light, plastic container, you need weight at the bottom because when your bulbs are in full flower it will become top-heavy.

Provided they have sufficient depth, a wide range of containers can be used for bulbs. Galvanized metal is cool and contemporary, while woven wicker containers give a country feel. Traditional terracotta pots look particularly good planted with sweet-scented *Gladiolus murielae*. Yellow tulips sing out when planted in glazed bowls of bright blue. If your heart is set on a container that does not have drainage holes, use it like a cache-pot. Plant your bulbs in a plain black plastic pot of the right size to fit inside the fancy pot. Set the inner pot on small blocks of wood so that its base is clear of any water that might collect at the bottom of the outer pot.

Window boxes can be a challenge, since they have to fit into a fixed space. Nonetheless, it often pays to get a wooden window box custom-made rather than use a plastic one. If overfilled, plastic window boxes may buckle and bow out in the middle. In sunshine, the plastic may become brittle and crack. A wooden window box (remember to get holes drilled in the bottom) can be stained a different colour each season. Try pale birch-grey with mauve or purple crocus, soft lichen-green with pale cyclamen or, for high drama, black with red tulips.

Pots provide a wonderful way of displaying flowers, of giving them extra prominence, but they offer practical advantages, too. On heavy ground, it is difficult to give bulbs the kind of sharp drainage they often need. In a pot, you can arrange this very easily with plenty of crocks and compost well mixed with grit. In our biggest tubs and containers, I use compost from our own heaps to fill at least half the space. It does not matter if it is only half cooked. The bits of twig and other debris help to keep the growing medium open and well-drained. I fill the top half of

OPPOSITE A huge old copper is crammed with tulips and wallflowers in Mary Keen's garden at The Old Rectory, Duntisbourne Rous, Gloucestershire.

each container with a mixture of bought loam-based compost and gravel or grit (two parts compost to one part 6mm/¼in gravel).

Planting depth and distance are not critical in a container. You can jam in more bulbs than you would if you were planting in open ground. Only with stem-rooting lilies do you need to make sure there is an extra-generous layer of compost over the bulbs. I usually sprinkle granules of slow-release fertilizer on the compost mix and always top off the containers with a layer of 6mm (¼in) gravel. It looks good, keeps the noses of the buds clean as they break through the surface and stops birds tossing the compost out of the pots. To a certain extent, it also deters slugs and snails, but not as much as you might hope.

ABOVE The long-necked goblet flowers of *Crocus etruscus* 'Rosalind' open wide in spring sunshine.

For spring, your first thought for containers might be dwarf iris and crocus, with tulips and lilies in bigger pots to follow on later in the season. But, depending on the pot and the situation, you might also use alliums of reasonable height, *Anemone coronaria* of the De Caen Group, arisaemas (which grow well in pots and fit beautifully into the kind of garden made from banana palms and tree ferns), eucomis, showy fritillaries such as *F. persica* 'Adiyaman', *Gladiolus × colvillii* 'The Bride' or *G. murielae* (a welcome late addition to any garden), hyacinths, some of the larger muscari such as *M. comosum* 'Plumosum', and daffodils. Do not be tempted to plant in the 'layers' that are so much written about, with for instance crocus, daffodils and tulips all planted at different depths in the same pot. It is a ghastly idea. None of the bulbs has the chance to grow really well, and each display will be spoiled by the dying foliage of the thing that came before. If you want three different things, put them in three different pots and give them a proper chance to show you how beautiful they are.

For the 40-odd years that I gardened on clay, I grew most of my tulips in pots as I learned that they did much better in the well-drained compost of a pot than in the ground. In the main the pots were not meant to be seen. They were made from black plastic, not less than 40cm (16in) across, lined out, when planted, in any spare space until the tulips began to push through in spring. Then I would drop the pots into our beds and borders, where 'Bleu Aimable' tulips, for instance, might look good next to *Hosta* 'Krossa Regal' or *Tulipa* 'Spring Green' next to the fountaining new growths of sweet cicely. You do not need to bury the pots themselves. During April and May when the tulips are at their height, there is plenty of other growth – fennel, *Geranium palmatum*, spurges – to disguise the pots. To all intents and purposes the tulips look as though they are springing from the ground. They seem taller, of course, but usually that is an advantage. What you cannot get, with this method, is the nice threading-through that happens when you plant direct in the ground. Your potted flowers are clumped rather than threaded. But if pots make the difference between having tulips or not having them, then clumps are better than nothing. When I was really well-organized (it did not happen often enough) I had pots of lilies waiting in the wings to drop into the spaces that the tulips had previously occupied.

While you will need to plant new tulips in fresh compost in your pots each year, lilies can stay in their containers. Each spring, you should scratch away the compost on top of the bulbs and replace it with a fresh mix, and a fresh sprinkling of slow-release fertilizer. Occasionally (perhaps every four or five years) you can tip out the whole potful and replant the lilies. This can be done either in spring or in autumn. If it is possible, drag your pots of lilies under cover for the winter. This will protect them from exceptional frosts and too much rain.

Bulbs in a greenhouse or bulb frame

Some bulbs included in this book are too tender to be kept out permanently in the garden and need the protection of a greenhouse. Others will be expensive jewels, demanding a regime (usually a summer without rain) that can best be accommodated by plunging them in individual pots in a bulb frame. Advanced gardeners will already have bulb frames, but you do not have to grow bulbs for many years before the lure of this special kind of playpen becomes irresistible.

Greenhouse specimens may include such show-off beauties as *Amaryllis belladonna* 'Purpurea', *Bessera elegans*, *Eucharis amazonica*, freesias, *Gloriosa superba* 'Rothschildiana', *Haemanthus albiflos*, hippeastrums in quantity, nerines, the sea daffodil (*Pancratium maritimum*), showy sprekelias and veltheimias. Specific instructions for growing these bulbs are given under each entry in this book. The advantage of bulbs that come from semi-tropical areas is that they are programmed to respond to wet seasons succeeding dry ones, not cold seasons succeeding warm ones. This means that you can manipulate their season of flowering just by giving water or withholding it.

None of the plants listed needs a tropical level of heat. All will survive in a greenhouse that is kept just a few degrees above freezing and are best kept lined out on a bench where plenty of air can move around them. The heat supply is best linked to a thermostat, which can kick in when temperatures start to fall. Electric fans are good as they keep the air within the house on the move and make it more difficult for fungus and moulds to settle. Group together pots of plants which need similar maintenance regimes. Some will die down for a complete rest. Others need to be kept growing as long as possible before they are allowed to become dormant. When bulbs are in flower, you can bring them into the house and admire them at close quarters. The cooler the temperature is indoors, the longer the flowers will last, though some such as sprekelia are by nature short-lived. Remember that more potted plants die from over watering than under watering. Do not be too liberal, especially during the bulbs' rest period. They will quickly rot if they sit in compost that is permanently wet. On the other hand, if they are too dry when they are coming up to flower the buds will abort.

Bulb frames do not provide heat, but are most useful for keeping rain off bulbs and corms that demand a very dry period of hibernation. In a bulb frame, too, you can more easily keep track of treasures, which will never perhaps be able to take the hurly-burly of life outside. The bulb frame can become a jewel box, a place to nurture some of the most beautiful plants that this book has to offer (especially crocuses and fritillaries). They may be more demanding to grow, but if you succeed in getting them to flower, the rewards are correspondingly high.

Effectively, a bulb frame is a raised bed enclosed within a structure that can be roofed with removable glass. You can adapt an existing cold frame, or build a frame from scratch with walls of brick, breeze block or lengths of heavy timber. The height can be whatever you want, but not less than 60cm (24in). If moles or mice are likely to a problem, cover the floor of the frame with fine wire netting. Fill the bottom of the frame with a layer of rubble, clinker or coarse gravel about 30cm (12in) deep. On top of this put garden compost or leaf mould in a layer about 10cm (4in) thick and finally the layer of potting compost that the bulb roots will actually penetrate. This should be a mixture of loam-based compost and fine 6mm (¼in) gravel laid on 20–30cm (8–12in) deep. (I am thinking of a reasonably deep bulb frame. If you want a smaller one, reduce the layers in proportion to the above.)

ABOVE The protected environment of a cool greenhouse is the perfect place to gently push on spring bulbs such as crocus and early-flowering narcissi.

You can plant bulbs direct into the frame, or plant them in clay pots and bury the pots up to their rims in the compost. As a kind of halfway house you can use the slatted baskets sold for aquatic plants and plant your bulbs in these before plunging them in the frame. Labels are critical. So is a top-dressing of grit 4–5cm (1½–2in) thick over everything you have planted.

It is likely that most of the bulbs in your bulb frame will be spring-flowering ones from the northern hemisphere. In this case, you should keep the glass roof (generally called 'lights') over the frame all summer to help the bulbs bake in whatever sun comes along. In early autumn, scatter bonemeal over the surface of the gravel and water the bulbs to stimulate root growth. Unless the autumn is unusually warm and dry you probably will not need to water again until early spring. Take the lights off during winter whenever the weather is reasonably dry and nights not too cold. By springtime, you can take the lights off permanently and leave them off until the foliage of the spring-flowering bulbs is beginning to wither. Then the lights need to go back on again. You should not need to replant more than once every four or five years.

If you want to grow summer-flowering bulbs in a frame (tigridia perhaps or species from Eastern Cape) you have to adopt a different regime, so it is probably best to grow these in a separate place. Leave the lights over these all winter, so the compost is kept as dry as possible. Take them off in spring and water the bulbs to tickle them into growth. Leave the lights off all summer until the leaves have begun to die down before covering the frame again for the winter.

Cultivating bulbs indoors

When great waves of sodden leaves wash up against the back door, when gales howl round the garden blowing down the artful arches and wigwams on which you grew your summer sweet peas and beans, the gardener tends to think, 'Hang outdoors. I'm going to garden inside.' And with a little forethought you can. Think of the smell of lily-of-the-valley or daffodils as you walk into your sitting room out of freezing fog and rain. Imagine the effect of a brilliant red bowl of tulips on a windowsill that looks out onto a world drained of colour.

Certain kinds of daffodils, hyacinths, some early tulips such as 'Generaal de Wet' and crocus can all be persuaded to flower indoors long before their outdoor cousins dare stick a nose above the winter parapet (though neither crocus, daffodils nor tulips can be forced as hard or as fast as hyacinths). Other bulbs such as hippeastrum, cyrtanthus and veltheimia are far too tender to have a place in gardens where winters bring regular bouts of frost, but are easy to grow in pots on a sunny windowsill. Nothing is quite as outrageously defiant as a hippeastrum in full bloom in January. And if you can coax four leaves out of a hippeastrum bulb as well as the flowering stem (and keep those leaves growing as long as possible through late spring), you have a good chance of getting flowers from that same bulb in the following season.

For 'forcing' flowers of bulbs that normally appear later in spring, you have to get hold of bulbs that have been specially doctored by growers; only certain varieties are amenable to treatment. Growers lift bulbs that are to be forced earlier than usual and store them in a special way giving them extra heat and humidity. Inside any bulb when it is lifted is a whole new plant in miniature waiting to burst out of its package in the next growing season. In a forced bulb, the embryo is encouraged to develop and grow inside the bulb before it is planted. By the time you come along and snatch them up, they are already well revved up.

Easiest of all are paper-white narcissi (*N. papyraceus*) which are usually available in August (see individual entries for specific details on forcing bulbs indoors). Like clockwork, the bulbs tick away for six weeks or so and then produce their flowers, smallish yes, too few for the amount of foliage yes, stems disproportionately tall for the size of head yes. But you forgive all that for the sake of the smell. So is 'Erlicheer' with double flowers in white and yellow.

Plant paper-whites at weekly intervals from late August onwards for a long display inside. Choose biggish containers (if you are careful with watering they need not have holes in the bottom) and plant the bulbs so that their noses are just below the surface of the compost. Set them quite close. A deepish container, such as an old china wash bowl, a soup tureen, a wicker basket, will provide good anchorage for the daffodil roots. I plant mine in zinc containers, 19cm (7½in) high, 27cm (11in) across, bought for £1 each at a junk place in the Fens, in eastern England, where they used to be used by the bulb growers. A container this size will take seven bulbs. 'Soleil d'Or' daffodils are not quite so quick but are equally sweetly scented.

At the end of August, too, the first of the treated hyacinths generally come out of store. These are probably the most popular of all forced bulbs, pale pink 'Anna Marie', darker 'Jan Bos', gentle 'Delft Blue'. Naturally early varieties such as these are the best ones to choose for forcing. Cool is what all potted bulbs need when they are first planted and, in a centrally heated flat, this may be difficult to provide. Take the planted bowls to someone else's cool if necessary. The bulbs cannot do without it, for they use this initial cool, dark growing period to develop the roots that will eventually support the shoots. In this context cool means 7–9°C (45–48°F). The safest (though messiest) way to provide the right conditions for the first half of the forcing process is to plunge the pots under the earth in some shady place in the garden. That way they will be kept at a steady temperature. They will also be dark and damp, which is equally vital.

You can use bulb fibre or multipurpose compost for planting. I generally use compost because the bulbs go out in the garden after they have done a season in the house and I feel the compost provides a few meals for them. It saves them from depleting their own food resources too savagely. Fibre though provides better drainage.

Set the hyacinth bulbs closely together, but not touching, with their noses just bumping out of the top of the compost. Water the bowls well. If you are burying them outside, you can swathe them in sheets of newspaper. This will keep the containers clean but still allow damp to penetrate through to the compost. The bulbs as they grow will be able to push through the damp newspaper.

At the beginning of December bring the bowls of hyacinths into the light, but keep them cool while they develop further. Finally when the flower spikes are beginning to colour, you can bring the bowls into the warmth. Central heating has a devastating effect on the life of flowers in bowls. If you can move them outside or on to a balcony for an occasional breath of cooler air, you will get a longer show.

If you miss the moment to buy hyacinth bulbs early on, you can pick them up later with flower spikes already showing. They are usually sold in foul plastic pots, too small to bring the flowers to maturity. Liberate them and plant them out in big groups in different containers, with moss or leaves scattered over the top of the compost. You can line the inside of a basket with a plastic carrier bag or bin bag, cut down to size. Put some pebbles, shards of clay pot or small stones at the bottom of the basket, then a layer of potting compost. Arrange the bulbs (tipped straight out of their pot, but not separated out) on top of the compost and fill in between the clumps with more compost until the basket is full. Firm the surface down gently. Water the basket and keep it in a light place until the flowers have developed fully. You can make the same kind of instant indoor garden with ready sprouting crocus (generally sold in pots of five) or dwarf daffodils (also sold in pots of five).

The container will catch the eye as much as the plants, so it needs to be worth looking at. Once you start thinking about planting, you can press the most unlikely things into service, but do not sink to plastic washing-up bowls. They cannot be disguised, however cunningly painted. Old enamelled tin bowls, even those with holes, are fine. Plug the hole with chewing gum and line the bowl with plastic as an extra precaution against leaking.

'Pips' of lily-of-the-valley (*Convallaria majalis*) can be brought into flower indoors too, and Victorian kitchen gardens had rows of them, dug up in rotation and brought under cover in peach and vine houses to be forced into flower, decorations for the dining table or bouquets for the boudoir. 'Pips' (the growing bud and roots) are sometimes available for forcing, and you would need a dozen plump 'pips' to fill a container roughly 15cm (6in) across. Plant them in a fast-draining potting compost and stand the container in a cool greenhouse or frame until January before bringing it into the warm. When they have finished flowering, plant them outside. It will take them a season to recover from their stint indoors, but meanwhile you will have had an early whiff of spring.

Forcing winter bulbs and flowers was once an important task for Edwardian and Victorian gardeners at large country houses. But even one single bowl of *Iris reticulata* can transform your mood and make winter seem more bearable. The wonderful thing about forcing indoor bulbs is that you do not need a garden to do it. A sunny windowsill is enough.

Propagating bulbs

Bulbs increase in two ways: one overground, one underground. All species can produce seed after flowering, but the plants that grow from that seed might vary slightly from the parent. Some bulbs can also split or produce daughter bulbs alongside themselves, which will be exact replicas of their parents. These may take a few years to grow to flowering size. Seed, of course, is even slower. A tulip may take seven years to develop from a seed to a flowering-size bulb. Tigridia is fast, often producing flowering-sized bulbs in a year. But though you need to be patient, growing bulbs from seed is not difficult.

Seed capsules of bulbs such as *Lilium regale* or *Tulipa sprengeri* take a surprisingly long time to develop fully. When the capsule starts to turn from bright green to a duller colour, you can cut it off with some of the stem and hang it upside down in a shed or greenhouse to finish ripening. Tie a paper bag round the head to catch the seeds as they fall from the three-chambered seedhead. Seed of many fritillaries and lilies looks like doll-sized cornflakes.

Sow seed as soon as you have it (there is some evidence that seed of bulbs from the Amaryllidaceae family loses viability sooner than that of bulbs from the other two big bulb families, the Liliaceae and the Iridaceae). Scatter it as thinly as you can on pots of loam-based compost, mixed with grit. Cover with more grit, which prevents moss and liverwort settling on top of the compost. Seed from plants used to a cold winter needs a similarly cold period to precipitate germination, but after that usually grows quite easily; the newly germinated seedlings of the Liliaceae tribe (it includes tulips and fritillaries as well as lilies) look like spears of bright grass.

What you do subsequently depends on your circumstances. If you have a spare piece of suitable ground to use as a nursery, you can plant out the seedlings in the year after they have germinated and grow them on undisturbed until they are of flowering size. Or you can plunge the pot in a bulb frame and let the seedlings grow on there, repotted each September into a slightly larger pot with fresh compost. Or you can just keep the seedlings in a pot, repotting them each September into a slightly larger container and giving them some slow-release fertilizer to feast on. Seed of tender species will of course have to be kept under cover during winter. In any event, you do not necessarily have to separate out the seedlings until they have reached flowering size. They often do better kept together, provided they have sufficient food and drink in season. And provided you have not sown too thickly in the first place.

Some tubers such as *Cyclamen hederifolium* and *Eranthis hyemalis* self-seed very satisfactorily in a garden, if they are in the right situation. The cyclamen can make a flowering-size tuber within two years, spread about by ants who like the sticky covering round the seed coat. Some seed (I am thinking of nerines) is so big that you can sow it singly, if you prefer. An egg box filled with compost makes a good nursery for nerines, with a seed pushed into each separate cavity.

Propagating lilies

Lilies produce seed in vast quantity (though are sadly slow to do anything with it; it may be two years before you see any growth above ground), but some of them such as *L. bulbiferum* and *L. lancifolium* also produce pea-sized bulbils in the axils of the leaves – the angle where the leaf meets the stem of the plant. You can break these off at the end of the growing season and grow them on, either in separate pots or lined out in a nursery bed until they reach flowering size (probably three or four years). Underground bulblets of all bulbs can be treated the same way. Or left where they are, which is often the best approach.

You can also propagate lilies from the scales of which the bulb is made up. Pull away a few scales and put them into a plastic bag half filled with damp multipurpose compost. Keep the bag somewhere warmish but shady until you see little bulblets forming along the edges of the scales. When they seem sufficiently robust, break them away and grow them on as you might a bulbil. You might get a flowering-size bulb within three years. You might have to wait seven.

ABOVE Without too much difficulty, lilies can be propagated from individual scales, broken apart from the bulb and set in pots of gritty compost.

Dividing bulbs

When clumps of bulbs such as daffodils become too crowded, they may stop flowering, go 'blind' as gardeners say. In this case, you can dig them up any time between the end of flowering in late spring and the start of new root growth in early autumn. The best time is July or August, but by then all the foliage will have died down and you will need a bamboo cane by the clump to remind you where to dig. Split up congested clumps, replanting bulbs in ground which you have refreshed with bonemeal.

If a daffodil is not increasing as fast as you would like, make two cuts at right angles through the basal plate of the dormant bulb, just into the scales. Push little pebbles or small pieces of slate into the cuts to keep them open. Plant the bulb in a pot of fresh potting compost. By the following season it should have produced little bulblets by the cuts, which you can break off and grow on as you might bulblets grown from seed. You can use this technique on alliums and hyacinths, too.

Fritillary bulbs, which are often made from just two fleshy semi-circular scales jammed together round a growing point, can be 'divided' by pulling the two halves apart. The half with the bud attached will probably grow on and flower as if nothing had happened. The other half will probably take a year to sort itself out.

Pests and diseases

If your bulbs, corms, tubers and rhizomes are happy, they will be less susceptible to disease. Happiness for them means a habitat that has been carefully chosen (or tweaked) to match as closely as possible their own wild homes: not too hot, not too cold, not too wet, not too dry. I prefer to concentrate on getting that right, rather than reaching for a bottle to try and correct something I have got wrong.

ABOVE Many bulbs, including crocuses such as this 'Vanguard', are subject to virus, for which there is no cure.

Bulb diseases

Viruses may be a problem, showing up as discolorations or malformations of leaf or flower. Here, the best course is to dig up and burn affected plants. Viruses are spread by aphids, and if you encourage enough of the aphid's predators into your garden (there are plenty of insects that love an appetizer of aphids) then an equilibrium should be established. If you kill all the aphids, the beneficial insects will have nothing to eat and will go elsewhere.

Fungal infections are a nuisance, but are often brought on or spread by adverse weather conditions, which you can do little about. Basal rot in daffodils, downy mildew on alliums, powdery mildew on anemones, grey mould on lilies, tulip fire in tulips, all are possible. Soil-borne problems such as tulip fire will not occur where you grow tulips in pots, in fresh potting compost each year. It builds up instead in borders where you grow tulips every year in the same place; it can be outwitted if you move your tulips around the garden. The symptoms are unmissable: leaves develop pale brown blotches which are later covered by a dense, grey fungus. The same kind of bleached spots appear on the petals of the flowers, and they, too, develop this fuzz of fungus on them. Sometimes buds are so badly affected that they do not open at all, but wither in a miasma of grey fungal growth. All this mayhem is caused by the fungus *Botrytis tulipae*. It is especially prevalent in wet seasons because the spores are spread by wind and rain. They settle in the soil and germinate when you plant your tulips next to them. There is little you can do to combat it. Burn affected tulips and plant in fresh ground the following season.

Bulb pests

Pests are generally more visible than diseases, though there are some microscopic ones such as the narcissus eelworm (*Ditylenchus dipsaci*) which can cause havoc in spreads of naturalized daffodils (they will go for bluebells and snowdrops, too). Growth is distorted and stunted, and affected bulbs eventually rot. The pest gradually works its way through a spread of bulbs, and there is no countermeasure except to dig up and burn all the affected plants, as well as any others growing within 1m (3ft) of them. Do not replant in the affected area for at least two years. If you think you might be harbouring this pest, dig up a bulb and cut it in half. If you see brown concentric rings between the layers of the bulb, you have probably got it.

Slugs, snails and lily beetles are more easily dealt with. I enjoy stamping on snails and lily beetles (a relatively new pest). Fortunately the latter is easy to see, as it is bright shiny red. It is easy to catch too, for it moves slowly. The beetle (*Lilioceris lilii*) and its larvae will attack fritillaries as well as lilies, eating both leaves and flowers. The larvae are disgusting, reddish brown with black heads, covered in their own excrement which they use as a disguise. Look out for them from mid summer onwards. Unfortunately the beetles themselves are active from spring when lily shoots first appear.

ABOVE A relatively new pest in the UK, the lily beetle feasts on fritillaries as well as lilies.

Slugs are a nightmare but dusk hunts with a torch at least make you feel you are facing up to the problem, even if you are not solving it entirely. The fresh shoots of lilies, emerging in spring, seem particularly vulnerable. But underground slugs, though small, can do even more damage than the monster overground ones and are more difficult to deal with. They love lilies and tulips. Planting with plenty of grit or sharp sand is probably the best defence.

In many ways the most maddening enemies are the mice that eat crocus bulbs and the squirrels that dig up tulip bulbs. Both bulbs are most at risk when they are first planted. Perhaps the mice and squirrels are more intent on hunting for them then, in order to fatten themselves up before winter. If the bulbs are planted in pots, you can lay fine-mesh wire netting over the top until the first growth shows through in spring. Protection is more difficult to arrange in an open border where bulbs are often threaded through herbaceous perennials and laying down wire is not so easy. Traps work (mice like chocolate), but a decent hunting cat is probably your best defence. A cat will not see off a badger, though, and in our garden badgers make regular raids on the juicy tubers of the dragon arum (*Dracunculus vulgaris*) and other Araceae. Why, I ask myself looking at yet another tragic scene of carnage, can't they eat the tubers of the wild arums with which the banks of our lanes are thickly covered? Why must they go for the expensive kinds, beautiful *Arum creticum* from Crete and Rhodes, fabulous *Arum nigrum* with its witchy spathes? The best defences are open-work bamboo cloches, pinned firmly down over the clumps. The badgers could easily push these over if they tried, but fortunately they do not.

Planting guide

The lists below are starting points only. Bulbs in containers and bulbs in a greenhouse will all be growing in artificial conditions, which can be an asset. In a greenhouse, you can tweak temperature; in a container, you can provide decent drainage. But both these groups of plants may need more watering and feeding than bulbs in open ground. The choice of bulbs for naturalizing will be the trickiest. Success here depends on understanding your soil.

Bulbs for naturalizing in grass
(depending on conditions)

Allium sphaerocephalon
Allium vineale 'Hair'
Anemone blanda ♀
Camassia leichtlinii
Colchicum autumnale
Colchicum speciosum
Corydalis solida
Crocus (especially *C. chrysanthus*) (right)
Cyclamen hederifolium ♀
Eranthis hyemalis ♀
Fritillaria meleagris
Galanthus (especially *G. nivalis*)
Gladiolus communis subsp. *byzantinus* ♀
Iris histrioides
Iris reticulata ♀
Leucojum aestivum
Leucojum vernum ♀
Muscari neglectum

Narcissus cyclamineus ♀
Narcissus poeticus var. *recurvus* ♀
Ornithogalum (especially *O. umbellatum*)
Scilla siberica ♀
Tulipa sprengeri ♀
Tulipa sylvestris

Bulbs for indoors or a greenhouse

Amaryllis belladonna 'Windhoek'
Babiana stricta ♀
Calochortus
Chasmanthe aethiopica
Cyclamen persicum
Cyrtanthus
Eucharis amazonica
Freesia
Gladiolus murielae ♀

Gloriosa superba
Habranthus robustus ♀
Haemanthus albiflos ♀
Hippeastrum
Hyacinthus
Hymenocallis × *festalis* ♀
Iris reticulata ♀
Ixia (left)
Lachenalia pustulata ♀
Moraea huttonii
Nerine filifolia
Ornithogalum arabicum
Ornithogalum thyrsoides ♀
Pancratium maritimum
Polianthes tuberosa ♀
Scadoxus multiflorus
Sparaxis
Sprekelia formosissima
Tecophilaea cyanocrocus ♀
Tigridia
Veltheimia bracteata ♀

Bulbs for containers

Allium
Amaryllis
Anemone coronaria
Arisaema
Chionodoxa
Crinum
Crocus
Cyclamen
Eucomis
Fritillaria
Gladiolus murielae ♀
Hyacinthus
Iris reticulata ♀
Lilium
Narcissus
Ornithogalum
Tulbaghia violacea
Tulipa (right)
Zigadenus nuttallii

Bulbs for a cutting garden

Allium (left)
Anemone coronaria (both De Caen and
    Saint Bridgid strains)
Arum
Chasmanthe aethiopica
Freesia
Fritillaria
Galanthus 'Atkinsii' ♀
Gladiolus
Hermodactylus tuberosus
Iris (especially the Dutch kinds)
Ixia
Lilium
Narcissus
Nerine bowdenii ♀
Ornithogalum arabicum
Ornithogalum thyrsoides ♀
Schizostylis coccinea
Sparaxis grandiflora ♀
Tulipa
Zantedeschia aethiopica

Bulbs by season

Plants are not regulated by timetables – an abomination we have invented. Sensibly, they respond to circumstances. If the weather in late winter is harsh, spring flowers will be delayed. If there is a sudden spell of hot weather in April, tulips that you might be expecting to furnish the garden in May will bring their act forward. So the list that follows must be taken as an indication only – the order in which you may expect flowers to appear during the year.

January

Crocus sieberi 'Violet Queen'
Eranthis hyemalis ♀
Galanthus 'Galatea'
Galanthus 'Magnet' ♀ (*right*)
Iris 'Cantab'
Iris histrioides 'Lady Beatrix Stanley'
Iris 'Katharine Hodgkin' ♀
Iris 'Purple Gem'

January
(indoors)

Hippeastrum 'Aphrodite'
Hippeastrum 'Apple Blossom'
Hippeastrum 'Fairytale'
Hippeastrum 'La Paz'
Hyacinthus orientalis 'Anna Marie' ♀
Hyacinthus orientalis 'Delft Blue' ♀
Hyacinthus orientalis 'Gipsy Princess' ♀
Hyacinthus orientalis 'Jan Bos'
Hyacinthus orientalis 'White Pearl'

January to February

Galanthus 'Atkinsii' ♀
Galanthus nivalis ♀

Galanthus nivalis 'Anglesey Abbey'

January to March

Crocus imperati

January to April (indoors)

Freesia cultivars

February

Crocus angustifolius ♀
Crocus 'Blue Bird'
Crocus 'Blue Pearl' ♀
Crocus chrysanthus 'Cream Beauty'
Crocus chrysanthus 'E A Bowles'
Crocus chrysanthus 'Gypsy Girl'

Crocus chrysanthus 'Ladykiller' ♀
Crocus chrysanthus 'Romance'
Crocus chrysanthus 'Zwanenburg Bronze' ♀
Crocus etruscus
Crocus tommasinianus 'Roseus'
Crocus tommasinianus 'Ruby Giant'

February
(continued)

Crocus tommasinianus 'Whitewell Purple'
Crocus 'Vanguard' ♀
Crocus vernus 'Grand Maître'
Crocus vernus 'Pickwick'
Eranthis hyemalis Cilicica Group
Eranthis hyemalis 'Guinea Gold' ♀
Galanthus 'Hill Poe'
Galanthus nivalis 'Flore Pleno' ♀
Galanthus nivalis 'Viridapice'
Galanthus 'S Arnott' ♀
Galanthus woronowii ♀
Iris 'George' ♀

Iris 'Gordon'
Iris 'Harmony'
Iris 'J S Dijt'
Iris reticulata ♀
Narcissus 'Bowles's Sulphur'
Narcissus 'Itzim' ♀
Narcissus 'Little Gem' ♀
Narcissus 'Tête-à-tête' ♀
Scilla mischtschenkoana ♀
Tulipa biflora (*T. polychroma*)
Veltheimia bracteata ♀

February
(indoors)

Hippeastrum 'Black Pearl'
Hippeastrum 'Chico'
Hippeastrum 'Lemon Lime'
Hippeastrum papilio ♀
Hippeastrum 'Picotee'

Hyacinthus multiflowered blue
Hyacinthus orientalis 'Carnegie'
Hyacinthus orientalis 'City of Haarlem' ♀
Hyacinthus orientalis 'Hollyhock'
Hyacinthus orientalis 'Woodstock'

February to March

Anemone blanda 'Radar' ♀
Anemone pavonina
Cyclamen libanoticum
Crocus biflorus 'Miss Vain'
Crocus malyi ♀
Crocus sieberi ♀
Crocus sieberi subsp. *sublimis* 'Tricolor' ♀
Crocus tommasinianus ♀
Crocus tommasinianus 'Barr's Purple'

Crocus vernus 'Jeanne d'Arc'
Crocus vernus 'King of the Striped'
Fritillaria raddeana
Galanthus elwesii ♀
Hermodactylus tuberosus
Iris histrioides 'Angel's Tears'
Iris unguicularis 'Mary Barnard' ♀
Narcissus 'February Gold' ♀

February to April

Corydalis caucasica

March

Allium paradoxum var. *normale*
Anemone apennina ♀
Anemone blanda ♀
Anemone blanda blue-flowered

Anemone blanda var. *rosea* ♀
Anemone blanda 'White Splendour' ♀
Anemone × *lipsiensis* 'Pallida' ♀
Anemone nemorosa ♀
Anemone nemorosa 'Lychette'
Chionodoxa forbesii
Chionodoxa luciliae ♀ (left)
Chionodoxa 'Pink Giant'
Chionodoxa sardensis ♀
Chionodoxa siehei ♀
× *Chionoscilla allenii*
Corydalis solida subsp. *solida* 'George Baker'
Corydalis solida 'White Swallow'
Crocus × *luteus* 'Golden Yellow' ♀
Crocus vernus 'Queen of the Blues'
Cyclamen pseudibericum ♀
Erythronium dens-canis 'Old Aberdeen'
Fritillaria assyriaca

March
(continued)

Fritillaria elwesii
Fritillaria michailovskyi ♀
Fritillaria persica 'Adiyaman' ♀
Galanthus plicatus ♀
Hyacinthus multiflowered blue
Hyacinthus orientalis 'Anna Marie' ♀
Hyacinthus orientalis 'Carnegie'
Hyacinthus orientalis 'Delft Blue' ♀
Hyacinthus orientalis 'Gipsy Princess' ♀
Hyacinthus orientalis 'Jan Bos'
Hyacinthus orientalis 'White Pearl'
Hyacinthus 'Woodstock'
Ipheion 'Alberto Castillo'
Ipheion uniflorum 'Charlotte Bishop'
Iris bucharica ♀
Leucojum vernum ♀
Muscari armeniacum ♀
Muscari armeniacum 'Valerie Finnis'
Muscari latifolium ♀
Muscari macrocarpum
Muscari neglectum
Narcissus bulbocodium Golden Bells Group
Narcissus 'Canaliculatus"
Narcissus cyclamineus ♀
Narcissus 'Geranium' ♀
Narcissus 'Hawera' ♀
Narcissus 'Ice Wings' ♀

Narcissus 'Jack Snipe' ♀
Narcissus 'Jenny' ♀
Narcissus jonquilla ♀
Narcissus 'Jumblie' ♀
Narcissus 'Little Beauty' ♀
Narcissus 'Mount Hood' ♀
Narcissus × odorus 'Double Campernelle'
Narcissus pseudonarcissus ♀
Narcissus 'Quail' ♀
Narcissus 'Rip van Winkle'
Narcissus 'Saint Keverne' ♀
Narcissus 'Suzy' ♀
Narcissus 'Trevithian' ♀
Narcissus 'White Lion' ♀
Narcissus 'Xit'
Ornithogalum nutans ♀
Puschkinia scilloides var. libanotica
Ranunculus ficaria 'Brazen Hussy'
Scilla bifolia ♀
Tulipa 'Berlioz'
Tulipa 'Cantata'
Tulipa 'Flaming Purissima'
Tulipa 'Für Elise'
Tulipa humilis
Tulipa humilis Violacea Group
Tulipa 'Purple Prince'
Tulipa 'Salut'

March (indoors)

Hippeastrum 'Pink Floyd'
Lachenalia aloides var. quadricolor ♀

March to April

Anemone nemorosa 'Robinsoniana' ♀
Anemonella thalictroides
Bulbocodium vernum
Corydalis solida
Crocus flavus subsp. flavus ♀
Cyclamen persicum
Gagea lutea
Hyacinthus orientalis 'Hollyhock' (right)
Hyacinthus orientalis 'Purple Sensation'
Ipheion 'Rolf Fiedler' ♀
Ipheion uniflorum 'Froyle Mill' ♀
Iris aucheri ♀
Iris winogradowii ♀
Narcissus 'Bell Song'
Romulea bulbocodium

March to April (indoors)

Hippeastrum 'Emerald'
Lachenalia pustulata ♀

March to May

Acis nicaeensis ♀
Crocus corsicus ♀

March to September

Anemone coronaria
Anemone coronaria 'Die Braut'
Anemone coronaria 'Hollandia'
Anemone coronaria 'Lord Lieutenant'

Anemone coronaria 'Mister Fokker'
Anemone coronaria 'Mount Everest'
Anemone coronaria 'Sylphide'
Anemone coronaria 'The Admiral'

April

Anemone nemorosa 'Allenii' ♀
Anemone nemorosa 'Blue Beauty'
Anemone nemorosa 'Bracteata Pleniflora'
Anemone nemorosa 'Vestal' ♀
Anemone nemorosa 'Virescens' ♀
Anemone ranunculoides ♀
Anthericum liliago 'Major'
Arum nigrum
Bellevalia paradoxa
Bellevalia romana
Erythronium californicum 'White Beauty' ♀
Erythronium dens-canis ♀
Erythronium 'Joanna'
Erythronium 'Pagoda' ♀
Erythronium revolutum ♀
Erythronium 'Sundisc'
Erythronium tuolumnense ♀
Fritillaria acmopetala ♀
Fritillaria davisii
Fritillaria imperialis
Fritillaria imperialis 'Maxima Lutea' ♀
Fritillaria imperialis 'William Rex'
Fritillaria meleagris
Fritillaria pallidiflora ♀
Fritillaria pontica ♀
Fritillaria pyrenaica ♀
Fritillaria uva-vulpis
Hyacinthus orientalis 'City of Haarlem' ♀
Hyacinthus orientalis 'Purple Sensation'
Iris graminea ♀
Iris kolpakowskiana
Iris 'Oriental Beauty'
Iris 'Professor Blaauw' ♀
Leucojum aestivum 'Gravetye Giant' ♀
Muscari armeniacum 'Blue Spike'
Muscari armeniacum 'Fantasy Creation'
Muscari azureum ♀
Muscari botryoides 'Album'
Muscari comosum 'Plumosum'
Narcissus 'Acropolis'
Narcissus 'Actaea' ♀
Narcissus 'Cheerfulness' ♀
Narcissus 'Eystettensis'
Narcissus 'Lothario'
Narcissus 'Minnow' ♀ (*above*)

Narcissus 'Passionale' ♀
Narcissus 'Petrel'
Narcissus 'Pipit' ♀
Narcissus 'Segovia' ♀
Narcissus 'Silver Chimes'
Narcissus 'Sun Disc' ♀
Narcissus 'White Lady'
Scilla litardierei ♀
Trillium erectum ♀
Trillium kurabayashii
Trillium luteum ♀
Trillium sulcatum
Tulipa 'Alice Leclercq'
Tulipa 'American Dream'
Tulipa 'Annie Schilder'
Tulipa 'Apricot Parrot' ♀
Tulipa 'Attila'
Tulipa 'Beau Monde' ♀
Tulipa 'Bestseller'
Tulipa 'Big Chief' ♀
Tulipa 'Black Hero'
Tulipa 'Blue Diamond'
Tulipa 'Capri'
Tulipa clusiana
Tulipa 'Couleur Cardinal'
Tulipa 'Doorman's Record'
Tulipa 'Douglas Bader'
Tulipa 'Dyanito'
Tulipa 'Fringed Elegance'

April (continued)	*Tulipa* 'Generaal de Wet'	*Tulipa orphanidea* 'Flava'
	Tulipa 'Georgette'	*Tulipa passeriniana*
	Tulipa 'Groenland'	*Tulipa* 'Recreado'
	Tulipa 'Gudoshnik'	*Tulipa* 'Sapporo'
	Tulipa 'Jan Reus'	*Tulipa saxatilis* Bakeri Group
	Tulipa linifolia Batalinii Group 'Bright Gem' ♀	*Tulipa* 'Snow Parrot'
		Tulipa 'Spring Green' ♀
	Tulipa 'Little Beauty' ♀	*Tulipa sylvestris*

April to May	*Arisaema griffithii*	*Hyacinthoides non-scripta*
	Arisarum proboscideum	*Iris magnifica* ♀
	Arum 'Chameleon'	*Trillium grandiflorum* ♀
	Arum creticum	*Trillium recurvatum*
	Arum italicum ♀	*Tulipa* 'Maytime'
	Bongardia chrysogonum	*Tulipa orphanidea* Whittallii Group ♀
	Convallaria majalis ♀	*Tulipa* 'Prinses Irene' ♀
	Cyclamen repandum	*Uvularia grandiflora* ♀

April to May (indoors)	*Sparaxis grandiflora* ♀	

April to June	*Arisaema speciosum*	*Dietes iridioides*
	Arisaema tortuosum	*Paris polyphylla* ♀
	Dietes grandiflora	

April to July	*Zantedeschia aethiopica*	*Zantedeschia aethiopica* 'Green Goddess' ♀
	Zantedeschia aethiopica 'Crowborough' ♀	

May	*Allium* 'Emperor'	*Brimeura amethystina* ♀
	Allium unifolium ♀	*Camassia leichtlinii* 'Alba Plena'
	Ambrosina bassii	*Camassia leichtlinii* subsp. *leichtlinii* ♀
		Camassia leichtlinii subsp. *suksdorfii*
		Camassia quamash
		Dracunculus vulgaris
		Gladiolus 'Charm'
		Gladiolus tristis
		Hyacinthoides italica ♀
		Iris 'Apollo'
		Iris cycloglossa
		Iris 'Gypsy Beauty'
		Iris 'Sapphire Beauty'
		Ixiolirion tataricum Ledebourii Group
		Lilium mackliniae
		Maianthemum bifolium
		Narcissus poeticus var. *recurvus* ♀
		Nectaroscordum siculum
		Ornithogalum arabicum
		Ornithogalum umbellatum
		Scilla peruviana

May
(continued)

Sprekelia formosissima
Trillium catesbyi
Triteleia ixioides 'Starlight'
Tulipa 'Angélique' 🏆
Tulipa 'Arma'
Tulipa 'Ballerina' 🏆
Tulipa 'Bleu Aimable'
Tulipa 'Blue Parrot'
Tulipa 'Blushing Girl'

Tulipa 'Estella Rijnveld'
Tulipa 'Fantasy' 🏆
Tulipa 'Magier'
Tulipa 'Negrita'
Tulipa 'Orange Favourite' (*opposite*)
Tulipa 'Rococo'
Tulipa sprengeri 🏆
Tulipa 'Weber's Parrot'

May to June

Allium 'Globemaster' 🏆
Allium hollandicum 'Purple Sensation' 🏆
Allium karataviense 🏆
Allium 'Lucy Ball'
Allium moly 'Jeannine' 🏆
Allium stipitatum 'Mars'
Allium stipitatum 'Mount Everest'
Arisaema concinnum

Arisaema consanguineum
Arisaema sikokianum
Babiana stricta 🏆
Calochortus superbus
Corydalis schanginii subsp. *ainii* 🏆
Dichelostemma ida-maia
Fritillaria camschatcensis
Ixia cultivars

June

Allium cristophii 🏆
Allium 'Firmament'
Allium giganteum 🏆
Allium 'Gladiator' 🏆
Allium narcissiflorum
Allium nigrum
Allium oreophilum 'Zwanenburg' 🏆
Allium 'Pinball Wizard'
Allium schubertii
Allium vineale 'Hair'
Arisaema saxatile
Arthropodium candidum
Camassia leichtlinii 'Semiplena'
Cyclamen purpurascens 🏆
Dichelostemma congestum
Dierama dracomontanum
Gladiolus communis subsp. *byzantinus* 🏆
Gladiolus 'Nymph'
Iris xiphium
Ledebouria cooperi

Lilium candidum 🏆
Lilium cernuum
Lilium × dalhansonii 'Mrs R O Backhouse'
Lilium martagon 🏆
Lilium martagon var. *album* 🏆
Lilium martagon var. *cattaniae*
Lilium Pink Perfection Group 🏆
Lilium pumilum 🏆
Lilium pyrenaicum
Lilium regale 🏆
Moraea huttonii
Nomocharis aperta
Ornithogalum dubium 🏆
Ornithogalum thyrsoides 🏆
Polianthes tuberosa 🏆
Roscoea cautleyoides 🏆
Roscoea cautleyoides 'Kew Beauty' 🏆
Triteleia 'Corrina'
Triteleia laxa 'Koningin Fabiola'
Zigadenus nuttallii

June
(October planting)

Gladiolus × colvillii 'The Bride'

June to July

Allium 'Ambassador'
Allium atropurpureum
Allium insubricum 🏆
Arisaema amurense
Arisaema candidissimum 🏆
Arisaema jacquemontii

Arisaema triphyllum
Calochortus venustus
Iris latifolia 🏆
Iris orientalis 🏆
Lilium nepalense

June to August	*Brodiaea californica*

June to September	*Tulbaghia violacea* 'Silver Lace'

July

Allium caeruleum ♀
Allium carinatum subsp. *pulchellum* ♀
Allium cernuum
Allium flavum ♀
Allium sativum var. *ophioscorodon*
Allium senescens var. *glaucum*

Allium sphaerocephalon
Eucomis bicolor ♀
Galtonia candicans ♀
Galtonia viridiflora
Gladiolus cardinalis
Lilium African Queen Group ♀
Lilium canadense
Lilium 'Casa Blanca' ♀
Lilium Citronella Group
Lilium davidii (*left*)
Lilium duchartrei
Lilium 'Gran Cru' ♀
Lilium leichtlinii
Lilium longiflorum 'White Heaven'
Lilium 'Netty's Pride'
Lilium pardalinum ♀
Lilium 'Pink Tiger'
Lilium 'Sterling Star'
Lilium 'Sweet Surrender'
Lilium 'White Tiger'
Lilium 'Yellow Star'
Roscoea auriculata
Roscoea 'Beesiana'

July (Spring planting)	*Gladiolus* × *colvillii* 'The Bride'

July to August

Allium angulosum
Caloscordum neriniflorum
Cardiocrinum giganteum
Chasmanthe aethiopica
Dierama 'Guinevere' (*right*)
Dierama 'Lancelot'
Dierama pendulum
Freesia cultivars
Gloriosa superba
Hymenocallis × *festalis* ♀
Notholirion bulbuliferum
Roscoea purpurea
Watsonia borbonica 'Arderne's White'
Watsonia pillansii

July to September	*Hippeastrum* 'Toughie'

July to November	*Cyclamen hederifolium* ♀ (right) *Cyclamen hederifolium* f. *albiflorum*

August	*Allium cyaneum* ♀ *Crinum moorei* *Crinum* × *powellii* ♀ *Crinum* × *powellii* 'Album' ♀ *Dierama pulcherrimum* *Eucomis autumnalis* ♀ *Eucomis bicolor* 'Alba' *Eucomis comosa* 'Sparkling Burgundy' *Eucomis vandermerwei* *Gladiolus murielae* ♀ *Gladiolus papilio* *Lilium* 'Anglia' *Lilium* 'Black Beauty' *Lilium henryi* ♀ *Lilium lancifolium* 'Splendens' ♀	*Lilium speciosum* var. *album* *Lilium* Triumphator *Scadoxus multiflorus* subsp. *katherinae* ♀ *Tigridia pavonia* *Zephyranthes candida*

August to September	*Colchicum agrippinum* ♀ *Cyrtanthus elatus* ♀ *Cyrtanthus falcatus* ♀ *Eucomis comosa* *Eucomis pole-evansii* *Pancratium maritimum*

August to October	*Allium tuberosum* *Scilla autumnalis* *Sparaxis grandiflora* ♀ (right)

August to November	*Cautleya spicata* 'Robusta'

September	*Amaryllis belladonna* 'Purpurea' *Amaryllis belladonna* 'Windhoek' *Colchicum autumnale* *Colchicum autumnale* 'Album' *Colchicum autumnale* 'Nancy Lindsay' ♀ *Colchicum* 'Pink Goblet' ♀ *Colchicum* 'Rosy Dawn' ♀	*Colchicum speciosum* ♀ *Colchicum tenorei* ♀ *Colchicum* 'Waterlily' ♀ *Cyclamen cilicium* ♀ *Habranthus robustus* ♀ *Haemanthus albiflos* ♀ *Nerine bowdenii* ♀

September to October	*Acis autumnalis* ♀ *Bessera elegans* *Colchicum byzantinum* ♀ *Colchicum cilicicum* *Crocus banaticus* ♀ *Crocus speciosus* 'Conqueror'	*Cyclamen mirabile* ♀ *Eucharis amazonica* ♀ *Eucomis pallidiflora* ♀ *Merendera montana* *Sternbergia lutea*

| September to November | *Schizostylis coccinea* 'Jennifer' ♀ | *Schizostylis coccinea* 'Sunrise' ♀ |
| | *Schizostylis coccinea* 'Major' ♀ | |

October	*Amaryllis belladonna* ♀	
	Colchicum speciosum 'Album' ♀	
	Crocus hadriaticus ♀	
	Crocus kotschyanus ♀	
	Crocus longiflorus ♀	
	Crocus nudiflorus	
	Crocus pulchellus ♀	
	Crocus sativus	
	Crocus speciosus ♀	
	Galanthus reginae-olgae	
	Nerine flexuosa 'Alba'	
	Nerine undulata (right)	

| October to November | *Crocus cartwrightianus* ♀ | *Crocus tournefortii* ♀ |
| | *Crocus medius* ♀ | *Nerine filifolia* |

| October to December (indoors) | *Narcissus papyraceus* | |

| November | *Crocus goulimyi* ♀ | *Crocus ochroleucus* ♀ |
| | *Crocus niveus* | |

November to March	*Iris unguicularis* ♀ (right)	
	Iris unguicularis 'Mary Barnard'	
	Iris unguicularis 'Walter Butt'	

| December | *Narcissus* 'Rijnveld's Sensation' ♀ | |

| December to February | *Iris lazica* ♀ | |

December to March	*Cyclamen coum* ♀	
	Cyclamen coum 'Maurice Dryden'	
	Cyclamen coum f. *pallidum* 'Album'	
	Cyclamen coum Pewter Group ♀	
	Cyclamen coum Silver Group	

| December to April | *Bowiea volubilis* | |

Reverse synonym index

Acidanthera bicolor, see *Gladiolus murielae* (page 241)

Allium azureum, see *Allium caeruleum* (page 27)

Allium ostrowskianum 'Zwanenburg', see *Allium oreophilum* 'Zwanenburg' (page 40)

Allium pulchellum, see *Allium carinatum* subsp. *pulchellum* (page 28)

Allium 'Purple Sensation', see *Allium hollandicum* 'Purple Sensation' (page 36)

Allium siculum, see *Nectaroscordum siculum* (page 396)

Arum dracunculus, see *Dracunculus vulgaris* (page 188)

Bellevalia pycnantha, see *Bellevalia paradoxa* (page 87)

Camassia esculenta, see *Camassia quamash* (page 100)

Iris ochroleuca, see *Iris orientalis* (page 299)

Iris stylosa, see *Iris unguicularis* (page 304)

Iris tuberosus, see *Hermodactylus tuberosus* (page 246)

Iris xiphioides, see *Iris latifolia* (page 296)

Ledebouria adlamii, see *Ledebouria cooperi* (page 311)

Lilium tenuifolium, see *Lilium pumilum* (page 337)

Muscari paradoxum, see *Bellevalia paradoxa* (page 87)

Narcissus old pheasant's eye, see *Narcissus poeticus* var. *recurvus* (page 386)

Narcissus 'Paper White', see *Narcissus papyraceus* (page 384)

Narcissus Queen Anne's double daffodil, see *Narcissus* 'Eystettensis' (page 374)

Narcissus 'Queen of Spain', see *Narcissus × johnstonii* (page 378)

Prospero autumnalis, see *Scilla autumnalis* (page 419)

Scilla 'Tubergeniana', see *Scilla mischtschenkoana* (page 420)

Tulipa bakeri, see *Tulipa saxatilis* Bakeri Group (page 489)

Tulipa batalinii 'Bright Gem', see *Tulipa linifolia* Batalinii Group 'Bright Gem' (page 486)

Tulipa didieri, see *Tulipa passeriniana* (page 474)

Tulipa 'Greenland', see *Tulipa* 'Groenland' (page 462)

Tulipa polychroma, see *Tulipa biflora* (page 454)

Tulipa pulchella 'Violacea', see *Tulipa humilis* Violacea Group (page 462)

Tulipa violacea, see *Tulipa humilis* Violacea Group (page 462)

Tulipa whittallii, see *Tulipa orphanidea* Whittallii Group (page 488

Vallota speciosa, see *Cyrtanthus elatus* (page 181)

Watsonia beatricis, see *Watsonia pillansii* (page 497)

Bibliography

Austin, C, *Irises: A Gardener's Encyclopaedia*, Portland: Timber Press, 2005

Bishop, M, Davis, A and Grimshaw, J, *Snowdrops. A Monograph of Cultivated Galanthus*, Maidenhead: Griffin Press, 2001

Blanchard, J W, *Narcissus – A Guide to Wild Daffodils*, Woking: Alpine Garden Society, 1990

Botschantzeva, Z P, *Tulips*, Rotterdam: A A Balkema, 1982

Bowles, E A, *A Handbook of Crocus and Colchicum for Gardeners*, London: Bodley Head, rev. edn 1952

Bowles, E A, *A Handbook of Narcissus*, London: Martin Hopkinson, 1934

Bown, D, *Plants of the Arum Family*, Portland: Timber Press, 2nd edn 2000

Boyce, P, *The Genus Arum*, London: HMSO, 1993

Bryan, J, *Bulbs*, Portland: Timber Press, rev. edn 2002

Case, F W J and Case, R B, *Trilliums*, Portland: Timber Press, 1997

Clark, T, 'Focus on Plants: Treasures of the East (Hyacinths)', *The Garden*, vol. 125, no. 9 (2000), pp.672–5

Clark, T and Grey-Wilson, C, 'Crown Imperials', *The Plantsman*, vol. 2, no. 1 (2003), pp.33–47

Coats, A M, *Flowers and Their Histories*, London: Adam & Charles Black, 1956

Dashwood, M and Mathew, B, *Hyacinthaceae – Little Blue Bulbs*: RHS Bulletin no. 11, Wisley: Royal Horticultural Society, 2006

Davies, D, *Alliums. The Ornamental Onions*, London: Batsford, 1992

Davis, A P, Mathew, B (ed.) and King, C (ill.), *The Genus Galanthus. A Botanical Magazine Monograph*, Portland: Timber Press, 1999

Duncan, G D, *The Lachenalia Hand Book*, Kirstenbosch: National Botanic Gardens, 1988

Dykes, W R, *The Genus Iris*, Cambridge: Cambridge University Press, 1913

Goldblatt, P, *The Genus Watsonia*, Kirstenbosch: National Botanic Gardens, 1989

Goldblatt, P, *The Moraeas of Southern Africa*, Kirstenbosch: National Botanic Gardens, 1986

Goldblatt, P and Manning, J, *Gladiolus in Southern Africa*, Vlaeburg: Fernwood Press, 1998

Grey, C H, *Hardy Bulbs*, London: Williams & Norgate, 3 vols 1937–8

Grey-Wilson, C, *Cyclamen. A Guide for Gardeners, Horticulturists & Botanists*, London: Batsford, 2003

Hillard, O M and Burtt, B L, *Dierama. The Harebells of Africa*, Johannesburg: Acorn Books, 1991

Hoog, M H, 'Bulbous Irises', *The Plantsman*, vol. 2, no. 3 (1980), pp.141–64

Jefferson-Brown, M, *Narcissus*, London: Batsford, 1991

Kohlein, Fritz, *Iris*, London: Christopher Helm, 1987

Leeds, R, *Autumn Bulbs*, London: Batsford/Alpine Garden Society, 2005

Leeds, R, *Bulbs in Containers*, Portland: Timber Press, 2005

Mathew, B, 'Hardy Hyacinthaceae Part 1: Muscari', *The Plantsman*, vol. 4, no. 1 (2005), pp.40–53

Mathew, B, 'Hardy Hyacinthaceae Part 2: Scilla, Chionodoxa and × Chionoscilla', *The Plantsman*, vol. 4, no. 2 (2005), pp.110–21

Mathew, B, *The Crocus*, London: Batsford, 1982

Mathew, B, 'The Genus Erythronium', *Bulletin Alpine Garden Society Great Britain*, vol. 66, no. 3 (1998), pp.308–21

Mathew, B, *The Iris*, London: Batsford, 1981

Mathew, B, *The Larger Bulbs*, London: Batsford, 1978

Mathew, B, *The Smaller Bulbs*, London: Batsford, 1987

Mathew, B, 'The Spuria Irises', *The Plantsman*, vol. 15, no. 1 (1993), pp.4–25

Mathew, B and Baytop, T, *The Bulbous Plants of Turkey*, London: Batsford/Alpine Garden Society, 1984

Mathew, B et al., *Fritillaria* issue. *Botanical Magazine*, vol. 17, no. 3 (2000), pp.145–85

Phillips, R and Rix, M, *Bulbs*, London: Pan Books, 1989

Pradhan, U C, *Himalayan Cobra Lilies*, Kalimpong: Primulaceae Books, 2nd edn 1997

Pratt, K and Jefferson-Brown, M, *The Gardener's Guide to Growing Fritillaries*, Newton Abbot: David & Charles, 1997

Read, V M, *Hippeastrum*, Portland: Royal Horticultural Society/Timber Press, 2004

Ruksans, J, *Buried Treasures*, Portland: Timber Press, 2007

Service, N, 'Iris unguicularis', *The Plantsman*, vol. 12, no. 1 (1990), pp.1–9

Sheasby, P, *Bulbous Plants of Turkey and Iran*, Pershore: Alpine Garden Society, 2007

Snijman, D, 'A Revision of the Genus Haemanthus', *J S African Bot.*, supp. vol. 12, 1984

The Species Group of the British Iris Society (ed.), *A Guide to Species Irises*, Cambridge: Cambridge University Press, 1997

Synge, P M, *Collins Guide to Bulbs*, London: Collins, 1961

Wilford, Richard, *Tulips*, Portland: Timber Press, 2006

Index

Acknowledgements

Photographic Acknowledgements

All photographs are by Andrew Lawson, with the exception of the following. Mitchell Beazley would like to acknowledge and thank these sources for supplying additional images.

9, 12, 15 Mary Evans Picture Library; 23 Rolf Nussbaumer/Alamy; 31a Photos Horticultural/Photoshot; 37a Garden World Images; 37b Howard Rice/GAP Photos; 38a Nigel Cattlin/Alamy; 39a A Descat/MAP/Garden World Images; 40b A Descat/MAP/Garden World Images; 41a Lee Thomas/Garden World Images; 43b Jason Ingram/GAP Photos; 49 Peter Chadwick/Gallo Images/Getty Images; 52 Ben Probert/Ben's Botanics; 53 Ian West/OSF/Photolibrary.com; 57a Lynn Keddie/GAP Photos; 59b Branko Stovanovij; 60a Paul S Drobot/www.plantstockphotos.com; 61a Visions/GAP Photos; 61c Anne Green-Armytage/Garden Picture Library/Photolibrary.com; 61b Visions/GAP Photos; 63b Roger Cope/Alamy; 64a Howard Rice/Garden Picture Library/Photolibrary.com; 74a Chris Wheeler/Garden World Images; 80 © 2009 www.NZPlantPics.com; 82 Peter Eastland; 82 Wildlife GmbH/Alamy; 84b Guy Gusman; 87b Visions/GAP Photos; 90 blickwinkel/Alamy; 94 Photos Horticultural/Photoshot; 95a A Baggett/Garden World Images; 97 Chris Cheadle/All Canada Photos/Photolibrary.com; 100 Mark Turner/Botanica/Photolibrary.com; 105 David Dixon/Garden Picture Library/Photolibrary.com; 111 Mary Evans Picture Library; 115b David Dixon, Garden Picture Library/Photolibrary.com; 128 Chris Burrows/Garden Picture Library/ Photolibrary.com; 132 courtesy eabowlessociety.org.uk; 134 nagelestock.com/Alamy; 137 Enzo & Paolo Ragazzini/Corbis; 144a, 145a Chris Burrows/Garden Picture Library/Photolibrary.com; 152b Sharon Pearson/GAP Photos; 155a, 159a Photos Horticultural/ Photoshot; 161a Chris Burrows/Garden Picture Library/Photolibrary.com; 167 Photoshot; 181b Liz Cole/Garden World Images; 183 Eric Crichton/Garden Picture Library/Photolibrary.com; 184b J S Sira/Garden Picture Library/Photolibrary.com; 186 Flora Toskana/ Garden World Images; 187a Liz Cole/Garden World Images; 189 Corbis; 193a courtesy Dr Andrew Ward/Norwell Nurseries; 206 RHS/Lindley Library; 210b Dr Alan Beaumont/Garden World Images; 224 courtesy H W G Elwes; 235 Juliette Spears/Garden World Images; 239b Chris Burrows/Garden Picture Library/Photolibrary.com; 248 Janet Johnson/GAP Photos; 250 CuboImages srl/Alamy; 252a Toshiko Gunter; 252bVisions/GAP Photos; 253a Floramedia/Garden World Images; 254-5 Gilles Delacroix/Garden World Images; 257a John Glover/Alamy; 259 Visions/GAP Photos; 262 Science Photo Library; 265 The Granger Collection/TopFoto; 267a Tom Hofferbert; 277a Botanicum/Alamy; 279 Classic Image/Alamy; 281 Science Photo Library; 286a Chris Burrows/Garden Picture Library/Photolibrary.com; 288b A Descat/MAP/Garden World Images; 290a Chris Ireland-Jones/www.avonbulbs.co.uk; 291b Photos Horticultural/Photoshot; 295 A Descat/MAP/Garden World Images; 301b J S Sira/Garden World Images; 206 Liz Coles/Garden World Images; 307 Andrew Ackerley/Garden Picture Library/Photolibrary.com; 312 Joerg Hauke/Picture Press/Photolibrary.com; 322b Visions/GAP Photos; 326a Photos Horticultural/Photoshot; 332b James Guilliam/Garden Picture Library/Photolibrary.com; 343a Mike Richardson;/ goodnessgrows.com; 344b Sunniva Harte/Garden World Images; 356 RHS/Lindley Library; 357 blickwinkel/Alamy; 360 Private Collection/The Stapleton Collection/The Bridgeman Art Library; 372 David Askham/Alamy; 374a Visions/GAP Photos; 378b Mark Smyth/www.marksgardenplants.com; 382a Liz Coles/Garden World Images; 390b Heather Angel/Natural Visions/Alamy; 400 Chris Burrows/Garden Picture Library/Photolibrary.com; 401 A Descat/MAP/Garden World Images; 406 Lola Claeys Bouuaert/Garden World Images; 416 John Glover/Garden Picture Library/Photolibrary.com; 429 Erin Paul Donovan/Alamy; 430a Don Johnston/Alamy; 430b Pat Thielen/Alamy; 433 Derek St Romaine/The Garden Collection; 436 Sarah Lee/Garden World Images; 439 blickwinkel/Alamy; 442 RHS/Lindley Library; 443 Private Collection/Stapleton Collection/Bridgeman Art Library; 454b Pernilla Bergdahl/Garden Picture Library/Photolibrary.com; 455b A Descat/MAP/Garden World Images; 456a Visions/GAP Photos; 457a Charles Hawes/Garden World Images; 464a Netherlands Flower Bulb Information Centre; 466b Frédéric Didillon/MAP/Garden World Images; 474b Laurent Lieser; 481b CuboImages srl/Alamy; 491 A Descat/MAP/Garden World Images; 497a John Sirkett; 501 Ladybird Johnson Wild Flower Center; 514 Ron Evans/Photolibrary/Getty Images; 518 Visions/Gap Photos; 520 Elke Borkowski/GAP Photos; 525 Sarah Cuttle/GAP Photos.

Andrew Lawson and Torie Chugg are most grateful to the following for providing plants for photography:

Paul Cumbleton and staff at the Alpine Department RHS Gardens, *Wisley*, Surrey

Richard Wilford and staff at the Alpine Department, *Royal Botanic Gardens*, Kew

Chris Ireland-Jones and Alan Street, *Avon Bulbs*, Somerset

Bob Brown, *Cotswold Garden Flowers*

Elaine Horton, *Tinpenny Plants*, Gloucestershire

Jacques Amand, Middlesex

Lady Skelmersdale, *Broadleigh Gardens*, Somerset

Timothy and Jane Whiteley, *Evenley Wood*, Northamptonshire

Fergus Garrett, *Great Dixter*, East Sussex

Gill and John Hazell, *Great Western Gladiolus*, Bristol

Julie and Robin Ritchie, *Hoo House Nursery*, Gloucestershire

Roger and Sue Norman, *Ivycroft Plants*, Herefordshire

Martin Davis Bulbs, Gloucestershire

RHS Gardens, *Rosemoor*, Devon

Sylvia and Tony Marden, *Shady Plants*, Gloucestershire

Keith and Ros Wiley, *Wildside Nursery*, Devon

Cerney House Gardens, Gloucestershire

Coughton Court, Warwickshire

Gothic House, Oxfordshire

Fiona Heywood, *Haseley Court*, Oxfordshire

Mary and Antony Haynes, Gloucestershire

The Inner Temple Gardens, London

John Lanyon and the National Trust, *Knightshayes Court*, Devon

Dr Ronald Mackenzie, Oxfordshire

John and Antoinette Moat, Devon

Gina Price, Oxfordshire